EMPLOYMENT LAW HANDBOOK

9TH EDITION

General Editor
Daniel Barnett

Contributors
Jeremy Scott-Joynt
Courtney Step-Marsden
Nicholas Bidnell-Edwards

ISBN 978-1-913925-15-4

This edition published by Employment Law Services Limited, Unit 3, Chequers House, Chequers Lane, Watford WD25 0LG.

ABOUT THE AUTHORS

Daniel Barnett is a leading employment barrister with 30 years' experience. He is the founder of the HR Inner Circle, the UK's leading membership organisation for smart, ambitious HR Professionals. He is the author or co-author of 20 books, two of which have been ranked as Amazon #1s for HR, and is the creator and presenter of Employment Law Matters, ranked #1 on the Apple Podcast Store for business podcasts in the UK. Daniel is a past chair of the Employment Lawyers' Association's publishing committee and electronic services working party. For the last 13 years, he has presented the LBC Legal Hour, a national radio show in which he answers caller's legal questions.

Jeremy Scott-Joynt is a barrister at Outer Temple Chambers specialising in employment law, commercial litigation, and business crime and regulatory matters. He regularly advises on employment claims (particularly those involving whistleblowing and discrimination) and investigations. Before coming to the Bar, he ran anti-corruption programmes and investigations for two international banks, and worked in intelligence at the Financial Services Authority. He started his working life as a reporter, spending six years covering economics, business and financial crime for BBC News.

Nicholas Bidnell-Edwards was called to the Bar in 2012. He specialises in employment law, and commercial work with an employment focus. In addition to advisory work, Nicholas appears frequently in Employment Tribunals, County Courts and in the Employment Appeal Tribunal. He has acted in the Court of Appeal, and has drafted successful pleadings, and Notices of Appeal.

Courtney Step-Marsden is a barrister at Outer Temple Chambers, and was called to the Bar in 2019. Courtney specialises in employment law, education law and Court of Protection matters. In employment matters, Courtney has a particular interest in discrimination claims. She has also appeared as junior Counsel in the Court of Appeal.

CONTENTS

ACKNOWLEDGMENTS

As a group of authors, we want to thank some people collectively, as well as each of individually thanking our nearest and dearest.

Thank you to those who have contributed to the preparation, editing and design of this book. There are many, but in particular we highlight Tincuta Collett, Eugenie Verney, Aaron Gaff, Rob Gibson, Jennie Hargrove and Christopher John Payne.

We also want to express our gratitude to Lord Neuberger, past president of the Supreme Court, for writing the foreword to the previous edition which we have reproduced on the following pages. We are flattered and humbled that one of the most eminent jurists in the UK has taken the time and trouble to set out his thoughts.

As general editor, Daniel Barnett has been involved from the first edition being published almost 25 years ago. Other authors have come and gone, but a special mention must go to Henry Scrope, now retired, who first developed this book and co-wrote the first six editions with Daniel Barnett. We also want to thank Keira Gore (who also co-wrote the sixth edition), Gus Baker & Stephen Butler (who co-wrote the seventh edition) and Stefan Liberadzki (who helped co-write the eighth edition).

Daniel Barnett would like to thank his family, Miranda, Tabby, Cressie and Rufus.

Jeremy Scott-Joynt would like to thank his wife, Angela, and their daughter Amara, for all their support, their love and their encouragement. He dedicates his work on this book to the memory of his late mother, Lou. Nicholas Bidnell-Edwards is grateful for all the support he continues to receive from his growing family, and for all the guidance provided by Shelley.

Courtney Step-Marsden would like to thank her parents, Cath and Maz, and her husband, Aleks, for their endless support. She would also like to thank her cats, Hamilton and Lady Justice, for their love and company. Courtney would also like to pay tribute to her late grandfather, Richard, whose support was instrumental in her coming to the Bar.

FOREWORD TO 8TH EDITION

My 21 years' experience as judge served to bring home to me the importance of employment law in the day-to-day lives of many people, even of the majority of people. A significant proportion of the population not only spend many of their waking hours at work, but they also gain a great deal of their sense of self-worth from their job, and from their ability to provide for those close to them. Most of us will spend, currently spend, or have spent a third of each day in close proximity to the same people in the same workplace, often for years. Some of those people may become very good friends, but some may not. Sometimes there is conflict, with anger and arguments, and occasionally something even worse, flowing from it.

We hope, even expect, each employer to be a guide, a coach, a conflict resolver and, sometimes, a disciplinarian. Yet those roles may be a distraction from the task of generating a profit for shareholders or providing essential public services. However much an employer may want to treat its workforce well, there is often a tension between that desire and the need to focus on running the business efficiently. Sometimes the conflict is stark: should the employer reprimand the successful but old-fashioned and brusque 50-year-old sales manager, risking her resignation? Or should it transfer out the inexperienced 22-year-old who complains that the manager is a bully? When sex, race or other protected characteristics are in play, the answer is often fairly clear; but, when they are not, the position is more opaque.

Since the introduction of discrimination and unfair dismissal law in the 1970s, Parliament and the courts have overseen the working relationship and provided some measure of protection for workers. That is plainly appropriate as they will almost always be in a relationship with their employer where they are the more economically vulnerable of the two parties. This is, of course, by no means the only area of law where the legislature intervenes to protect the more vulnerable party in a contractual relationship — examples are also to be found in landlord and tenant law and consumer protection.

One of the main battlegrounds in employment law in recent years has been the extension of employee and workers' rights to as many individuals as possible. During my time in the Supreme Court, I sat on cases including *Reyes v Al-Malki* [2017] UKSC 61, where we decided a diplomat engaged in trafficking his domestic servant was not entitled to shield behind diplomatic immunity, and *Bates van Winkelhof v Clyde & Co LLP* [2014] IRLR 641, where we held that a member of an LLP was a 'worker' and thus entitled to some level of legal protection. But there are limits. In *X v Mid-Sussex Citizens' Advice Bureau* [2013] IRLR 146, we were unable to extend the protection of the discrimination statutes to a CAB volunteer because the domestic and European legislation did not go that far. The battle continues: as I write this foreword, the Supreme Court is deciding whether or not to uphold the majority decision of the Court of Appeal that Uber drivers are 'workers'.

Closely aligned to workers' rights is the question of employers' responsibility, or vicarious liability. In *Cox v Ministry of Justice* [2016] IRLR 370 we held that the Prison Service was vicariously liable for injuries sustained by a catering manager when a prisoner negligently dropped a sack of rice on her. And in *Mohamud v WM Morrison Supermarkets plc* [2016] IRLR 362, we decided a supermarket was vicariously liable for the acts of a petrol station attendant who committed an unprovoked and racially aggravated assault on a customer. These cases show how the law has evolved: it is almost unthinkable that vicarious liability would have extended to these situations 20 years ago.

Another fascinating area of the last decade has been the conflict of rights, particularly in the discrimination field. When I was Master of the Rolls, I said in *Islington Borough Council v Ladele* [2010] IRLR 211 that 'it cannot constitute direct discrimination to treat all employees in precisely the same way'. In that case, we rejected the argument of a strongly-committed Christian registrar that she had been discriminated against for refusing to conduct civil partnerships, despite her deep-rooted conviction they were against her beliefs. In *Bull v Hall* [2014] 1 All ER 919, the Supreme Court held that a bed and breakfast owners' religious beliefs did not allow them to refuse a room to a gay couple. More recently, shortly after I retired from the bench, the Supreme Court decided *Lee v Ashers Baking Company* [2018] IRLR 1116, in which it was held that a bakery did not discriminate on grounds of sexual orientation when refusing to decorate a cake with a message supporting gay marriage. The conflict of religious beliefs and other rights is one which is likely to continue troubling practitioners and judges over the next few years.

Sometimes we have seen the Government overstep, normally (but, unfortunately not always) with the best of intentions. One of the most constitutionally significant cases of the last decade was *R (on the application of the UNISON) v Lord Chancellor* [2017] IRLR 911, where I agreed with Lord Reed that the fees imposed by the Lord Chancellor in respect of proceedings in employment tribunals and the Employment Appeal Tribunal were unlawful because of their effect on access to justice. Although nothing in our judgment prevents a future government from introducing a similar scheme, I suspect — and I certainly hope — there is little political appetite for doing so at the moment.

This book makes employment law simple. It covers everything, and can be read by any employee or employer, as well as the experienced employment lawyer. The authors avoid debate and arid analysis, and just say what the law is and what it requires employers to do. I commend it as a reliable, user-friendly and clear guide to anyone with an employment law problem.

David Neuberger
President of the Supreme Court 2012-2017
Arbitrator, One Essex Court

CHAPTER 1
EMPLOYMENT STATUS

1.0 OVERVIEW

Employment law can in some ways be seen as a creature of contract law. The relationship between an individual and who they work for is almost always contractual, whether it is an express written document or a collection of implied terms. However, for many hundreds of years, legislators have recognised that the relationship between people and their employers is fundamentally different in nature to that between commercial parties to contracts.

A central tension therefore permeates almost all employment law disputes: to what extent should individuals and organisations be free to make agreements related to work on terms of their own choosing, and to what extent should the law intervene to protect the more vulnerable party?

Historically, the majority of statutory protection existed to protect employers from their employees. For example, the *Statute of Labourers 1351*, passed by King Edward III in the wake of a labour shortage following the Black Death, provided that:

> 'If any reaper, mower, or other workman or servants, of what estate or condition that he be, retained in any man's service, do depart from the said service without reasonable cause or license, before the term agreed, he shall have pain of imprisonment; and no one, under the same penalty, shall presume to receive or retain such a one in his service.'

Similarly, throughout much of the 19th century, the *Master and Servant Acts* criminalised breaches of contract by employees against their employers.

Now, the situation is rather different. The core statute from which most employment rights derive, the *Employment Rights Act 1996* (ERA 1996), provides a wide variety of measures designed to protect employees and workers against unfair terms imposed by their employers. The *Equality Act 2010* (EqA 2010) is a comprehensive code prohibiting discrimination, including at work. Further, there are various regulations that implement

1

European Union legislation protecting individuals at work, which have been retained under provisions of the *European Union (Withdrawal) Act 2018*.

The courts and tribunals also readily recognise that contracts to do work are not the same as ordinary commercial contracts. The terms of the agreement between employer and employee/worker will – in addition to the statutory provisions – also be interpreted with regard to the bargaining positions of the parties. In *Autoclenz v Belcher [2011] ICR 1157 SC*, Lord Clarke approved the following dicta of Aikens LJ from the same case in the Court of Appeal (*Autoclenz v Belcher [2010] IRLR 70*):

> 'I respectfully agree with the view ... that the circumstances in which contracts relating to work or services are concluded are often very different from those in which commercial contracts between parties of equal bargaining power are agreed. I accept that, frequently, organisations which are offering work or requiring services to be provided by individuals are in a position to dictate the written terms which the other party has to accept. In practice, in this area of the law, it may be more common for a court or tribunal to have to investigate allegations that the written contract does not represent the actual terms agreed and the court or tribunal must be realistic and worldly wise when it does so.'

In the highly publicised case of *Uber BV v Aslam [2021] ICR 657 SC*, the Supreme Court took this principle further, stating that the terms of a written contract should not be the starting point in determining an individual's worker status, as the employer will often dictate the contractual terms, whilst the individual will have little or no ability to influence the terms. Thus, whilst advisers must be alert to the terms of any contract, the relevant legislation and the context in which the work was done must be the central focus in determining employment status.

1.1 THE IMPORTANCE OF EMPLOYMENT STATUS

An individual's employment status determines what rights they are entitled to at work, with the most extensive employment rights limited to 'employees'. Individuals who qualify for 'worker' status are entitled to some core rights, while those who are genuinely self-employed are entitled to very few statutory protections at work.

People describe their employment status in many ways in everyday language – for example as an 'employee', a 'worker', a 'member of staff', a 'freelancer' or a 'contractor'. The contracts individuals sign with an employer will often contain clauses which purport to determine an employee's status. Following the Supreme Court's decision in *Autoclenz Ltd v Belcher and ors [2011] UKSC 41*, what matters is what was actually agreed by the parties and the 'real' relationship between them.

The core definitions for the different types of employment status are found within section 230 of the ERA 1996. However, each different legislative instrument covering employment rights will generally contain an 'interpretation' provision defining the employment status of the individuals to whom it applies. Although the definitions generally remain consistent across statutes, it is always worth consulting the relevant instrument to check to whom it affords the relevant rights.

The main statutory definitions, and the most significant rights that go with them, are as follows.

Employee

The term 'employee' is defined in section 230(1) of the ERA 1996 as:

> 'an individual who has entered into or works under (or, where the employment has ceased, worked under) a contract of employment'.

A 'contract of employment' is defined as 'a contract of service or apprenticeship, whether express or implied, and (if it is express) whether oral or in writing' (section 230(2) of the ERA 1996).

For the purposes of regulation 2(1) of the Transfer of Undertakings (Protection of Employment) Regulations 2006 (TUPE Regulations 2006), an employee is:

> 'any individual who works for another person whether under a contract of service or apprenticeship or otherwise, but does not include anyone who provides services under a contract for services'.

Employees are exclusively entitled to:

a) Protection from unfair dismissal under part X of the ERA 1996

b) Redundancy payments under part XI of the ERA 1996

c) A minimum notice period on termination under part IX of the ERA 1996

d) Maternity, paternity, parental, shared parental and adoption leave (paid and unpaid) under part VIII of the ERA 1996

e) Time off for antenatal care under part VI of the ERA 1996

f) The right to request flexible working under part 8A of the ERA 1996

g) Paid time off work for trade union or representative duties under section 168 of the *Trade Union and Labour Relations (Consolidation) Act 1992* (TULR(C)A 1992)

h) Protection of contractual rights on the transfer of their employer's undertaking, under the TUPE Regulations 2006

Worker

The term 'worker' is defined in section 230(3) of the ERA 1996 as:

'an individual who has entered into or works under (or, where the employment has ceased, worked under) –

a) a contract of employment; or

b) any other contract, whether express or implied and (if it is express) whether oral or in writing, whereby the individual undertakes to do or perform personally any work or services for another party to the contract whose status is not by virtue of the contract that of a client or customer of any profession or business undertaking carried on by the individual'.

Therefore, all employees are workers but not all workers are employees. This is an intermediate category between an employee and the truly self-employed which confers a number of basic rights. All workers are entitled to:

a) The National Minimum Wage and the National Living Wage under the *National Minimum Wage Act 1998* (NMWA 1998) and related provisions

b) Regulated hours of work and annual leave under the *Working Time Regulations 1998, SI 1998/1833* (WTR 1998)

c) Protection from discrimination due to part-time worker status under the *Part-time Workers (Prevention of Less Favourable Treatment) Regulations 2000, SI 2000/1551*

d) Protection from detriment on the grounds of trade union membership or activities under section 146 of the TULR(C)A 1992

e) Protection from detriment when 'whistleblowing' under section 47B of the ERA 1996

f) The right to a written statement of particulars of employment under section 1 of the ERA 1996 from April 2020 (this was previously restricted to employees)

Employment

Unhelpfully, the EqA 2010 uses the term 'employment' to describe the categories of individuals protected from discrimination under the Act. The term 'employment' in this context will encompass both 'employees' and 'workers', as described above. Section 83(2) of the EqA 2010 provides that 'employment' means:

a) 'employment under a contract of employment, a contract of apprenticeship or a contract personally to do work;

b) Crown employment;

c) employment as a relevant member of the House of Commons staff;

d) employment as a relevant member of the House of Lords staff.'

The definition of 'employment' in the EqA 2010 will include those who would otherwise be workers under the ERA 1996, but will *not* include those who are truly self-employed (see the judgment of Lady Hale at paragraph 31 in *Bates Van Winkelhof v Clyde & Co LLP [2014] ICR 730*).

Self-employment

Very few employment rights are granted to genuinely self-employed individuals. The definition of 'worker' in section 230(3) of the ERA 1996 expressly excludes those who perform work or services for another party whose status is 'that of a client or customer of any profession or business undertaking carried on by the individual'.

Other categories of employment

Parliament has created some special employment categories that are outside the norm. Individuals who are employed in roles defined as falling within one of these statutory categories are not entitled to ordinary employment rights and will fall under specific schemes. These categories include share fishermen, Crown employment, employment as a member of House of Commons or House of Lords staff and police constables. Ministers of religion also have a curious status, with the case law emphasising the fact-sensitive nature of deciding whether there is a contract between them and their religious organisation.

1.2 DETERMINING EMPLOYMENT STATUS

The question of whether someone is an employee is a question of fact, which ultimately is for an employment tribunal to decide, and difficult to successfully challenge on appeal. Different authorities may reach different conclusions on whether someone amounts to an employee based on the same set of facts. For example, an employment tribunal may determine that someone classifies as an employee for the purposes of unfair dismissal, despite HMRC classifying the same employee as self-employed for tax purposes.

1.2.1 WHO IS AN EMPLOYEE?

The statutory definition – an individual who works under 'a contract of service or apprenticeship' – is unhelpful by itself. There is no 'magic formula' to determine whether somebody is an employee, but the courts have identified a number of indicators over the years. Employment lawyers and tribunals usually start with the judgment of McKenna J in *Ready Mixed Concrete v Minister of Pensions [1968] 2 QB 497*, in which it was held:

> 'A contract of service exists if these three conditions are fulfilled: (i) The servant agrees that, in consideration of a wage or other remuneration, he will provide his own work and skill in the performance of some service for

his master; (ii) He agrees, expressly or impliedly, that in the performance of that service he will be subject to the other's control in a sufficient degree to make that other master; (iii) The other provisions of the contract are consistent with its being a contract of service.'

Thus, case law determines that there must be an 'irreducible minimum' for a contract of service to exist: control, mutuality of obligation and personal performance.

Control

'Control' is a necessary, but insufficient, condition of an employment contract (see *Ready Mixed Concrete* at p517). If an individual has a significant degree of control over their contractual obligations, an inference may be made that they are less likely to be an employee. However, as HHJ David Richardson noted in *White v Troutbeck SA* (2013) UKEAT/0177/12:

'the key question is whether there is, to a sufficient degree, a contractual right of control over the worker. The key question is not whether in practice the worker has day to day control of his own work'.

This reflects the fact that an individual – particularly a skilled craftsperson or a professional adviser – may be able to exercise a significant degree of judgement over the manner in which they carry out their instructions without this preventing them being an employee.

If there is no contractual right to issue an individual with instructions about the tasks they are to perform, the individual is less likely to be an employee. A good example is *UPVC Designs Ltd v Latimer (2007) UKEAT/0431/07*, where a sales consultant at a garden centre, who was paid entirely by commission, was held to be self-employed. The key finding was that under the contract, the company could not require her to follow up a particular lead, work at particular times or come into the centre to help at peak periods.

Mutuality of obligation

'Mutuality of obligation' means a requirement on the employer to offer work and on the employee to accept it. If the employer does not have to offer work, or the individual is free to refuse it, there will not be a contract of employment.

Most contracts for work are for a period of time which will generally either extend over a fixed period or be indefinite in duration. The aim of these contracts will generally be to fulfil a role rather than to carry out a discrete task. Individuals will usually work during agreed contractual hours, but the relationship will persist whether the individual is actually working or not. The existence of 'mutuality of obligation' in such cases is obvious.

However, a significant number of contracts cover situations where an individual works intermittently for an employer, carrying out discrete separate engagements – and these contracts are becoming increasingly common. The so-called 'gig economy' relies on individuals who do not work set hours but are assigned engagements as and when both work is available and they are available. In these cases, a question often arises over whether there is sufficient mutuality of obligation *between* assignments for an individual to be an employee.

The clearest summary of how mutuality of obligations affects employment status is provided in *Stephenson v Delphi Diesel Systems Ltd [2003] ICR 471 EAT*, as subsequently approved by the Court of Appeal in *Quashie v Stringfellow Restaurants Ltd [2013] IRLR 99 CA*. It can be summarised as follows:

a) Mutuality is significant as it determines 'whether there is a contract in existence at all'.

b) Where an employee works intermittently for an employer, 'it is often necessary then to show that the contract continues to exist in the gaps between the periods of employment'.

c) The question will often be whether there is an umbrella contract, 'which remains in existence even when the individual concerned is not working'.

d) It is in answer to this question that the phrase 'mutuality of obligations' becomes relevant. The court will consider whether there is something from which a contract can be properly inferred when the individual is not working.

In *Hellyer Brothers v McLeod [1987] 1 WLR 728 CA*, despite a long-term arrangement whereby the employer offered the individuals short-term assignments, the individuals could not establish that there was any umbrella (or global) contract of employment between assignments. Had there been one, it would have allowed the individuals to accrue the necessary continuity of employment to claim redundancy pay.

In contrast, in *Wilson v Circular Distributors Ltd [2006] IRLR 38*, the Employment Appeal Tribunal (EAT) held that despite a clause which specified that there might be occasions when no work was available, the clause really meant that 'if there is work available, it must be offered' and the individual would have been required to accept it. On that basis, there was sufficient mutuality of obligation for the individual to be an employee.

Personal service/substitution

For a contract of employment to exist, it must be an individual's *own* work and skill that is provided. This is known as the requirement of personal service. Thus, a right to substitute an individual's labour for that of another will not be consistent with a contract of employment. This was the case in *Express & Echo Publications Ltd v Tanton [1999] ICR 693 CA* where a newspaper delivery driver was held not to be an employee because his contract allowed him to arrange for another trained and suitable person to cover for him if he was 'unable or unwilling to perform the services himself'.

However, the requirement of personal service is not absolute: a limited or occasional power to delegate work to somebody else can be consistent with employee status. In *MacFarlane v Glasgow City Council [2001] IRLR 7 EAT*, a gym instructor could arrange for a replacement, but only if she was 'unable' to take a session. The replacement had to be another instructor who was already on the Council's books, and the Council would pay the replacement directly instead of her. She was found to be an employee.

If the individual must secure the employer's approval before arranging for a replacement, this will also be consistent with employee status because, in reality, the employer still decides who is doing the work. It will not matter that the right of substitution has never been exercised in practice. However, a clause which provides for rights to substitute that could never conceivably be used is liable to be found to be a 'sham' which does not reflect the true agreement between the parties (*Consistent Group Ltd v Kalwak [2007] IRLR 560 CA*).

'Consistent with a contract for services'

Beyond the 'irreducible minimum', *Ready Mixed Concrete* laid down the third condition that the contractual relationship must be 'consistent with a contract for services'. In *Revenue and Customs Commissioners v Atholl House Productions Ltd [2022] EWCA Civ 501* and *Kickabout Productions Limited v The Commissioners for Her Majesty's Revenue and Customs [2022] EWCA Civ 502*, the Court of Appeal addressed this limb in appeals from the Upper Tribunal (Tax and Chancery Chamber). The Court of Appeal held that this third condition was not limited to express and implied contractual terms, but that all relevant factors should be examined, both consistent and inconsistent with employment, to determine whether an employment relationship existed. This will include factors such as integration into the workforce and economic reality.

Integration into the workforce

Courts will look at the extent to which the worker is integrated into the employer's organisation. This might include, for example, whether they wear a uniform, are subject to a disciplinary or grievance procedure or are included in an occupational benefit scheme. However, it is not usually as significant a factor as 'control'.

Economic reality

Courts have sometimes asked whether the individual is 'in business on his/her own account' – that is, to what extent do they bear the financial risks (and reap the rewards) of their work? Payment solely by commission or per task, rather than a fixed wage, will point towards self-employment. So will the fact that an individual has to pay for their own equipment in order to carry out their job (for example, a vehicle, tools or premises).

Any individual who receives remuneration directly from customers is unlikely to be an employee. In *Quashie v Stringfellow Restaurants Ltd [2013] IRLR 99 CA*, a lap dancer was not an employee because she negotiated her own fees with clients, took the risk that she might be out of pocket on any particular night and received back from the venue only the money paid by clients after deductions.

A person's tax status is also relevant, but HMRC's opinion on whether they are employed or self-employed is rarely conclusive for employment purposes. See, for example, *Enfield Technical Services Ltd v Payne, BF Components Ltd v Grace [2008] ICR 1423 CA* and *O'Kelly and ors v Trusthouse Forte plc [1983] ICR 728 CA*, where the employment status of the individuals was found to be the opposite of their tax status. However, registration for VAT will normally be a strong indicator of self-employment.

1.2.2 WHO IS A WORKER?

Section 230(3)(b) of the ERA 1996 provides that an individual will be a worker if they work under:

> 'any other contract, whether express or implied and (if it is express) whether oral or in writing, whereby the individual undertakes to do or perform personally any work or services for another party to the contract whose status is not by virtue of the contract that of a client or customer of any profession or business undertaking carried on by the individual'.

People who run their own businesses as sole traders, where the parties they contract with are their 'clients' rather than their employers, do not qualify as 'workers'. Worker status is perhaps best understood as a halfway house between employee status and these self-employed individuals.

As noted above, this category also covers the extended definition of 'employment' used in section 83(2) of the EqA 2010. Although that section does not explicitly contain the 'client or customer of any profession or business undertaking' exception, the Supreme Court has held that it applies in the same way (*Bates van Winkelhof v Clyde & Co LLP [2014] ICR 730*, at paragraph 25).

Relevant factors

Assessing whether or not an individual is running their own business, with the organisation as their client, will involve many of the same factors considered for employee status: control, integration and economic reality. However, the overall threshold or 'pass mark' is lower than for employee status (*Byrne Brothers (Formwork) Ltd v Baird & ors [2002] ICR 667 EAT*). This means that an individual who fails to establish employee status may still be able to show that they are a worker.

In particular, there is no requirement for an irreducible minimum of obligation as a pre-requisite for worker status. Worker status will exist when the individual undertakes work for someone who is not their customer or their client and is required to perform that work personally (*Nursing and Midwifery Council v Somerville [2022] EWCA Civ 229*). The points discussed in **1.2.1** under 'Personal service/substitution' are just as relevant to worker status as to employee status.

Recent case law

Worker status is a rapidly evolving area of case law, particularly in the 'gig economy'. Some businesses seek to organise their workforce on a self-employed basis, avoiding the need to provide rights such as paid holidays or the National Minimum Wage, while also marketing 'their' workers' (often drivers' or couriers') services to customers. The courts have been increasingly willing to treat carefully drafted 'freelancer' agreements as a sham and instead look at the reality of the parties' relationship.

The Supreme Court has held that Pimlico Plumbers operatives have worker status (*Pimlico Plumbers Ltd v Smith [2018] ICR 1511*). Although their contracts enabled them to send a substitute for a job not just when they were unable to work but also if another more lucrative job arose, the substitute had to be another Pimlico Plumbers operative. This was still consistent with a requirement for personal service.

In *Uber BV v Aslam [2021] ICR 657 SC*, the Supreme Court held that those who provided their driving services through the Uber smartphone application were 'workers' under section 230 of the ERA 1996. Whilst the court acknowledged that Uber drivers had some level of autonomy in independence (in that they were free to choose when to work, how much to work and where to work), the reality of the relationship demonstrated that the drivers were, in fact, workers:

a) The remuneration paid to drivers for their work was fixed by Uber and the drivers had no say in it. Whilst the drivers did have the ability to charge less than the app calculated, this was not of benefit to the drivers as any pay cut came out of the driver's pocket.

b) The contractual terms on which drivers performed their services were dictated by Uber.

c) Once a driver logged into the app, a driver's choice about whether to accept requests for rides was constrained by Uber.

d) Uber exercised a significant degree of control over the drivers, in particular through controlling the technology which is integral to the service.

e) Uber restricted the communication between the passenger and driver to the minimum necessary and took active steps to prevent drivers from establishing any relationships with passengers capable of extending beyond an individual ride.

There have also been numerous first-instance decisions finding courier drivers or riders to have worker status, none of which were appealed. Among these are *Dewhurst v Citysprint UK Ltd (ET 2202512/2016)*, *Leyland v Hermes Parcelnet Ltd (ET 1800575/2017)*, and *Boxer v Excel Group Services Ltd (ET 3200365/2016)*. Similar claims against Deliveroo and Royal Mail have been settled for significant sums.

Claims have also been brought in the adult entertainment industry, where dancers and hostesses have traditionally been understood to be self-employed. Employment tribunals reached differing conclusions on the status of dancers in *Kyriazopoulou v Pearl Restaurants Ltd (ET 1600695/2019)* and *Nowak v Chandler Bars Group Ltd (ET 3200538/2019)*.

An application to the Central Arbitration Committee by the Independent Workers Union of Great Britain to be recognised for collective bargaining on behalf of Deliveroo riders was rejected on the grounds that the riders were not workers. A subsequent judicial review in the High Court also failed (*R (IWGB) v Central Arbitration Committee [2019] IRLR 249*). The key issue was, again, personal service: in this case, a contractual clause allowing riders to send a substitute of their choice was held to be genuine because it was, in fact, sometimes exercised.

1.2.3 SELF-IMPOSED LABELS

The tribunal may depart from a self-imposed label if it does not reflect the reality of the relationship – particularly where there is significant inequality of bargaining power or where the label has been imposed to defraud HMRC. Note, however, that in such a case, an employee may be unable to benefit from many employment rights because of the doctrine of illegality (considered further in Chapter 2).

The formation of a one-person limited company as an intermediary between employer and worker does not automatically prevent employee status (*Catamaran Cruisers v Williams [1994] IRLR 386 EAT*). What matters is the reality of the situation. Thus, an individual who provides services to an end-user via their own service company can be the 'employee' of that end-user even though the arrangement is set up through an independent employment agency and even though the contract expressly states that they are 'self-employed' (*Cable & Wireless plc v Muscat [2006] ICR 975 CA*).

It should be noted that other cases have suggested that if the parties choose to impose a corporate intermediary, this is likely to prevent employment status arising (*Costain Building & Engineering v Smith [2000] ICR 215 EAT* and

Hewlett Packard v O'Murphy [2002] IRLR 4 EAT, neither of which are referred to in the *Cable & Wireless plc v Muscat* judgment).

1.2.4 PRACTICAL CONSIDERATIONS

Below are lists of general and specific considerations that may help in assessing whether somebody is self-employed, a worker or an employee. The Government provides helpful guidance at www.gov.uk/employment-status. However, it should be remembered that tribunals will not adopt a 'checklist' approach: they will look at all the factors to form an overall picture.

General indicators

- What the job advertisement said.
- What any written contract or job offer letter says.
- The tax status of the worker: Schedule E is an indicator of employment and Schedule D of self-employment. However, this is not determinative, particularly for 'worker' status where there is no equivalent intermediate category for tax purposes between employee and self-employed.
- Whether there are others doing similar duties for the employer and whether they are employed or self-employed.
- The extent of control exercised by the employer over the worker. Note that a low level of day-to-day control does not preclude an employment relationship, particularly where an agreement provides the employer with the contractual right to control the worker.
- Who arranges a replacement if the individual does not attend work. If the employer arranges a replacement, this will normally indicate employee or worker status. If the individual can arrange his/her own replacement, this will normally indicate self-employed status (unless it is limited to situations where the worker is *unable* to work, or the employer exercises tight control over the choice of substitute).
- Who provides the equipment.
- Who pays for any professional insurance.
- Who carries the financial risk.

Specific pointers towards employee or worker status

- The existence of a staff handbook or collective agreement which governs the individual's work.
- The employer provides a formal induction process or training.
- The employer moves the worker around from job to job.

- The worker receives sick or holiday pay.
- The employer can overrule the worker in respect of how or when the job is done.
- The employer has exercised disciplinary powers over the worker or the worker has used a grievance procedure.
- The contract contains restrictive covenants, such as non-compete or non-solicitation clauses (either during the employment period or post termination).

Specific pointers towards self-employed status

Here, the individual:

- Works from his/her own premises
- Is responsible for his/her own expenses rather than being able to reclaim them from the employer
- Works for other employers/organisations
- Issues invoices before receiving payment
- Stands to make (or lose) money depending on how well they do the job (such a contractor should not be confused with an employee who is paid commission)
- Has invested his/her own money in being able to perform the job properly (for example, buying equipment or paying for training)
- Has their own business cards (rather than company business cards) or advertisements
- Has some influence over their rate of pay (for example, by tendering for the work)

1.3 OTHER CATEGORIES OF WORKERS

1.3.1 AGENCY WORKERS

This category covers people who work for a business but whose contracts are with a separate employment agency. Typically, the employment agency has people seeking work on its books. The agency places a worker with a client (the principal) typically on a short-term (or sometimes a longer-term) contract. The agency pays the worker's remuneration directly, and the principal pays the agency a sum of money which covers the worker's remuneration and a profit element for the agency.

An agency worker's arrangement typically has two distinctive features:

a) The agency has contracts with its end-user client and with the worker (giving rise to what is often referred to as a 'triangular relationship'), but the worker has no contract with the end-user.

b) Control over the work done by the worker is exercised by the end-user and not by the agency.

For some years, the courts consistently held that agency workers were not employees of the end-user (as there was no contract, there was no contract of employment). Agency workers were not considered employees of the agency either due to a lack of day-to-day control by the agency and of mutual obligations to provide and accept work. The current legal position, however, is more complex and less predictable. An agency worker may be an employee of either, both or neither.

Relationship with end-user

Several earlier cases have suggested that a worker might be an employee of an end-user. In *Frank v Reuters Ltd [2003] ICR 1166* and *Dacas v Brook Street Bureau (UK) Ltd [2004] ICR 1437*, the Court of Appeal held that tribunals must consider whether there is an implied contract of employment between the agency worker and the end-user. A number of factors might give rise to such an implied contract, in particular, how long the agency worker works for the end-user. Indeed, at least in theory, the same individual could conceivably be the employee of both the agency *and* the end-user (*Cairns v Visteon UK Ltd [2007] IRLR 175 EAT*). Even where a written agreement provides that it contains the entire agreement between the parties and that no contract of employment exists, this will not be determinative (*Royal National Lifeboat Institution v Bushaway [2005] IRLR 674 EAT*).

More recent case law, however, has moved away from the position in *Frank v Reuters* and *Dacas v Brook Street Bureau (UK) Ltd* despite neither case being overruled. In *James v Greenwich Council [2008] ICR 545*, the Court of Appeal reminded tribunals that the test for implying a contract between an agency worker and end-user was whether it was *necessary* to do so. If the relationship – including the element of control by the end-user – could be explained by a straightforward agency agreement, there would be no necessity to imply a contract between worker and end-user. The judgment concluded with a stern warning to practitioners not to bring cases asserting that agency workers were employed by the end-user unless there was something other than the normal agency relationship in place which demonstrated it was necessary to imply such a contract exists. In *Tilson v Alstom Transport [2011] IRLR 169*, the Court of Appeal held that the fact that a worker is 'integrated' into an end-user's operations and workforce does not mean that the worker automatically becomes its employee.

14

Relationship with the agency

Some agencies expressly agree that their staff are employees. However, attempts to assert employment status in the face of contractual agreements stating the opposite have largely failed, as the agreement often does not have the 'irreducible minimum' factors required for a contract of service to exist. Whilst there may be mutuality of obligation with regard to specific assignments (as noted in *Montgomery v Johnson Underwood Ltd and anor [2001] ICR 819* at [40]), the agency is under no obligation to provide work, and the worker is under no obligation to accept any work offered.

Further, the worker will often struggle to demonstrate the necessary control required in a contract of service, as the agency will not have daily oversight over the agency worker. However, there have been some cases where there has been an exceptional or unusual level of control by the agency over the individual's work for the end-user, thus establishing employment status. One example is *Augustin v Total Quality Staff Ltd* (2008) UKEAT/0343/07, where the individual worked under the supervision of an employee of the agency. Even then, he was only held to be employed under a series of daily contracts rather than an umbrella contract because he was not obliged to accept the work offered to him on a daily basis.

Other rights

The Agency Workers Regulations 2010, SI 2010/93 (implementing Directive 2008/104/EC) do not affect the employment status of agency workers, but they do ensure that after 12 weeks working for a 'hirer', an agency worker is entitled to the same basic rights – notably pay and holiday rights – as the hirer's other employees.

The scope of some employment rights is specifically extended to cover agency workers. This includes protection for whistleblowers (section 43K(1)(a) of the ERA 1996), non-discrimination (section 241 of the EqA 2010) and the national minimum wage (section 34(2) of the NMWA 1998).

1.3.2 APPRENTICES

Apprentices fall within the definition of employee under the EqA 2010 and the TUPE Regulations 2006. They do not, strictly, fall within the definition of employee for the purposes of the ERA 1996 (including the right to claim unfair dismissal), or the *Maternity and Parental Leave Regulations 1999*. However, 'contract of employment' is defined in section 230(2) of the ERA 1996 so as to include a (common law) apprenticeship, thus granting apprentices the right to claim unfair dismissal – although establishing the two-year qualifying period is often a challenge for them.

An apprenticeship agreement is to be treated as being a contract of service as per section A5 and section 35 of the *Apprenticeships, Skills, Children,* and *Learning Act 2009.* The result under section 35 is that apprentices will generally be treated as 'employees' provided they are working under an 'apprenticeship agreement' as defined in section 32. That definition requires that the agreement must be in a 'prescribed form'. This means that the apprentice must be supplied with a written statement of particulars of employment, or a document in the form of a contract of employment or letter of engagement, which must include a statement of the skill, trade or occupation for which the apprentice is being trained (*Apprenticeships (Form of Apprenticeship Agreement) Regulations 2012, SI 2012/844*).

1.3.3 VOLUNTARY WORKERS

Volunteers working for no remuneration for charities and similar organisations are specifically excluded from the right to the National Minimum Wage by section 44(1) of the NMWA 1998. This applies if a volunteer for a charity or voluntary organisation receives:

- a) No monetary payments of any description, or no monetary payments except in respect of expenses:

    - ii) Actually incurred in the performance of his duties; or

    - iii) Reasonably estimated as likely to be or to have been so incurred; and

- d) No benefits in kind of any description, or no benefits in kind other than the provision of some or all of his subsistence or of such accommodation as is reasonable in the circumstances of the employment.

The eligibility of volunteers for other statutory employment law rights depends simply on whether or not they come within the definition of 'employee' or 'worker' under the requirements of the relevant statute. As a general rule, they come within neither definition.

However, payments paid regardless of whether any expenses have actually been incurred, even if called 'expenses', will in law generally be regarded as wages (and will indicate that the recipient is an employee, not a volunteer). For example, in *Migrant Advisory Service v Chaudri (1998) UKEAT/1400/97*, the EAT said 'one must look through the labels to the realities of the relationship. Mrs Chaudri was engaged at a flat rate of £25 per week which, although stated to be in respect of travel and subsistence expenses, bore no relation to the expenses which she actually incurred in travelling to and from work or having meals at work'.

The Supreme Court has ruled that non-remunerated work by a volunteer does not fall within the definition of 'work' or 'occupation' in the *Equal Treatment Framework Directive 2000/78/EC* (*X v Mid Sussex CAB and Challis [2012] UKSC 59*). This decision confirmed that volunteers – unless they have a contract to work personally for those to whom they provide their services –

do not fall within the wide definition of 'employment' in section 83 of the EqA 2010 and cannot bring a discrimination claim.

1.3.4 INTERNS

There is no legal definition of an 'intern'. Essentially, an intern is someone who works in a temporary position with an emphasis on training rather than merely employment. In some ways, an intern is therefore like an apprentice. Some interns are paid but a substantial number are not. Internship arrangements have traditionally been associated with the medical professions but are now much more widely used, particularly in the media.

Whether an intern is a 'worker' – and therefore entitled to be paid the minimum wage (amongst other rights) – turns on whether there is a contract to personally perform work or services. Some interns merely shadow others as part of work experience and will not therefore meet this definition. If, however, they are expected to carry out tasks for the employer, they are likely to have worker status. There does need to be a contract – that is, some form of valuable consideration provided in return for the intern's services – but this need not be monetary. It could, for example, include the provision of training or a promise of paid work on successful completion of the placement.

It is therefore likely that a large number of unpaid interns are, based on the work they do, entitled to be paid the National Minimum Wage. This was the finding of the Social Mobility Commission in its *State of the Nation 2014* report. Part of the problem is a lack of enforcement action, whether by HMRC or through individuals being unable or unwilling to bring claims for non-payment of the minimum wage. In their *Good Work Plan 2018*, the Government stated that they were taking steps against exploitative internships through an HMRC campaign to 'promote greater compliance, including awareness-raising, publicity material and information and guidance'. Government guidance for employers on this issue is available at www.gov.uk/guidance/national-minimum-wage-work-experience-and-internships and www.gov.uk/government/publications/good-work-plan.

Note, however, that the *National Minimum Wage Regulations 2015* contain exemptions for persons on specified training schemes and programmes which are Government-funded, part of an educational course or provided by charities for homeless people (regulations 51 to 56).

1.3.5 WORKERS UNDER 'ZERO-HOURS CONTRACTS'

Zero-hours contracts have been the subject of intense political and media debate in recent years. However, they have little formal significance in employment law and were not even recognised in legislation until 2015. In recent 'gig economy' cases over worker status, the zero-hours nature of a contract has rarely been decisive.

Section 27A of the ERA 1996 defines a zero-hours contract as:

'a contract of employment or other worker's contract under which:

  a) the undertaking to do or perform work or services is an undertaking to do so conditionally on the employer making work or services available to the worker, and

  b) there is no certainty that any such work or services will be made available to the worker'.

A zero-hours contract thus enables employers to call on staff at any time but without guaranteeing any minimum amount of work if it is not available. Because such individuals are not guaranteed to have any work made available to them, there will typically be no mutuality of obligation between them and their employer. Therefore, they are unlikely to be working under a 'contract of employment' for the purposes of section 203(3)(a) of the ERA 1996.

However, a person working under a zero-hours contract may be able to claim employment status and accrue continuity of employment if, in practice, they work regularly. Thus in *Colley v Corkindale [1995] ICR 965 EAT*, an employee worked only once a fortnight – every other Friday – but was held to accrue continuity of employment.

In *Pulse Healthcare Ltd v Carewatch Care Services Ltd (2012) UKEAT/0123/12*, workers who had signed a document entitled 'Zero Hours Contract Agreement' were nonetheless employees on the basis that the documents 'did not reflect the true agreement between the parties'. The factors that the EAT cited as demonstrating that there was sufficient mutuality of obligations were as follows:

'Once the rota was prepared they were required to work and the employer was required to provide that work. They were subject to control and discipline; they had to provide personal services; they were provided with uniforms and equipment; they were paid on a PAYE basis; they had all worked regularly over a number of years and had only taken time off for holidays, sickness and when suspended for which they received payment; it was not established that there were gaps in the continuity of employment. The claimants required regular work and this was provided by the first respondent'.

Further, as discussed above, individuals working under a zero-hours contract may still have 'worker' status, which does not require the same mutuality of obligation as 'employee' status.

Despite calls for tighter regulation and even the outright banning of zero-hours contracts, legislative intervention has been limited to a restriction on exclusivity clauses. Under section 27A(3) of the ERA 1996, any requirement in a zero-hours contract not to work for another employer is unenforceable. The worker also has protection against any detriment or dismissal on the ground that they are working for another employer (*Exclusivity Terms in Zero Hours Contracts (Redress) Regulations 2015, SI 2015/2021*). This covers situations where an employer punishes a zero-hours worker's perceived disloyalty by offering them no further work.

However, a loophole remains in that an employer could (arguably) escape the legislation simply by guaranteeing an extremely limited number of hours, for example, one hour per month. It is also unclear exactly what is meant by 'no certainty' that work will be offered.

1.3.6 COMPANY DIRECTORS

A director may be an employee as well as a director, but this is not automatic. Indeed, it is common practice for companies to have non-executive directors who are not employees and have no service agreement or employment relationship of any sort with the company.

Whether a director of a company is an employee depends on the facts of each case. Relevant considerations include the reasons for the contract, whether it was made when insolvency loomed, what each party actually did pursuant to the contract and – importantly – the degree of control exercised by the company over the individual. Ultimately, the most important single test is likely to be whether the individual concerned is, in reality, answerable only to themselves. If 'yes', the tribunal can find that the contract under which they work is not, in reality, a 'contract of service', and therefore they are not an employee.

A controlling shareholding is not on its own determinative of the issue (*Nesbitt v Secretary of State for Trade and Industry [2007] IRLR 847 EAT*), but it may raise doubts as to whether the individual concerned is truly an employee. In *Secretary of State for Business, Enterprise and Regulatory Reform v Neufeld [2009] IRLR 475*, the Court of Appeal issued fresh and detailed guidance on determining whether a majority shareholder is a director or an employee. In essence, the court stated that all the evidence as to whether there is a contract of employment must be considered. The controlling shareholding is simply one of the background factors to be taken into account.

In *Clark v Clark Construction Initiatives Ltd & anor [2008] IRLR 364*, the EAT also said that if a contract purports to be a contract of employment, the onus is on the party seeking to deny its effect to satisfy the court that it is not what it appears to be. This is particularly so where the individual has paid PAYE and National Insurance as an employee 'as on the face of it he has earned the right to take advantage of the benefits which employees may derive from such payments'.

The fact that the individual has guaranteed a company's debts to a bank is not inconsistent with their being its employee (*Neufeld v A&N Communication in Print Ltd (2008) UKEAT/0177/07* – which is also authority for the proposition that the individual's status has to be considered as it was at the time relevant to the case in point, not at the date when they first began working for the company).

All employees are subject to a duty of fidelity, implied into all employment contracts. However, only those who are in a fiduciary position – such as directors – owe a fiduciary duty (an equitable obligation born of a particular relationship) to their company. From this, it follows that, unlike normal employees, company directors generally have a duty to report their own misconduct, or that of colleagues, to their company (*Lonmar Global Risks Ltd v West & ors [2011] IRLR 138 QBD* – in which the court pointed out that 'the hallmark of a fiduciary duty is a requirement that a person pursues the interests of another at the expense of his own').

1.3.7 PARTNERS

Partners in a firm, other than salaried partners, are not normally employees. Rather, they are 'persons carrying on a business in common with a view of profit' (section 1 of the *Partnership Act 1890*). No minimum voting rights or share of profits are required before a person can be a partner (*Tiffin v Lester Aldridge LLP [2012] ICR 647 CA*). The status of a partner is different from (say) an executive director of a company, who will usually be an employee.

While most employment protection legislation does not apply to partners, discrimination legislation does. Section 44 of the EqA 2010 prohibits discrimination, victimisation and harassment by firms against prospective and established partners.

Salaried partners – who, usually, will not be partners within the strict meaning of the *Partnership Act 1890* – are normally employees and qualify for all employment rights.

Limited liability partnerships (LLPs), established under the *Limited Liability Partnerships Act 2000* (LLP Act 2000), are different from the traditional partnership relationship in that an LLP exists as a distinct legal person, which limits the individual liability of each of its members. Section 4(4) of the LLP Act 2000 states that an LLP member shall not be regarded as employed 'unless, if he and the other members were partners in a partnership, he would be regarded for that purpose as employed by the partnership'. In the case of *Tiffin v Lester Aldridge LLP*, referred to above, Mr Tiffin was held to be a 'partner' within the meaning of the *Partnership Act 1890*, working under the LLP membership agreement. Accordingly, he was not an employee.

However, in *Clyde & Co LLP v Bates van Winkelhof [2014] ICR 730 SC*, the Supreme Court held that a partner in an LLP was a 'worker' for the purposes of a whistleblowing claim under the definition in section 230(2) of the ERA 1996.

1.3.8 ARBITRATORS

The definition of employment under the EqA 2010 is broad but not without its limits, as the case of *Jivraj v Hashwani [2011] UKSC 40* demonstrates. Here, the Supreme Court held that although appointing an arbitrator involved the retention of their services, they were not 'employed' and not covered by the *Employment Equality (Religion or Belief) Regulations 2003, SI 2003/1660* (which contained substantially the same definition of 'employment' as section 83 of the EqA 2010). Applying the principles from the European Court of Justice (ECJ) case of *Allonby v Accrington and Rossendale College and ors (Case C-256/01) [2004] ECR I-873*, the court reasoned that arbitrators are not employed 'under a contract of work' as they are not in subordination to the person receiving the service nor under their direction. Rather, they are independent service providers.

1.3.9 CIVIL SERVANTS

There is debate about whether civil servants should properly be regarded as office holders or as ordinary employees – or even as both (*R v Lord Chancellor's Department, ex parte Nangle [1991] ICR 743 CA*). However, this question is largely academic as section 191 of the ERA 1996 expressly provides that the majority of rights under that Act (including the right to claim unfair dismissal) apply to Crown servants. In addition, the EqA 2010 expressly applies to civil servants. However, Crown servants are not entitled to written particulars of employment, a statutory minimum notice period or a statutory redundancy payment.

1.3.10 MINISTERS OF RELIGION

Traditionally, ministers of religion did not normally come within the definition of 'employee'. This was on the basis that an undertaking to perform religious duties was not a contractual relationship but a calling which stemmed from the beliefs and ethics of the individual.

However, *Percy v Church of Scotland Board of National Mission [2005] UKHL 73* changed that. By a majority, the House of Lords ruled that a Church of Scotland Minister's relationship with her church constituted employment for purposes of the *Sex Discrimination Act 1975*. That Act gave a wider meaning to 'employment' than the ERA 1996, which was not then under consideration as Ms Percy had earlier dropped an unfair dismissal claim. Nevertheless, two of the five Law Lords suggested that the traditional position might need to be reconsidered. This happened the following year, in 2006, when the EAT ruled that a minister, this time of the New Testament Church of God, was an employee and could claim unfair dismissal. The decision was later upheld by the Court of Appeal (*New Testament Church of God v Stewart [2008] ICR 282*).

The Supreme Court revisited the employment status of ministers of religion in *Preston (formerly Moore) v President of the Methodist Conference [2013] UKSC 29*. The court held unanimously that there is no presumption against an intention to create legal relations in the appointment of a minister of religion. Rather, the question of a minister's employment status involves consideration of the manner in which they are engaged and the terms governing their service. After analysis of the internal arrangements of the Methodist Church, the court held by majority that in this case, there was no intention to create a legally binding contract: the minister's entry into the church was covenantal, not contractual.

In addition to this case law, the *Ecclesiastical Offices (Terms of Service) Regulations 2009, SI 2009/2108*, ensure that as a general rule, Church of England clergy have the same employment law rights as employees.

1.3.11 POLICE

Police service is not 'employment' for the purposes of the ERA 1996. Accordingly, police officers do not qualify for the statutory protections against unfair dismissal, redundancy and/or unlawful deduction from wages. However, special rules extend discrimination legislation (section 42 of the EqA 2010) and health and safety rules to police officers.

Police officers have whistleblowing protection in the same way as other workers (section 43KA of the ERA 1996). The Independent Police Complaints Commission has been added to the list of 'prescribed persons' to whom disclosures concerning the conduct of police officers can be made.

1.3.12 JUDGES

Judges have traditionally been regarded as officeholders unprotected by employment law. However, this position is no longer certain. In *O'Brien v Ministry of Justice [2010] UKSC 34*, the Supreme Court was asked to consider whether part-time recorders could satisfy the definition of 'worker' in the *Part-time Workers Regulations*. The court referred the issue of the EU definition of worker to the ECJ, which said that while it was for member states to define who is a worker for the purpose of the regulations, and in particular to determine whether judges fall within that concept, such a determination must not arbitrarily exclude judges from the protection of the *Equal Treatment Framework Directive*. In addition, the ECJ observed that the fact that judges are labelled as 'judicial office holders' rather than 'employees' is insufficient in itself to exclude them from protection against discrimination. When the case returned to the Supreme Court, it confirmed that part-time recorders are 'workers' for the purposes of the UK regulations (*O'Brien v Ministry of Justice [2013] UKSC 6*).

The issue was considered again in *Gilham v Ministry of Justice [2019] ICR 1655*, where the Supreme Court held that a district judge was a 'worker' for the purposes of bringing a whistleblowing claim under the ERA 1996. Although she did not meet the literal definition in section 230(3), the statute had to be interpreted broadly to comply with Article 14 (prohibition of discrimination in the application of human rights) and Article 10 (freedom of expression) of the *European Convention on Human Rights*.

CHAPTER 2
CONTRACTS OF EMPLOYMENT

2.0 OVERVIEW

Every employee has a contract of employment. It may be in writing or verbally agreed (or a combination of both), and the employer and employee may disagree about some of the terms. Nevertheless, the relationship is contractual. Where the terms are not expressed, they are those standard in the trade or as can be inferred from the parties' conduct.

Although the contract of employment itself does not need to exist in writing, all employers are obliged to provide a written statement of particulars of employment which contains basic information for the employee (sections 1-6 of the *Employment Rights Act 1996* (ERA 1996)). This right was previously limited to employees only, but for any contract commencing on or after 6 April 2020, it has been extended to cover all workers (*Employment Rights (Miscellaneous Amendments) Regulations 2019, SI 2019/731*).

Employers have previously had two months from the start of employment to provide written particulars, but any employee or worker whose contract started on or after 6 April 2020 is entitled to receive the particulars on day one.

2.1 WRITTEN PARTICULARS OF EMPLOYMENT

2.1.1 WHAT SHOULD BE INCLUDED?

The list of matters required to be included in the particulars is extensive. Details such as dates of employment, pay, hours, holidays, sickness absence, pensions, notice periods, the place of work, a brief description of the job role and disciplinary and grievance procedures must all be included. The full list is in section 1 of the ERA 1996, and note that further matters must be included for workers who started on or after 6 April 2020.

The statement must also be kept up to date. Any changes in the matters specified in section 1 must be notified to the employee at the earliest opportunity and no later than one month after the change (section 4 of the ERA 1996).

2.1.2 LEGAL STATUS OF WRITTEN PARTICULARS

The statement of particulars is not itself a contract of employment. If the parties have agreed the contractual terms in a separate document, that will always take precedence and the statement of particulars cannot override it in the case of any differences. In fact, provided the written contract or letter of engagement contains all the information required by section 1, and a copy has been given to the employee/worker, there is no need to provide a separate statement of particulars (sections 7A and 7B of the ERA 1996).

However, in the absence of a complete written agreement, the statement of particulars can provide important evidence of the terms the parties may be taken to have agreed. An employer that seeks to persuade a court that the statement of particulars does not accurately reflect the 'real' contractual terms will face an uphill struggle if those terms are not set out in any other written record.

2.1.3 FAILURE TO PROVIDE WRITTEN PARTICULARS

Under section 11 of the ERA 1996, an employee can apply to a tribunal to determine what particulars ought to have been included in a missing or incomplete statement. This may require the tribunal to look for an express contractual term that has been agreed verbally or in some other document, or imply a term from the circumstances and how the contract has been performed in practice (*Mears v Safecar Security Ltd [1982] ICR 626 EAT*). However, the tribunal cannot simply invent a term where there was no express or implied agreement at all (*Eagland v British Telecommunications plc [1993] ICR 644 EAT*). The Court of Appeal has also ruled that the tribunal cannot use its power under section 11 of the ERA 1996 to resolve a dispute between the parties over the interpretation of a vague or unclear contractual term (*Southern Cross Healthcare Co Ltd v Perkins & ors [2011] ICR 285*). The Law Commission has recommended that tribunals be given the express power to rule on disputed contractual terms in such cases (Report on Employment Law Hearing Structures, April 2020).

There is no freestanding financial penalty for an employer that fails to provide a written statement. However, if an employee successfully brings another type of tribunal claim, an additional two or four weeks' pay may be awarded if the employer has not provided a written statement of terms and conditions in accordance with sections 1-3 of the ERA 1996 (section 38 of the *Employment Act 2002*).

Employees also have the right not to be dismissed for requesting a statement of particulars or complaining that they have not been given a full or accurate statement. A dismissal for this reason will be automatically unfair. There is no minimum qualifying service for bringing such a claim (section 104 of the ERA 1996, which covers dismissal for asserting any statutory right).

2.2 ILLEGALITY

Like all contracts, a contract of employment can be tainted with illegality – either inherently (because it requires the parties to commit illegal acts) or in the way the parties perform it. The most common example is where employer and employee attempt to unlawfully evade income tax (*Colen v Cebrian (UK) Ltd [2004] ICR 568 CA*). The employee will, however, normally only be precluded from relying on the provisions of a contract tainted with illegality where they were involved in illegal performance (*Hall v Woolston Hall Leisure Co. [2001] ICR 99 CA* and *Vakante v Addey and Stanhope School (No.2) [2005] ICR 231 CA*). Further, notwithstanding arguments to the contrary by HMRC, the employee must have been aware that there was some form of misrepresentation or some attempt to conceal the true facts of the relationship before the contract is rendered illegal. Simply miscategorising the arrangement as self-employment is not enough (*Enfield Technical Services Ltd v Payne; Grace v BF Components Ltd [2008] ICR 1423 CA*).

How a court approaches an argument of illegality has changed following the Supreme Court's decision in *Patel v Mirza [2017] UKSC 42*. The key question is whether enforcing the claim would harm the integrity of the legal system and whether denying the claim is a proportionate response to the illegality. This involves considering the underlying purpose of the law that has been breached, the seriousness of the illegal conduct, its significance to the contract, whether it was intentional and whether one party is more culpable than the other. However, the new approach is likely to produce the same result as in many earlier cases, particularly where the employee was uninvolved in, or unaware of, the illegal conduct.

If a contract is tainted with illegality but it is possible to sever the legal from the illegal parts, then the employee may be able to enforce their employment rights relating to the lawful parts (*Blue Chip Trading Ltd v Helbawi [2009] IRLR 128 EAT*).

2.3 THE SOURCE OF CONTRACTUAL TERMS

2.3.1 STATUTE

A number of terms are implied into the contract of employment by statute. For example, an equality clause is implied into all contracts of employment to ensure men and women receive the same remuneration for like work or work of equal value (sections 64-66 of the *Equality Act 2010* (EqA 2010)). Also implied by statute is the right to a minimum period of paid holiday (*Barber v RJB Mining (UK) Ltd [1999] ICR 679 QBD*) and the right to minimum notice periods (section 86 of the ERA 1996).

An employee cannot contract out of basic statutory employment rights and any attempt to do so is void under section 203 of the ERA 1996. It is possible to contract out of some subsidiary rights – for example, the 48-hour maximum working week (regulation 5 of the *Working Time Regulations 1998 SI 1998/1833*).

2.3.2 EXPRESS TERMS

Where a contract of employment is in writing, the majority of the terms will be expressly set out. Employment contracts range from basic statements – thereby complying merely with the obligation to set out basic particulars of employment (see 2.1) – to complex and lengthy documents, such as service contracts for company directors. Express terms can also be agreed verbally.

Express terms are often incorporated into a contract of employment by reference to other documents. However, a lack of clear drafting can lead to confusion and, ultimately, litigation.

An employee who has signed a written contract of employment will not normally succeed in a claim that one of its terms was unduly onerous (*Peninsula Business Services Ltd v Sweeney [2004] IRLR 49*). There is no general rule that the terms of employment have to be 'fair' or 'reasonable'.

Collective agreements

These are agreements between the employer and – generally – a recognised trade union. A collective agreement is not legally enforceable by the trade union against the employer (or vice-versa) unless it is in writing and contains a provision stating that the parties intend it to be a legally enforceable contract (section 179 of the Trade Union and Labour Relations (Consolidation) Act 1992 (TULR(C)A 1992)).

The usual means of giving legal effect to collective agreements is by incorporating their terms into individual contracts of employment. This can be achieved through an express clause stating that specific collective agreement terms are incorporated into the contract. Not all of the collective agreement will necessarily be incorporated this way: some aspects, such as a collective bargaining procedure to be followed by the union and employer, are not suitable for inclusion because they do not confer any rights on individual employees. Where incorporation would lead to disastrous commercial consequences for an employer, an intention to incorporate is unlikely to be found (see *Malone v British Airways plc [2011] ICR 125 CA*).

Alternatively, a court may imply a term into the individual contract that the collective agreement is to be incorporated. This cannot be done simply because it would be fair or reasonable. There must be evidence from the parties' conduct that they intend the collective agreement to be binding – for example, where wages have always been set in accordance with the agreement and without protest by the employees, or where there is a clearly established custom and practice. The Court of Appeal has stressed the need for clear evidence to establish a custom and practice of incorporating collectively negotiated terms in a particular industry (*Henry v London General Transport Services Ltd [2002] ICR 910*).

A collective agreement negotiated by a union for its members can apply for the benefit of all employees, even non-union members (*Stewart v The Moray Council [2006] IRLR 168 CAC*).

Staff handbooks

Whether or not the terms of a staff handbook are incorporated into the contract will depend on the handbook's provisions and how they are dealt with within the contract. If there is no contractual term referring to the handbook, it is difficult to predict whether courts will regard the handbook's contents as having contractual status. A useful starting point is the judgment of the Court of Appeal in *Keeley v Fosroc International Ltd [2006] IRLR 961*.

Policies not formally set out in a staff handbook are less likely to be found to be contractual terms. The most important factor appears to be clarity: a vague statement of intent is less likely to achieve contractual status than a clearly defined and detailed policy. However, a sufficiently serious breach of a non-contractual policy may amount to a breach of the implied term of trust and confidence.

2.3.3 IMPLIED TERMS

The law of contract recognises implied terms in a variety of situations: because they are necessary to give business efficacy to an agreement, because they are customary in the trade or because the term is so obvious that the courts assume the parties must have intended it (the 'officious bystander' test). Employment contracts are no different.

The traditional test for an implied term arising from custom and practice is that it must be 'reasonable, notorious and certain' (*Devonald v Rosser & Sons [1906] 2 KB 728*). In *Park Cakes Ltd v Shumba and ors [2013] IRLR 800 CA*, at paragraph 35, Underhill LJ described how a court should approach the question of whether a practice which has been followed in a particular workplace amounts to a contractual term:

'The essential question in a case of the present kind must be whether, by his conduct in making available a particular benefit to employees over a period, in the context of all the surrounding circumstances, the employer has evinced to the relevant employees an intention that they should enjoy that benefit as of right. If so, the benefit forms part of the remuneration which is offered to the employee for his work (or, perhaps more accurately in most cases, his willingness to work) and the employee works on that basis. (The analysis by reference to offer and acceptance may seem rather artificial, as it sometimes does in this field, but it was not argued before us that if the employer had indeed sufficiently conveyed an intention to afford the benefits claimed as a matter of contract, he would not thereby be bound.) It follows that the focus must be what the employer has communicated to the employees. What he may have personally understood or intended is irrelevant except to the extent that the employees are, or should reasonably have been, aware of it.'

2.4 COMMON CONTRACTUAL TERMS

A number of terms are central to the employment relationship and are implied into all contracts. Sections 2.5 and 2.6 relate to terms involving fidelity – such as the duty of confidentiality – and restrictive covenants. The law will only imply limited terms relating to fidelity; anything more should be regulated by express provision.

2.4.1 MUTUAL TRUST AND CONFIDENCE

Neither an employer nor an employee may 'without reasonable and proper cause conduct itself in a way calculated or likely to destroy or seriously damage the relationship of trust and confidence between employer and employee' (*Malik v BCCI [1997] IRLR 462 HL*, as clarified in *Baldwin v Brighton and Hove City Council [2007] IRLR 232 EAT*). The term has been described by Bernard Livesy QC in *RDF Media Group PLC v Alan Clements [2008] IRLR 207,* at paragraph 102:

> 'The implied obligation as formulated is apt to cover a great diversity of situations in which a balance has to be struck between an employer's interests in managing his business as he sees fit and the employee's interest in not being unfairly and improperly exploited. It is a mutual obligation, though it seems that the implied term adds little to the employee's implied obligations to serve his employer loyally and not to act contrary to his employer's interests.'

Therefore, it is far more likely that a breach of the implied term of trust and confidence will be relied upon by an employee rather than an employer.

The existence of the implied term of mutual trust and confidence arguably comes close to an obligation on employers to act 'reasonably'. Indeed, the term has been called an obligation of 'fair dealing' (*Shiner Ltd v Hilton [2001] IRLR 727 EAT*). However, it does not go so far as to impose a general obligation on employers to act sensitively in its dealings with an employee – although the employer must, of course, be careful not to breach the common law duty to take reasonable care to avoid causing foreseeable harm to the employee, including psychological injury (*Deadman v Bristol City Council [2007] IRLR 888 CA*).

It has been held that a breach by an employer of the implied term of trust and confidence will always be repudiatory and therefore will always entitle the employee to resign in response to that breach (*Morrow v Safeway Stores plc [2002] IRLR 9 EAT*). Therefore, this term often forms the basis of constructive unfair dismissal claims.

Examples in which an employer has been in breach of trust and confidence include:

- Verbal abuse of an employee (*Palmanor Ltd v Cedron [1978] IRLR 303 EAT* and *Cantor Fitzgerald International v Bird [2002] IRLR 867 QBD*)

- Arbitrary refusal to award a pay increase (*FC Gardner Ltd v Beresford [1978] IRLR 63 EAT*)

- Failing to provide support for employees, for example, against ill-treatment or bullying (*Wigan Borough Council v Davies [1979] IRLR 127 EAT*)

- unreasonable accusations of theft (*Robinson v Crompton Parkinson Ltd [1978] IRLR 61 EAT*)

- Undermining a supervisor in front of subordinates (*Hilton International Hotels v Protopapa [1990] IRLR 316 EAT*)

- Persistently trying to vary an employee's terms and conditions of employment (*Woods v WM Car Services (Peterborough) Ltd [1982] IRLR 413 EAT*)

- Failing to investigate allegations of sexual harassment (*Bracebridge Engineering v Darby [1990] IRLR 3 EAT*)

- Failing to make reasonable adjustments for a disabled employee (*Greenhof v Barnsley MBC [2006] IRLR 98 EAT*)

The mutual trust and confidence term is particularly important in regulating how an employer exercises a discretion with respect to an employee, for example, when awarding a bonus (*Horkulak v Cantor Fitzgerald International [2005] ICR 402, Commerzbank AG v Keen [2007] ICR 623 CA* and *Ridgway v JP Morgan Chase Bank National Association [2007] EWHC 1325*) or providing a bridging loan for relocation expenses (*French v Barclays Bank plc [1998] IRLR 646 CA*). However, there is no general implied obligation on an employer to advise the employee about their economic well-being, such as ways to maximise pension or insurance benefits (*Crossley v Faithful and Gould Holdings [2004] IRLR 377 CA*).

In exceptional circumstances, it can be a breach of the implied term of trust and confidence for an employer to insist on strict compliance with express terms of an employment contract. In *GMB Union v Brown (2007)*

31

UKEAT/0621/06/ZT, the GMB's insistence on strict compliance with its standard grievance procedures amounted to breach of trust and confidence as it was unreasonable to require the employee to discuss her grievance with the manager perceived as the source of her problems.

If an employer treats one employee less well than others in a particular case, this may amount to a breach of the term of trust and confidence: the duty extends to failing to take positive steps (for example, not offering generous redundancy terms to one employee), as well as taking those positive steps (*Transco v O'Brien [2002] ICR 721 CA*). However, an argument that there was no breach of trust and confidence because the employer, and others in the industry, treat all employees poorly is unlikely to succeed (*McBride v Falkirk Football and Athletic Club [2012] IRLR 22 EATS*).

The first part of the term – 'without reasonable and proper cause' – can be important. An employer may act in a way that damages trust and confidence, but with a good reason to do so. In *Amnesty International v Ahmed [2009] ICR 1450 EAT*, the employer refused a promotion that would have involved travel to Sudan because the employee's Northern Sudanese ethnic origin would put her safety at risk. Although this was direct race discrimination it was not a breach of the implied term because, while the employee felt offended and discriminated against, the employer's reason was genuine and serious.

A constructive dismissal case can be brought by an employee on the basis that a course of conduct by the employer culminated in a 'last straw' and cumulatively amounted to a breach of the implied term of trust and confidence. In such a case, it is not necessary for the incidents which make up the course of conduct to be by themselves serious enough to breach the implied term (*Lewis v Motorworld Garages Ltd [1986] ICR 157 CA*). Nevertheless, the resignation must be in response to an act which contributed something to the chain of events and which was not 'entirely innocuous' (*Omilaju v Waltham Forest LBC [2005] IRLR 35 CA* and *Williams v The Governing Body of Alderman David Church in Wales Primary School (2020) UKEAT/0108/19/LA*).

2.4.2 REASONABLE DISCIPLINARY AND GRIEVANCE PROCEDURES

There is no statutory requirement to conduct disciplinary and grievance procedures 'without unreasonable delay'. However, the courts may imply a term that grievances must be resolved within a reasonable period. Accordingly, an employer who failed to hear a grievance over a two-month period, despite repeated requests from two employees, was found to be in breach of contract (*WA Goold (Pearmak) Ltd v McConnell [1995] IRLR 516 EAT*). In *McLory v Post Office [1993] IRLR 159 QBD*, an employer who suspended three employees for six months while investigating charges of violence was found to be in breach of contract. The court implied a term that an employer would only suspend on reasonable grounds and would continue the suspension only for so long as there were reasonable grounds for doing so.

In *Burn v Alder Hey Children's NHS Foundation Trust [2022] ICR 492*, the Court of Appeal raised the 'strong provisional view' that there may be an implied duty on an employer to act with procedural fairness in the disciplinary process, arising from the nature of the disciplinary process rather than as an aspect of the implied duty of trust and confidence (per Lord Justice Underhill, at [42]).

2.4.3 PROVIDING A SAFE WORKING ENVIRONMENT

Employers must provide a reasonably safe system and place of work, including ensuring that the equipment and fellow employees are reasonably safe. Resignation in response to an employer's failure to comply, or to offer alternative employment when it is not practical to comply, may amount to a constructive dismissal (*Marshall Specialist Vehicles v Osborne [2003] IRLR 672 EAT* and *Flatman v Essex County Council UKEAT/0097/20/BA*).

2.4.4 PAYING WAGES

An employer cannot avoid paying wages by asserting that no wages were ever agreed. The Court of Appeal confirmed in the case of *Driver v Air India Ltd [2011] IRLR 992* that if a contract of employment does not specify a contractual level of payment – in this case, for working overtime – then the law will imply a contractual right to 'a reasonable sum'.

2.4.5 PROVIDING WORK

The courts have not recognised a general 'right to work'. The traditional view is of a 'work-wage bargain'. The employee is entitled only to their wages. As Asquith J put it in *Collier v Sunday Referee Publishing Co Ltd [1940] 2 KB 647*: 'Provided that I pay my cook her wages regularly, she cannot complain if I take all or any of my meals out.'

The position is different where the employee needs to be able to exercise their skills – either to maintain them or to protect the employee's reputation (*Herbert Clayton and Jack Waller Ltd v Oliver [1930] AC 209* and *Land Securities Trillium Ltd v Thornley [2005] IRLR 765 EAT*). Suspension of a professional person, even on full pay, 'inevitably casts a shadow over the employee's competence' and the courts can interfere by granting an injunction in appropriate cases (*Mezey v South West London and St George's Mental Health NHS Trust [2007] IRLR 244 CA*).

Further, an employer must not, without reasonable or proper cause, arbitrarily or capriciously deny the employee the opportunity to work (see *Langston v Amalgamated Union of Engineering Workers [1974] IRLR 15 CA* and *William Hill Organisation Ltd v Tucker [1999] ICR 291 CA*).

2.4.6 DOING THE WORK

An employee is obliged to work, and – except to an extent specifically agreed – may not delegate their duty to someone else. However, an employee is not obliged to obey instructions to do a job different from the one they were employed to do (*Bull v Nottinghamshire and City of Nottingham Fire and Rescue Authority [2007] ICR 1631 CA*).

2.4.7 EXERCISING REASONABLE CARE

Employees must take reasonable care when performing their duties. In principle, an employee who causes loss to their employer by failing to take reasonable care could be sued by the employer (*Janata Bank v Ahmed [1981] IRLR 457 CA*). However, it is unlawful for an employer to make deductions from the employee's wages for any losses caused unless the requirements of part II of the ERA 1996 have been complied with.

2.4.8 OBEYING INSTRUCTIONS

An employee is under an implied obligation to carry out the employer's reasonable and lawful orders. Failure to do so will place them in breach of contract, and this is usually listed as a disciplinary offence in the employee's contract. An order is lawful if it falls within the employee's job description and does not break the law. For example, an instruction to a lorry driver to drive at 100mph would be an unlawful order, and the driver could not be justifiably disciplined for refusing to follow it (*Morrish v Henlys (Folkestone) Ltd [1973] IRLR 61 NIRC*).

Where a written contract clearly defines an employee's contractual duties, there can be an implied obligation on them to carry out duties outside the express terms. This arises if – but only if – there are exceptional circumstances justifying the requirement, the work is suitable, the employee suffers no detriment in terms of contractual benefits or status and the change in duties is only temporary (*Luke v Stoke on Trent City Council [2007] IRLR 305 CA*).

Whether an instruction is reasonable will depend on all the circumstances. The classic case involves an instruction to an employee to visit Turkey, where he had been sentenced to be executed (*Ottoman Bank v Chakarian [1930] AC 277*). Unsurprisingly, this was held to be an unreasonable instruction. In other words, the employer will be subject to the implied obligation of trust and confidence when giving instructions and is likely to be in breach of that obligation if the employer demands of the employee an impossible, criminal or ludicrous act.

2.5 DUTIES OF FIDELITY

This is a complex and rapidly developing area of common law, often involving litigation of some urgency. Although this section summarises the relevant principles, reference to specialist practitioners' textbooks for a detailed study of these duties is recommended.

2.5.1 CONFIDENTIAL INFORMATION

Employers should express unambiguously any information to be kept confidential and make it clear that the obligation of confidence persists after the employment relationship has ended. Such information might include customer lists or trade secrets. If the clause is sufficiently precise, injunctive relief will be granted to prevent employees from misusing this confidential information during, or after, their employment.

The law may imply a term preventing employees from misusing confidential information during their employment, for example, by passing customer lists to competitors or using them for their own gain.

If employees disclose confidential information during their employment, this can justify summary dismissal. Whether it will depends on the level of confidentiality/importance of the information and whether this is listed as a dismissible offence in the employer's disciplinary code. However, employees are afforded considerable protection under whistleblowing legislation if they disclose confidential information in order to reveal some misdeed by the employer (see **Chapter 6**). Further, a current or ex-employee who breaches a confidentiality clause may be able to rely on the 'just cause' defence if disclosure of the particular information is in the public interest (*Lion Laboratories Ltd v Evans [1985] QB 526 CA*).

The duty of confidentiality owed by an ex-employee to their former employer is considerably less onerous than that owed by a continuing employee to their employer. Ex-employees are permitted to use their full skill and knowledge for their own benefit, even if that is in competition with the ex-employer, and once the employment finishes, the law will protect only the trade secrets of the ex-employer. In the absence of an express term (a 'restrictive covenant'), it will not restrict the use by ex-employees of other information accumulated during their employment. What amounts to a trade secret is a question of fact and degree, making it difficult to define (*Faccenda Chicken v Fowler [1986] IRLR 69 CA*). The courts will not imply a confidentiality term which goes beyond that set out above no matter how reasonable it might be to do so (*Brooks v Olyslager OMS (UK) Ltd [1998] IRLR 590 CA*).

An area of concern is the use of 'gagging clauses' or 'non-disclosure agreements' (NDAs) in employment contracts or exit agreements, particularly to prevent victims of alleged workplace harassment from making disclosures. In July 2019, the Government indicated that it wants to legislate to ensure that such clauses cannot prevent someone from making a disclosure to the police, or to a healthcare or legal professional, and that the limitations of any confidentiality clause are clearly spelt out in the agreement. The Solicitors Regulation Authority has also issued a warning notice reminding practitioners not to use NDAs to prevent disclosures that are protected by whistleblowing legislation or are reportable to regulators.

2.5.2 COMPETITION DURING EMPLOYMENT

An implied term prevents employees from setting up in competition with the employer or working for a competitor. This applies even outside working hours, if such employment truly competes with the employer, while the employment subsists. Often, contracts include restrictive covenants which define the geographic areas or type of work in which the employee is prohibited from competing. The law distinguishes between, on the one hand, actual competition – which an employee cannot engage in – and on the other, steps taken in anticipation of competition – that is, preparing to compete. The law does not imply a term to prevent the latter (*Hivac Ltd v Park Royal Scientific Instruments [1946] All ER 350 CA, Marshall v Industrial Systems [1992] IRLR 294 EAT* and *Foster Bryant Surveying Ltd v Bryant [2007] IRLR 425 CA*).

2.5.3 COMPETITION AFTER EMPLOYMENT

On termination of employment, subject to any enforceable post-termination restrictive covenant in the contract, an employee is free to compete with their employer. Further, if the termination resulted from a breach of contract by the employer – for example, in a constructive dismissal situation – the general rule is that any restrictive covenants, even if otherwise reasonable and enforceable, will fall away with the rest of the contract and so not be enforceable (*General Billposting Co Ltd v Atkinson [1909] AC 118 HL*, but see *Rock Refrigeration v Jones [1997] ICR 938 CA* and *Campbell v Frisbee [2003] ICR 141 CA*).

Where a former employee takes confidential information, such as client lists, to use as a 'springboard' in their new employment, an employer may seek an injunction under the 'springboard doctrine'. To succeed, the employer must show that the ex-employee has obtained an unfair and ongoing competitive advantage by taking the information. The principles governing the period and scope of a springboard injunction are helpfully summarised in the case of *QBE Management Services (UK) Ltd v Dymoke and ors [2012] IRLR 458 QBD*.

2.6 RESTRICTIVE COVENANTS

The courts will not imply restrictive covenants – they must be express terms (*Wallace Bogan & Co Ltd v Cove [1997] IRLR 453 CA*).

2.6.1 LEGITIMATE BUSINESS INTERESTS

The onus is on the employer to demonstrate it is seeking to protect a legitimate business interest. Logically, the covenant becomes unenforceable when an employer has ceased to carry out the trade or business in question at the time the restriction is to be applied (*Phoenix Partners Group LLP v Asoyag [2010] IRLR 594 QBD*).

Customers and suppliers

To establish that the employer is seeking to protect a legitimate business interest, the restrictive covenant should normally identify – either as a class or, ideally, by name – the customers and suppliers with whom the ex-employee has had contact in the recent past. Given these might change as time goes on, it is common to agree that the employer can provide a list at regular intervals. If the ex-employee has had no contact with particular customers, then the employer may have no business interest to protect in relation to them, and a clause that purports to give such protection will go further than is necessary to protect the employer's interests (*Herbert Morris Ltd v Saxelby [1916] 1 AC 688 HL*).

Staff

Courts are likely to recognise that employers have a legitimate business interest in maintaining a stable workforce. It may therefore be permissible to restrain ex-employees from soliciting people they used to work with to join their new enterprise. However, as with customers and suppliers, the clause must be carefully drafted (*CEF Holdings Ltd and anor v Mundey and ors [2012] IRLR 912 QBD*).

2.6.2 NO MORE THAN IS REASONABLE TO PROTECT THE EMPLOYER'S INTERESTS

The doctrine of 'restraint of trade' requires that post-termination restrictive covenants – which inevitably do restrain an ex-employee's freedom to trade – must be no more than is reasonable to protect the ex-employer's legitimate business interest. If a restrictive covenant is held to be unreasonable, it is void and unenforceable. Minor phrases or clauses can be severed, leaving the remainder of the clause intact. However, in the absence of any ambiguity, the courts cannot 'read down' an otherwise unreasonable covenant to render it enforceable (*TFS Derivatives v Morgan [2005] IRLR 246 QBD*).

Extent of covenants

Courts may permit a prohibition on a senior ex-employee from working for a direct competitor, but in order to be upheld, such a clause will have to be subject to strict geographical and temporal limits (*Dentmaster (UK) Ltd v*

Kent [1997] IRLR 636 CA). As Sir Christopher Slade said in *Office Angels Ltd v Rainer-Thomas and anor [1991] IRLR 214 CA* at paragraph 54:

> 'A covenant which prohibits wholly the carrying on of business by a former employee in a specified area for a specified time will always be approached with caution by the court, since it amounts to a covenant against competition.'

In this case, the Court of Appeal found that a restriction preventing the employees from working within a small radius comprising the City of London was inappropriate because it was wider than necessary for protection and would exclude the employees from working in a 'particularly fertile area for persons carrying on this class of business'.

In contrast, in *Hollis & Co v Stocks [2000] IRLR 712*, the Court of Appeal found that the judge at first instance was entitled to conclude that a restraint of trade within a 10-mile radius around the town of Sutton-in-Ashfield in Nottinghamshire was reasonable, considering the 'nature of the area' and the fact the restriction did not cover the cities of Nottingham and Derby.

The reasonableness of any geographical restriction will depend on the nature of the trade and the competition. A court might uphold a restrictive covenant preventing a print shop manager in Yorkshire from competing within seven miles of an ex-employer's premises, but a one-mile radius clause in central London is likely to be struck down. That would effectively prohibit a print shop manager from earning a living anywhere in central London (*Scully UK Ltd v Lee [1998] IRLR 259 CA*). A solicitor's post-termination six-mile geographical competition restriction was void as too wide, but a 12-month anti-client-poaching restriction was valid in *Allan Janes LLP v Johal [2006] IRLR 742 ChD*. A 12-month post-termination restrictive covenant in the employment contract of the managing director of a firm of insurance brokers was valid in *Thomas v Farr plc & anor [2007] ICR 932 CA*.

When drafting a restrictive covenant clause, the employer should carefully consider how the geographical and temporal restrictions will affect the individual employee, taking into account the employee's occupation or profession. Two important factors are the seniority of the employee and the effect that the restriction will have on the employee's ability to earn a living. Courts will be more willing to enforce a restrictive covenant against a senior employee than a junior one. It is not sufficient that the clause is reasonably necessary to protect the employer's interests. The court will undertake a balancing act to weigh the prejudice to the employer in striking down the covenant against the prejudice to the employee in enforcing it (*Empire Meat Co Ltd v Patrick [1939] 2 All ER 85*).

Clauses that prohibit holding any kind of financial interest in a competitor, in addition to working for one, are more difficult to justify. In *Tillman v Egon Zehnder Ltd [2019] ICR 1223 SC*, a covenant that an ex-employee should not 'be interested in' any competitor in the first six months after leaving was held to be void because it prohibited holding even a minority share in another business.

Dismissal of an employee for refusing to accept new reasonably required restrictive covenants can potentially count as 'some other substantial reason' for dismissal and thus be potentially fair (*Willow Oak Developments Ltd t/a Windsor Recruitment v Silverwood & ors [2006] ICR 1552 CA*). However, this principle should be approached with caution. The imposition of a new restrictive covenant is a significant variation in an employee's employment contract (see **2.7**), and much will depend on the employer's business justification and the impact of the proposed covenants.

Standard form clauses

It is important that the employer provides evidence that it has weighed up the need for the clause, and the extent to which it impacts on the ex-employee. In *Wincanton Ltd v Cranny [2000] IRLR 716 CA*, a post-termination non-competition clause failed mainly because the wording was the company's standard form and not tailored to the employee's specific field of work.

Specific consideration

The fact that the employer makes a specific termination payment to an ex-employee – a golden handshake – to secure their agreement to restrictive covenants does not override the public interest test that the clause go no further than is reasonable to protect the employer's legitimate business interests (*Turner v Commonwealth & British Minerals Ltd [2000] IRLR 114 CA*). However, the employee's agreement in these circumstances will be a factor in determining what is reasonable (*TSC Europe (UK) Ltd v Massey [1999] IRLR 22 ChD*, at paragraph 49).

2.6.3 TUPE TRANSFERS

Following a transfer under the Transfer of Undertakings (Protection of Employment) Regulations 2006 (TUPE Regulations 2006), all contracts of employment will be transferred to the purchaser. The basic position is that valid restrictive covenants in the employees' contracts can be enforced by the new owner of the business. However, it is unlikely the scope of the restrictive covenant will be widened by the transfer to cover the whole business of the new employer (*Morris Angel & Son Ltd v Hollande [1993] ICR 71 CA*). The transferee will be able to enforce the 'same restriction' as was envisaged prior to the transfer (see Dillon LJ at paragraph 24 of *Morris Angel*).

Any introduction of, or variation to, a restrictive covenant that is because of the TUPE transfer will be rendered void by regulation 4(4) of the TUPE Regulations 2006 (see **Chapter 11**).

2.7 VARYING CONTRACT TERMS

Employers frequently need to vary contract terms, for example, due to business reorganisation or to harmonise employment contracts among different workers. Any unilateral change of terms and conditions operating to the employee's detriment will usually entitle them to resign and claim constructive dismissal.

2.7.1 EMPLOYEE'S OPTIONS

An employee faced with a unilateral change in their terms to which they do not agree must decide whether to carry on working, but under protest, or resign and claim constructive dismissal. If they take the first route – sometimes called the 'stand and sue' option – they should make clear that they are only continuing to work under protest or duress (as in *Hepworth Heating Ltd v Akers (2003) EAT/13/02/MAA*, where the employee signed a new agreement but added the words 'under duress'). An employee who continues to work without objection may be held to have accepted the change, as discussed at 2.7.4.

However, an employee who wishes to work on 'under protest' while reserving the right to resign and claim constructive dismissal if the employer insists on enforcing the changes must be very careful. If, under protest, they work under the new terms and then subsequently refuse to do so, the employer will have grounds to dismiss them and successfully resist a claim of unfair dismissal simply because the employee did not keep their side of the bargain (*Robinson v Tescom Corporation [2008] IRLR 408 EAT*).

If the change is sufficiently fundamental to amount to a wholesale withdrawal of the old contract and replacement with a new contract, the employee may be able to continue to work under new terms under protest and, at the same time, claim unfair dismissal on the basis that they were dismissed from their 'old' job. This was found in *Hogg v Dover College [1990] ICR 39 EAT*, where the head of history at Dover College was demoted, his teaching hours and salary were halved and he was required to teach other subjects as well as history.

2.7.2 DOES THE VARIATION NEED THE EMPLOYEE'S CONSENT?

Sometimes, the employer will change policy rather than contractual terms. The latter requires consent, but the former does not. However, when considering the variation of policy terms that bestow an entitlement on an employee, an employer must be alive to the possibility that the contents of that policy may have obtained contractual force (see *Keeley*, referred to at 2.3.2).

In addition, some contracts of employment contain or incorporate a clause entitling the employer to make changes without the employee's express consent. If so, the employee's consent need not be obtained, provided that the changes are implemented so as not to breach the implied term of trust and confidence (*Bateman & others v Asda Stores Ltd [2010] IRLR 370 EAT*).

In *Dresdner Kleinwort Ltd and anor v Attrill and ors [2013] IRLR 548 CA*, an employer was found to have exercised its express power to unilaterally vary its employees' contracts when it announced that it had established a discretionary bonus scheme. The announcement was intended to help retain staff in a period of uncertainty before part of the business was sold. The subsequent introduction of a 'material adverse change clause' in an attempt to avoid paying the bonuses was held to be a breach of the implied duty of mutual trust and confidence.

2.7.3 CONSULTATION

If agreement to a variation is yet to be obtained, the employer should explain the proposed changes, the reasons behind them and the consequences of them not being implemented. Employees should be encouraged to raise concerns, and these should be assessed and considered. It is prudent to consult with employees' representatives at this stage because if, eventually, any employees do not agree to the changes and are dismissed, the duty of collective consultation will arise prior to the dismissal (*Information and Consultation of Employees Regulations 2004, SI 2004/3426*). If changes are made to more than 20 contracts, failure to engage in collective consultation could result in a protective award of up to 90 days' pay per employee being made against the employer (section 188 of the TULR(C)A 1992).

2.7.4 OBTAINING AGREEMENT

Any variation should be supported by consideration. This can take the form of a pay rise or, when that is not practical, a one-off incentive, such as a bonus or an extra day's paid holiday. If the employee's agreement is not supported by consideration, it may be invalid, although the employer may still be able to argue that the employee's employment on the old terms was terminated and a new contract came into existence on the new terms.

Employees who agree changes, however reluctantly, will be bound by them. Agreement can be inferred by continuing in employment on the altered terms without raising any objection (see, for example, *GAP Personnel Franchises Ltd v Robinson (2007) UKEAT/0342/07*), but this is not automatic and such an inference will not be drawn lightly (see *Khatri v Cooperative Centrale Raiffeisen-Boerenleenbank BA [2010] IRLR 715 CA*). In *Abrahall v Nottingham County Council [2018] ICR 1425*, paragraphs 83-89, the Court of Appeal held that the inference must arise 'unequivocally' from the employee's conduct. Put another way, the employee's conduct by continuing to work must be 'only referable to his having accepted the new terms imposed by the employer' (the test set out by Elias J in *Solectron Scotland Ltd v Roper and ors [2004] IRLR*

4 EAT). Therefore, if a change concerns an issue which will only be relevant in the future, such as pension rights or sickness benefits, continued working cannot be taken as acceptance of the variation.

2.7.5 IF AGREEMENT CANNOT BE OBTAINED

Changes should not simply be imposed, as that would risk giving the employee the right to resign and claim unfair and/or wrongful constructive dismissal. However, if a good, sound business reason for an important change can be shown and proper consultation has been undertaken – particularly if a sizeable proportion of the workforce has agreed to the change – then the constructive dismissal is likely to be fair. (See *Willow Oak Developments Ltd t/a Windsor Recruitment v Silverwood & ors [2006] ICR 1552 CA*, in which an employee had resigned after refusing to accept a new restrictive covenant.)

The safest route for the employer is to comply with the general law of contract: to give notice of termination to all employees who have refused to consent to the change, coupled with an offer of a new contract, with the variations, to start immediately on termination of the old contract ('fire and rehire'). However, this can be highly damaging to staff morale and, of course, may result in unfair dismissal claims being brought – although, as set out above, the employers have a good argument that the dismissal was fair. An employee who is offered a new contract on reasonable terms without substantial changes is unlikely to be awarded much (if anything) by way of compensatory award if they succeed in claiming unfair dismissal. The tribunal will, however, normally award the basic award in full. Knowing this, employers and employees sometimes agree cash sweeteners calculated by reference to the basic award formula in return for accepting changes in terms of employment. If more than 20 employees are dismissed, collective consultation is required.

It must be noted that there has been increased criticism of the practice of 'fire and rehire' in light of P&O Ferries sacking 800 workers on the spot without consultation. On 29 March 2022, the Labour Markets Minister announced in Parliament a new statutory code to seek to clamp down on this practice 'when parliamentary time allows'. The Supreme Court has also granted permission to hear an appeal related to fire and rehire practices from the Court of Appeal judgment of *USDAW and ors v Tesco Stores Ltd [2022] EWCA Civ 978*.

2.7.6 WRITTEN STATEMENT OF CHANGES

An employer must provide an employee, or a worker whose contract commenced on or after 6 April 2020, with a written statement of any changes to the main terms and conditions of employment within one month of the variation (section 4 of the ERA 1996).

2.7.7 VARIATIONS FOLLOWING A TUPE TRANSFER

It is unlawful to vary any terms and conditions, except those relating to pension rights, for any reason related to a TUPE transfer.

There is an exception, and this is where the reason for the variation is an economic, technical or organisational (ETO) reason entailing changes in the workforce. However, European Court of Justice rulings have made this all but impossible to establish, as 'entailing changes in the workforce' has been limited to changes in the *numbers* or the *functions* of the workforce (*Delabole Slate Ltd v Berriman [1985] IRLR 305 CA* and *Green v Elan Care (2002) EAT/18/01* but see also *Crawford v Swinton Insurance Brokers Ltd [1990] IRLR 42 EAT*). See **11.6.2** for more on the ETO defence.

If the employer purports to vary contractual terms, the variation will be void and the employee can insist on the old terms. Further, any variation (unless trivial) that adversely affects employees will entitle them to claim constructive dismissal and this will be automatically unfair (regulation 7(1) of the TUPE Regulations 2006).

Courts dislike this restrictive approach. As a result, when fixed-term transferred employees' contracts expire and are renewed on different terms which harmonise with those routinely used by the transferee, the variation has been held not to be prohibited under the TUPE Regulations 2006. This is because new terms in new contracts resulted from the expiry of the previous fixed-term contracts rather than from the TUPE transfer (*Ralton v Havering College [2001] IRLR 738 EAT*).

2.8 CLAIMS FOR BREACH OF CONTRACT

Contractual claims can be brought in the county court or High Court or in employment tribunals (*Employment Tribunals Extension of Jurisdiction (England and Wales) Order 1994, SI 1994/1623*) (the 1994 Order). Only employees can commence breach of contract claims in the employment tribunal, although an employer can counterclaim once a contract claim has been raised. A claim can only be brought in a tribunal once the employment contract has terminated (article 3(c) of the 1994 Order). Tribunals cannot award more than £25,000. Any excess over this statutory maximum of £25,000 cannot be recovered in a civil court, even if the claimant expressly reserved the right to pursue a civil court claim for the excess (*Fraser v HLMAD Ltd [2006] ICR 1395 CA*).

It is worth noting that an equal pay claim is technically a claim for breach of contract and so can be brought in either a court or an employment tribunal. This can be useful if a claim would be out of time in a tribunal but not in a court: an equal pay claim at a tribunal must be brought within six months after leaving employment, but the normal six-year limitation period applies to a breach of contract claim in a county court or the High Court. While a court would normally refer an equal pay case to an employment tribunal (section 128 of the EqA 2010), it need not do so if the case would be time-barred there (*Birmingham City Council v Abdulla & others [2012] UKSC 47*).

In its report on Employment Law Hearing Structures (April 2020), the Law Commission recommended that tribunals' jurisdiction to hear breach of contract claims should be widened to cover (a) claims by workers as well as employees; (b) claims that arise during employment; and (c) claims worth up to £100,000. The intention is to reduce the number of cases that must be brought in the civil courts. In June 2021, the Government responded to the report, largely deferring the recommendations for later consideration, particularly in light of the Government's legislative focus on Covid-19 and the increased pressure that this has had on the employment tribunals.

CHAPTER 3

PROBLEMS DURING EMPLOYMENT

3.0 OVERVIEW

Problems during employment are best dealt with as swiftly and informally as possible. Relaxed support from a supervisor is likely to be more effective than a formal warning for poor performance, and an employee being able to discuss their difficulties in an informal and supportive setting can eliminate tension, reduce stress and ultimately lead to a positive work environment.

However, difficulties inevitably arise on both sides of the employment relationship. Employers sometimes need to invoke disciplinary proceedings, and employees have grievances they want to be resolved. The importance of clear lines of communication cannot, therefore, be overstated.

The *Acas Code of Practice on Disciplinary and Grievance Procedures* (the Acas Code) sets out guidance for employers and employees on the process to adopt and principles to follow when handling disciplinary proceedings and grievances. Section 207 of the *Trade Union and Labour Relations (Consolidation) Act 1992* provides that, while a failure to follow a Code of Practice will not have the effect of causing someone to be automatically liable to proceedings, the Acas Code is admissible in evidence. It states that 'any provision of the Code which appears to the tribunal or Committee to be relevant to any question arising in the proceedings shall be taken into account in determining that question'. It is frequently cited by employees claiming unfair dismissal (especially in misconduct cases) or arguing that they were constructively dismissed because their employer failed to deal with a grievance properly.

An unreasonable failure to comply with the Acas Code gives an employment tribunal the power to impose an uplift (where the employer has not complied) or reduction (where the employee has not complied) on any award it makes. The maximum uplift or reduction is 25%.

3.1 THE RIGHT TO BE ACCOMPANIED

It has always been a basic principle of a reasonable disciplinary procedure for an employee to have a right to be accompanied by a companion. This right was codified by sections 10-15 of the *Employment Relations Act 1999* (ERA 1999).

All workers – including agency workers and homeworkers – have the right to be accompanied during any disciplinary hearing, and an employer should advise the employee of this right.

A disciplinary hearing is widely defined in section 13 of the ERA 1999 as a hearing which could result in:

- The administration of a formal warning to a worker by the employer

- The taking of some other action in respect of a worker by the employer

- The confirmation of a warning issued or some other action taken

The right to a companion accordingly extends to any appeal hearing.

The employer must permit the worker to be accompanied by a companion that is chosen by the worker. The companion can be a trade union representative or another of the employer's workers. The companion is entitled to 'address the hearing' and to 'confer with the worker during the hearing' but is not permitted to 'answer questions on behalf of the worker', and so can be there to provide guidance and support but not to act as an advocate.

The ERA 1999 does not entitle a worker to insist on any other type of representative, such as a lawyer, a family member or a friend who is not a work colleague. However, the worker's contract of employment may sometimes provide for wider rights of representation.

Any attempt to contract out of the right to be accompanied is void (section 14 of the ERA 1999).

A worker may invoke the right to legal representation at a disciplinary hearing based on Article 6 of the *European Convention on Human Rights* (right to a fair trial) in some limited circumstances. The general rule is that an argument for legal representation based on Article 6 will not succeed (*R v Securities & Futures Authority Ltd, ex parte Fleurose [2002] IRLR 297 CA*). However, where the employer is a public authority or a private employer carrying out a public function and the employee's ability to get other work is at stake, Article 6 may be engaged (*Kulkarni v Milton Keynes Hospital NHS Foundation Trust [2010] ICR 101 CA* and *Ministry of Justice v Parry [2013] ICR 311 EAT*).

Where an employee's civil right to practise their profession is to be determined by a separate decision-making body – for example, the Disclosure and Barring Service or the General Medical Council – the employee will need to show that their employer's disciplinary proceedings would exert a substantial influence over that body's decision before their Article 6 rights are engaged (*R (on the application of G) v X School Governors [2011] UKSC*

30 and *Mattu v University Hospitals of Coventry and Warwickshire NHS Trust [2013] ICR 270 CA*). In practice, this means reliance on Article 6 rights will fail in the majority of cases.

If a worker 'reasonably' requests to be accompanied by a union representative or work companion at a disciplinary or grievance hearing, the request for a particular companion does not have to be reasonable (*Toal v GB Oils Ltd [2013] IRLR 696 EAT*). The Acas Code was updated to reflect this. However, the request itself must be reasonable. The Acas Code suggests that the worker 'should provide enough time for the employer to deal with the companion's attendance at the meeting', and this may include giving the companion's name in advance and identifying whether they are a fellow worker or union representative.

There is no duty on a fellow worker or trade union official to accept a request to accompany a worker and no pressure should be brought to bear on a person if they do not wish to act as a companion.

Employers must allow companions a reasonable amount of time off during working hours to attend the hearing (section 10(6) of the ERA 1999). If a companion cannot attend on the proposed date, the employer must adjourn the hearing date for up to five working days, if this will enable the companion to be present, provided the alternative time proposed by the employee is reasonable (sections 10(4) and (5) of the ERA 1999).

3.1.1 WHAT IF THE EMPLOYER BREACHES THE RIGHT TO BE ACCOMPANIED?

If an employer fails to allow a worker to be accompanied, the worker is entitled to complain to an employment tribunal, which can award up to two weeks' pay. A week's pay is capped under the statute.

Of more significance is that dismissal of a worker for exercising rights under section 12 of the ERA 1999, whether the worker is the person being accompanied or the companion, amounts to automatic unfair dismissal.

Withholding the right to be accompanied even at the informal oral warning stage can be a breach of the employee's statutory right (*London Underground Ltd v Ferenc-Batchelor* and *Harding v London Underground Ltd [2003] IRLR 252 EAT*).

3.2 DISCIPLINARY PROCEDURES

An employer is obliged to include in the written particulars of employment a note setting out details of any disciplinary rules and procedures applying to an employee. The note must also identify the person to whom an employee can appeal any disciplinary decision (section 3(1) of the *Employment Rights Act 1996* (ERA 1996)).

The Employment Appeal Tribunal (EAT) has emphasised the importance of particularly careful investigation where there are serious allegations of criminal misbehaviour, and it has suggested that the obligation on the investigator is just as much to look for evidence which exculpates the individual as evidence which implicates that individual (*A v B [2003] IRLR 405*).

Employers should be careful not to lean too heavily on HR advisers when carrying out investigations. A dismissal is unlikely to be fair if the investigating officer is subject to pressure or revision from individuals who are not the nominated officer. As was noted in *Ramphal v Department for Transport [2015] ICR D23 EAT*:

> 'A claimant facing disciplinary charges and a dismissal procedure is entitled to expect that the decision will be taken by the appropriate officer, without having been lobbied by other parties as to the findings he should make as to culpability, and that he should be given notice of any changes in the case he has to meet so that he can deal with them.'

In our experience, *Ramphal* has led to many HR professionals refusing to express any views to disciplinary officers, which we think is an excessively harsh reading of the case. As long as the disciplinary officer clearly understands that the decision is ultimately theirs and that they would be the one having to defend the fairness of the process at a tribunal, there is no reason why an HR professional should not express a view on the evidence.

If a dismissal is unfair because the employer followed unfair procedures – for example, an unfair redundancy selection process – the likelihood that the employee might have been dismissed anyway even if proper procedures had been followed can, in some circumstances, be relevant in assessing the compensatory award (see *Software 2000 Ltd v Andrews, Trinder, Prowse and Lawrence [2007] IRLR 568 EAT*).

How to deal with confidential informers

A basic principle of a fair disciplinary process is that the employee should know who is making the allegations against them so that they can challenge the veracity of the accuser. Many defences turn on cross-allegations that the accuser has a grudge against the accused and has manufactured the evidence. Whether the employer accepts this or not, it remains a fundamental principle of natural justice that the employee should know who accuses them.

However, sometimes, the accuser wishes to keep their identity confidential. This may be for a variety of reasons, but the most common is a fear of retribution. The EAT has laid down guidelines on how to approach such a situation. *Linfood Cash & Carry Ltd v Thomson [1989] IRLR 235* should be read in full, but the salient points are, in summary:

1) A formal written statement should be taken from the informer, dealing in detail with the opportunities the informer had to see the disciplinary offence, why the informer was present and whether the

informant has suffered at the hands of the accused or has any other reason to fabricate evidence.

2) The employer should then carry out further investigations with a view to corroborating or undermining the informer's evidence.

3) A decision should then be made, depending on the employer's view of the strength of the evidence, whether or not to carry on with the disciplinary process.

4) The written statement of the informant, with identifying details removed, should be made available to the accused employee.

5) If the accused employee raises any questions about the informer's statement, the disciplinary hearing should be adjourned so that the questions can be put to the informer.

It is important to note that although the *Linfood* guidelines are persuasive, they are not legally binding and in limited circumstances, departure from them is permissible (see, for example, *Ramsey v Walkers Snack Foods Ltd [2004] IRLR 754 EAT*).

Useful guidance on the process of disclosure and redaction in employment tribunal cases involving confidential witnesses is set out in *Asda Stores Ltd v Thompson [2002] IRLR 245 EAT*.

3.3 WRITTEN STATEMENT OF REASONS FOR DISMISSAL

The general rule is that an employee is entitled to request written reasons for the dismissal (section 92 of the ERA 1996). A written statement must then be provided within two weeks. As explained in *Health Development Agency v Parish [2004] IRLR 550 EAT*, if the employee so requests, the law 'requires an employer to lay his cards on the table when he dismisses an employee. Whatever may have been said orally or informally or in negotiations, the reason for dismissal has to be set out with due formality'.

A request may be verbal or written. If the employer unreasonably fails to provide a written statement of the reasons for dismissal within two weeks, the employee can complain to an employment tribunal. The tribunal is entitled to make an award equal to two weeks' pay. The tribunal may also make a declaration as to the reasons for the dismissal.

The general rule does not apply in two situations:

1) If the employee has less than two years' continuous employment, in which case the right to a written statement does not exist (section 92(3) of the ERA 1996).

2) If the employee is pregnant or on maternity, parental or adoption leave, in which case the employee is entitled to a written statement without making any request (section 92(4) of the ERA 1996).

3.4 APPEALS

The Acas Code requires employers to provide employees with an opportunity to appeal against a sanction (see paragraphs 26 to 29). The appeal should be dealt with impartially by a manager who has not been involved in the case previously, if this is possible. The right to be accompanied applies to an appeal, and an employer should inform the employee in writing of the results of the appeal.

Where an employee successfully appeals against a sanction, the ordinary effect (subject to the contract detailing any other procedure), is that the sanction is retrospectively altered (*Roberts v West Coast Trains Ltd [2005] ICR 254 CA*). Where an employee successfully appeals against a dismissal, the dismissal does not take place. In *Salmon v Castlebeck Care (Teesdale) Ltd [2015] ICR 735 EAT*, Langstaff J held that:

> 'It must be implicit in any system of appeal, unless otherwise stated, that the appeal panel has the right to reverse or vary the decision made below. Where a decision is to dismiss, being the most draconian of sanctions, any success on appeal means that the decision is one in which dismissal does not take effect, though some lesser sanction might.'

Note that when an employee appeals, the appeal panel will generally not have the power to increase the original sanction on appeal unless such a power has been expressly provided for (*McMillan v Airedale NHS Foundation Trust [2015] ICR 747 CA*).

CHAPTER 4
WORKING TIME AND TIME OFF WORK

4.0 OVERVIEW

Before the *Working Time Regulations* (WTR 1998), employers and employees were generally free to negotiate the hours of work and holiday they wanted. However, employers were, and still are, subject to a general implied duty to protect the health and safety of workers which could be used to prevent them from requiring excessive hours of work (*Johnstone v Bloomsbury Health Authority [1991] ICR 269 CA* and *Marshall Specialist Vehicles Ltd v Osborne [2003] IRLR 672 EAT*).

There were already some statutory rules in place before the WTR 1998 came into effect and in special cases, these continue. For example, separate statutory provisions apply in respect of children and young persons, lorry drivers and farm workers. It is therefore always important to check whether any additional relevant legislation applies.

This chapter addresses employees' entitlement to have their hours at work regulated. It also addresses their entitlement to time off for various purposes, the most common of which are holiday, sickness and trade union activities. A number of less common entitlements are also dealt with in this chapter. **Chapter 5** considers time off for family reasons.

4.1 SCOPE OF WORKING TIME LEGISLATION

The WTR 1998 implement in UK law EC Directives introduced in the early 1990s, now consolidated as the *Working Time Directive*. This has been retained via the *European Union (Withdrawal) Act 2018*.

There are also separate 'sector-specific' regulations: the *Merchant Shipping (Hours of Work) Regulations 2002*; the *Merchant Shipping (Working Time: Inland Waterways) Regulations 2003*; the *Civil Aviation (Working Time) Regulations 2004*; the *Fishing Vessels (Working Time: Sea-fishermen) Regulations 2004*; and the *Road Transport (Working Time) Regulations 2005*.

Workers covered by these regulations are excluded under regulation 18 of the WTR 1998.

The working time limits set out in the WTR 1998 take effect as implied contractual terms. As a result, workers can enforce their rights to paid holiday or rest breaks in the same way that they can enforce any other contractual right (*Barber v RJB Mining (UK) Ltd [1999] ICR 679 QBD*).

The provisions of the WTR 1998 apply to 'workers', not just to 'employees'. A worker is defined in regulation 2(1) of the WTR 1998 as:

> 'an individual who has entered into or works under (or, where the employment has ceased, worked under) —
>
> a) a contract of employment; or
>
> b) any other contract, whether express or implied and (if it is express) whether oral or in writing, whereby the individual undertakes to do or perform personally any work or services for another party to the contract whose status is not by virtue of the contract that of a client or customer of any profession or business undertaking carried on by the individual'.

In other words, the regulations apply to all employees and self-employed individuals unless they are sole traders running a business on their own account.

The EAT has found that regulation 2(1)(b) of the WTR 1998 created a 'hybrid' category of worker, falling between the position of the individual employee and the individual who is a genuinely self-employed contractor, and stated that as long as someone who falls into this hybrid category was not carrying on a profession or business undertaking, they would be a 'worker' for the purposes of the WTR 1998 (*Torith Ltd v Flynn [2003] All ER 45*). The important question is not 'whether the individual is in business on his own account' but, as the regulations state, whether the other party to the contract is a 'client or customer of any profession or business undertaking carried on by the individual' (*Byrne Brothers (Formwork) Ltd v Baird & ors [2002] ICR 667 EAT* and *Redrow Homes (Yorkshire) Ltd v Wright [2004] ICR 1126 CA*). For further detail, see **1.2**.

4.2 MAXIMUM 48-HOUR WORKING WEEK

Regulation 4(1) of the WTR 1998 provides:

> 'Unless his employer has first obtained the worker's agreement in writing to perform such work, a worker's working time, including overtime ... shall not exceed an average of 48 hours for each seven days.'

The legislation goes further than a ban on employers requiring their workers to work more than the 48-hour limit: they must also take 'all reasonable steps' to ensure that workers comply (regulation 4(2) of the WTR 1998). The Health and Safety Executive (HSE) is responsible for enforcing this wider duty.

4.2.1 CALCULATING THE NUMBER OF HOURS

The regulations concern limiting the average number of hours in a working week. This average is calculated over a rolling 17-week period (regulation 4(3) of the WTR 1998).

Alternatively, the employer can agree a different period with the workforce in a workforce agreement, a collective agreement or a worker's contract of employment. However, this can only be done for 'objective or technical reasons concerning the organisation of work' and is subject to a maximum reference period of 52 weeks (regulation 4(3) read with regulation 23(b) of the WTR 1998). Such an agreement can also provide for fixed successive reference periods, rather than a rolling period.

For certain categories of workers, regulations 4(5) and 21 of the WTR 1998 provide for a 26-week rather than a 17-week reference period. These include:

- Workers who live a long distance from their place of work (including offshore workers, for whom the reference period is 52 weeks (regulation 25B of the WTR 1998).

- Security guards in roles where a permanent presence is required.

- Where there is a need for continuity of service (such as work at hospitals, docks or airports, or in the media, communications or utilities industries).

- Where there are periodic surges of activity (such as in the agriculture, tourism, or postal industries).

- Where the worker's working time is spent on board trains with intermittent activities and their hours are linked to transport timetables. If the worker has been employed for less than 17 (or, if applicable, 26 or 52) weeks, the weekly working hours are averaged out from when employment started (regulation 4(4) of the WTR 1998). Employers should therefore take particular care to ensure that new workers do not exceed the 48-hour average during their first weeks of employment.

Adjustments are made to the number of days within the reference period to take account of any absences owing to 'excluded days'. These are days comprising any period of annual leave taken as part of the statutory right to four weeks' leave; any period of sick leave; any period of maternity, paternity, adoption or parental leave; or any period when the 48-hour limit was disapplied because the worker opted out (regulations 4(6) and (7) of the WTR 1998). The end date of the reference period is extended by the equivalent number of days in order to calculate the weekly average. Note that absences for other reasons (for example, compassionate leave or additional statutory or contractual annual leave) do not count as 'excluded days'.

The regulations do not address how time is calculated if an individual has more than one employer, outside of the context of young workers. However, considering the purpose of the legislation is to protect the health and safety of employees, it is likely that the 48-hour limit is a maximum even if the employee has multiple jobs.

4.2.2 WHAT TIME COUNTS?

'Working time' is defined in regulation 2 of the WTR 1998 as 'any period during which [a worker] is working, at his employer's disposal *and* carrying out his activity or duties' (emphasis added). It also includes time spent on work-related training. Collective or workforce agreements can provide for other periods of time to count as well.

The European Court of Justice (ECJ) has ruled that all time spent by a doctor on call in a hospital constitutes working time for the purposes of the *Working Time Directive* (*Sindicato de Medicos de Asistencia Publica (SIMAP) v Conselleria de Sanidad y Consumo de la Generalidad Valenciana (Case C-303/98) [2000] ECR I-7963*), even if sleeping facilities are provided (*Landeshaupstadt Kiel v Jaeger (Case C-151/02) [2003] IRLR 805*). Similarly, the EAT has held that on-call time spent by a care worker was working time for the purposes of WTR 1998, even though she was allowed to sleep while on call. The worker in question was provided with tied accommodation at her workplace but was required to be available on site to answer calls at any time (*MacCartney v Oversley House Management [2006] ICR 510*).

On-call time spent at accommodation near the workplace can also count. In *Truslove v Scottish Ambulance Service [2014] ICR 1232 EATS*, relief paramedics had to take accommodation within a three-mile radius of their ambulance station and respond to calls within three minutes. Langstaff P reviewed the domestic and European authorities regarding rest breaks and on-call working and concluded that 'the question is whether the individual is obliged to be present and remain available at the place determined by the employer'. In *DJ v Radiotelevizija Slovenija [2021] ICR 1109 ECJ*, the ECJ held that a period of stand-by time was not working time unless the constraints imposed on the worker very significantly affected the worker's ability to manage their free time during that period. In that case, DJ was required to answer telephone calls during his stand-by time and be able to attend his work locations within one hour. Due to the distance of these locations from DJ's home, he stayed in accommodation provided by his employer. The court ruled at paragraph 40 that 'organisational difficulties that a period of stand-by time may generate for the worker, which are not the result of such constraints but are, for example,

54

the consequence of natural factors or of his or her own free choice, may not be taken into account' for the purposes of working time.

For workers with a fixed place of work, time spent travelling between their home and workplace is not 'working time', although travel during the working day would count – for example, to meet a client. Peripatetic workers, however, are entitled to count travel between their home and the first and last customers of the day (*Federación de Servicios Privados del sindicato Comisiones obreras (CCOO) v Tyco Integrated Security SL [2015] ICR 1159 ECJ*). The Supreme Court has also held that Uber drivers are 'working' whenever they have the app switched on and are ready to accept trips, and not just when carrying a passenger or travelling to a pick-up (*Uber BV v Aslam [2021] ICR 657 SC*).

For overtime, the test is whether the employer has asked or required the worker to do it. A worker who voluntarily stays late or takes work home would not be 'working' because they are not 'at their employer's disposal'. Similar considerations would apply to working lunches or work-related social events.

4.2.3 KEEPING RECORDS

There is an obligation to keep records (and to retain them for two years) to see whether the 48-hour maximum working week is being complied with (regulation 9 of the WTR 1998). However, the Court of Justice of the EU has held that the *Working Time Directive* requires employers to maintain an 'objective, reliable and accessible system enabling the duration of time worked *each day* by each worker to be measured' (emphasis added) (*Federacion de Servicios de Comisiones Obreras (CCOO) v Deutsche Bank SAE [2020] ICR 48*). This goes significantly further than required by regulation 9 of the WTR 1998, and the decision implies that the WTR 1998 do not meet the standards required by EU law in this respect. However, in the context of Brexit, it remains to be seen whether the Government will take steps to tighten up the regulations.

There is also an obligation to keep records identifying workers who have signed an 'opt-out' agreement from the 48-hour maximum working week (see **4.2.5**), but the wording of the regulations suggests there is no requirement to keep records of time worked by such workers (regulations 9 and 4(2) of the WTR 1998).

4.2.4 EXCLUSIONS AND SPECIAL PROVISIONS

As well as the blanket exemption from the WTR 1998 for certain sectors covered by specific legislation (see above) , some workers are excluded from the maximum 48-hour working week provisions:

- *Unmeasured working time.* Workers whose working time is neither measured nor predetermined, or whose hours can be determined by the workers themselves, are excluded. The regulations give examples of managing executives or others with autonomous decision-making powers, family workers and ministers of religion (regulation 20 of the WTR 1998).

- *Domestic workers.* Those employed as domestic servants in private households are excluded (regulation 19 of the WTR 1998).

- *Opting out.* See **4.2.5** (regulation 5 of the WTR 1998).

- *Armed forces and police.* These workers are excluded 'where characteristics peculiar to' their services inevitably conflict with the WTR 1998 (regulation 18(2) of the WTR 1998).

Regulation 5A of the WTR 1998 provides extra protection for young workers (those who have attained the age of 15 but not the age of 18 and are over compulsory school age (regulation 2(1) of the WTR 1998)). Their working time must not exceed eight hours per day or 40 hours in any calendar week, and it is not permitted to use a weekly average over a period. If a young worker has more than one employer, these limits apply to their total working hours in a given week. However, this extra protection can be disapplied if the work is necessary to maintain continuity of service or production or to respond to a surge in demand, no adult worker is available and the work would not adversely affect the young worker's education or training (regulation 27A(1) of the WTR 1998).

4.2.5 OPTING OUT

An individual worker and their employer can validly agree to opt out of the permitted working hours limits imposed by the WTR 1998 (regulation 5 of the WTR 1998).

An opt-out agreement must be in writing (regulation 4(1) of the WTR 1998). A worker's consent to the opt-out agreement must be by the individual concerned and cannot be 'given by trade union representatives in the context of a collective or other agreement' (*SIMAP v Conselleria de Sanidad y Consumo de la Generalidad Velenciana (Case C-303/98) [2000] ECR I-7963 ECJ*).

Note that the opt-out at regulation 5 of the WTR 1998 is restricted to the right under regulation 4 of the WTR 1998 to a maximum working week. It is not a general freestanding right to opt out of the other provisions of the regulations.

Any opt-out agreement must be cancellable on not more than three months' written notice (seven days' notice if nothing else has been agreed) (regulation 5(2)(b) of the WTR 1998).

Workers have the right not to be dismissed or subjected to a detriment because they refuse to enter into or continue an opt-out agreement (sections 45A(1)(c) and 101A(1)(c) of the *Employment Rights Act 1996* (ERA 1996)).

However, the protection does not cover job seekers who are refused employment for this reason.

4.3 REST BREAKS AND WEEKLY REST PERIODS

Minimum rest breaks and rest periods for all workers are provided under the WTR 1998. The provisions differ for adult workers and young workers.

4.3.1 DAILY REST PERIODS

A worker must have a minimum of 11 consecutive hours' rest during each 24-hour period for which they work for an employer. A young worker must have at least 12 consecutive hours' rest during each 24-hour period (regulations 10(1) and 10(2) of the WTR 1998). A 'rest period' is defined in the WTR 1998 and the *Working Time Directive* as any period which is not 'working time' or a 'rest break'.

4.3.2 WEEKLY REST PERIODS

Workers must have an 'uninterrupted rest period' of not less than 24 hours in each seven-day period they work for their employer. This is extended to 48 hours for young workers (regulation 11(1) and (3) of the WTR 1998). The seven-day period runs from midnight between Sunday and Monday (unless a relevant agreement provides otherwise), but the timing of the rest period within each week can be determined by the employer. Employers cannot count a daily rest period towards the weekly rest period unless this is justified by objective or technical reasons concerning the organisation of work.

Employers have the alternative option with adult workers of using a two-week base period, in which case the rest period must be at least 48 uninterrupted hours or two separate uninterrupted 24-hour periods (regulation 11(2) of the WTR 1998).

4.3.3 REST BREAKS

Every worker must have an uninterrupted rest break of not less than 20 minutes (or such longer period as may be agreed in a collective or workforce agreement) where their working time exceeds six hours. A young worker is entitled to not less than 30 minutes of rest break where their working time exceeds four and a half hours (regulation 12 of the WTR 1998). The legislation does not stipulate when the rest break should be taken, but it is implicit in the term 'break' that it should not be at the start or end of the working day.

The Court of Appeal in England and Wales has held that a rest break must be a period that does not count as 'working time': the worker should be free to use it as they please and should know at the start of the break that it will be uninterrupted. 'Downtime' between tasks, when the worker is still expected to remain at the employer's disposal, does not constitute a rest break, even if, in fact, it often results in an uninterrupted 20-minute period of rest (*Gallagher v Alpha Catering Services Ltd [2005] ICR 673*).

The Northern Ireland Court of Appeal reached a somewhat different conclusion in *Martin v Southern Health and Social Care Trust [2010] IRLR 1048*, where a nurse's rest breaks were held *not* to count as 'working time' even though they were often interrupted by emergencies or routine practical matters. However, the ruling is not binding on courts in Great Britain. Further, the European Commission has subsequently issued guidance advising that rest breaks should have the same qualities as daily or weekly rest periods – that is, workers should not be obliged to remain at their employer's disposal or carry out their duties (Interpretative Communication on the Working Time Directive of the European Parliament and of the Council concerning certain aspects of the organisation of working time).

Regulation 12(3) of the WTR 1998 stipulates that, unless a collective or workforce agreement provides otherwise, the worker is entitled to spend a rest break away from their workstation if they have one. However, this does not mean that workers must be free to leave their *place* of work.

The EAT has held that there is no right to a second rest break if a worker's shift exceeds 12 hours: the legislation does not provide for one break *per* six hours worked (*Hughes v The Corps of Commissionaires Management Ltd [2009] ICR 345*).

If the pattern according to which an employer organises work may put the health and safety of a worker at risk – in particular because the work is monotonous or the work-rate is predetermined – the employer must ensure that the worker is given 'adequate rest breaks' (regulation 8 of the WTR 1998). It is unclear how this differs from the minimum entitlements under regulation 12 of the WTR 1998, but a precautionary view is that employers should afford such workers longer and/or more frequent breaks than one 20-minute break per shift.

4.3.4 RECORDS

There is no statutory obligation to keep a record of breaks, although it is an ancillary task to the exercise of keeping records of worked time for the purpose of the 48-hour maximum working week. As discussed above, the decision in *Federacion de Servicios de Comisiones Obreras (CCOO) v Deutsche Bank SAE [2020] ICR 48 ECJ* suggests that UK law is insufficiently strict to meet EU law standards on record-keeping.

4.3.5 SPECIAL RULES AND EXCLUSIONS

There are special rules for workers covered by 'sector-specific' regulations as noted above. Workers employed in a domestic capacity in a private household are excluded from the statutory entitlement to rest breaks deriving from monotonous work putting their health and safety at risk, and from the limits on night work (see 4.4). They remain entitled to rest breaks, daily rest and weekly rest (regulation 19 of the WTR 1998).

Workers whose working time is not measured, or who determine it by themselves, are excluded from the statutory entitlement to rest breaks, daily rest, weekly rest and the limits on night work (regulation 20 of the WTR 1998).

Certain 'special cases' – and workers covered by a collective or workforce agreement which derogates from the statutory rules – are exempt from rest breaks, daily rest, weekly rest and the limits on night work. The 'special cases' in regulation 21 of the WTR 1998 cover circumstances where:

- The worker's activities are such that their place of work and place of residence, or different places of work, are distant from one another.

- The worker is engaged in security and surveillance activities requiring a permanent presence in order to protect property and persons.

- The worker's activities involve the need for continuity of service or production.

- There is a foreseeable surge of activity.

- The worker's activities are affected by 'force majeure' or accident.

- The worker works in railway transport, in certain prescribed circumstances.

However, the employer must provide 'an equivalent period of compensatory rest', unless exceptional circumstances make this impossible for objective reasons (regulation 24 of the WTR 1998). The Court of Appeal has held, in relation to rest breaks, that 'equivalent' does not mean identical to the normal rest entitlement, but it should have the same value in terms of contributing to the worker's well-being (*Network Rail Infrastructure v Crawford [2019] ICR 1206*). In that case, a railway signalman could take short breaks from his workstation during naturally occurring gaps in work, which, over a shift, amounted to far more than 20 minutes, but he could not take a continuous 20-minute break. This was held to be equivalent.

There is no domestic case law on equivalent compensatory rest periods for daily or weekly rest, but the ECJ held in *Landeshauptstadt Kiel v Jaeger [2004] ICR 1528* that, if the *daily* rest period is reduced:

- The reduction 'must in principle be offset by the grant of equivalent periods of compensatory rest made up of a number of consecutive hours corresponding to the reduction applied'.

- The compensatory rest must follow immediately from the working time which it is supposed to counteract.

- The worker must be free to pursue his own interests without interruption or any obligation towards his employer.

A further exemption from daily or weekly rest periods (but not rest breaks) applies under regulation 22 of the WTR 1998 in two situations, again with a requirement to provide equivalent compensatory rest:

- A shift worker changes shifts and cannot take the rest period in between the two shifts.

- A worker is engaged in activities involving periods of work split up over the day (an example being cleaning staff).

4.4 NIGHT WORK

4.4.1 WHO IS A NIGHT WORKER?

A 'night worker' is defined as a worker 'who, as a normal course, works at least three hours of his daily working time during night time' (regulation 2(1) of the WTR 1998). Alternatively, a collective or workforce agreement can set the definition based on a proportion of *annual* working time that takes place during night time.

'Night time' is defined in regulation 2(1) of the WTR 1998 as a period:

'(a) the duration of which is not less than seven hours, and

 (b) which includes the period between midnight and 5 am

which is determined for the purposes of these Regulations by a relevant agreement, or, in default of such a determination, the period between 11 pm and 6 am'.

A worker on a rotating shift who, one week out of every three weeks, worked at least three hours at night, fell within the above definition (*R v Attorney General for Northern Ireland, ex parte Burns [1999] IRLR 315*). The court stated that 'as a normal course' means 'as a regular feature of employment' – a worker does not have to work all or even the majority of their shifts at night to qualify for protection. However, a worker who is 'on call' at night is not *automatically* thereby a 'night worker' for the purposes of the WTR 1998 (*SIMAP v Conselleria de Sanidad y consumo de la Generalidad Valenciana (Case C-303/98) [2000] ECR I-7963 ECJ*).

4.4.2 WHAT RIGHTS DO NIGHT WORKERS HAVE?

An employer is required to 'take all reasonable steps, in keeping with the need to protect the health and safety of workers, to ensure that' the normal hours of work of any night worker do not exceed an average of eight for each 24 hours in any applicable reference period (regulation 6(1) and 6(2) of the

WTR 1998). This eight-hour limit applies to the worker's total hours, not just the hours worked at night. The reference period is the same 17-week (or 26-week) rolling period used for the computation of the 48-hour maximum working week. 'Normal hours of work' is not defined, but the Health and Safety Executive's Guidance states that it should include regular overtime but not occasional overtime.

If the night work involves a significant risk to the health and safety of workers employed by the employer (note: not just to the worker involved) or involves special hazards or heavy physical or mental strain, then there is an absolute limit of eight hours' work (of any kind) in any period of 24 hours during which the individual performs night work (regulation 6(7) and 6(8) of the WTR 1998).

An employer must ensure that each night worker has the opportunity of a confidential, free health assessment before starting night work and at regular intervals 'of whatever duration may be appropriate in his case' (regulation 7 of the WTR 1998).

Where possible, a night worker has the right to be transferred to suitable day work if a registered medical practitioner informs the employer that the worker is suffering from health problems connected with working at night (regulation 7(6) of the WTR 1998).

4.4.3 YOUNG WORKERS AND NIGHT WORK

Young workers are generally precluded from working during the 'restricted period' between 10pm and 6am (regulation 6A of the WTR 1998). However, regulation 27A of the WTR 1998 provides that a young worker may:

- Work at any time of night in a hospital or similar establishment, or in connection with cultural, artistic, sporting or advertising activities
- Work outside of the period between midnight and 4am in agriculture, retail, postal or newspaper deliveries, catering, hotels, bars, pubs, restaurants or bakeries

In either case, the exemption only applies if the work is necessary to maintain continuity of service or production or to respond to a surge in demand, no adult worker is available and the work would not adversely affect the young worker's education or training.

4.4.4 KEEPING RECORDS

There is an obligation to keep records to show that the limits on night work are being complied with and to retain them for two years. The same applies to records concerning offers of free health assessments (regulation 9 of the WTR 1998).

4.5 ANNUAL LEAVE AND HOLIDAY PAY

4.5.1 HOW MUCH HOLIDAY?

Regulation 13 of the WTR 1998 provides that workers are entitled to four weeks' 'basic' annual leave in any leave year. A leave year is deemed to commence on either the date specified in a workforce or collective agreement or individual written contract, or the date that employment started (and each successive anniversary). If the worker began work prior to 1 October 1998, their leave year will begin each year on 1 October (regulation 13 of the WTR 1998).

Regulation 13A, introduced by the *Working Time (Amendment) Regulations 2007, SI 2007/2079*, provides for entitlement to 'additional' annual leave. In any leave year, the additional entitlement is 1.6 weeks. Note that, while this additional entitlement is intended to reflect the number of public holidays in England and Wales, there is no statutory requirement to allow workers to take those specific days as holiday. Basic and additional leave together provide a worker who works five days a week with 5.6 × 5 days' paid annual holiday *(*28 days).

Workers who work more or less than five days per week

The maximum amount of aggregate leave is capped at 28 days (regulation 13A(3) of the WTR 1998), so workers who work more than five days per week are not entitled to extra leave. Part-time workers are entitled to the same 5.6 weeks' leave as their full-time colleagues but based on the number of days they normally work per week. A move from full-time to part-time work does not affect the annual leave entitlement already accumulated (*Zentralbetriebsrat der Landeskrankenhäuser Tirols v Land Tirol [2010] IRLR 631 ECJ*).

Part-year workers

In *Harpur Trust v Brazel [2022] UKSC 21*, the Supreme Court addressed the issue of part-year workers, in the context of a school. The Supreme Court held that part-year workers are entitled to the full entitlement of 5.6 weeks' annual leave, as set out in section 224 of the ERA 1996.

New workers

The right to paid holiday accrues from the first day of employment, and workers are entitled to take 1/12th of their annual holiday entitlement (rounded up to the next half or full day) for every month that they have worked in their first 12 months (regulation 15A of the WTR 1998). After 12 months of employment, their full annual entitlement becomes available to take at the start of each leave year (subject to notice requirements).

A worker who starts employment part-way through a contractual leave year is entitled to a proportionate amount of the full entitlement based on the unexpired portion of the leave year (regulations 13(5) and 13A(5) of the WTR 1998).

4.5.2 WHEN CAN HOLIDAY BE TAKEN?

Subject to any agreement to the contrary, a worker must give the employer notice of intention to take holiday, and the notice must be at least twice as long as the amount of holiday to be taken (regulations 15(1) and (4)(a) of the WTR 1998). So, if the worker is taking two weeks' holiday, the regulations provide that they should give their employer four weeks' advance notice. The employer then has half that amount of time to object and refuse permission for the holiday to be taken at that time (regulation 15(4)(b) of the WTR 1998).

An employer can require workers to take holiday to which they are entitled on a particular date (regulation 15(2)(a) of the WTR 1998). This can be especially relevant on dismissal when a worker may prefer to take pay in lieu rather than holiday (see below) . If the employer is unhappy about this, they can require the worker to take the holiday subject to giving appropriate notice, which, again, must be at least twice the amount of holiday involved (regulation 15(4)(a) of the WTR 1998).

These notice requirements may, if operated properly and reasonably by the employer, result in a worker losing their unused leave entitlement for the year. However, the case law on unpaid holiday pay upon termination (see below) suggests that employers should be proactive, by encouraging workers to take their annual leave entitlement and reminding them that they will lose it if they do not.

Carrying over leave

Basic annual leave can only be taken in the leave year to which it relates and cannot be carried over (regulation 13(9)(a) of the WTR 1998). However, a collective or workforce agreement or an individual contract may allow for additional annual leave to be carried over to the next leave year (but not beyond) (regulation 13A(7) of WTR 1998).

The ECJ has developed a line of case law (starting with *Stringer v Revenue and Customs Commissioners [2009] ICR 932*) to the effect that workers absent on sick leave remain entitled to benefit from paid basic annual leave. This is a complex and rapidly evolving subject, on which employers would be wise to seek specialist advice.

The basic position is that a worker can choose to take paid annual leave during a period of sickness absence if they wish, but their employer cannot compel them to do so (*Pereda v Madrid Movilidad SA [2009] IRLR 959 ECJ*). This allows a worker who is absent on long-term sick leave to request to take a 'notional' period of paid annual leave, which may be to their financial advantage if their sick pay entitlement has expired. Alternatively, and contrary to the express wording of the WTR 1998, the worker may carry their entitlement over into the next leave year and take it then and/or receive payment in lieu of the unused leave if their employment is terminated (*NHS Leeds v Larner [2012] ICR 1389 CA*).

The ECJ's case law also covers situations where a worker falls sick before or during a pre-booked period of annual leave: they may ask their employer to treat them as being on sick leave and to reschedule the annual leave to a later date (subject to business requirements), even if this means carrying it over into the next leave year.

The EAT's judgment in *Plumb v Duncan Print Group Ltd [2016] ICR 125* clarified that this right extends to private as well as public sector workers, and that sick workers do not need to show that they are physically unable to take annual leave in order to carry it over. The EAT also confirmed that the carry-over period required by the *Working Time Directive* is not unlimited: the carried-over leave must still be taken within 18 months of the end of the leave year to which it relates, failing which it will be lost.

The Court of Appeal held in *NHS Leeds v Larner [2012] ICR 1389 CA* that sick workers can carry over their unused holiday entitlement even if they did not make an express request to take holiday during the relevant leave year.

It should be noted that the principles above only apply to basic annual leave and not additional statutory leave or any extra-contractual leave entitlement (*Dominguez v Centre Informatique du Centre Ouest Atlantique and anor [2012] ICR D23 ECJ*).

Annual leave during the Coronavirus Job Retention Scheme

During the Coronavirus pandemic, the Government introduced the Coronavirus Job Retention Scheme (CJRS), which allowed employers to furlough staff and claim back 80% of their wages. The effect of this on annual leave was:

- Workers continued to accrue annual leave while on furlough.

- Workers could take annual leave during furlough.

- Employers could block workers from taking holiday by giving counter-notice in response to holiday requests.

- Employers could require workers to take holiday during furlough.

- Any annual leave would be paid at the normal rate of remuneration.

- The *Working Time (Coronavirus) (Amendment) Regulations 2020* enabled workers to carry holiday forward where, due to the impact of COVID-19, it was not 'reasonably practicable' for them to take leave in the leave year to which it related. The worker could then carry up to four weeks' holiday forward into the following two leave years. Government guidance was that workers who were furloughed were unlikely to have needed to carry forward their leave as they were able to take this during furlough, but it highlighted that the correct holiday pay needed to be paid.

4.5.3 HOLIDAY PAY

Calculating holiday pay

The statutory holiday under the WTR 1998 is to be paid 'at the rate of a week's pay in respect of each week of leave' (regulation 16(1) of the WTR 1998). This is to be calculated in accordance with sections 221-224 of the ERA 1996 as at the beginning of the period of leave.

A series of ECJ decisions have held that this method of calculation is not fully compliant with the *Working Time Directive*. Individuals are entitled to have their holiday pay calculated by reference to their 'normal remuneration' (see *British Gas Trading Ltd v Lock [2017] ICR 1 CA*). This will ordinarily require commission and overtime to be taken into account, even if the rights to these benefits were not contractual and would not usually count towards 'a week's pay' under the ERA 1996.

There has been a significant volume of litigation over the extent to which remuneration other than basic contractual pay should be taken into account in assessing 'normal remuneration'. A rough summary is as follows:

- Pay for compulsory but non-guaranteed overtime (including standby and call-out payments) is taken into account (*Bear Scotland Ltd v Fulton [2015] ICR 221 EAT*). Purely voluntary overtime should also be counted, provided that it forms part of a broadly regular and predictable pattern of work (*East of England Ambulance Service NHS Trust v Flowers [2019] ICR 1454 CA*). However, for some workers, it may be difficult to draw the line between this and more sporadic or occasional overtime work, and the position may need to be re-assessed each time they take holiday.

- A worker's typical income from commission is counted, on the basis that workers should not be deterred from taking holiday by the prospect of being unable to generate commission (*British Gas Trading Ltd v Lock [2017] ICR 1 CA*). However, if taking annual leave would not cause any shortfall in commission (for example, because the sales leads would remain open to the worker on their return to work), this may not be necessary.

- Bonuses linked to individual performance and paid regularly should be taken into account but not if they are based solely on the company's performance.

To calculate normal remuneration for holiday taken on or after 6 April 2020, a reference period of 52 weeks leading up to the start of the leave period applies (Employment Rights (Employment Particulars and Paid Annual Leave) (Amendment) Regulations 2018). Earlier weeks are brought into account if the 52-week period contains any weeks for which no remuneration was payable, subject to a cap of 104 weeks.

For holiday that started before 6 April 2020, the ERA 1996 provided for a reference period of 12 weeks, but it was doubtful whether this always met the EU law requirement of a 'representative reference period', particularly for casual or seasonal workers.

Note that the above case law on 'normal remuneration' only applies to the four weeks of annual leave guaranteed by regulation 13 of the WTR 1998 and not to any additional contractual annual leave, nor to the additional 1.6 weeks of annual leave provided for by regulation 13A of the WTR 1998. That said, most employers will find it too difficult to distinguish the two when calculating pay and will use one uniform rate for holiday pay.

Payment in lieu of holiday

Neither the WTR 1998 nor EU law permit statutory holiday entitlement to be swapped for cash (*Federatie Nederlandse Vakbeweging v Staat der Nederlanden (Case C-124/05) [2006] ICR 962 ECJ*). The logic is that this would be tantamount to encouraging a practice which runs counter to the Working Time Directive's basic health and safety objectives.

The position is different when employment is terminated. The worker is then entitled to compensation for loss of holiday pay in respect of holiday accrued but untaken at the date of termination. This will, by default, be calculated in accordance with regulation 16 of the WTR 1998, as discussed above, as at the date the contract comes to an end. The contract of employment, or a workforce or collective agreement, may provide for a different basis of compensation (regulation 14 of the WTR 1998). However, such agreements cannot be used to forfeit outstanding holiday pay entirely, for example, where a worker is dismissed for gross misconduct (*Witley and District Mens Club v Mackay [2001] IRLR 595 EAT*). There is no statutory cap on the amount of a week's pay for this purpose (and, specifically, section 227 of the ERA 1996 does not apply).

The general prohibition on carrying over unused leave from one leave year to the next applies equally on termination: a worker cannot claim payment for unused leave from previous years. As discussed above, this rule is relaxed in favour of workers who have been on long-term sickness absence. ECJ case law has established two further qualifications:

- The worker must have had an 'effective opportunity' to take leave. An employer who has not exercised all due diligence to ensure the worker can take their full annual leave entitlement will be expected, on termination, to compensate the worker for the leave which remains untaken as a result. This includes leave from previous leave years (*Max-Planck-Gesellschaft zur Forderung der Wissenschaften v Shimizu (Case C-684/16) [2019] 1 CMLR 35*). Employers should therefore provide adequate opportunities to take leave, encourage workers to use it and inform them in good time that it will be lost if they do not.

- An employer who refuses to provide paid holiday will have to reimburse the worker on termination, not just for any leave taken but also for any leave entitlement that the worker did not take as a consequence (*King v Sash Window Workshop [2018] ICR 693*). This ruling has significant implications for employers who mis-classify their workforce as 'independent contractors' and provide no paid holiday.

There is nothing to prevent workers from 'selling' any contractual leave that goes above the statutory minimum if their contracts allow for this.

4.5.4 ROLLED-UP HOLIDAY PAY

'Rolled-up' holiday pay refers to remuneration paid on account of holiday pay as a regular sum throughout the course of a year as part of a worker's hourly, daily or weekly wage. This can be administratively convenient, especially in industries such as construction where there can be a frequent turnover of workers, on the basis that the employer will then not have to pay holiday pay when the workers are taking leave.

The position regarding rolled-up holiday pay is not straightforward. In *Robinson-Steele v RD Retail Services Ltd [2006] ICR 932*, the ECJ concluded that:

'[A]rticle 7 of the Directive precludes the payment for minimum annual leave within the meaning of that provision from being made in the form of part payments staggered over the corresponding annual period of work and paid together with the remuneration for work done, rather than in the form of a payment in respect of a specific period during which the worker actually takes leave'.

However, the Court went on to hold that where 'rolled-up' payments were made, the employer *might* be able to set any claim for holiday pay off against them. The Court stated that:

'[A]rticle 7 of the Directive does not preclude, as a rule, sums additional to remuneration payable for work done which have been paid, transparently and comprehensibly, as holiday pay, from being set off against the payment for specific leave'.

The net practical effect is thus that rolling up statutory holiday pay is unlawful but that an employee cannot get away with claiming it twice over, provided the arrangement is completely transparent and comprehensible. The burden of proof is expressly on the employer to show that the arrangement was 'transparent and comprehensible'. If this can be shown, it seems that the employer may be entitled to set off rolled-up holiday pay against amounts due to an employee who is absent on basic statutory annual leave.

A useful case to consider is *Lyddon v Englefield Brickwork [2008] IRLR 198 EAT*, in which Elias J upheld a decision dismissing an employee's claim for unpaid annual leave on the basis that the requirement for a clear and transparent arrangement had been met.

4.5.5 TIME LIMIT FOR CLAIMS

In *Inland Revenue Commissioners v Ainsworth/Stringer [2009] UKHL 31*, the House of Lords confirmed that a worker who has not received holiday pay in respect of periods of sickness absence can bring his claim as one for unlawful deductions from wages under the ERA 1996 rather than as a claim under the WTR 1998. This is advantageous for the worker because the time limit for bringing a claim for unlawful deduction from wages is three months from the last default by the employer. This gives workers greater possibilities of bringing 'back claims' than under the WTR 1998, provided that there has been a 'series of deductions'.

However, the *Deduction from Wages (Limitation) Regulations 2014* impose a two-year limit on the backdating of unlawful deduction from wages complaints. Further, following the judgment in *Bear Scotland*, if there is a gap of more than three months between non-payment of holiday or deductions , this will break the chain in the series of deductions and the deductions before the 'gap' will therefore be out of time.

The Northern Ireland Court of Appeal has since held that the Northern Ireland equivalent of the ERA 1996 does *not* impose such a three-month break and that the EAT was wrong about this point in *Bear Scotland*. The decision is not binding in Great Britain but is likely to be persuasive if *Bear Scotland* is challenged in a future appeal.

The two-year limit in the *Deduction from Wages (Limitation) Regulations 2014* is also open to challenge on the basis that it breaches the EU law requirement of equivalent and effective remedies. An employment tribunal reached this conclusion in *Singh v First Stop (Wombourne Common Road) Ltd [2018] UKET 1301376/2017*), but the point has not yet been considered at appeal level, and, in light of Brexit, it is perhaps unlikely that such an argument would succeed.

4.5.6 ENFORCEMENT

There are four main ways of enforcing rights provided by the WTR 1998.

First, the local authority or the HSE is entitled to bring prosecutions arising from breaches of regulations imposing the 48-hour maximum working week, night work, record-keeping and some of the rest break provisions (regulations 28 and 29 of the WTR 1998 and *Health and Safety (Enforcing Authority) Regulations 1998*).

Second, a worker can lodge a complaint with an employment tribunal alleging that their rights have been infringed. If a complaint is well founded, a tribunal must make a declaration to that effect and may make an award of compensation. No upper limit for compensation is specified (regulation 30 of the WTR 1998). Compensation is not mandatory but is expressly a matter for the tribunal's discretion to be considered in the light of financial loss suffered by the worker and the 'default of the employer' (*Miles v Linkage Community Trust Ltd [2008] IRLR 602 EAT*).

Third, the worker can bring a tribunal claim if they suffer a detriment because of asserting, or attempting to assert, a right under the WTR 1998. It does not matter whether they actually have that right, provided they purport to exercise it in good faith (section 45A of the ERA 1996).

Fourth, if the worker is dismissed because they assert, or attempt to assert, their rights under the WTR 1998, the dismissal will be automatically unfair (section 101A of the ERA 1996).

A fifth possible method exists in the case of public sector employees: direct enforcement of the *Working Time Directive*. In *Fuss v Stadt Halle (Case C-429/09) [2011] IRLR 176*, the ECJ held that a worker employed by a public authority who had worked for a period exceeding the maximum laid down under the Directive had a directly enforceable right to 'reparation' for loss or damage caused by the breach. It was for the national courts to decide whether the form of reparation should be time in lieu or financial compensation.

Additionally, a worker may have rights under general law resulting from a breach by their employer of the WTR 1998. The worker may, for example, bring a claim for breach of contract, although financial loss or personal injury would have to be demonstrated (*Barber v RJB Mining (UK) Ltd [1999] ICR 679 QBD*).

The Government's Good Work Plan, published in December 2018 in response to the Taylor Review of Modern Working Practices, committed to state enforcement of vulnerable workers' holiday pay rights so that workers can raise a complaint with a Government agency rather than having to make a tribunal claim. In June 2021, the Government issued their response to the consultation, which ended in October 2019, entitled 'Establishing a new single enforcement body for employment rights'. This report confirmed the Government's commitment to create a new single labour market enforcement body which would also have new powers to tackle non-compliance with holiday pay and statutory sick pay. No time frames for this project have been given.

4.6 SICKNESS LEAVE

4.6.1 TIME OFF WORK FOR SICKNESS

There is no statutory right to be off work when sick. However, in the absence of suspicion of malingering, no reasonable employer would insist an employee attend work when ill. Such a requirement would probably be a breach of the term of trust and confidence, and any dismissal (whether actual or constructive) would likely be unfair.

4.6.2 SICK PAY

The employee is entitled to statutory sick pay (SSP), payable to most employees for 28 weeks at a rate determined by statute after the first three days of sickness absence. After seven days of absence, the employer is entitled to demand a 'fit note' signed by a doctor (*Social Security Contributions and Benefits Act 1992*, Part XI; *Statutory Sick Pay (Medical Evidence) Regulations 1985*; *Social Security (Medical Evidence) and Statutory Sick Pay (Medical Evidence) (Amendment) Regulations 2010*). The employer must issue a form SSPI(T) by the end of the 23rd week to let the employee know when SSP will be ending. Incapacity benefit may then be claimed by an employee who is still too ill to work.

In practice, many employers offer enhanced sickness rights. Care must be taken to ensure that any contractual provisions and the way they are applied do not amount to unjustified less favourable treatment of persons with a disability, or a failure to make reasonable adjustments for disability, thereby breaching the EqA 2010 (see **Chapter 13**).

4.7 TIME OFF WORK FOR OTHER PRESCRIBED REASONS

4.7.1 TRADE UNION DUTIES AND ACTIVITIES AND EMPLOYEE REPRESENTATIVES

Trade union officials

Employees who are trade union officials have the statutory right to reasonable time off their normal work for attending to specified trade union duties. This includes conducting negotiations with the employer on terms and conditions of employment. There is an Acas Code of Practice on Time Off for Trade Union Duties and Activities (section 168 of the Trade Union and Labour Relations (Consolidation) Act 1992 (TULR(C)A 1992); Employment Protection Code of Practice (Time Off) Order 1998).

The right to pay during time off under section 169 of the TULR(C)A 1992 is for trade union officials only: ordinary trade union members have a separate right to time off work for trade union activities, but this does not carry any statutory right to pay during the time off (see section 170 of the TULR(C)A 1992).

Dismissal for attempting to exercise the statutory rights given by sections 168 and 169 of the TULR(C)A 1992 is automatically unfair dismissal (section 104(4)(c) of the ERA 1996).

Trade union members

An employee who is a member of an independent, recognised trade union is entitled to reasonable unpaid time off during working hours to take part in trade union activities (section 170 of the TULR(C)A 1992).

There is no definition of what constitutes 'trade union activities' for this purpose. Attending union meetings and acting as a union representative are examples of 'activities' for which time off can be claimed, but trade union activities for this purpose specifically exclude strikes or other industrial action (section 170 of the TULR(C)A 1992; *Employment Protection Code of Practice (Time Off) Order 1998*). It seems clear that a person does not have to be a union representative to be engaged in trade union activities (*Hamilton v Arriva Trains Northern Ltd ((2004) UKEAT/0310/04*), a case under section 146 of the TULR(C)A 1992 'Right not to be subjected to detriment for a trade union related reason', but presumably the same is true for the purposes of section 170 of the TULR(C)A 1992.

Dismissal for attempting to exercise the statutory rights given by section 170 of the TULR(C)A 1992 is automatically unfair dismissal (section 104(4) (c) of the ERA 1996), as is dismissal on other grounds related to trade union membership or activities (section 152 of the TULR(C)A 1992).

4.7.2 TIME OFF FOR PUBLIC DUTIES

An employer is obliged to allow employees to take a reasonable amount of time off work for performing certain public duties. The employee does not need to have achieved any qualifying period of employment. The time off work is not paid.

The duties are tightly defined in section 50 of the ERA 1996, but can be summarised as follows:

- A justice of the peace
- A member of a local authority
- A member of a statutory tribunal
- A member of a police authority
- A member of a board of prison visitors or a prison visiting committee
- Related to a health authority, an education authority, the Environment Agency or a water authority

Justices of the peace are permitted time off work for discharging any of their functions. Employees falling within the other categories are permitted time off only for attendance at committee meetings or undertaking duties authorised by the body (section 50(1) and (3) of the ERA 1996). Guidance on 'Time Off for Public Duties' is available at www.gov.uk/time-off-work-public-duties.

There is no statute requiring an employer to allow employees time off work for jury service (but there are sanctions for failing to do so – see **4.7.7**).

What amounts to a reasonable amount of time off for public duties must be determined in accordance with section 50(4) of the ERA 1996. This specifies three 'circumstances', which can be summarised as:

1) How much time off will be needed to perform a particular duty compared to how much time off is needed to perform the duties of the office generally

2) How much time off the employee has already had for public duties or for trade union duties/ activities

3) The effect on the employer's business of the employee taking time off

It is for the tribunal to determine reasonableness by an objective consideration of these and any other factors it considers relevant (*Riley-Williams v Argos (2003) EAT/811/02/RN*).

4.7.3 TIME OFF FOR PENSION FUND TRUSTEES AND MEMBERS

An employer which operates an occupational pension fund is obliged to permit a reasonable amount of time off to employees who are trustees of that pension fund. The time off should be paid at normal pay rates. Time off is permitted for performing duties as a trustee and for training in connection with those duties (sections 58 and 59 of the ERA 1996).

Employees can complain to a tribunal if they are denied a reasonable amount of time off, or if they are not paid during such time off. Employees also have a right not to be subjected to any detriment for performing their duties as pension fund trustees and any dismissal for that reason is automatically unfair (sections 46, 60 and 102 of the ERA 1996).

There are analogous provisions entitling employees to time off work, with pay, for acting as 'consulted representatives' of employees under the *Occupational and Personal Pension Schemes (Consultation by Employers and Miscellaneous Amendment) Regulations 2006* (see the Schedule).

4.7.4 TIME OFF FOR STUDY OR TRAINING

General right

Employees of more than 26 weeks' standing, working for large businesses (250+ employees), have a legal right to request time away from their core duties to undertake any training that will help them to be more productive and effective at work and will help their employer to improve productivity and business performance. The main provisions are in sections 63D-63J and 47F of the ERA 1996.

The right to request training works in a similar way to that already in operation in relation to the right that employees have to request flexible working. Employers are not required to pay for training when they agree to a request for time to train, although many employers will be happy to do so. The training may be on site or elsewhere.

16- and 17-year-olds

There is a freestanding right to time off for training for 16- and 17-year-olds in Wales and Scotland who have left school but have not attained a satisfactory standard of achievement while at school/college (section 63A of the ERA 1996). The provisions of section 63A do not apply to 16- and 17-year-olds in England, who are under a duty to participate in education or training until they turn 18 (by virtue of Part 1 of the Education and Skills Act 2008).

In essence, 16- and 17-year-olds in Wales or Scotland who have failed to reach a prescribed standard of academic achievement are entitled to paid time off work to attend courses at specified institutions. Although there are minor exceptions, in general, they are entitled to be paid by the employer at their normal rate (section 63B of the ERA 1996). An 18-year-old who commenced a course under these provisions while younger is entitled to finish the course (and continue to be paid while doing so). Once they reach 19 years old, they lose the right to paid time off for study (section 63A(4) of the ERA 1996).

Employees can complain to an employment tribunal if the employer fails to allow time off or fails to pay them in respect of that time off. Moreover, employees have a right not to be subjected to any detriment for invoking these rights (sections 63C and 47A of the ERA 1996).

4.7.5 ACCOMPANYING A WORKER AT A DISCIPLINARY OR GRIEVANCE HEARING

Employees are entitled to be represented by a trade union official or workplace colleague during any disciplinary or grievance hearings, as introduced by the *Employment Relations Act 1999* (ERA 1999). Such a right would be ineffective unless the accompanying employee was entitled to time off work to discharge this function. Employees can complain to an employment tribunal if the employer fails to allow them time off to accompany a colleague or subjects them to a detriment for doing so. Moreover, any dismissal for accompanying a colleague at a disciplinary or grievance hearing will be automatically unfair (sections 10(6) and 12 of the ERA 1999).

4.7.6 TIME OFF FOR REDUNDANT WORKERS TO SEEK NEW WORK

An employee who has been given notice of dismissal due to redundancy is entitled to take a reasonable amount of time off work to look for new employment or make arrangements for retraining (note: warnings about impending redundancies are insufficient). To qualify for this right, the employee must have been employed for two years at the date on which notice expires.

The time off work is paid but limited to 40% of a week's pay. This is a cap on the total amount paid, irrespective of the number of weeks during which the employee is searching for a new job while under notice, rather than a cap on the total amount to be paid per week (section 53 of the ERA 1996). An employee can complain to an employment tribunal if the employer refuses to allow reasonable time off work or to pay them during such time. However, the maximum compensation is, again, limited to 40% of a week's pay for the employee (section 54 of the ERA 1996).

4.7.7 JURY SERVICE

Surprisingly, no statute requires an employer to allow employees time off work for jury service. However, any dismissal for taking time off work for jury service is automatically unfair (section 98B of the ERA 1996), subject to exceptions and safeguards should the employer's business be badly affected by allowing the employee to take time off. There is no qualifying period of employment required.

Individual jurors can claim various amounts for expenses and financial loss from the court (including loss of earnings) up to a specific maximum. Details of up-to-date rates can be found at www.gov.uk/jury-service/what-you-can-claim. No payment to employers is made by the state or the courts in respect of employees absent on account of jury service.

CHAPTER 5
FAMILY AND FLEXIBLE LEAVE

5.0 OVERVIEW

The rights parents have to work flexibly and take time off to look after children have changed significantly in recent years as Parliament has sought to recognise the diversity in how modern families operate. The result is that the law relating to parental leave is not simple, nor is it contained in one consolidated statute.

This chapter attempts to summarise key principles and rights that employees have when seeking to take time off work to look after dependants and to work flexibly. However, the complexity and the sheer volume of statute law in this area means that those advising employers and employees must always look afresh at each request for leave and check the rights that individuals may have.

Whether an individual is a single parent, is adopting, is expecting an unusual pregnancy or has chosen to split parental leave with their partner will impact on the rights they have to pay and time off. Every scenario is different, and the relevant statutes will always need to be reviewed to establish who is entitled to what.

The phrase 'family leave' is used to refer to maternity leave, parental leave, paternity leave, adoption leave and shared parental leave. These schemes apply to different people and in different situations, but they share common principles and provisions.

5.1 ANTENATAL CARE

5.1.1 TIME OFF FOR ANTENATAL CARE FOR A PREGNANT WOMAN

According to section 55(1) of the *Employment Rights Act* (ERA 1996), a pregnant employee who 'has, on the advice of a registered medical practitioner, registered midwife or registered nurse, made an appointment to attend at any place' for antenatal care is entitled 'to be permitted by her employer to take time off during the employee's working hours in order to enable her to keep the appointment'. This means that the focus is not simply on the length of time of the appointment but also on the travelling and waiting time. No minimum qualifying service is necessary.

The employer is entitled to request a certificate confirming pregnancy before allowing the employee to take time off, with the exception of the first appointment during her pregnancy (since, at that stage, the employee may yet to have had the pregnancy formally confirmed) (section 55(2) and 55(3) of the ERA 1996).

Where an employer has been found to have 'unreasonably refused' to allow a woman to take time off under section 55 of the ERA 1996, the tribunal 'shall also order the employer to pay to the employee an amount that is twice the amount of the remuneration to which she would have been entitled under section 56 if the employer had not refused' (section 57(4) of the ERA 1996). The focus here is on whether the refusal to permit time off is 'unreasonable'. There is little guidance on what this means, but it is likely that a tribunal would consider whether the pregnant woman could have scheduled appointments outside of working hours or at a more convenient time for her employer's business.

Where the employer has allowed the employee to take the leave but has failed to pay her, the tribunal will 'order the employer to pay to the employee the amount which it finds due to her' (section 57(5) of the ERA 1996). A woman is entitled to be paid at her normal hourly rate while absent for antenatal appointments (section 56 of the ERA 1996).

It is likely that a complaint for an unreasonable refusal to allow paid time off for antenatal care would be accompanied by a complaint for pregnancy discrimination under section 18 of the *Equality Act 2010* (EqA 2010).

This right does not apply to those employed in the armed forces (section 192 of the ERA 1996), those employed in share fishing (section 199(2) of the ERA 1996) and those employed in the police service (section 200 of the ERA 1996).

5.1.2 ACCOMPANYING A PREGNANT WOMAN TO ANTENATAL APPOINTMENTS

The right to attend antenatal appointments is not restricted to the pregnant woman. Employees who have 'a qualifying relationship with a pregnant woman or her expected child' are entitled to time off to accompany her to the appointment (section 57ZE(1) of the ERA 1996). The provision details what counts as a 'qualifying relationship', which includes the father of the baby and the partner or spouse of the pregnant woman.

There is no right to pay for individuals who take time off to accompany a woman to an antenatal appointment. Further, an employee is not entitled to take time off under this section more than twice in relation to any particular pregnancy. The maximum time that the employer is required to permit for each appointment is six and a half hours.

Under section 57ZF of the ERA 1996, if an employer has unreasonably refused to permit the person to accompany the mother-to-be to an antenatal appointment, and a complaint is brought to the tribunal, the tribunal must make a declaration and must order the employer to pay twice the hourly rate of the employee's pay, multiplied by the number of hours the employee would have been entitled to take off to attend the appointment.

5.1.3 AGENCY WORKERS

Agency workers also have the right to take time off for antenatal appointments and to be remunerated at their 'appropriate hourly rate' (sections 57ZA to 57ZD of the ERA 1996). However, this is subject to the qualifying period under regulation 7(2) of the *Agency Workers Regulations 2010* – essentially, working in the same role with the same hirer for 12 continuous calendar weeks.

Persons who have a 'qualifying relationship' with an agency worker may also be entitled to time off after their qualifying period (section 57ZG(1) of the ERA 1996).

5.2 MATERNITY LEAVE AND PARENTAL LEAVE

This section deals with maternity and parental leave. It is important to differentiate maternity leave from maternity pay. It is also important to differentiate parental leave from paternity leave and shared parental leave. They are separate concepts despite their similar names.

Part VIII of the ERA 1996 and the *Maternity and Parental Leave Regulations 1999* (MPLR 1999), provide a statutory code under which new mothers are entitled to take maternity leave and parents of children under 18 are entitled to take parental leave. This section will not attempt to summarise the entirety of this statutory code, nor will it attempt to deal with each and every scenario that could arise regarding maternity and parental leave.

5.2.1 WHO HAS THE RIGHT TO MATERNITY LEAVE?

Women who are pregnant or have given birth are entitled to maternity leave if they are employees (regulations 2(1) and 4 of the MPLR 1999). This means that a woman would still be entitled to maternity leave in the event of a stillbirth after 24 weeks or more, or if her child only survived for a short time after the birth. There is no qualifying length of service.

The rights of those in Crown employment are dealt with at part XIII of the ERA 1996.

To benefit from the right to maternity leave, a woman must notify her employer of her pregnancy within 15 weeks before the expected week of birth or as soon as is reasonably practicable (regulation 4(1) of the MPLR 1999).

5.2.2 HOW LONG DOES MATERNITY LEAVE LAST?

Ordinary maternity leave

An employee is entitled to ordinary maternity leave (OML) provided she informs her employer of her pregnancy, the expected week of childbirth, and the date on which she intends her OML to start. The period of OML lasts for 26 weeks (regulation 7 of the MPLR 1999).

The period of OML commences on the earliest of the following three dates:

- The day that the employee specifies she intends that her OML will start (regulation 6(1)(a) of the MPLR 1999).

- 'The day which follows the first day after the beginning of the fourth week before the expected week of childbirth on which she is absent from work wholly or partly because of pregnancy' (regulation 6(1)(b) of the MPLR 1999).

- The day which follows the day on which the employee's childbirth occurs (regulation 6(2) of the MPLR 1999).

Additional maternity leave

Employees are also entitled to 'additional maternity leave' (regulation 4(1) of the MPLR 1999). The period of additional maternity leave commences 'on the day after the last day of her ordinary maternity leave period' (regulation 6(3) of the MPLR 1999) and 'continues until the end of the period of 26 weeks from the day on which it commenced' (regulation 7(4) of the MPLR 1999).

Therefore, if an employee elects to take the full period of OML (26 weeks) plus additional maternity leave (26 weeks), her total time off work will equal one year.

5.2.3 HEALTH AND SAFETY FOR NEW MOTHERS

Compulsory maternity leave

It is a criminal offence for an employer to permit an employee to work during the 'compulsory maternity leave period' (section 72 of the ERA 1996). The compulsory maternity leave period is the period of two weeks commencing on the day on which childbirth occurs (regulation 8 of the MPLR 1999).

Risk assessments and suspension from work

Under regulation 16 of the Management of Health and Safety at Work Regulations 1999, an employer is obliged to undertake assessments of the risk of working to new or expectant mothers if women of childbearing age work at the workplace and the work is of a kind which could involve risk to employees who are pregnant or their babies. A new mother is defined as one who has given birth within the last six months or is breastfeeding.

When an employee gives written notice to their employer that she is pregnant, has given birth within the last six months or is breastfeeding, under regulation 18(1) of the *Management of Health and Safety at Work Regulations 1999*, the employer must consider whether the general risk assessment is sufficient to avoid risks to the employee. If not, the employer must take additional actions to avoid those risks.

If a risk is identified which cannot be averted by altering working hours or conditions of work, the employer is obliged to suspend the employee from work, but it will be automatically unfair to dismiss her.

If a pregnant night worker has a certificate from her doctor stating that she cannot work at night for health and safety reasons, she must be suspended from work.

Obviously, an employer should not be penalised for failing to employ a person when health and safety rules make it illegal for it to do so. Accordingly, special rules apply if an employee is suspended on 'maternity grounds'. The effect is that they only cover suspensions required by law or which are recommended in a Code of Practice issued under section 16 of the *Health and Safety at Work etc. Act 1974*, if specified by the Secretary of State as a 'relevant provision' (section 66(1) of the ERA 1996) and see *Iske v P & O European Ferries (Dover) Ltd [1997] IRLR 401 EAT*. Relevant provisions are contained within the *Suspension from Work (on Maternity Grounds) Order 1994*.

The employer is required to record the findings of the risk assessment and give information about the findings. There is no stipulation regarding the form the information must take and no requirement that the assessment must be in writing (*Stevenson v J M Skinner & Co (2008) UKEAT/0584/07*).

Suspension must be on full pay unless the worker unreasonably refuses suitable alternative work (section 68 of the ERA 1996).

A failure to conduct a risk assessment may also amount to discrimination (*Hardman v Mallon (t/a Orchard Lodge Nursing Home) [2002] IRLR 516 EAT*). No male comparator is needed because of the rule that a pregnant woman seeking to establish sex discrimination related to her pregnancy need not point to a male comparator simply because pregnancy is a uniquely female condition (the rule in *Webb v Emo Air Cargo (UK) Ltd [1995] ICR 1021 ECJ*).

5.2.4 PARENTAL LEAVE

Employees of either sex who have one year's continuous employment and who have (or expect to have) responsibility for a child have the right 'to be absent from work on parental leave for the purpose of caring for that child' (regulation 13(1) of the MPLR 1999). There is no right to be paid for this leave.

Employees are entitled to up to 18 weeks' leave in respect of each child (regulation 14(1) of the MPLR 1999). The right must be exercised before a child's 18th birthday (regulation 15 of the MPLR 1999).

Schedule 2 of the MPLR 1999 provides for default provisions for parental leave where no contractual provision, collective agreement or workforce agreement has been made regarding parental leave (regulation 16 of the MPLR 1999). This schedule provides information regarding notification requirements and minimum and maximum periods of leave.

5.2.5 WHAT RIGHTS DO EMPLOYEES HAVE ASSOCIATED WITH MATERNITY AND PARENTAL LEAVE?

The right to return

An employee has the right to 'return to the job in which she was employed before her absence' after a period of parental leave which lasts for four weeks or less or having taken OML (regulation 18(1) of the MPLR 1999).

The situation is different if the employee has taken a period of additional maternity leave or a longer period of parental leave, or combined their leave (as described at regulation 18(2) of the MPLR 1999). In this case, the individual has the right to:

'... return from leave to the job in which she was employed before her absence or, if it is not reasonably practicable for the employer to permit her to return to that job, to another job which is both suitable for her and appropriate for her to do in the circumstances'.

Regulation 18A of the MPLR 1999 provides details of what is meant by the right to return. Put simply, it is to return without any diminution in seniority, rights and terms and conditions.

The right not to be subjected to detriment or dismissal

Employees who have taken maternity or parental leave have the right not to be subjected to a detriment or dismissed because of doing so (regulations 19(1) and 20 of the MPLR 1999). There is some overlap between this right and the prohibition in the EqA 2010 against discrimination on the grounds of pregnancy and maternity (see **Chapter 14**).

The right to favourable redundancy conditions

If during an employee's maternity leave 'it is not practicable by reason of redundancy for her employer to continue to employ her under her existing contract of employment', she has a right to be offered 'a suitable alternative vacancy' with her original employer or a successor or an associated employer, if such a vacancy exists (regulation 10 of the MPLR 1999). Note that this right does not apply in respect of parental leave.

5.3 PATERNITY AND ADOPTION LEAVE

The *Paternity and Adoption Leave Regulations 2002* (PAL 2002) provide for a statutory code under which fathers (or the mother's partner) and adopters are entitled to take leave from work. As with the previous section, this section will not attempt to summarise the entirety of this statutory code, nor will it attempt to deal with each and every possible scenario.

5.3.1 PATERNITY LEAVE: WHO IS ENTITLED TO THE RIGHT?

The right to paternity leave is restricted to employees who have been continuously employed for a period of not less than 26 weeks ending with the week immediately preceding the 14th week before the expected week of birth (regulation 4(2)(a) of the PAL 2002). Where a child is born prematurely, an employee will be entitled to paternity leave if he would have been continuously employed for a period of 26 weeks up until the 14th week before the child was expected to be born (regulation 4(3) of the PAL 2002).

To claim paternity leave, the employee must be one of the following:

- The father of the child, and expect to have responsibility for the upbringing of the child.
- The mother's spouse, civil partner, or partner and expect to have the main responsibility (apart from the mother's responsibility) for the upbringing of the child (regulation 4(2) of the PAL 2002).

To benefit from the right, employees must give notice of their intention to take paternity leave and provide adequate evidence if required (regulation 6 of the PAL 2002).

Individuals will also be entitled to take paternity leave when their spouse, civil partner or partner adopts a child and they expect to have the main responsibility (apart from the responsibility of the adopter) for the upbringing of the child (regulation 8 of the PAL 2002).

5.3.2 PATERNITY LEAVE: WHAT ARE THE RELEVANT RIGHTS?

Leave

The core right is to take one week or two consecutive weeks' leave (regulation 5(1) of the PAL 2002). The period in which paternity leave may be taken starts with the child's birth and ends 56 days later (regulation 5(2) of the PAL 2002). This rule is slightly amended if a child is born prematurely.

Right to return

Individuals who have taken paternity leave are entitled to return to their previous jobs (regulation 13(1) of the PAL 2002).

However, note that if certain statutory maximums are exceeded, an individual will have the right to 'the job in which he was employed before his absence, or, if it is not reasonably practicable for the employer to permit him to return to that job, to another job which is both suitable for him and appropriate for him to do in the circumstances' (regulation 13(2) of the PAL 2002).

The 'right to return' means a right to return to work 'on terms and conditions not less favourable than those which would have applied if he had not been absent' (regulation 14(1)(b) of the PAL 2002).

Rights that are dependent on seniority – such as pension rights – are preserved during paternity leave. If the leave is taken as part of 'consecutive periods of statutory leave which included a period of additional adoption leave or additional maternity leave', then the accrued rights are left as they would have been if the leave had not been taken. In any other case, the accrued rights are treated as if the employee had not been absent (regulation 14(1)(a) of the PAL 2002).

5.3.3 ADOPTION LEAVE: WHO IS ENTITLED TO THE RIGHT?

The right to adoption leave is restricted to employees. The employee must be the child's adopter and comply with the notification and evidence requirements contained within the regulations (regulations 15 and 17 of the PAL 2002).

There is no requirement for continuity of service for an employee to take adoption leave. Further, 'an employee's entitlement to leave … shall not be affected by the placement for adoption of more than one child as part of the same arrangement' (regulation 15(4) of the PAL 2002).

An employee may choose to begin a period of adoption leave, under regulation 16(1) of the PAL 2002, on:

'(a) the date on which the child is placed with him for adoption, or

(b) a predetermined date, specified in a notice under regulation 17, which is no more than 14 days before the date on which the child is expected to be placed with the employee and no later than that date'.

Where employees are adopting children from overseas, the *Paternity and Adoption Leave (Adoption from Overseas) Regulations 2003* should be consulted.

5.3.4 ADOPTION LEAVE: WHAT ARE THE RELEVANT RIGHTS?

Leave

An employee's ordinary adoption leave period lasts for 26 weeks (regulation 18 of the PAL 2002). Employees may also take a period of additional adoption leave. Mirroring the maternity leave provisions, additional adoption leave lasts 26 weeks and commences immediately after ordinary adoption leave ends (regulation 20(2) of the PAL 2002).

Problems with the adoption

The regulations provide the employee with some protection should the adoption of the child not go according to plan. If the child is not placed with the employee when the employee has already begun adoption leave, the child dies during the leave or the child is returned to the agency while the employee is on leave, then the employee's adoption leave will end eight weeks after the week in which one of the above has happened (regulation 22 of the PAL 2002) or, if earlier, at the end of the ordinary or additional adoption leave period.

Redundancy and right to return to work

If an employee takes an isolated period of ordinary adoption leave which does not exceed the statutory limits provided for at regulation 26(1)(b) of the PAL 2002, the employee will be 'entitled to return from leave to the job in which he was employed before his absence' (regulation 26(1)(a) of the PAL 2002).

An employee who takes consecutive periods of leave which exceed the statutory maximums will be entitled to return 'to the job in which he was employed before his absence, or, if it is not reasonably practicable for the employer to permit him to return to that job, to another job which is both suitable for him and appropriate for him to do in the circumstances' (regulation 26(2) of the PAL 2002).

Detriment and dismissal

It is unlawful to subject any employee to a detriment for a reason connected with taking adoption leave (regulation 28 of the PAL 2002). If an employee is dismissed for taking or seeking to take adoption leave, the dismissal will be automatically unfair (regulation 29 of the PAL 2002).

5.3.5 TIME OFF FOR ADOPTION APPOINTMENTS

Sections 57ZJ to 57ZS of the ERA 1996 provide for a scheme under which employees are entitled to time off to attend adoption appointments.

Employees can take paid time off for adoption appointments if they have been notified by an adoption agency that a child is to be placed for adoption with them, whether they are adopting alone or jointly with another person (section 57ZJ of the ERA 1996).

This right is similar, but not (for obvious reasons) the same as the right to attend an antenatal appointment and the right to accompany a woman to an antenatal appointment. The statutory scheme in sections 57ZJ to 57ZS of the ERA 1996 provides an exhaustive guide as to the scope of the right, the notification requirements relating to adoption appointments and the calculation of the pay individuals are entitled to when the time off is to be paid.

5.4 SHARED PARENTAL LEAVE

Shared parental leave (SPL) was introduced in sections 75E to 75K of the ERA 1996. The *Shared Parental Leave Regulations 2014* (SPLR 2014), provide for leave from work which can be divided between parents up to the child's first birthday. While this is simple in principle, the application can be complex.

As this is not a guidebook on the management of family leave, this section will not detail each of the procedural steps, notifications and evidential requirements employers need to follow. Instead, this section will provide a precis of the entitlements involved. In dealing with individual cases and queries, this section refers to the relevant regulations.

The 'Employers' Technical Guide to Shared Parental Leave and Pay' (https://assets.publishing.service.gov.uk/government/uploads/system/uploads/attachment_data/file/881347/shared-parental-leave-and-pay-employers-technical-guide.pdf), as revised by the Department for Business, Energy & Industrial Strategy in April 2020, and the Acas 'Shared Parental Leave and Pay' guide (https://www.acas.org.uk/shared-parental-leave-and-pay) offer useful guidance on SPL and pay.

The SPLR 2014 covers SPL in relation to birth and adoption. The focus in this section is on birth. The adoption rules broadly mirror the rules on birth.

SPL is optional. The mother may opt out of the maternity leave/statutory maternity pay system and opt into the SPL and pay system. SPL can be taken consecutively or concurrently between parents, provided they do not take more than the total SPL available to them.

5.4.1 WHO IS ENTITLED TO SHARED PARENTAL LEAVE?

The 'continuity of employment' and 'employment and earnings' tests

Regulations 35 and 36 of the SPLR 2014 provide two tests, which are used as criteria for eligibility for SPL, as detailed below.

The continuity of employment test at regulation 35 of the SPLR 2014 provides that:

'(1) For the purposes of entitlement to shared parental leave (see regulations 4, 5, 20 and 21), an employee satisfies the continuity of employment test if the employee –

(a) has been continuously employed with an employer for a period of not less than 26 weeks ending with the relevant week (see paragraph (3)); and

(b) remains in continuous employment with that employer until the week before any period of shared parental leave taken by the employee.'

The employment and earnings test at regulation 36 of the SPLR 2014 provides that:

'(1) An individual satisfies the employment and earnings test if that individual –

(a) has been engaged in employment as an employed or self-employed earner for any part of the week in the case of at least 26 of the 66 weeks immediately preceding the calculation week; and

(b) has average weekly earnings (determined in accordance with paragraph (2)) of not less than the amount set out in section 35(6A) of the 1992 Act in relation to the tax year preceding the tax year containing the calculation week.'

Note that the continuity of employment test requires an individual to be an employee, whereas the employment and earnings test requires that the individual 'has been engaged in employment as an employed or self-employed earner'. The practical effect of this is that where an employed mother has a partner who is self-employed (or vice versa), the leave may be split and so the self-employed partner benefits from SPL pay.

The mother

Regulation 4 of the SPLR 2014 deals with the mother's entitlement to SPL.

For a mother to be entitled to SPL, she must satisfy the continuity of employment test at regulation 35 (regulation 4(2)(a) of the SPLR 2014), and the father or partner must satisfy the employment and earnings tests at regulation 36 (regulation 4(3)(a) of the SPLR 2014). She must be entitled to statutory maternity leave in respect of her child (regulation 4(2)(c) of the SPLR 2014) and must have ended the entitlement to statutory maternity leave by curtailing the leave (regulation 4(2)(d) of the SPLR 2014). The notice and evidentiary requirements in regulations 8 and 10 must be met. The mother and the father or partner must have the main responsibility for the care of the child (regulations 4(2)(b) and 4(3)(b) of the SPLR 2014).

The father or partner

Regulation 5 of the SPLR 2014 deals with the father or partner's entitlement to SPL.

For a father or partner to be entitled to SPL, they must satisfy the continuity of employment test at regulation 35 (regulation 5(2)(a) of the SPLR 2014) and the mother of the child must satisfy the employment and earnings test (regulation 5(3)(a) of the SPLR 2014). The notice and evidentiary requirements in regulations 9 and 10 must be met. The mother and the father or partner must have the main responsibility for the care of the child (regulations 5(2)(b) and 5(3)(b) of the SPLR 2014).

The mother of the relevant child must be entitled to statutory maternity leave, maternity pay or maternity allowance (regulation 5(3)(c) of the SPLR 2014) and must have curtailed or ended her enjoyment of those benefits (regulation 5(3)(d) of the SPLR 2014).

Period when leave may be taken

SPL may be taken between the date on which the child is born and the day before the child's first birthday. It must be taken in complete weeks. It may be taken as one continuous period or in discontinuous periods (regulation 7 of the SPLR 2014).

5.4.2 WHAT IS THE ENTITLEMENT?

Duration

The total SPL that may be shared between the mother and the father or partner in relation to their child is 52 weeks, minus the time in maternity leave taken by the mother (regulation 6(1) of the SPLR 2014). Similar provisions occur where the mother is entitled to maternity allowance or maternity pay but not maternity leave in relation to maternity pay and maternity allowance (regulations 6(2) and 6(3) of the SPLR 2014). Regulations 6(4) and 6(5) of the SPLR 2014 detail how SPL is calculated for the mother and the father or partner.

Redundancy during SPL

Where a redundancy situation arises during a period in which an employee is taking SPL, if there is a suitable alternative vacancy, the employee is entitled to be offered alternative employment with the employer, the employer's successor or an associated company (regulation 39 of the SPLR 2014). This effectively mirrors the right within the MPLR 1999.

Right to return after SPL

An employee taking SPL will have a right to return after they have finished their period of leave (regulation 40 of the SPLR 2014). Similar to the provisions in the MPLR 1999, where the period of SPL is 26 weeks or less and is not taken together with any other statutory leave, the employee will be entitled to return to the same job in which they were employed before the absence (regulation 40(1) of the SPLR 2014). In other cases, the employee may be entitled to return to the same job or, if it is not reasonably practicable, to another job which is both suitable and appropriate in the circumstances (regulation 40(2) of the SPLR 2014).

Detriment and dismissal

It is unlawful to subject any employee to a detriment for a reason connected with taking SPL (regulation 42 of the SPLR 2014). If an employee is dismissed for taking or seeking to take SPL, the dismissal will be automatically unfair (regulation 43 of the SPLR 2014).

5.5 PARENTAL BEREAVEMENT LEAVE

From 6 April 2020, bereaved parents are entitled to two weeks' paid leave. This right was introduced by sections 80EA to 80EE of the ERA 1996 and the *Parental Bereavement Leave Regulations 2020* (PBLR 2020).

5.5.1 WHO IS ENTITLED TO PARENTAL BEREAVEMENT LEAVE?

The right applies to all employees, with no minimum period of service. As well all legal parents, it covers (regulation 4 of the PBLR 2020):

- Adoptive and intended adoptive parents
- Natural parents whose child has been adopted subject to a post-adoption contact order
- Any person who, for at least four weeks before the child's death, lived with the child and had day-to-day caring responsibility
- The partner of any of the above persons

The right arises when a child under the age of 18 dies or is stillborn after 24 or more weeks of pregnancy. There are notification requirements in regulation 6 of the PBLR 2020, but there is no requirement to provide evidence of the death or stillbirth.

5.5.2 WHAT IS THE ENTITLEMENT?

Bereaved parents are entitled to two weeks of leave in the 56 weeks following the death or stillbirth (the 56-week period is intended to allow parents to mark the anniversary of the death if they wish). The weeks can be taken consecutively or separately (regulation 5 of the PBLR 2020).

As with the other forms of parental leave, the employee's terms and conditions, seniority, pension and similar rights remain unchanged during parental bereavement leave (regulations 9 and 11 of the PBLR 2020). There is a right to return to the same job after leave (regulation 10 of the PBLR 2020).

It is unlawful to subject an employee to a detriment or dismiss them for requesting or taking parental bereavement leave (regulations 12 and 13 of the PBLR 2020).

5.6 PAY DURING FAMILY LEAVE

5.6.1 STATUTORY MATERNITY PAY

Qualification

A woman will be entitled to statutory maternity pay if she meets the criteria prescribed under the Statutory Maternity Pay (General) Regulations 1986 (SMP 1986) and the Social Security Contributions and Benefits Act 1992 (SSCBA 1992).

1) She must have ceased working for her employer (that is, for reasons of maternity leave) (section 164 (2)(a) of the SSCBA 1992).

2) She must have been employed for a period of 'at least 26 weeks ending with the week immediately preceding the 14th week before the expected week of confinement' (section 164(2)(a) of the SSCBA 1992).

3) Her 'normal weekly earnings for the period of eight weeks ending with the week immediately preceding the 14th week before the expected week of confinement are not less than the lower earnings limit' (section 164(2)(b) of the SSCBA 1992).

4) She must have 'become pregnant' and 'reached, or been confined before reaching, the commencement of the 11th week before the expected week of confinement' (section 164(2)(c) of the SSCBA 1992).

5) She must have given notice in the correct way (section 164(4)-(5) of the SSCBA 1992).

6) She must have provided the requisite evidence (regulation 22 of the SMP 1986).

Confinement is defined as '(a) labour resulting in the issue of a living child, or (b) labour after [24 weeks] of pregnancy resulting in the issue of a child whether alive or dead' (section 171(1) of the SSCBA 1992).

Entitlement

Where a pregnant employee meets qualification requirements based on average earnings and length of service, she will be entitled to receive Statutory Maternity Pay (SMP) for up to 39 weeks (regulation 2(2) of the SMP 1986).

Under the SSCBA 1992, the rate of statutory maternity pay is at the 'earnings-related rate' for the first six weeks of SMP (section 166(1)(a) of the SSCBA 1992), and at the lower of the earnings-related rate and a fixed rate prescribed by statute for the remainder of the maternity pay period (section 166(1)(b) of the SSCBA 1992).

The earnings-related rate is 90% of the woman's normal weekly earnings, calculated using the eight weeks before the 'expected week of confinement' (section 166(1)(b) of the SSCBA 1992).

5.6.2 STATUTORY PATERNITY PAY AND STATUTORY ADOPTION PAY

Where an individual is entitled to statutory paternity leave, he will generally be entitled to statutory paternity pay. Part XIIZA of the SSCBA 1992 and the *Statutory Paternity Pay and Statutory Adoption Pay (General) Regulations 2002* provide a code for the payment of statutory paternity and adoption pay.

Qualification and notice requirements are similar to those for maternity pay and must be met before statutory paternity or adoption pay is due. The rate of pay is prescribed by statutory instrument.

5.6.3 STATUTORY SHARED PARENTAL PAY

The *Statutory Shared Parental Pay Regulations 2014* (SSPPR 2014), provide a statutory scheme whereby the father or partner is entitled to be paid for time spent on statutory SPL.

Various qualifications and requirements are specified by the SSPPR 2014 relating to earnings and length of service.

The key qualification particular to shared parental pay is that the mother has curtailed her entitlement to statutory maternity pay (section 165(3A) of the SSCBA 1992) or maternity allowance (section 35(3A) of the SSCBA 1992). The extent of entitlement to statutory shared parental pay is set out at regulation 10 of the SSPPR 2014. Effectively, the entitlement is to 39 weeks less the number of weeks in which maternity allowance or maternity pay has been paid to the mother if the notification requirements have been met.

5.6.4 STATUTORY PARENTAL BEREAVEMENT PAY

Entitlement is governed by part 12ZD of the SSCBA 1992 and the *Statutory Parental Bereavement Pay (General) Regulations 2020*. Essentially, there is a qualifying period of 26 weeks' continuous employment with the same employer, ending with the week before the child's death or stillbirth. The rate of pay for the two weeks' leave is the same as for paternity pay, with similar notification requirements.

5.7 TIME OFF TO LOOK AFTER DEPENDANTS

Under section 57A(1) of the ERA 1996, an employee is permitted:

'a reasonable amount of time off work during [their] working hours in order to take action which is necessary –

a) to provide assistance on an occasion when a dependant falls ill, gives birth or is injured or assaulted;

b) to make arrangements for the provision of care for a dependant who is ill or injured;

c) in consequence of the death of a dependant;

d) because of the unexpected disruption or termination of arrangements for the care of a dependant;

e) to deal with an incident which involves a child of the employee and which occurs unexpectedly in a period during which an educational establishment which the child attends is responsible for him'.

Item (c) above does not give a right to compassionate leave, as such, on the death of a dependant. Although it may be in consequence of the death, it is not 'action which is necessary', which refers to matters such as making funeral arrangements, registering the death and applying for probate (see *Forster v Cartwright Black [2004] IRLR 781 EAT*).

The time off must be 'to take action which is necessary' for one of the listed purposes. Earlier Employment Appeal Tribunal (EAT) decisions had suggested that nothing short of a genuine and unforeseen emergency would suffice (for example, *Cortest Ltd v O'Toole (2007) UKEAT/0470/07*). However, the EAT took a somewhat broader view in *Royal Bank of Scotland v Harrison [2009] ICR 116*, stating that the words 'necessary' and 'unexpected' should be given their ordinary meaning and there was no implied requirement of a 'sudden' event.

'Dependant' is defined as meaning an employee's spouse, civil partner, child or parent. It also includes any person who lives in the same household as the employee (other than their employee, tenant, lodger or boarder). Further, it includes anybody who reasonably relies on the employee for assistance on occasions when they fall ill or for assistance with care arrangements. This would include, for example, an elderly neighbour or relative (section 57A(3)-(5) of the ERA 1996).

The time off work is unpaid. Employees must tell their employer the reason for the absence as soon as reasonably practicable (which does not necessarily have to be before the employee leaves work) and, unless they have already returned to work, give an estimate of the length of their absence (section 57A(2) of the ERA 1996).

What is reasonable?

The question of what is 'reasonable' for the purposes of the legislation was considered by the EAT in *Qua v John Ford Morrison Solicitors [2003] IRLR 184*. The following propositions emerged:

1) An employer should always take account of the individual circumstances of the employee seeking to exercise the right.

2) It is not possible to specify maximum periods of time which are reasonable in any particular circumstance.

3) An employer may take into account the number and length of previous absences in order to determine whether the time taken off or sought to be taken off is reasonable or necessary.

4) The legislation was passed in order to deal with 'unforeseen' problems (however, as discussed above, the later *Harrison* decision suggests this is not a requirement in all cases).

5) The disruption or inconvenience caused to an employer's business are irrelevant factors which should not be taken into account.

5.8 FLEXIBLE WORKING

5.8.1 REQUESTS FOR FLEXIBLE WORKING ARRANGEMENTS

The *Flexible Working Regulations 2014* (FWR 2014) and part VIIIA of the ERA 1996 provide a statutory scheme for flexible working. There is no longer a requirement, as there was before 2014, to be a carer. The procedure for making a request has been simplified, with less stringent procedural requirements on employers but a new requirement to act in a 'reasonable manner'.

Eligibility

Employees must have been employed for 26 consecutive weeks in order to make a flexible working application (regulation 3 of the FWR 2014). Applications must be in writing, specify whether an application has previously been made and be dated (regulation 4 of the FWR 2014).

What changes can be requested?

The scope of the changes that can be requested is broad. Section 80F(1)(a) of the ERA 1996 provides that a qualifying employee may apply for a change in his terms and conditions if the change relates to:

'(i) the hours he is required to work,

(ii) the times when he is required to work,

(iii) where, as between his home and a place of business of his employer, he is required to work, or

(iv) such other aspect of his terms and conditions of employment as the Secretary of State may specify by regulations'.

Acting 'in a reasonable manner'

An employer must deal with an application 'in a reasonable manner' (section 80G(1)(a) of the ERA 1996). The employer must reply within the decision period (three months, or a longer period if agreed) and shall only be entitled to refuse the application on the basis of any of the following grounds, as set out in section 80G(1)(b) of the ERA 1996:

(i) The burden of additional costs

(ii) Detrimental effect on ability to meet customer demand

(iii) Inability to re-organise work among existing staff

(iv) Inability to recruit additional staff

(v) Detrimental impact on quality

(vi) Detrimental impact on performance

(vii) Insufficiency of work during the periods the employee proposes to work

(viii) Planned structural changes

(ix) Such other grounds as the Secretary of State may specify by regulations

The reasonableness requirement was introduced by the FWR 2014, so case law pre-dating the FWR 2014 (when there was no test of reasonableness) should be treated with caution. Employers and individuals would be well advised to start by considering the statutory *Acas Code of Practice on handling in a reasonable manner requests* (see www.acas.org.uk/acas-code-of-practice-on-flexible-working-requests) to work flexibly, which provides a relatively comprehensive guide. In *Whiteman v CPS Interiors ET/2601103/2015*, an employment tribunal expressed the view that the employer is required to follow a reasonable procedure, act in good faith and give real thought to the request. A tribunal will not, however, assess the reasonableness of the decision itself.

Useful Acas guidance exists on flexible working policies and homeworking. While this does not have the same statutory force as the Code of Practice, it is likely to be persuasive.

5.8.2 REFUSAL TO GRANT REQUEST

An employee may complain to an employment tribunal of a failure to grant flexible working on the grounds that the employer has failed to comply with its duty under section 80G of the ERA 1996, that the decision was based on incorrect facts or that the employer's rejection of the flexible working request did not satisfy the statutory criteria for refusal (section 80H of the ERA 1996).

Section 80I of the ERA 1996 entitles the tribunal to grant compensation which is 'just and equitable' up to the statutory maximum, which is currently eight weeks' pay (regulation 6 of the FWR 2014).

5.8.3 DETRIMENT, DISMISSAL AND DISCRIMINATION

It is unlawful to subject an employee to a detriment or dismiss them for making a flexible working request (sections 47E and 104C of the ERA 1996). Equally, it is unlawful to discriminate against an employee in deciding whether to grant a request.

5.9 PROPOSED LAW REFORM

5.9.1 STATUTORY NEONATAL LEAVE AND PAY

In March 2020, the Department for Business, Energy & Industrial Strategy published its response to consultation on a proposed scheme for neonatal leave and pay. The document indicates that parents of babies who are admitted to hospital within 28 days of birth, and who remain hospitalised for at least seven days, will be eligible for a maximum of 12 weeks' leave, with similar pay entitlements as for other forms of family leave.

It was thought that this entitlement would be introduced in an Employment Bill. However, the Government has decided to support a Private Members' Bill – *the Neonatal Care (Leave and Pay) Bill*. At the time of writing, this is at the report stage, and there is no set timetable for implementation.

CHAPTER 6

WHISTLEBLOWING, TRADE UNION ACTIVITIES AND HEALTH AND SAFETY AT WORK

6.0 OVERVIEW

This chapter covers in detail the essential elements in protected disclosure claims – claims brought by 'whistleblowers' – and discusses in broader terms individual trade union and health and safety at work provisions.

Whistleblowing detriment and dismissal claims are explored by reference to five main questions:

1) What amounts to a protected disclosure?

2) Who qualifies as a whistleblower?

3) What amounts to whistleblowing detriment?

4) When will a whistleblower be automatically unfairly dismissed?

5) What compensation can a whistleblower claim in respect of detriments and unfair dismissal?

These questions provide the headings for the sections below. The focus is on individual claims before employment tribunals. Regulatory requirements, as well as other legal obligations related to whistleblowers, are outside the scope of this book.

The definition of 'protected disclosure' is common to both detriment and dismissal claims, but it is useful to summarise how the central statutory provisions divide:

- Those provisions concerning detriment – that is, 'protection from suffering detriment in employment' – contained in part V of the *Employment Rights Act 1996* (ERA 1996), including sections 43A-43L.

- Those provisions concerning unfair dismissal contained in part X of the ERA 1996.

This chapter regularly refers to the distinction between a detriment claim under part V of the ERA 1996 and an unfair dismissal claim under part X of the ERA 1996. This distinction is found in the statutory language (section 47B of the ERA 1996), and in case law (*Timis v Osipov [2019] IRLR 52*, paragraph 60). The distinction explains why it is only possible to claim for unfair dismissal under part X, but it is possible to bring a claim that the act of dismissal was a detriment under part V. This is as (a) a claim against a named individual who took the decision; and (b) a claim against the employer on the basis that it is vicariously liable for the actions of the named individual. This distinction is also useful when considering the remedies a whistleblower may pursue using either route.

6.1 WHAT AMOUNTS TO A PROTECTED DISCLOSURE?

The requirements of a protected disclosure are the same for a whistleblower claimant pursuing a detriment or an unfair dismissal claim, although the burden of proof provisions differ.

In broad terms, there are five requirements for a disclosure to qualify for the purposes of section 43B of the ERA 1996:

1) There needs to be a disclosure of information.

2) The information disclosed must, in the reasonable belief of the worker making the disclosure, tend to show one or more of the things listed under section 43B(1) of the ERA 1996.

3) The disclosure of the *relevant* information must, in the reasonable belief of the worker making the disclosure, be in the public interest.

4) The disclosure must be made by the worker in a manner that accords with the scheme set out in sections 43C-43H of the ERA1996.

5) The act of disclosing the information must not amount to a criminal offence.

6.1.1 A DISCLOSURE OF INFORMATION

A qualifying disclosure is defined in section 43B of the ERA 1996, which provides that a qualifying disclosure must be a 'disclosure of information'. The Employment Appeal Tribunal (EAT) noted in *Cavendish Munro Professional Risk Management v Geduld [2010] IRLR 38* that this means the disclosure must convey a statement of facts. Slade J said at paragraph 24:

'Further, the ordinary meaning of giving "information" is conveying facts. In the course of the hearing before us, a hypothetical was advanced regarding communicating information about the state of a hospital. Communicating "information" would be: "The wards have not been cleaned for the past two weeks. Yesterday, sharps were left lying around." Contrasted with that would be a statement that: "You are not complying with health and safety requirements." In our view, this would be an allegation, not information.'

It is worth noting that while *Cavendish Munro* remains good law, the EAT has warned in *Kilraine v London Borough of Wandsworth [2016] IRLR 422* that care should be taken in distinguishing between 'information' and an 'allegation'. In *Kilraine*, Langstaff J noted at paragraph 30 that:

'It would be a pity if tribunals were too easily seduced into asking whether it was one or the other when reality and experience suggest that very often information and allegation are intertwined. The decision is not decided by whether a given phrase or paragraph is one or rather the other, but is to be determined in the light of the statute itself. The question is simply whether it is a disclosure of information. If it is also an allegation, that is nothing to the point.'

It is possible for a number of communications to be read together to form a protected disclosure, even where each individual communication would not do so (*Norbrook Laboratories v Shaw [2014] ICR 540*). However, in each case, a tribunal will have to apply the relevant law to determine 'whether or not a particular statement or disclosure does contain sufficient content or specificity[,] [and this] is a matter for evaluative judgment by the tribunal in light of all the facts of the case' (Choudhury J, President of the EAT, *Simpson v Cantor Fitzgerald Europe [2020] ICR 236*).

6.1.2 WHAT THE DISCLOSURE MUST TEND TO SHOW

The information disclosed must, in the reasonable belief of the worker making the disclosure, tend to show one or more of the things listed under section 43B(1) of the ERA 1996, namely:

'(a) that a criminal offence has been committed, is being committed or is likely to be committed;

(b) that a person has failed, is failing or is likely to fail to comply with any legal obligation to which he is subject;

(c) that a miscarriage of justice has occurred, is occurring or is likely to occur;

(d) that the health or safety of any individual has been, is being or is likely to be endangered;

(e) that the environment has been, is being, or is likely to be damaged; or

(f) that information tending to show any matter falling within any one of the preceding paragraphs has been, is being or is likely to be deliberately concealed.'

This is further clarified by section 43B(2) of the ERA 1996, which says:

'For the purposes of subsection (1), it is immaterial whether the relevant failure occurred, occurs or would occur in the United Kingdom or elsewhere, and whether the law applying to it is that of the United Kingdom or of any other country or territory.'

The reference to a 'reasonable belief' means that the test for belief is a subjective one. The question is whether the particular worker making the disclosure would reasonably believe the information disclosed tends to show one of the matters listed under section 43B(1) of the ERA 1996. The information disclosed does not need to be true (*Darnton v University of Surrey [2003] IRLR 133 EAT*). Where information has been received from a third party and then disclosed by a whistleblower, this also does not need to be true. The question will be whether the worker has a reasonable belief that the disclosure of that information tends to show one of the matters listed under section 43B(1) of the ERA 1996. The extent of a worker's technical knowledge and understanding will be highly relevant to the statutory question.

6.1.3 THE PUBLIC INTEREST TEST

Workers must persuade a tribunal that they had a reasonable belief that making the protected disclosure was in the 'public interest' (section 43B of the ERA 1996).

It is not the role of the tribunal to consider whether, in fact, a disclosure is (or was) in the public interest. Instead, the tribunal must consider whether the claimant subjectively reasonably believed that the disclosure was in the public interest *(Morgan v Royal Mencap Society [2016] IRLR 428)*.

The meaning of 'in the public interest' was considered in *Chesterton Global v Nurmohamed [2015] ICR 920*, where Underhill LJ held at paragraph 37:

'In a whistleblower case where the disclosure relates to a breach of the worker's own contract of employment (or some other matter under section 43B(1) where the interest in question is personal in character), there may nevertheless be features of the case that make it reasonable to regard disclosure as being in the public interest as well as in the personal interest of the worker. Doctors' [disclosing excessive working] hours is particularly obvious, but there may be many other kinds of case where it may reasonably be thought that such a disclosure was in the public interest. The question is one to be answered by the tribunal on a consideration of all the circumstances of the particular case, but [the list of four] relevant factors comprising:

a) the numbers in the group whose interests the disclosure served;

b) the nature of the interests affected and the extent to which they are affected by the wrongdoing disclosed;

c) the nature of the wrongdoing disclosed – disclosure of deliberate wrongdoing is more likely to be in the public interest than the disclosure of inadvertent wrongdoing affecting the same number of people;

d) the identity of the alleged wrongdoer – the larger or more prominent the wrongdoer (in terms of the size of its relevant community), the more obviously should a disclosure about its activities engage the public interest.'

6.1.4 THE MANNER OF DISCLOSURE

For a *qualifying* disclosure to be a *protected* disclosure, it must be made in accordance with one or more of sections 43C-43H of the ERA 1996. These sections provide details regarding to whom, and how, the disclosure must be made. These sections and subsections are detailed, and ideally, each should be consulted individually. The following is a brief summary of the differing ways in which a qualifying disclosure may be made.

- Section 43C of the ERA 1996 provides that a qualifying disclosure may be made to the worker's employer or another person who has legal responsibility for the conduct to which the relevant failure relates.

- Section 43K(2) of the ERA 1996 defines an 'employer' broadly, and – depending on the 'worker' – in terms that may include the person who substantially determines or determined the terms on which a worker is or was engaged, the National Health Service Commissioning Board, the Local Health Board or the person providing work experience or training.

In *McTigue v University Hospital Bristol NHS Foundation Trust [2016] ICR 1155*, the EAT held that a worker could have two employers for the purposes of the whistleblowing litigation. On the facts of the case, a forensic nurse examiner had worked under a contract of employment with an agency at a medical centre operated by an NHS Trust. Additionally, she was issued with an honorary contract by the trust, authorising her to carry out duties and requiring her cooperation in relation to health and safety, clinical governance and working time while on trust premises. The EAT held that if both the supplier and the end user of a worker had substantially determined the terms of engagement, then both were the 'employer' for the purposes of section 43K(2)(a) of the ERA 1996, regardless of whether one had substantially determined the terms to a greater extent than the other.

In *Gilham v Ministry of Justice [2020] IRLR 52*, the Supreme Court held that district judges could suffer detriments as whistleblowers. To reach this conclusion, it was necessary to construe the provisions of the ERA 1996, by reference to the *European Convention on Human Rights* (ECHR), taking into account article 14. On the facts of the case, this meant the right of District

Judge Gilham not to suffer discrimination in the enjoyment of her right to freedom of expression.

The remaining provisions are more specialised, and are summarised briefly below:

- Section 43D of the ERA 1996 provides that a qualifying disclosure complies with the section if it is made 'in the course of obtaining legal advice'.

- Section 43E of the ERA 1996 provides that a qualifying disclosure may be made to a Minister of the Crown if the worker's employer is an individual appointed under any enactment or a body 'any of whose members are so appointed'.

- Section 43F of the ERA 1996 provides that the worker may make the disclosure to a person prescribed by an order made by the Secretary of State. The statutory list of persons to whom disclosures may be made is found within the *Public Interest Disclosure (Prescribed Persons) Order 2014*.

- Section 43G of the ERA 1996 provides for 'disclosure in other cases'. This provision entitles a worker to make the disclosure if 'in all the circumstances of the case, it is reasonable for him to make the disclosure' (section 43G(1)(e) of the ERA 1996) and if certain conditions listed in section 43G(1) and section 43G(2) of the ERA 1996 are met. Perhaps the most common scenario in which a worker will rely on this provision is where 'the worker reasonably believes that he will be subject to a detriment by his employer if he makes a disclosure to his employer' or the prescribed person under section 43F (section 43G(2)(a) of the ERA 1996.

- Lastly, a qualifying disclosure will be made in accordance with section 43H of the ERA 1996 if the worker reasonably believes the information is substantially true and does not make the disclosure for personal gain, it is reasonable for them to make the disclosure and 'the relevant failure is of an exceptionally serious nature'.

Under section 43J of the ERA 1996, any contractual duty of confidentiality is void 'in so far as it purports to preclude a worker from making a protected disclosure'.

A worker can complain of suffering a detriment by reason of making a protected disclosure even though the disclosure was made while they were working for a previous employer (*BP plc v (1) Elstone (2) Petrotechnics [2010] ICR 879*).

In *Catt v English Table Tennis Association Ltd and ors [2022] IRLR 1022*, the EAT has emphasised that the factual enquiry to determine whether a non-executive director claimant is a limb (b) worker involves asking whether there was a contract between the claimant and the alleged employer whereby the former undertook to perform work or services for the latter. Mrs Justice Eady DBE, President, likened the approach to that identified in *Gilham v Ministry of Justice [2020] IRLR 52*, where general guidance was provided for other cases concerning office holders, and the factual enquiry to determine whether the parties had intended to enter into a contractual relationship, defined at least in part by their agreement.

6.1.5 THE MAKING OF THE DISCLOSURE MUST NOT BE A CRIME

An alleged disclosure is not a qualifying disclosure if, by making it, the person commits an offence, and the information must not be such that a claim to legal professional privilege (or, in Scotland, to confidentiality as between client and professional legal adviser) could be maintained in legal proceedings.

6.2 WHO QUALIFIES AS A WHISTLEBLOWER?

In brief, a whistleblower is a 'worker' who makes a qualifying protected disclosure to their employer or another responsible person. Although only an employee can bring a claim under section 103A of the ERA 1996, a 'worker' can bring a claim of whistleblowing detriment under section 47B of the ERA 1996. The term 'employee' is explained in Chapter 1.

Unlike in the discrimination context, the protection of whistleblowers extends only to the employment context. In *Tiplady v City of Bradford Metropolitan District Council [2020] IRLR 230*, the Court of Appeal held that the approach required by the discrimination legislation (which divides the protection between different kinds of relationships) should also be applied to the whistleblower legislation. Despite the differences in their particular structure and language, the whistleblower legislation and the discrimination legislation are fundamentally of the same character. Parliament must be taken to have intended, when using the terminology of detriment in the discrimination legislation and in part V of the ERA 1996, that it should have the same scope in both. The whistleblower provisions of the ERA 1996 apply only in relation to the employment field. In general, whether a detriment is to be recognised as arising, or not arising, can be answered by asking in what 'capacity' the detriment was suffered – or, to put the same thing another way, whether it was suffered by the claimant 'as an employee'.

6.2.1 THE MEANING OF THE TERM 'WORKER'

The term 'worker' refers to both (a) the 'regular' definition of 'worker' under section 230(3) of the ERA 1996 and (b) as specifically extended under section 43K of the ERA 1996. The meaning of 'worker' under section 230(3) of the ERA 1996 is addressed in **Chapter 1**. The extension of the definition under section 43K of the ERA 1996 includes certain classes of individuals who would not otherwise be workers. Broadly, this includes agency workers, homeworkers, individuals who provide services to the NHS in certain circumstances and people who are provided with work experience connected to a training course with the Nursing and Midwifery Council.

The main extensions under section 43K of the ERA 1996 are phrased in terms that 'for the purposes of [whistleblowing claims] a "worker" includes an individual who is not a worker as defined by section 230(3) but who –

(a) works or worked for a person in circumstances in which –

(i) he is or was introduced or supplied to do that work by a third person, and

(ii) the terms on which he is or was engaged to do the work are or were in practice substantially determined not by him but by the person for whom he works or worked, by the third person or by both of them,

(b) contracts or contracted with a person, for the purposes of that person's business, for the execution of work to be done in a place not under the control or management of that person and would fall within section 230(3)(b) if for "personally" in that provision there were substituted "(whether personally or otherwise)",

(ba) works or worked as a person performing services under a contract entered into by him with [the National Health Service Commissioning Board]...'

Importantly, under section 43K(1) of the ERA 1996 the definition of worker for the purpose of whistleblowing includes those who would have qualified as 'workers' but for the requirement that they provide services personally – that is, individuals who are contractually entitled to send a replacement. This provision may mean that those who might consider themselves freelancers or self-employed will nonetheless receive protection when making protected disclosures.

Someone employed by their own company which supplies their services to an employment agency, which in turn provides their services to an end-user, still counts as a 'worker' for whistleblowing law purposes and can bring a claim against the end-user (*Croke v Hydro Aluminium Worcester Ltd [2007] ICR 1303*).

A member of an LLP may be a 'worker' for the purposes of section 230(3) of the ERA 1996 and thus will be entitled to whistleblowing protection (*Clyde & Co LLP and another v Bates van Winkelhof [2014] UKSC 32*).

Note, however, that despite the wide ambit of section 43K of the ERA 1996, the Court of Appeal held in *Sharpe v Worcester Diocesan Board of Finance Ltd and anor [2015] ICR 1241* that a contract must be in existence for an individual to be a 'worker' (see paragraph 115).

6.3 WHAT AMOUNTS TO WHISTLEBLOWING DETRIMENT?

A worker has the right not to be subjected to any detriment done on the ground that they have made a protected disclosure (section 47B(1) of the ERA 1996). Workers can bring claims against their co-workers, or agents of their employers, and their employers directly, as well as against employers on the ground that they are vicariously liable for the actions of co-workers and/ or agents. The term 'worker' is explained in paragraph **6.2.1**.

The term 'detriment' is very broad, and the Court of Appeal in *Timis v Osipov [2019] IRLR 52* confirmed that it includes the detriment of an individual taking the decision to dismiss a worker or employee. However, it is a defence for the employer to show that it took all reasonable steps to prevent one worker subjecting another to a detriment (section 47B(1D) of the ERA 1996).

In *Edinburgh Mela Ltd v Purnell [2021] IRLR 874*, the EAT upheld a finding of post-termination dismissal, namely, reporting an employee to the police, and emphasised that the threshold to find a detriment was not a high one.

6.3.1 THE RIGHT NOT TO BE SUBJECTED TO A DETRIMENT

A worker has a right not to be subjected to any detriment by another worker, or an agent of their employer on the ground that they have made a protected disclosure (section 47B(1A) of the ERA 1996).

Since the *Enterprise and Regulatory Reform Act 2013* came into effect in 2013, it has been possible under section 47B(1A) of the ERA 1996 for a worker to bring a claim of whistleblowing detriment not only against their employer but also against an agent of the employer or an individual co-worker.

The precise wording of the provisions means that it is 'immaterial whether [the detriment] is done with the knowledge or approval of the worker's employer' (section 47B(1C) of the ERA 1996).

Further, under section 48(2) of the ERA 1996, the burden is on the respondent to prove the reason the claimant has suffered any detriment: 'It is for the employer to show the ground on which any act, or deliberate failure to act, was done'. However, it is a defence for the employer to show that it took all reasonable steps to prevent one worker subjecting another to a detriment (section 47B(1D) of the ERA 1996).

6.3.2 DETRIMENT AND DISMISSAL

The term 'detriment' is very broad. The Court of Appeal in *Jesudason v Alder Hey Children's NHS Foundation Trust [2020] IRLR 374* provided the following clarification of the meaning of the term 'detriment' as follows:

'The concept [of detriment] is well established in discrimination law and it has the same meaning in whistleblowing cases. In *Derbyshire v St Helens MBC [2007] UKHL 16, [2007] ICR 841, [2007] IRLR 540*, paras [67]-[68], Lord Neuberger described the position thus:

'[67] ... In that connection, Brightman LJ said in *Ministry of Defence v Jeremiah [1980] ICR 13 at 31A* that "a detriment exists if a reasonable worker would or might take the view that the [treatment] was in all the circumstances to his detriment".

[68] That observation was cited with apparent approval by Lord Hoffmann in *Chief Constable of West Yorkshire Police v Khan [2001] ICR 1065*, para 53. More recently it has been cited with approval in your Lordships' House in *Shamoon v Chief Constable of the Royal Ulster Constabulary [2003] ICR 337*. At para 35, my noble and learned friend, Lord Hope of Craighead, after referring to the observation and describing the test as being one of "materiality", also said that an "unjustified sense of grievance cannot amount to 'detriment'". In the same case, at para 105, Lord Scott of Foscote, after quoting Brightman LJ's observation, added: "If the victim's opinion that the treatment was to his or her detriment is a reasonable one to hold, that ought, in my opinion, to suffice".'

Some workers may not consider that particular treatment amounts to a detriment; they may be unconcerned about it and not consider themselves to be prejudiced or disadvantaged in any way. But if a reasonable worker might do so, and the claimant genuinely does so, that is enough to amount to a detriment. The test is not, therefore, wholly subjective.'

The Court of Appeal in *Timis v Osipov [2019] IRLR 52* confirmed that the term detriment includes the detriment of an individual taking the decision to dismiss a worker or employee. This may seem surprising since section 47B(2) of the ERA 1996 precludes a claim for dismissal as a detriment. However, the wording of section 47B(2) expressly refers only to a 'dismissal within the meaning of part X' – that is, the termination of the contract of employment, which can only be claimed as an automatically unfair dismissal claim contrary to section 103A of the ERA 1996 against the employer (see paragraph 60 of *Osipov*). The action of a co-worker in taking the decision to dismiss is separate from the actual termination of employment and therefore can be pursued as a detriment claim.

In full, Lord Justice Underhill held in *Osipov* that:

'I start by saying that I agree with Simler P that a construction of section 47B(2) which prevented a claimant from bringing a claim against an individual co-worker based on the detriment of dismissal would produce an incoherent and unsatisfactory result and is accordingly unlikely to conform to Parliament's intention. Once the decision was taken to make co-workers personally liable for whistleblower detriment it is hard to see any reason in principle why they should, uniquely, not be so liable in a case where the detriment amounts to dismissal. Such a state of affairs produces the obvious anomalies identified by Simler P at paras 156-158 of her judgment, namely, in short:

(a) that co-workers whose unlawfully motivated acts short of dismissal cause the claimant to be dismissed will be liable for those acts (and, subject to the point considered at paras 77-82 below, for compensation for the losses caused by the dismissal) while an individual with the same motivation who decides on the actual dismissal escapes scot-free; and

(b) that there is no such bar to individual liability in the case of a claimant who is a worker rather than an employee and who has his or her contract of employment terminated, even though the two situations might be thought to be substantially identical.'

Where an employee has been dismissed, they are able to claim (a) that the actions of the dismissing officer were a detriment; (b) that the employer is vicariously liable for the actions of the dismissing officer applying section 47B(1A-C) of the ERA 1996; and, as set out below, (c) that they were automatically unfairly dismissed contrary to section 103A of the ERA 1996.

However, it is a defence for the employer to show that it took all reasonable steps to prevent one worker subjecting another to a detriment (section 47B(1D) of the ERA 1996).

6.3.3 WHEN WILL A WHISTLEBLOWER BE AUTOMATICALLY UNFAIRLY DISMISSED?

Unlike claims for whistleblowing detriments, only an employee can bring this claim. Section 103A of the ERA 1996 provides that an 'employee who is dismissed shall be regarded for the purposes of part [X] as unfairly dismissed if the reason (or, if more than one, the principal reason) for the dismissal is that the employee made a protected disclosure'. So where a tribunal finds the sole, or principal, reason for the dismissal of an employee was the making of a protected disclosure, the dismissal is automatically unfair.

There is no qualifying service requirement, so the employee need not have been employed for at least two years, unlike 'ordinary' unfair dismissal claims under sections 94-98 and section 108(3) of the ERA 1996. The definition of employee is covered in **Chapter 1**.

6.3.4 THE BURDEN OF PROOF

Although qualifying service is not a prerequisite to bringing a claim under section 103A of the ERA 1996, it does affect how the burden of proof is applied. Where the claimant has two years' qualifying service under section 108 of the ERA 1996, the burden of proving the reason or principal reason remains on the employer (as it does in a claim for ordinary unfair dismissal contrary to sections 94-98 of the ERA 1996). Where a claimant has not been continuously employed for two years, the burden of proof should be approached as described by Lord Justice Mummery in *Kuzel v Roche Products Ltd [2008] IRLR 530*:

> 'When an employee positively asserts that there was a different and inadmissible reason for his dismissal, he must produce some evidence supporting the positive case, such as making protected disclosures. This does not mean, however, that, in order to succeed in an unfair dismissal claim, the employee has to discharge the burden of proving that the dismissal was for that different reason. It is sufficient for the employee to challenge the evidence produced by the employer to show the reason advanced by him for the dismissal and to produce some evidence of a different reason.

> Having heard the evidence of both sides relating to the reason for dismissal it will then be for the ET to consider the evidence as a whole and to make findings of primary fact on the basis of direct evidence, or by reasonable inferences from primary facts established by the evidence, or not contested in the evidence.

> The ET must then decide what was the reason or principal reason for the dismissal of the claimant on the basis that it was for the employer to show what the reason was. If the employer does not show to the satisfaction of the ET that the reason was what he asserted it was, it is open to the ET to find that the reason was what the employee asserted it was. But it is not correct to say, either as a matter of law or logic, that the ET must find that, if the reason was not that asserted by the employer, then it must have been for the reason asserted by the employee. That may often be the outcome in practice, but it is not necessarily so.'

To summarise, this means that first, a claimant must raise a *prima facie* case that the reason for dismissal was their making of a protected disclosure, instead of the reason advanced by the respondent. Then, the tribunal must determine whether the respondent has proved its reason. Finally, if the respondent has not done so, the tribunal may, or may not, find the reason to have been the claimant's making of a protected disclosure.

Where a claimant has brought both a claim under section 103A of the ERA 1996 and an 'ordinary' unfair dismissal claim, the tribunal must not make inconsistent findings, and if it upholds the claim under section 103A of the ERA 1996, it need go no further in considering the 'ordinary' unfair dismissal claim (*London Borough of Wandsworth v CRW (2016) UKEAT/0322/15*).

6.3.5 THE SEPARABILITY PRINCIPLE

Employers may seek to defend a whistleblowing claim on the basis that even if an employee has made a disclosure, the reason for the detriments or dismissal is a feature of the employee's conduct that is separable from the protected disclosure. The label for what can be a necessary step in determining the real reason for the impugned treatment is referred to as the 'Separability Principle'.

In *Kong v Gulf International Bank (UK) Limited [2022] ICR 1513* the claimant was found to have made a protected disclosure, but in doing so, she had also questioned the professional awareness or competence of the respondent's Head of Legal. The claimant's conduct towards the Head of Legal was found by the employment tribunal, and the EAT, to have been a separate explanation for the claimant's dismissal, for which the sole, or principal, reason test applies. By contrast, the claimant had discharged the burden of proving the requisite level of causation for two of her detriment claims; the detriment claims did not succeed, ultimately, because of limitation. The Court of Appeal upheld the rejection of the automatically unfair dismissal claim on the ground of whistleblowing, and Lady Justice Simler gave the following guidance on the approach to the Separability Principle, emphasising that:

> 'the "separability principle" is not a rule of law or a basis for deeming an employer's reason to be anything other than the facts disclose it to be. It is simply a label that identifies what may in a particular case be a necessary step in the process of determining what as a matter of fact was the real reason for impugned treatment. Once the reasons for particular treatment have been identified by the fact-finding tribunal, it must evaluate whether the reasons so identified are separate from the protected disclosure, or whether they are so closely connected with it that a distinction cannot fairly and sensibly be drawn. Were this exercise not permissible, the effect would be that whistleblowers would have immunity for behaviour or conduct related to the making of a protected disclosure no matter how bad, and employers would be obliged to ensure that they are not adversely treated, again no matter how bad the associated behaviour or conduct.

> 'Likewise, what was said in *Martin v Devonshires Solicitors [2011] ICR 352*, about being slow to allow purported distinctions between a protected complaint and ordinary unreasonable behaviour, is also not a rule of law. There is no objective standard against which behaviour must be assessed to determine whether the separability principle applies in a particular case, nor any question of requiring behaviour to reach a particular threshold

of seriousness before that behaviour or conduct can be distinguished as separable from the making of the protected disclosure itself. The phrases used in the authorities (in the context of trade union activities, victimisation and whistleblowing) capture the favour of the distinction, but were not intended to be treated as defining, and do not define, those cases where separability would or would not apply.

'The statutory question to be determined in these cases is what motivated a particular decision-maker; in other words, what reason did he or she have for dismissing or treating the complainant in an adverse way. This factual question is easy to state; but it can be and frequently is difficult to decide because human motivation can be complex, difficult to discern and subtle distinctions might have to be considered. In a proper case, even where the conduct of the whistleblower is found not to be unreasonable, a tribunal may be entitled to conclude that there is a separate feature of the claimant!s conduct that is distinct from the protected disclosure and is the real reason for impugned treatment.

All that said, if a whistleblower's conduct is blameless, or does not go beyond ordinary unreasonableness, it is less likely that it will be found to be the real reason for an employer's detrimental treatment of the whistleblower. The detrimental treatment of an innocent whistleblower will be a powerful basis for particularly close scrutiny of an argument that the real reason for adverse treatment was not the protected disclosure. It will "cry out" for an explanation from the employer, as Elias LJ observed in Fecitt, and tribunals will need to examine such explanations with particular care'.

In *Jesudason v Alder Hey Children's NHS Foundation Trust [2020] IRLR 374*, the Court of Appeal upheld a finding that the respondent trust's action in sending letters was a detriment, but the objective was, so far as was possible, to nullify the adverse, potentially damaging and, in part at least, misleading information that the claimant had chosen to put in the public domain. That both explained the need to send the letters and the form in which they were cast. The trust was concerned with damage limitation; in so far as the appellant was adversely affected as a consequence, it was not because he was in the direct line of fire. Although sending letters in the way they were drafted did constitute a detriment to the claimant, it was not a detriment on the grounds that the claimant had made a protected disclosure or disclosures.

6.3.6 KNOWLEDGE

In larger organisations, the eventual dismissing officer may be unaware of an employee's protected disclosures, though they may have been provided with tainted information by a co-worker. In *Royal Mail Group Ltd v Jhuti [2019]*

UKSC 55, the Supreme Court clarified that even where this is the case, there are circumstances when it is possible for a claimant to succeed in a claim for automatically unfair dismissal.

In brief, Ms Jhuti made protected disclosures to Mr Widmer, her line manager. He then (a) raised performance concerns with the claimant for the first time; (b) set up 'intense weekly meetings' to monitor her performance; and (c) placed her on a six-week performance improvement plan (paragraphs 6-13). The claimant was signed off with anxiety and depression. Whether the claimant's employment would continue was reviewed by Ms Vickers, who took the decision to dismiss the claimant. Ms Vickers was found not to have made her decision because of the claimant's protected disclosures but to have reached the decision on the basis of Mr Widmer's performance concerns, and an 'e-mail trail [created by Mr Widmer, which made it] inevitable that Ms Vickers would, as she did, dismiss the claimant' (paragraph 34).

Lady Justice Hale explains the rationale in the following terms in paragraph 60:

> '[I]f a person in the hierarchy of responsibility above the employee (here Mr Widmer) determines that, for reason A (here the making of protected disclosures), the employee should be dismissed, but that Reason A should be hidden behind an invented Reason B, which the decision-maker adopts (here, inadequate performance), it is the court's duty to penetrate through the invention rather than allow it also to infect its own determination. If limited to a person placed by the employer in the hierarchy of responsibility above the employee, there is no conceptual difficulty about attributing to the employer that person's (i.e. the colleague more senior than the claimant's) state of mind rather than that of the deceived decision-maker'.

The Supreme Court expressly explained the rationale behind the decision to find that this was a dismissal for the sole, or principal, reason of a protected disclosure, on the bases that (a) Mr Widmer had been senior to the claimant, (b) he had concealed that the protected disclosures were the reason he wished to dismiss the claimant, (c) the invented reason had been accepted by the dismissing officer and (d) the tribunal of fact had a duty to see past the invention to the real reason.

6.3.7 AUTOMATICALLY UNFAIR DISMISSAL IN REDUNDANCY SITUATIONS

The automatic right not to be dismissed for having made a protected disclosure is expressly protected in a redundancy situation in the following terms in section 105 ERA 1996:

> '(1) An employee who is dismissed shall be regarded for the purposes of this Part as unfairly dismissed if –

109

(a) the reason (or, if more than one, the principal reason) for the dismissal is that the employee was redundant,

(b) it is shown that the circumstances constituting the redundancy applied equally to one or more other employees in the same undertaking who held positions similar to that held by the employee and who have not been dismissed by the employer, and...

'(6A) the reason (or, if more than one, the principal reason) for which the employee was selected for dismissal was that specified in section 103A.'

[section 103A being whistleblowing]

6.4 WHAT COMPENSATION CAN A WHISTLEBLOWER CLAIM IN RESPECT OF DETRIMENTS AND UNFAIR DISMISSAL?

In brief, a whistleblower can recover for a successful detriment claim:

- An injury to feelings award
- Consequential financial losses, such as loss of earnings
- Interest
- An award for personal injury caused by whistleblowing detriment (which is distinct from an injury to feelings award)

For an unfair dismissal claim, a whistleblower can recover the remedies usually provided for such a claim, comprising:

- A basic award
- A compensatory award (with no statutory cap on the amount (section 124(1A) of the ERA 1996))

Reinstatement and re-engagement (though these outcomes are highly unlikely)

Both claims are capable of reductions amounting to 25% for a lack of 'good faith' in respect of protected disclosures. Similarly, both claims can be increased or decreased by up to 25% to reflect the extent to which the parties have complied with the *Acas Code of Practice on Disciplinary and Grievance Procedures* (Acas Code). Note that this only applies where a detriment claim is brought by an employee.

A claimant pursuing a claim under section 103A of the ERA 1996 can also apply for interim relief under section 128(1) of the ERA 1996.

With the exception of the disapplication of the statutory cap for the compensatory award, the principles relating to compensation for an automatically unfair dismissal are the same as those set out in **Chapter 16**. Similarly, the principles relating to financial compensation for injury to feelings or personal injury are the same as in discrimination claims and are also set out in **Chapter 16**.

6.4.1 INJURY TO FEELINGS AWARDS

The reason injury to feelings is available for a claim under section 47B of the ERA 1996 and not under section 103A of the ERA 1996 is summarised by Underhill LJ in *Timis v Osipov [2019] IRLR 52* in the following terms:

> 'I should note one divergence which has emerged in the case-law. It has from the early days of the unfair dismissal legislation been held, and it was confirmed by the House of Lords in *Dunnachie v Kingston-upon-Hull City Council [2004] UKHL 36, [2004] IRLR 727*, that the reference to "loss" in what is now section 123(1) refers only to pecuniary loss and thus excludes injury to feelings. However, there is EAT authority, reviewed by HHJ Ansell in *Virgo Fidelis Senior School v Boyle [2004] IRLR 268*, to the effect that "loss" in section 49(2) has a wider meaning which does extend to injury to feelings; and such awards are almost invariably made in whistleblower cases.'

6.4.2 DISCLOSURES NOT MADE IN GOOD FAITH

While the requirement for the protected disclosure to be made in good faith has been removed, an employment tribunal is nonetheless entitled to reduce a compensatory award by up to 25% if it appears to the tribunal that the disclosure was not made in good faith and it considers that it is just and equitable in all the circumstances to do so (section 123(6A) of the ERA 1996). Where it appears to the tribunal that the protected disclosure was not made in good faith, and it considers it just and equitable in all the circumstances to do so, it may reduce any award made to the worker in respect of detriments by no more than 25% (section 49(6A) of the ERA 1996).

6.4.3 UPLIFTS FOR BREACHING THE ACAS CODE

An uplift of up to 25% is available for damages awarded in respect of an automatically unfair dismissal for the employer's failure to follow the Acas Code. By the same token, if a claimant fails to follow the Acas Code, a tribunal may reduce damages by the same amount.

In *Osipov* (before the EAT, and not challenged in the Court of Appeal) it was held that compensation for whistleblowing detriment could be awarded together with a 12.5% uplift on damages against the two individual respondents under section 207A of the *Trade Union and Labour Relations (Consolidation) Act 1992* (TULR(C)A 1992) for failing to use the procedures laid down in the Acas Code.

6.5 TRADE UNIONS

This book is concerned with individual employment rights. Therefore, it does not cover the law relating to trade union recognition, industrial action or collective bargaining.

The statutory provisions relating to trade unions were consolidated into one Act in 1992 – the TULR(C)A 1992. This has frequently been amended (notably by the *Trade Union Reform and Employment Rights Act 1993*, the *Employment Relations Act 1999*, the *Employment Act 2002*, the *Employment Relations Act 2004* and the *Employment Act 2008*).

6.5.1 RIGHT NOT TO BE SUBJECTED TO DETRIMENT FOR A TRADE UNION-RELATED REASON

A worker has the right not to 'be subjected to any detriment as an individual by any act, or any deliberate failure to act, by his employer' done to prevent them from, or penalise them for, joining or taking part in the activities of an independent trade union. The worker also has the right not to be compelled by the employer to join a trade union or a particular trade union (section 146 of the TULR(C)A 1992).

In *Mercer v Alternative Future Group Ltd and anor [2022] IRLR 517 CA*, the Court of Appeal held that in the TULR(C)A 1992, the words the 'activities of an independent trade union', qualifying for protection under section 146(1)(b) of the TULR(C)A 1992, do not include participation in lawful industrial action. On ordinary principles of statutory interpretation, section 146 of the TULR(C) A 1992 did not provide protection against detriment short of dismissal for taking part in or organising industrial action. To avoid impermissible judicial legislation, Lord Chief Justice Burnett held it was not appropriate to grant a declaration of incompatibility in this case when (a) it was a lacuna in the law rather than a specific statutory provision which was incompatible, (b) the extent of the incompatibility was unclear and (c) the legislative choices were far from being binary questions.

Compensation for breach of this right can be awarded without limit on a 'just and equitable' basis, and an employment tribunal has the power to order a trade union to pay or contribute to compensation if it pressurised the employer into subjecting the individual to the detriment which has led to a complaint (section 149 and section 150 of the TULR(C)A 1992). In assessing compensation for injury to feelings in a case under section 146 of the TULR(C) A 1992, the EAT held that the same sort of considerations apply as in race and sex discrimination cases, and similar levels of compensation are appropriate (*London Borough of Hackney v Adams [2003] IRLR 402*).

An example of the effect of these provisions is the successful claim made by an employee elected to be a full-time branch secretary of her trade union, who found that she would not be entitled to a salary increase from her employer until she ceased full-time union activities (*Southwark LBC v Whillier [2001] ICR 1016*).

6.5.2 RIGHT NOT TO BE DISMISSED FOR A TRADE UNION-RELATED REASON

Separate from, but similar to, the right of a worker not to be subjected to a detriment is the right not to be dismissed for a trade union-related reason. Dismissal because the employee is not a member of an independent trade union, or of a particular trade union, is thus automatically unfair dismissal. Selection for redundancy on these grounds is also automatically unfair dismissal (section 152(1)(c) and section 153 of the TULR(C)A 1992).

Dismissal is also automatically unfair if the principal reason was that the employee 'had taken part, or proposed to take part, in the activities of an independent trade union at an appropriate time', or that the employee 'had made use, or proposed to make use, of trade union services at an appropriate time', or had turned down an offer made by their employer in an attempt to influence them in matters relating to their union membership or activity. Selection for redundancy on these grounds is also automatically unfair dismissal (section 152(1) and section 153 of the TULR(C)A 1992).

Dismissal relating to industrial action

Dismissal is automatically unfair if the principal reason is that the employee took part, or is taking part, in 'protected industrial action' and the dismissal takes place during what is called 'the protected period'. Protected industrial action carries immunity from action in tort because of section 219 of the TULR(C)A 1992. This refers, for most practical purposes, to official strikes called after a proper balloting process has been carried out. The protected period is 12 weeks from the start of the protected industrial action plus an extension equal to the length of any lock-out the employer might impose (section 238A of the TULR(C)A 1992).

Refusal of employment

It is unlawful for an employer to refuse someone employment 'because he is, or is not, a member of a trade union'. This is a specific, separate, right since, by definition, the claim cannot be for unfair dismissal (section 137 of the TULR(C)A 1992). The argument that a refusal to employ a person was because of their past trade union activity rather than because of their trade union membership is unlikely to succeed as it will normally be impossible to draw a sensible distinction between the two (*Fitzpatrick v British Railways Board [1992] ICR 221* and *Harrison v Kent County Council [1995] ICR 434*).

6.6 HEALTH AND SAFETY

The intention of this section is not to provide a detailed exposition of the various criminal and civil sanctions and liabilities employers may incur for failing to take reasonable care of the health and safety of workers. Instead, it looks just at the common law and statutory duties as they relate to individual employers and those working for them.

6.6.1 COMMON LAW DUTIES

An employer owes a duty of care to employees to (a) select proper staff, (b) provide adequate materials, (c) provide safe premises and (d) provide a safe system of work (*Wilsons and Clyde Coal Co Ltd v English [1938] AC 57*). Not only are these duties in tort but they are also implied under the contract of employment, so if an employer breaches any of these terms (and the breach is sufficiently serious), the employee can resign and claim constructive dismissal (*Graham Oxley Tool Steels Ltd v Firth [1980] IRLR 135* and *Marshall Specialist Vehicles Ltd v Osborne [2003] IRLR 672*).

In *Johnstone v Bloomsbury Health Authority [1991] IRLR 118*, the Court of Appeal held that an employer cannot require an employee to work such excessively long hours that it was reasonably foreseeable that the work might damage their health, irrespective of the fact that an express term required the employee to work such long hours.

The duty to take care of the wellbeing of employees extends to mental health as well as physical health (*Walker v Northumberland County Council [1995] IRLR 35*).

6.6.2 STATUTORY DUTIES

The statutory position is governed by the *Health and Safety at Work etc. Act 1974* (HSWA 1974) and the *Management of Health and Safety at Work Regulations 1999* (MHSWR 1999). A vast number of industry-specific and other regulations exist, which are largely outside the scope of this book.

6.6.3 HEALTH AND SAFETY POLICIES

Every employer with five or more employees has a statutory obligation to prepare and keep up to date a 'written statement of his general policy with respect to the health and safety at work of his employees ... and to bring the statement and any revision of it to the notice of all of his employees' (section 2(3) of the HSWA 1974 and the *Employers' Health and Safety Policy Statements (Exception) Regulations 1975*).

In addition, all employers (irrespective of the number of employees) must provide an approved leaflet or health and safety poster at a place reasonably accessible to all employees, or provide all employees with a copy (*Health and*

Safety Information for Employees Regulations 1989 and the *Health and Safety Information for Employees (Modifications and Repeals) Regulations 1995*).

6.6.4 RISK ASSESSMENTS

Each employer (irrespective of the number of employees) must carry out a risk assessment 'for the purpose of identifying the measures he needs to take to comply with … the relevant statutory provisions' (regulation 3 of the MHSWR 1999). An employer's duty to carry out a risk assessment is non-delegable (*Uren v Corporate Leisure (UK) Ltd [2011] EWCA Civ 66*).

The Health and Safety Executive (HSE) has produced a range of useful resources, all available at www.hse.gov.uk/risk/controlling-risks.htm. The areas covered include:

- Identifying the hazards
- Deciding who might be harmed and how
- Evaluating the risks and deciding on precautions
- Recording the findings and implementing them
- Reviewing the assessment and updating if necessary

6.6.5 HEALTH AND SAFETY REPRESENTATIVES/CONSULTATION WITH EMPLOYEES

Employers are obliged to consult on health and safety matters with any duly elected safety representatives of the workforce. If there are no elected safety representatives, then the employer is obliged to consult all employees. It is therefore in the employer's interests to ensure representatives are elected. There is no 'small employer' exemption (*Safety Representatives and Safety Committees Regulations 1977*).

The consultation must be 'in good time' and must cover health and safety matters generally, including the provision of health and safety information, planning and organising of health and safety training and consultation regarding the health and safety implications of any new technologies in the workplace (regulation 3 of the *Health and Safety (Consultation with Employees) Regulations 1996*).

Employee representatives have the right to paid time off work for training and carrying out their duties. They are protected against victimisation – that is, being subjected to a detriment for performing their functions – and any dismissal connected with their duties will be automatically unfair. Victimisation and dismissal are also prohibited for employees – not necessarily elected employee representatives – who exercise their rights under health and safety legislation. Those who bring health and safety issues to the employer's attention if there is no safety representative to whom they could have reported their concerns are also protected.

Finally, victimisation and dismissal are prohibited in respect of any employees who leave (or propose to leave) their place of work, or take appropriate steps, because they reasonably believe there to be 'serious and imminent' danger within the workplace (section 44(1) and section 100 of the ERA 1996). No qualifying period of continuous employment is required to bring a claim of unfair dismissal on these grounds (section 108(3)(c) of the ERA 1996).

If at least two safety representatives ask the employer in writing to establish a 'safety committee', the employer must do so within three months (regulation 9(1) of the *Safety Representatives and Safety Committees Regulations 1977*).

Employers should take note of the HSE Guidance on worker involvement (see www.hse.gov.uk/involvement).

In *Sinclair v Trackwork Ltd [2021] IRLR 557*, the EAT gave guidance on the test for causation in cases involving section 100(1)(a) of the ERA 1996. The EAT overturned the decision of the employment tribunal on the basis that it could not be said that the claimant carried out his activities as a designated employee in a malicious or extraneous way that was irrelevant to the task in hand so as to deprive him of the protection afforded by section 100(1)(a) of the ERA 1996. The tribunal had erred in law in reaching its conclusions as it relied upon a matter (namely, the upset caused to the workforce) that was not properly separable from the carrying out of the activity itself, and the conclusion that the dismissal was other than for the carrying out of health and safety activities was not a permissible option. Accordingly, a finding would be substituted that the reason for the dismissal was the carrying out of activities under section 100(1)(a) of the ERA 1996.

6.6.6 REPORTING OBLIGATIONS

Employers must report all work-related health and safety incidents specified in the *Reporting of Injuries, Diseases and Dangerous Occurrences Regulations 2013* (RIDDOR 2013). The HSE has set up a dedicated reporting centre for this purpose, and reports can be logged via www.hse.gov.uk/riddor.

CHAPTER 7

PAY AND NOTICE PERIODS

7.0 OVERVIEW

Employers are subject to a range of statutory duties regarding both the payments they make to those working for them and the payments they are entitled to withhold. There is also a significant body of case law surrounding this issue, as there is with the National Minimum Wage and notice periods.

7.1 DEDUCTIONS FROM WAGES

Under part II of the *Employment Rights Act 1996* (ERA 1996), employers are forbidden by statute from making deductions from wages except in specific cases. The rules do not mean an employer has no right to recover money properly due from an employee – for example, to recover an overpayment of expenses. They merely mean that employers are generally not allowed to recover the money by making deductions without consent from future wages.

Under section 13 of the ERA 1996, a worker has the right not to suffer an unlawful deduction from wages 'unless –

a) the deduction is required or authorised to be made by virtue of a statutory provision or a relevant provision of the worker's contract, or

b) the worker has previously signified in writing his agreement or consent to the making of the deduction'.

Further, if an employer reduces wages without agreement, this is an unlawful deduction contrary to the statute, as well as a breach of contract.

Employees may, in rare circumstances, be taken to have waived their right to complain if they continue to work at the lower wage for a reasonable length of time without making it plain that they are doing so 'under protest' (see, for example, *Henry & ors v London General Transport Services Ltd [2002] ICR 910*, in which bus conductors worked on at reduced pay for two years before making an unsuccessful claim). However, a worker's breach of contract is not a good defence to a claim for unlawful deduction of wages (*Asif v Key People Ltd UKEAT/0264/07*).

'Wages' includes fees, commissions, bonuses, holiday pay, statutory sick pay and statutory maternity pay but does not include pension contributions. Pay in lieu of notice counts as 'wages' if payable under a contractual provision but not if genuinely paid as compensation for failing to give notice (*Delaney v Staples [1992] ICR 483*). The loss of a chance to earn a bonus or allowance does not count (*Lucy & ors v British Airways (2009) UKEAT0033/08*).

An employment tribunal has no jurisdiction to rule on whether a person is entitled to statutory sick pay or similar statutory payments – that is HMRC's job – and an employee cannot get around that by trying to use the 'unlawful deductions from wages' rules (*Taylor Gordon & Co Ltd v Timmons [2004] IRLR 180*).

In practice, the provisions can be surprisingly valuable to an employee in dispute with their employer. For example, an employer is not entitled to deduct overpaid holiday from an employee's final salary payment in the absence of a 'relevant agreement' under the *Working Time Regulations 1998* (WTR 1998) authorising such a deduction (*Hill v Howard Chapell [2003] IRLR 19*). Similarly, the amount an employer is entitled to deduct because the employee has been on strike is the same sum the employee would be entitled to seek if the deduction was unlawful. The employer is therefore not able to take holidays into account in calculating the deduction (*Cooper & ors v The Isle of Wight College [2007] EWHC 2831*).

A claim by a former employee that he was dismissed for complaining about unauthorised deductions from wages will amount to an assertion of a statutory right within the meaning of section 104(4)(c) of the ERA 1996, with the result that if the claim is proved, the dismissal will be automatically unfair (*Pearce and Pearce v Dyer (2004) UKEAT/0465/04*).

Exceptions to the general rule forbidding deductions from wages are:

- Deductions required or authorised by law (such as PAYE or under an attachment of earnings order) or by the worker's contract (section 13(1)(a) of the ERA 1996)

- Deductions authorised by the employee in advance of the event in respect of which they are made (section 13(1)(b) of the ERA 1996)

- Deductions to reimburse the employer for overpayment of wages or expenses (section 14(1) of the ERA 1996)

- Deductions made 'on account of the worker's having taken part' in a strike or other industrial action (section 14(5) of the ERA 1996)

The concept of 'estoppel' can (very) occasionally arise here. If an employer overpays in error and the employee – genuinely not realising that there has been a mistake – changes their position as a result, the employer may not be entitled to recover the overpayment (see *Lipkin Gorman (a firm) v Karpnale Ltd [1992] 4 All ER 512*).

118

Errors in the computation of wages which result in an underpayment do not count as 'deductions' and so a tribunal will have no jurisdiction if a deficiency in wages results. The deficiency must, of course, be made good, but the statutory remedies for unlawful deductions will not apply (see *Morgan v Glamorgan County Council [1995] IRLR 68*).

To be covered by the unlawful deduction from wages rules, the amount of the deduction must be quantified. If the amount claimed to have been deducted is uncertain, the claim has to be for breach of contract rather than for unlawful deduction from wages (*Tradition Securities & Futures SA v Mouradian [2009] EWCA Civ 60*). An employee should seek to claim an award of more than £25,000 in a contractual claim in the county court or the High Court; employment tribunals cannot award more than £25,000 in a contract claim, such that £25,000 is an effective 'cap' on those damages: article 10 of the *Extension of Jurisdiction (England & Wales) Order* 1994. It is not permissible for a claimant to bring a contract claim in the employment tribunal and then seek to recover the amount above the £25,000 'cap' by means of a county court or High Court claim (*Fraser v HLMAD Ltd [2006] IRLR 687*).

7.2 ITEMISED PAY STATEMENTS

Employees have the right to a written itemised pay statement at the time, or before, a wages or salary payment is made. This must contain details of gross and net wages or salary and any deductions (section 8 of the ERA 1996). Employees are entitled to a section 8 pay statement whether it is requested or not (*Coales v John Wood & Co [1986] ICR 71*).

Writing includes typing, printing, lithography, photography and 'other modes of representing or reproducing words in a visible form' (Schedule 1 of the *Interpretation Act 1978*). Presumably, therefore, an email pay statement satisfies the requirements.

Where an employer fails to provide an itemised pay statement, an employee can apply to an employment tribunal for a declaration and compensation for unnotified deductions in pay (section 9 of the ERA 1996).

7.3 THE NATIONAL MINIMUM WAGE AND THE NATIONAL LIVING WAGE

What is the right?

The *National Minimum Wage Act 1998* (NMWA 1998) provides for the right for workers to be paid a minimum hourly rate of pay.

Who is entitled to the right?

A person qualifies for the National Minimum Wage (NMW) if they ordinarily work in the UK under their contract and have ceased to be of compulsory school age. Workers, as defined, qualify for the NMW even if they are not employees (section 1(2) of the NMWA 1998).

The fact that there is no mutuality of obligation when the work is not being performed is of little significance in determining the status of the relationship when the person is actually at work. It is simply one of the factors to take into account in deciding whether a person is a worker, an employee or 'self-employed' (*James v Redcats (Brands) Ltd [2007] IRLR 296*).

The following types of workers qualify:

- Agency workers (section 34 of the NMWA 1998).

- Apprentices aged under 19 or who are within the first 12 months of their employment or engagement. Separate from the regulations, an apprentice may sometimes be able to show that, as a matter of contract, they are entitled to be paid at a higher rate (*Garrett Electrical Ltd v Cotton UKEAT/0547/05*).

- Homeworkers, even if they do not come within the normal definition of 'worker' because they are not obliged to perform their work personally (section 35 of the NMWA 1998 and *Bridges & ors v Industrial Rubber plc (2004) UKEAT/0150/04* (the case of 'the Gosport Nine')). In *James v Redcats (Brands) Ltd*, the final decision (in February 2008) of the employment tribunal to which the EAT remitted the case was that Mrs James was not only a 'worker' but also a 'homeworker' for NMW purposes.

Trainees on government training schemes are excluded (*National Minimum Wage Regulations 2015*), and voluntary workers are also generally excluded (section 44 of the NMW 1998).

The National Living Wage

Since 2022, employers have been obliged to pay workers aged 23 and above a new top rate of the NMW – the National Living Wage rate (regulation 4 of the NMWR SI 2015/621). Since 1 April 2023, the rate has been £10.40 per hour. In reality, this is nothing more than an additional age band for the NMW, despite the catchy title.

Records and the National Minimum Wage

Records must be kept for at least three years and must be in a form capable of being produced in a single document to cover a specific pay reference period. A worker has the right to require their employer to produce records and to inspect and copy those records (section 10 of the NMWA 1998). This applies even if at the time of the request, the worker has ceased to work for the employer (*Madani v Spirit SSR Ltd (2003) EAT/0641/03*). There is a presumption that the NMW has *not* been paid to a worker unless the employer can prove that it *has* been paid.

Payments from the employer not included in the calculation of the NMW

Regulation 10 of the *National Minimum Wage Regulations 2015* lists payments which are not to be counted towards remuneration for the purposes of the NMW. Of particular note, these include:

- Pension payments (regulation 10(b) of the *National Minimum Wage Regulations 2015*)

- Redundancy payments (regulation 10(d))

- Benefits in kind other than living accommodation (regulation 10(f))

- 'Payments paid by the employer to the worker representing amounts paid by customers by way of a service charge, tip, gratuity or cover charge' (regulation 10(m))

- Payments relating to income tax-deductible travel expenses (regulation 10(n))

An employer who pays these sums to a worker cannot therefore offset them against the NMW.

7.4 NOTICE PERIODS

Any employees who have completed one month or more of continuous employment with the same employer (or an associated employer) are entitled to a statutory minimum period of notice. They will, of course, be entitled to longer notice than the statutory minimum if the contract so provides – either expressly or by implied term (section 86 of the ERA 1996). If an employee is employed for less than one month, a common law requirement of reasonable notice applies.

According to section 86(1) of the ERA 1996, '[t]he notice required to be given by an employer to terminate the contract of employment of a person who has been continuously employed for one month or more –

- is not less than one week's notice if their period of continuous employment is less than two years

- is not less than one week's notice for each year of continuous employment if his period of continuous employment is two years or more but less than twelve years, and

- is not less than twelve weeks' notice if his period of continuous employment is twelve years or more.'

An employee being dismissed by reason of redundancy is entitled to the same notice period as they would were they being dismissed for any other reason.

Quite apart from the minimum statutory notice periods required by the ERA 1996, common law requires that – subject to any express agreement – an employment contract may only be lawfully terminated by either party if reasonable notice is given. What is reasonable will depend on all the facts and circumstances, including the employee's status and, if relevant, the notice arrangements agreed for other employees in similar positions with the same employer.

When notice starts to run

In *Haywood v Newcastle upon Tyne Hospitals NHS Foundation Trust [2018] ICR 882*, the Supreme Court held that in the absence of an express provision, a term was implied into all contracts of employment such that notice would not take effect until an employee had a reasonable opportunity to know that they had been given notice of dismissal.

Dismissal without notice

Section 86(6) of the ERA 1996 provides that 'this section does not affect any right of either party to a contract of employment to treat the contract as terminable without notice by reason of the conduct of the other party'. Thus, where a party has committed a repudiatory breach of contract, there will be no requirement to give notice and thus no entitlement to receive notice pay (*Lancaster & Duke Ltd v Wileman [2019] ICR 125*).

CHAPTER 8
TERMINATION OF EMPLOYMENT

8.0 OVERVIEW

Contracts of employment can be terminated in a number of ways. The classic examples involve dismissal, resignation or retirement. However, termination can also occur by the death or insolvency of one of the parties, by frustration of the contract or by mutual agreement, such as the expiry of a fixed-term contract.

Particular problems arise when an employee resigns in the heat of the moment and then asks for their job back. Other problems are seen when the wording of dismissal/resignation is ambiguous – for example, when an employer tells the employee to 'get out of here'. Is that a dismissal, or is it an instruction to take the rest of the day off? A variety of issues also surround pressured resignations and ultimatums to resign – 'resign or be sacked'.

For the purposes of unfair dismissal or a redundancy payment, an employee must establish that they were dismissed within the definition of a dismissal in section 95 and section 136 of the *Employment Rights Act 1996* (ERA 1996). And where notification of dismissal has been provided by post, or another written form, then the effective date of termination is the date from which the claimant had a reasonable opportunity to be aware of the dismissal (*Gisda Cyf v Barratt [2010] ICR 1475*).

8.1 UNAMBIGUOUS DISMISSALS AND RESIGNATIONS

We deal here with straightforward dismissals and resignations, where the employer says 'you are dismissed', or the employee utters words to the effect of 'I resign'. Such terminations can be either with notice or, in the case of summary dismissal or wrongful dismissal, without notice.

The contract can be terminated on notice by either side (section 86 of the ERA 1996). The length of the notice period will be set out in the contract – subject to the minimum notice periods imposed by statute (see **7.4**) or, if not set out, implied as being of a 'reasonable' length (*Hill v C.A. Parsons [1972] Ch 305*). Usually, the contract will terminate on the date that the notice period expires. Occasionally – for example, when the dismissal or resignation is without notice and it is made clear that it is meant to take effect immediately – it will take place on the date the termination is communicated to the other side. This date is important because many employment claims have to be brought within three or six months of the effective date of termination of employment (section 97 of the ERA 1996).

A straightforward dismissal, as envisaged here, will count as a dismissal for the purposes of unfair dismissal and redundancy rights. A straightforward resignation will not.

8.2 AMBIGUOUS AND HEAT-OF-THE-MOMENT DISMISSALS

Sometimes, an employer will utter words in the heat of the moment which were not intended to amount to a dismissal, but the employee takes them as such and leaves. Is that a dismissal, enabling the employee to claim unfair dismissal? Or was there no dismissal, and the employee should be regarded as having resigned (and hence have no claim for unfair dismissal, unless constructive dismissal can be established)?

In a case from the 1970s, the foreman in a fish filleting factory said to a worker: 'If you don't like the job, fuck off'. The worker thought he had been dismissed, but the foreman said not. The employment tribunal held that there was no dismissal because that was common language in the fish market and the employee should have known that the dismissal process was a much more formal one (*Futty v D&D Brekkes Ltd [1974] IRLR 130 IT*). However, in another case in which a manager had told an employee during an argument that 'you're fucking sacked', a tribunal held that although the manager spoke in the heat of the moment and had no intention of dismissing the employee, the employee had nevertheless been dismissed (*Atkins v Coyle Personnel plc [2008] IRLR 420*).

The authorities emphasise that ambiguous dismissals must be determined in their specific contexts. Where the employer uses words which are genuinely ambiguous, a tribunal will decide what an objective and reasonable listener (who knows all the facts and circumstances) would have thought was meant. The test is a purely objective one: the tribunals will not look at what the employer secretly intended, nor at what the employee unreasonably understood. This approach does not lend itself to certainty when advising litigants, but it must be correct (*Sothern v Franks Charlesly [1981] IRLR 278, J & J Stern v Simpson [1983] IRLR 52*, and *Atkins v Coyle Personnel plc [2008] IRLR 420*).

It is not easy for an employer to retract a clearly expressed dismissal. Where unambiguous words of dismissal amount to a repudiatory breach of contract, that breach cannot be remedied by the employer so as to preclude the employee's acceptance of the breach, though it may be waived by the employee (*Buckland v Bournemouth University Higher Education Corporation*

[2010] ICR 908, and *Willoughby v CF Capital plc [2011] ICR 88*). In this situation, all is not lost for the employer. An offer to withdraw a dismissal may be treated as an offer of reinstatement and an employee who unreasonably refuses such an offer may be treated as failing to mitigate their loss, disentitling them to a compensatory award.

8.3 AMBIGUOUS AND HEAT-OF-THE-MOMENT RESIGNATIONS

A problem sometimes occurs when the employee, in a moment of anger, shouts 'I resign' (usually adopting more colourful language). Ordinarily, an unambiguous resignation should be taken at face value, so the employee should be taken to have resigned and not to have been dismissed. This means the employee would be unable to claim unfair dismissal unless they could establish constructive dismissal. However, the courts have held that if an employee utters words of resignation in circumstances where the employer knew, or ought to have known, that the employee might not have meant them, then the employer is obliged to give the employee a reasonable opportunity to clarify their resignation. If the employee makes it clear within that reasonable period that they did not intend to resign, then the employer must have the employee back. If the employer refuses to have the employee back, that refusal amounts to a dismissal (and, probably, an unfair dismissal) (*Sovereign House Security Services Ltd v Savage [1989] IRLR 115*).

So, what is a reasonable period? It is likely to be relatively short. The employer is obliged to hold the employee's job open for a day or two to see if they come back and make clear that they did not really intend to resign. An employer is not obliged to investigate whether the resignation is genuinely intended (*Kwik-Fit (GB) Ltd v Lineham [1992] IRLR 156*).

8.4 PRESSURED RESIGNATIONS AND ULTIMATUMS TO RESIGN

Often, employers pressure their employees to resign, or offer them the choice of 'resign or be sacked'. They may then attempt to shelter under the letter of resignation as a defence to an unfair dismissal claim. But matters are rarely so straightforward.

In *Jones v Mid Glamorgan County Council [1997] ICR 815*, Waite LJ noted the following regarding when a tribunal will hold that a dismissal has taken place in circumstances in which the employee has been pressured to resign:

'Courts and tribunals have been willing, from the earliest days of the unfair dismissal jurisdiction, to look, when presented with an apparent resignation, at the substance of the termination for the purpose of inquiring whether the degree of pressure placed on the employee by the employer to retire amounted in reality to a dismissal ... It is a principle of the utmost flexibility which is willing in all instances of apparent voluntary retirement to recognise a dismissal when it sees it, but is by no means prepared to assume that every resignation influenced by pressure or inducement on the part of the employer falls to be so treated.'

One example is where an employee faces serious disciplinary proceedings likely to result in dismissal. An employer's invitation to resign, rather than go through the disciplinary process, would not necessarily convert the employee's subsequent resignation into a dismissal (*Staffordshire County Council v Donovan [1981] IRLR 108*).

8.5 EXPIRY OF A FIXED TERM CONTRACT

The coming to an end of a fixed-term contract counts as dismissal for unfair dismissal and redundancy purposes according to section 95 and section 136 of the ERA 1996. Whether a particular dismissal is unfair must then be decided according to the normal rules.

If a genuine purpose can be shown for setting up the contract as a fixed-term contract – and the employee was aware of this – and the specific purpose no longer exists, the employer may have grounds for dismissing on expiry. They could argue that the dismissal was for 'some other substantial reason' and the employee may then not be able to win a claim that it was unfair dismissal (*North Yorkshire County Council v Fay [1985] IRLR 247*).

Before allowing a fixed-term contract to elapse, employers should consult with employees about whether there is any alternative employment available for them.

Note that under the *Fixed-term Employees (Prevention of Less Favourable Treatment) Regulations 2002*, a fixed-term contract is normally automatically converted by law into a contract of indefinite duration once the employee has completed four years' continuous employment under the contract or under renewals of the contract (regulation 8 of the *Fixed-term Employees (Prevention of Less Favourable Treatment) Regulations 2002*). Note that this automatic conversion does not apply if there was objective justification for setting up the contract for a fixed term only (regulation 8(2)(b) of the *Fixed-term Employees (Prevention of Less Favourable Treatment) Regulations 2002* and *Duncombe, Fletcher & ors v Secretary of State for Children, Schools and Families [2011] UKSC 14*).

8.6 CONSTRUCTIVE DISMISSAL

8.6.1 OVERVIEW

Constructive dismissal is the name commonly given to a form of dismissal. It is not a separate cause of action. According to section 95(1)(c) and section 136(1)(c) of the ERA 1996, an employee is constructively dismissed if:

'he terminates the contract under which he is employed (with or without notice) in circumstances in which he is entitled to terminate it without notice by reason of the employer's conduct'.

The classic statement of the law on constructive dismissal is that of Lord Denning in *Western Excavating (ECC) Ltd v Sharp [1978] ICR 221*, in which he said:

'If the employer is guilty of conduct which is a significant breach going to the root of the contract of employment, or which shows that the employer no longer intends to be bound by one or more of the essential terms of the contract, then the employee is entitled to treat himself as discharged from any further performance. If he does so, then he terminates the contract by reason of the employer's conduct. He is constructively dismissed.'

For a constructive dismissal claim to succeed, an employment tribunal will only need to find that a claimant has resigned, at least in part, in response to the fundamental breach (*Nottinghamshire County Council v Meikle [2004] IRLR 703*, at paragraph 708). A constructive dismissal could be the basis of an unfair dismissal claim by an employee, but it could also be the basis of a discrimination claim by a worker. Equally, a constructive dismissal may be fair or unfair. This is an important point because it is often assumed that employees are entitled to a finding of unfair dismissal just because they have been constructively dismissed.

First, a resignation in response to conduct by the employer which falls short of being a breach of a fundamental term would simply be a resignation. But note the 'last straw' doctrine: resignation in response to a final, relatively minor act which forms part of a series can sometimes entitle an employee to resign and claim constructive dismissal (see **8.6.3**). Secondly, although it is relatively uncommon, a tribunal can sometimes find that the employer's breach of contract was itself a response to misconduct by the employee, with the result that the constructive dismissal was reasonable – thus fair – in all the circumstances of the case (*Savoia v Chiltern Herb Farms Ltd [1982] IRLR 166*).

Because unfair dismissal, unlike wrongful dismissal, does not necessarily involve any breach of contract, it follows that all constructive unfair dismissals are also constructive wrongful dismissals. At one stage, the Employment Appeal Tribunal (EAT) suggested that there could be constructive unfair dismissal even if there was no breach of contract, and therefore no wrongful dismissal, but the Court of Appeal pointed out that this was wrong (*Rossiter v Pendragon plc [2002] ICR 1063*).

To claim constructive dismissal, the employee must establish that:

- The employer was in breach of a term of the contract of employment.
- The breach was a repudiatory one, entitling the employee to resign.

- The employee resigned because of that breach of contract.

The burden of proof is on the employee to establish each of the above. If they fail at any stage, they will not establish a constructive dismissal and will be held to have resigned.

It is also worth noting that section 111A of the ERA 1996 provides that evidence of pre-termination negotiations is inadmissible in ordinary unfair dismissal claims (but not automatically unfair dismissal claims). In general terms, this means that an offer to terminate employment cannot be used by the employee as evidence that their subsequent resignation was, in fact, constructive dismissal.

8.6.2 EMPLOYER'S BREACH OF CONTRACT

An employee must demonstrate that the employer has committed a repudiatory breach of the contract of employment. This could be an express term, such as a failure to pay wages, or a breach of the implied term of trust and confidence as defined in *Malik v BCCI [1997] ICR 606*, and modified by *Baldwin v Brighton and Hove City Council (2006) UKEAT/0240/06*. That is whether, assessed objectively, the respondent, without reasonable and proper cause, has acted in a manner either calculated or likely to destroy or seriously undermine the implied term of trust and confidence.

The 'range of reasonable responses' test is not relevant when considering whether an employer was in fundamental breach of contract entitling an employee to resign and claim constructive dismissal (*Buckland v Bournemouth University Higher Education Corporation [2010] ICR 908*).

It should be emphasised that apart from breaches of the implied term, what will constitute a repudiatory breach of contract is fact-dependent. Not every breach of contract will be repudiatory in nature. The following examples of breaches which may be repudiatory are indicative, not exhaustive.

Wages

The most obvious breach of contract is the failure to pay wages, or a unilateral decision by the employer to reduce wages.

Trust and confidence

This is the most common implied term that is used in constructive dismissal claims. It is addressed in detail at **2.4.1**. A breach of the duty of trust and confidence will always be repudiatory (*Morrow v Safeway Stores plc [2002] IRLR 9*).

Duties

An employer is entitled to issue lawful and reasonable orders. The employer may also be entitled to vary a worker's job description if there is a contractual right to do so. However, a significant unilateral variation of an employee's job duties will amount to a breach of contract.

Working hours

The insistence that an employee works overtime when there is no contractual obligation to do so, or a unilateral variation of an employee's working hours, will be a breach of contract (*Derby City Council v Marshall [1979] IRLR 261*).

Job location

There may be a breach of contract if employees are required to change their place of work, beyond a reasonable commuting distance from their home, unless there is an express mobility clause in the contract of employment (*Courtaulds Northern Spinning Ltd v Sibson & TGWU [1988] IRLR 305*).

Unlawful discrimination

The EAT has specifically confirmed that an employee who resigns because of unlawful discrimination can, in appropriate circumstances, have a claim for constructive dismissal (*Shaw v CCL Ltd (2007) UKEAT/0512/06*).

Suspension without pay

Suspension without pay during a disciplinary process will always be a breach of contract unless there is an express right in the contract to suspend without pay.

Swearing at or criticising employees

Unjustified or excessive swearing at an employee may be a breach of the implied term of mutual trust and confidence (*Palmanor Ltd v Cedron [1978] ICR 1008*). Likewise, humiliating criticism of an employee in front of other staff may be a breach of trust and confidence. The likelihood of a breach is increased if the swearing or criticism is directed at a manager in the presence of his subordinates (*Hilton International Hotels v Protopapa [1990] IRLR 316*).

Refusing a pay rise

The arbitrary refusal to award a pay rise to a particular employee could be a breach of trust and confidence (*F C Gardner Ltd v Beresford [1978] IRLR 63*).

The Court of Appeal has held that an assurance of a pay increase made at a Christmas party was not intended to create a legally binding obligation. There was, accordingly, no breach of contract, let alone a repudiatory breach, when the employer later changed his mind (*Judge v Crown Leisure Ltd [2005] IRLR 823*).

Inadequate support

In appropriate circumstances, not giving adequate support to a member of staff might amount to a breach of trust and confidence (*Seligman v McHugh [1979] IRLR 130*).

Dealing with grievances and disciplinary matters promptly

If the employer fails to deal with grievances and disciplinary matters promptly – particularly if the employee is suspended without pay – this may be a breach of contract (see **2.4.2**). Issuing an unjustified final written warning may also amount to a repudiatory breach, entitling a constructive dismissal claim (*Stanley Cole (Wainfleet) Ltd v Sheridan [2003] IRLR 52*).

8.6.3 REPUDIATORY BREACH

Not every breach of contract will entitle an employee to resign and claim constructive dismissal. The breach must be a serious, or a repudiatory, one.

Failure to pay wages

A failure to pay wages is highly likely to be a repudiatory breach of contract. As Browne-Wilkinson J (as he then was) noted in *RF Hill Ltd v Mooney [1981] IRLR 258* at p260:

> 'The obligation on an employer to pay remuneration is one of the fundamental terms of a contract. In our view, if an employer seeks to alter that contractual obligation in a fundamental way, such as he has sought to do in this case, such attempt is a breach going to the very root of the contract and is necessarily repudiation.'

However, note that a mistake or a delay in paying wages due to problems with technology, an accounting error, or unexpected events would leave it open to a court to conclude that the breach did not go to the root of the contract (*Cantor Fitzgerald v Callaghan [1999] ICR 639*).

Mutual trust and confidence

A breach of the term of mutual trust and confidence will always amount to a repudiatory breach of contract (*Morrow v Safeway Stores plc [2002] IRLR 9*).

A repudiatory breach by the employer will usually release the employee from all obligations under the contract, including confidentiality and restrictive covenant clauses (see **2.4.1** for more detail).

Termination on acceptance

A party's repudiation of a contract of employment does not automatically terminate the contract. The contract is only terminated once the other party accepts the repudiatory breach (*Société Generale, London Branch v Geys [2012] UKSC 63; [2013] IRLR 122*).

Cumulative acts — the last straw doctrine

The cumulative effect of a series of incidents, leading to a 'last straw', can amount to a repudiatory breach of the implied term of trust and confidence even if the individual incidents would not have qualified had only one of those incidents occurred. Lord Justice Underhill, at Paragraph 55 of *Kaur v Leeds Teaching Hospitals NHS Trust [2019] ICR 1*, gave the following helpful guidance on assessing last straw cases:

'In the normal case where an employee claims to have been constructively dismissed it is sufficient for a tribunal to ask itself the following questions:

1) What was the most recent act (or omission) on the part of the employer which the employee says caused, or triggered, his or her resignation?

2) Has he or she affirmed the contract since that act?

3) If not, was that act (or omission) by itself a repudiatory breach of contract?

4) If not, was it nevertheless a part (applying the approach explained in *Omilaju [2005] ICR 481*) of a course of conduct comprising several acts and omissions which, viewed cumulatively, amounted to a (repudiatory) breach of the Malik term? (If it was, there is no need for any separate consideration of a possible previous affirmation, for the reason given at the end of para 45 above.)

5) Did the employee resign in response (or partly in response) to that breach?'

Underhill LJ also expressly referred to the theoretical distinction at paragraph 45 of Kaur in these terms:

'[E]ven when correctly used in the context of a cumulative breach, there are two theoretically distinct legal effects to which the "last straw" label can be applied. The first is where the legal significance of the final act in the series is that the employer's conduct had not previously crossed the Malik threshold: in such a case the breaking of the camel's back consists in the repudiation of the contract.

In the second situation, the employer's conduct has already crossed that threshold at an earlier stage, but the employee has soldiered on until the later act which triggers his resignation: in this case, by contrast, the breaking of the camel's back consists in the employee's decision to accept, the legal significance of the last straw being that it revives his or her right to do so. I have thought it right to spell out this theoretical distinction because Lewis J does so in his judgment in *Addenbrooke v Princess Alexandra Hospital*

131

NHS Trust, 2 December 2014, which I discuss below; but I am bound to say that I do not think that it is of practical significance in the usual case. If the tribunal considers the employer's conduct as a whole to have been repudiatory and the final act to have been part of that conduct (applying the Omilaju test), it should not normally matter whether it had crossed the Malik threshold at some earlier stage: even if it had, and the employee affirmed the contract by not resigning at that point, the effect of the final act is to revive his or her right to do so.'

It is important to note that there is no particular timescale within which the various incidents culminating in a 'last straw' must take place. The Court of Appeal has held that an employment tribunal was wrong when it decided that a gap of 18 months between the acts complained of and the complaint was too long for the 'last straw' doctrine to apply (*Logan v Commissioners of Customs & Excise [2004] IRLR 63*).

Acceptance of repudiation

While an employer's repudiatory conduct is an essential condition of a constructive dismissal claim, it is the employee's acceptance of the repudiation that causes the dismissal (*Société Generale, London Branch v Geys [2012] UKSC 63*). It follows that damage – for example, stress – caused by antecedent breaches of the implied term of trust and confidence is not damage suffered 'in consequence' of the dismissal (section 123 of the ERA 1996) but rather is damage that the employee has already accrued as a cause of action to sue for damages. Compensation for such damage cannot therefore be awarded as part of a compensatory award if the constructive dismissal was unfair.

8.6.4 EMPLOYEE MUST RESIGN IN RESPONSE TO THE BREACH

It is not enough for the employee to resign soon after the employer's breach of contract. In order to fall within the definition of constructive dismissal, the resignation must be, at least in part, *because* of the repudiatory breach (*Nottinghamshire County Council v Meikle [2004] IRLR 703*, at paragraph 708). In *Wright v North Ayrshire Council [2014] ICR 77*, the Court of Appeal endorsed the dicta of Elias P in *Abbycars (West Horndon) Ltd v Ford (2008) UKEAT/0472/07*, in which he said at paragraph 35:

'It follows that, once a repudiatory breach is established, if the employee leaves [and] even if he may have done so for a whole host of reasons, he can claim that he has been constructively dismissed if the repudiatory breach is one of the factors relied upon.'

There is no statutory requirement for the employee to tell the employer of the reason for resignation at the time of leaving, although a failure to do so might throw into doubt their reasons if they are challenged later (*Weathersfield Ltd v Sargent [1999] IRLR 94*).

132

Waiving the breach

The employee does not have to resign immediately on becoming aware of the breach. Employees are permitted a reasonable time to consider their position. However, if they wait too long, they are regarded as having waived the breach and therefore would be unable to resign and claim constructive dismissal.

The classic statement of the law regarding affirmation is that of Lord Denning in *Western Excavating ECC Ltd v Sharp [1978] QB 761*:

> 'He must make up his mind soon after the conduct of which he complains: for, if he continues for any length of time without leaving, he will lose his right to treat himself as discharged. He will be regarded as having elected to affirm the contract.'

How long can the employee wait? There is no fixed rule. Delay by the employee in resigning is by itself neutral. It may indicate that the employee is not resigning in response to the employer's breach of contract, but it does not by itself constitute affirmation of contract (*Bass v Travis Perkins Trading Company Ltd (2005) UKEAT/0598/05*).

Factors to be taken into account include the employee's length of service, whether the employee has protested the breach, how serious the breach is and whether the employee has been taking steps to mitigate their loss – for example, by using a grievance procedure or by looking for another job. The employee is entitled to a reasonable time to decide whether to leave or not (*Air Canada v Lee [1978] IRLR 392* and *G W Stephens & Son v Fish [1989] ICR 324*), but three weeks has been held to be too long (*Cow v Surrey and Berkshire Newspapers Ltd (2003) EAT/0716/02*).

It is also possible for an employee to give longer than their minimum notice period and still claim constructive unfair dismissal (*Buckland v Bournemouth University Higher Education Corporation [2010] ICR 908*).

8.7 TERMINATION BY MUTUAL AGREEMENT

Theoretically, the employer and employee can agree to terminate the employment contract. However, as this avoids a dismissal – and hence a claim for unfair dismissal – courts strain to avoid finding that a consensual dismissal has taken place. In practice, unless the initiative for the termination has come from the employee, courts and tribunals are likely to find that it was a classic dismissal by the employer because the employer was the effective cause of the termination.

The legal rationale for this approach is as follows. Employees cannot contract out of their employment rights unless they comply with one of the two recognised methods of compromising claims, namely a settlement via Acas or a formal settlement agreement (section 203 of the ERA 1996). Therefore, an agreement to terminate employment cannot be effective to sign away the right to claim unfair dismissal – unless the agreement complies with the requirements for a settlement agreement, which it often will not (*Igbo v Johnson Matthey Chemicals [1986] IRLR 215*).

Occasionally, however, a tribunal will find that there was a genuine, mutually agreed termination, for example, when university lecturers applied for their employment to be terminated early in order to receive the benefit of an enhanced early retirement scheme. The Court of Appeal held that their dismissal under the scheme was a genuine mutual termination, not a dismissal at the behest of the employer (*Birch & Humber v University of Liverpool [1985] IRLR 165*).

8.7.1 FIXED-TERM CONTRACTS

A contract for a fixed period will terminate when that period expires, and this is deemed a dismissal. Under the *Fixed-term Employees (Prevention of Less Favourable Treatment) Regulations 2002*, those on task-related contracts share the same protection as those working on fixed-term contracts. The expiry of such a contract is deemed to be a dismissal for the purposes of unfair dismissal and redundancy legislation (section 95(1)(b) and section 136(1)(b) of the ERA 1996). A tribunal then needs to consider whether the dismissal is fair or unfair. This prevents employers from trying to avoid unfair dismissal legislation by awarding a series of short fixed-term contracts. Under the regulations, a fixed-term contract is normally automatically converted into a contract of indefinite duration once the employee has completed four years' continuous employment under it, or renewals of it (regulation 8 of the *Fixed-term Employees (Prevention of Less Favourable Treatment) Regulations 2002*).

8.8 DEATH AND INSOLVENCY

8.8.1 DEATH OF EMPLOYEE

An employee is obliged to provide personal service, and death will frustrate the contract of employment. A particular exception is when the employee is already under notice of dismissal. In that case, death does not frustrate the contract, but the dismissal is treated as having occurred on the date of death. This is so that the employee's estate is not prevented from bringing a claim of unfair dismissal simply because the employee died while already under notice (section 133(1) of the ERA 1996).

An estate is able to bring claims for breach of contract, unfair dismissal or discrimination after the employee's death. Likewise, claims issued before death can be pursued by the employee's estate after death (section 1 of the *Law Reform (Miscellaneous Provisions) Act 1934*, section 206 of the ERA 1996 and *Lewisham & Guy's Mental Health NHS Trust v Andrews [2000] ICR 707*).

8.8.2 DEATH OF EMPLOYER

The death of an employer – where the employer is an individual as opposed to a limited company – will frustrate the contract of employment. At common law, this would mean that no monies were payable. However, statute provides that in these circumstances, a termination is deemed to be a dismissal due to redundancy. A redundancy award will then be payable unless the employer's personal representatives make an offer of suitable alternative employment within eight weeks of death. Notice pay will not be payable (section 136(5)(b), section 138 and section 174 of the ERA 1996).

Partnerships

The death of a partner presents a theoretical problem. Technically, the partnership changes its identity and the old employer no longer exists. The contract should be frustrated and the right to a redundancy payment triggered. In practice, a tribunal might find – on the officious bystander test – an implied term that the parties intended the employment relationship to continue when periodic changes in the partnership take place. The position is different when a partnership dissolves, although it is not entirely clear whether this amounts to a frustrating event or an ordinary dismissal (*Briggs v Oates [1990] IRLR 473 ChD*).

8.8.3 INSOLVENCY/DISSOLUTION OF COMPANY

Winding up

A compulsory winding-up order will terminate any employment contracts (*Re Oriental Bank Corpn (1886) 32 Ch D 366)*. An employee will usually have a claim for redundancy and notice pay, which will be met by the Department for Business, Energy and Industrial Strategy (BEIS) if the company lacks sufficient funds (see 'The National Insurance Fund', below). A voluntary winding-up order, passed by members, will not automatically terminate employment contracts (*Midland Counties Bank v Attwood [1905] 1 Ch 357 ChD*).

Appointment of an administrator/receiver

Administrators and administrative receivers appointed by debenture holders act as agents of the company concerned (section 14(5) and section 44(1)(a), respectively, of the Insolvency Act 1986). In both cases, they are personally liable in respect of employment contracts 'adopted by' them. They have 14 days from their appointment to make other arrangements (section 19(5) and section 44(2) of the Insolvency Act 1986). Their appointment does not automatically terminate employment contracts of the company with its employees (*Griffiths v Secretary of State for Social Services [1974] QB 468*).

A court-appointed receiver, on the other hand, is an officer of the court and is not the agent of the company. Their appointment terminates any employment contracts (*Reid v The Explosives Co Ltd (1887) 19 QBD 264*) and therefore may give rise to unfair and/or wrongful dismissal claims.

An administrator or a receiver becomes personally liable for employment contracts 'adopted' by them – that is, where they have acted in a way which indicates the employment contract is ongoing. The administrator is 'entitled in respect of that liability to an indemnity out of the assets of the company' for liabilities that have been incurred in respect of contracts of employment that have been adopted (section 44(1) of the *Insolvency Act 1986*).

'Wages or salary' are payable prior to the administrator's own fees and expenses (Schedule B1, paragraph 99 of the *Insolvency Act 1986*), so administrators are rightly cautious about adopting employment contracts. Neither statutory redundancy pay nor unfair dismissal compensation count as 'wages or salary' for this purpose (*Re Allders Department Stores (in administration) [2005] EWHC 172 Ch*). Similarly, damages for wrongful dismissal do not count as 'wages or salary' for this purpose (*Re Leeds United Association Football Club Ltd [2007] EWHC 1761 Ch*), nor do amounts payable to employees in respect of a protective award or genuine pay in lieu of notice (*Re Ferrotech & other cases [2006] ICR 205*).

The National Insurance Fund

Subject to various limits, the fund (administered by the BEIS) will pay certain sums to employees which an employer is unable to pay by reason of its insolvency/dissolution, etc. (section 182 of the ERA 1996). In outline, the important limits are:

- Up to eight weeks' wages
- Any unpaid pay for the minimum statutory notice period
- Up to six weeks' unpaid holiday pay in respect of the last 12 months
- Basic award for unfair dismissal (*DTI v Walden [2000] IRLR 168*)

For this purpose, a week's pay is limited to £571.00 per week for terminations on or after 6 April 2022 (*Employment Rights (Increase of Limits) Order 2022*).

The EAT has said of the state guarantee of protective award that 'it is not subject, apparently, to the statutory cap … in a week's pay provided for by section 227 of the ERA 1996,' (*Evans, Motture and Hutchins v Permacell Finesse Ltd (in administration) (2007) UKEAT/0350/07*). While technically correct, this can best be described as misleading – the cap *does* apply in such a case, but it is imposed by a different section – section 186 of the ERA 1996 – which was not mentioned.

The cap provided for by section 186 of the ERA 1996 is normally adjusted annually to ensure it is the same as the cap in a week's pay provided by section 227 of the ERA 1996. It must be applied before deductions for tax and national insurance (*Titchener v DTI [2002] IRLR 195*).

8.9 RETIREMENT

Termination of employment by reason of retirement has taken on new significance since the abolition in 2011 of the so-called 'default retirement age'. The *Employment Equality (Repeal of Retirement Age Provisions) Regulations 2011* removed the previous rule which enabled an employer to require an employee to retire at age 65 or over without the risk of facing an age discrimination or unfair dismissal claim. Now, any imposed retirement is prima facie age discrimination, which will require justification by the employer.

8.10 PILON CLAUSES AND THE 'LEAST BURDENSOME RULE'

In *MacKenzie v AA Ltd and anor [2022] IRLR 985*, the Court of Appeal upheld the decision of the High Court that an employer was entitled to exercise a payment in lieu of notice (PILON) clause, where there were several ways in which the contract might be performed. Lord Justice Bean upheld the High Court's decision in terms that:

> 'In the context of contracts of employment I find it difficult to imagine a clearer case of the application of the [Least Burdensome] Rule than where the contract expressly gives the employer a choice between dismissal with a requirement that the employee works out his notice and dismissal with payment in lieu of notice. The whole point of a PILON clause is to give the employer that choice and to avoid the argument that dismissal with pay in lieu is a repudiation.'

It was simply not open to the court to depart from a consistent line of authority going back 150 years and recently cited with approval at the highest level.

However, also in *MacKenzie*, the Court of Appeal recognised that there is no rule of law that in every case the cheapest or quickest mode of termination of a contract of employment will be the least burdensome. In most cases, it will be, but there is no special free-standing rule to that effect. In some cases, it may be open to reasonable debate what is the less or least burdensome mode of performing or terminating a contract.

CHAPTER 9

UNFAIR AND WRONGFUL DISMISSAL

9.0 OVERVIEW

Unfair dismissal claims comprise a significant proportion of employment tribunal workloads across the UK. The range of circumstances that can give rise to an unfair dismissal claim is broad. This chapter aims to cover most eventualities and look more briefly at wrongful dismissal, which – unlike statute-driven unfair dismissal – arises from a breach of contract.

The chapter starts with unfair dismissal.

9.1 QUALIFICATIONS

There are a number of conditions that must be satisfied before somebody can bring a claim for unfair dismissal. The claimant must be an employee (as defined by section 230 of the *Employment Rights Act 1996* (ERA 1996)) and must have sufficient continuity of service to bring a claim, although this requirement is subject to exceptions.

9.1.1 IS THE CLAIMANT AN EMPLOYEE?

The definition of 'employee' in the ERA 1996 is not particularly helpful. It refers to 'an individual who has entered into or works under (or, where the employment has ceased, worked under) a contract of employment' (section 230(1) of the ERA 1996). The ERA 1996 defines 'contract of employment' as 'a contract of service or apprenticeship, whether express or implied, and (if it is express) whether oral or in writing' (section 230(2) of the ERA 1996). This is considered in more detail at 2.3.

9.1.2 QUALIFYING PERIOD OF EMPLOYMENT

The general rule is that an employee must have sufficient continuity of service before obtaining the right to claim unfair dismissal (section 108 of the ERA 1996). The qualifying period for unfair dismissal claims is two years. However, there are exceptions, meaning that in some cases (generally, cases in which a dismissal is automatically unfair), there is no qualifying period, and in a few special cases, it is just one month.

Continuous employment

In determining whether employment is continuous, each individual week must, theoretically, be examined, but in practice, a more global view is usually taken (section 210 of the ERA 1996).

Section 212(1) of the ERA 1996 states: 'Any week during the whole or part of which an employee's relations with his employer are governed by a contract of employment counts in computing the employee's period of employment.' There is no exclusion of part-time work in this wording. A teacher employed to work one half-day per week was therefore held to have had a continuous contract of employment (*Metropolitan Borough Council of Calderdale v Wells (2009) UKEAT/0340/09*).

In order to qualify as a week of continuous employment, the week in question must have been governed – in part or in full – by a contract of employment. However, if the employee is incapable of work due to sickness or injury, or is absent due to a temporary cessation of work, the week still counts as a 'filler' week of continuous employment even if there is no governing contract of employment. This applies equally in circumstances where, by arrangement or custom, the employee is regarded as continuing in employment while absent. No more than 26 filler weeks can count before continuity of employment is broken (section 212 of the ERA 1996), even if the employer has guaranteed re-employment at the end of a career break (*Curr v Marks & Spencer [2003] ICR 443*).

Employment with the same employer, or an associated employer, during any period is presumed to be continuous unless the contrary is shown (section 210(5) of the ERA 1996).

The employee must have worked for the same employer during the period of continuous employment, or the clock resets to zero. The employee is deemed to have been working for the same employer where there has been a transfer of undertakings, a move between associated employers, a change of partners in a partnership or the employee is kept on by personal representatives after the death of an employer (section 218 of the ERA 1996).

If an employee was on strike during any week, or part of a week, then the entire week is excluded for the purpose of calculating the number of weeks of continuous employment. This does not, however, reset the clock to zero. Likewise, any period during which an employee is locked out by the employer does not count when calculating the number of weeks of continuous employment (section 216 of the ERA 1996).

It is established law that continuity of employment is preserved where there is a temporary cessation of a school or college teacher's work during school or college holidays (*Ford v Warwickshire County Council [1983] ICR 273*). If, in particular circumstances, there is doubt that this general rule applies, it is necessary to look at the effective cause of the cessation and consider whether or not the parties expect the teacher to be offered further work after temporary cessation (*Hussain v Acorn Independent College Ltd [2011] IRLR 463*).

It is worth noting that failure to state on the claim form the date on which employment started – and thus demonstrate the required continuous employment – is not in itself fatal to a claim. The Employment Appeal Tribunal (EAT) has ruled that a tribunal should only reject a claim if it is sure that it does *not* have jurisdiction to entertain the claim (*Young v Hexion Speciality Chemicals UK Ltd (2009) UKEATS/0024/09*).

Extension of period

If an employee is dismissed without notice after 103 weeks of employment – but before a full two years' employment has been achieved – the statutory minimum period of notice of one week, as set out in section 86 of the ERA 1996, is added to the actual time worked so that they are 'deemed' to have the necessary qualifying service. This takes the employee past the minimum threshold and enables a claim for unfair dismissal to be brought (section 97 of the ERA 1996).

However, the 'deeming provision' of section 97 of the ERA 1996 does not apply to extend time where (a) an employer has dismissed a claimant without notice for gross misconduct or (b) a tribunal finds that 'the claimant had been guilty of gross misconduct such that the employer would have been entitled to terminate the contract of employment without notice' (*Lancaster & Duke Ltd v Wileman [2019] ICR 125*, at paragraph 38). Put simply, where (a) a claimant has been dismissed without notice for alleged gross misconduct and (b) the claimant would only have qualifying service to bring an unfair dismissal claim if the statutory notice of one week is added, then a tribunal must hear the evidence in the case. In so doing, the tribunal must first determine whether the claimant has, in fact, committed gross misconduct. If they have, then the tribunal will have no jurisdiction to consider the unfair dismissal claim.

Section 97 of the ERA 1996 only extends the period of employment by the statutory minimum period of one week, not the contractual notice period. An employee who has worked for 21 months, and who is summarily dismissed in breach of a three-month notice clause, cannot therefore extend the period of employment by three months to claim unfair dismissal. Furthermore, if a dismissed employee has not completed sufficient continuous employment to qualify for unfair dismissal but would have done so if they had been given the contractual notice to which they were entitled, they are not entitled to damages for loss of the chance to claim unfair dismissal (*Wise Group v Mitchell [2005] ICR 896* and *Virgin Net v Harper [2003] IRLR 831*).

Exceptions to the qualification requirement

There are a number of exceptions to the qualifying period, and for the most part, they are for dismissals that are automatically unfair. These include:

1) Reasons set out in section 154(1) of the *Trade Union and Labour Relations (Consolidation) Act 1992* (TULR(C)A 1992) regarding dismissal on grounds related to trade union membership, non-membership or activities.

2) Dismissal for any of the reasons set out in section 108(3) of the ERA 1996. These are essentially:

   a) Dismissal relating to pregnancy, childbirth or maternity.

   b) Dismissal relating to compulsory, ordinary or additional maternity leave.

   c) Dismissal relating to ordinary or additional adoption leave.

   d) Dismissal relating to paternity or parental leave.

   e) Dismissal for certain health and safety reasons.

   f) Dismissal in connection with a health and safety representative's role.

   g) Dismissal of a protected shop worker, an opted-out shop worker or a betting shop worker who refuses to work on Sundays.

   h) Dismissal for refusing to comply with a requirement imposed in contravention of the *Working Time Regulations 1998* (WTR 1998) or to forgo a right conferred under the regulations.

   i) Dismissal of an employee who is a trustee of their employer's pension scheme for performing their duty.

   j) Dismissal of employee representatives, or candidates for election, for performing their functions.

   k) Dismissal relating to an employee's role as a member of, or candidate for election to, a 'special negotiating body' or European Works Council.

   l) Dismissal relating to part-time status.

   m) Dismissal for exercising rights as a fixed-term worker.

   n) Dismissal for 'assertion of a statutory right'.

   o) Dismissal for making a 'protected disclosure'.

p) Dismissal for enforcing the right to be paid the National Minimum Wage.

q) Dismissal for enforcing the right to tax credits.

r) Selection for redundancy for any of the reasons set out in (a) to (q) above.

s) Dismissal as a result of carrying out jury service (section 98B of the ERA 1996).

t) Dismissal on grounds relating to the right to request flexible working.

u) Dismissal for exercising or attempting to exercise various statutory consultation rights, for example, under the *Information and Consultation of Employees Regulations 2004*, the *European Public Limited-Liability Company (Employee Involvement) (Great Britain) Regulations 2009*, and the *Companies (Cross-Border Mergers) Regulations 2007*.

v) Dismissal for exercising rights under the *Agency Workers Regulations 2010*.

Note that the normal qualifying period is required under the *Transfer of Undertakings (Protection of Employment) Regulations 2006* (TUPE 2006). Although a TUPE dismissal is automatically unfair (regulation 7(1) of TUPE 2006), the effect of regulation 7(6) of TUPE 2006 is that the employee must have completed the normal qualifying period of employment.

9.2 EXCEPTIONS

9.2.1 ILLEGAL CONTRACTS

Where a contract has been 'tainted' with illegality, the parties to that contract may not be able to rely on it. A tribunal may decide that it will not hear the claim because the contract has been formed, or performed, illegally. Taking an extreme example, a contract killer would not be able to sue their employer in the employment tribunal or the county court for unpaid wages.

Two key judgments of the Supreme Court have clarified the law regarding illegality. In both *Patel v Mirza [2016] UKSC 42* and *Hounga v Allen [2014] IRLR 811*, the Supreme Court has emphasised that the doctrine is based on public policy.

The test set out by Lord Toulson in *Patel v Mirza*, (with whom Baroness Hale, Lord Kerr, Lord Wilson and Lord Hodge agreed), supersedes much of the previous case law on when tribunals should refuse to hear claims on the basis of illegality. At paragraph 120, he said:

'The essential rationale of the illegality doctrine is that it would be contrary to the public interest to enforce a claim if to do so would be harmful to the integrity of the legal system ... In assessing whether the public interest would be harmed in that way, it is necessary (a) to consider the underlying purpose of the prohibition which has been transgressed and whether that purpose will be enhanced by denial of the claim, (b) to consider any other relevant public policy on which the denial of the claim may have an impact, and (c) to consider whether denial of the claim would be a proportionate response to the illegality, bearing in mind that punishment is a matter for the criminal courts.'

Tribunals may apply this test based on an assessment of proportionality and public policy. This marks a departure from previous case law, which focused on whether the illegality was present at the outset of the contract or only in the performance.

Illegality in discrimination claims

In *Hounga v Allen*, the Supreme Court redefined the way in which illegality should be approached in claims of tort and specifically applied its reasoning to the claim of dismissal as an act of discrimination on the ground of the claimant's nationality then before it. The Court of Appeal had applied previous case law to find that the illegality of the contract of employment had 'formed a material part of Miss Hounga's complaint and that to uphold it would be to condone the illegality' (paragraph 4).

However, Lord Wilson, delivering the majority verdict in the Supreme Court, held that the matter should be resolved by considering two questions: first, 'What is the aspect of public policy which founds the defence?' and second, 'But is there another aspect of public policy to which application of the defence would run counter?' (paragraph 42). In answer to the first question, Lord Wilson summarised his reasoning in respect of the aspect of public policy which founds the defence in these terms:

'Concern to preserve the integrity of the legal system is a helpful rationale of the aspect of policy which founds the defence even if the instance given by McLachlin J of where that concern is in issue may best be taken as an example of it rather than as the only conceivable instance of it. I therefore pose and answer the following questions:

a) Did the tribunal's award of compensation to Miss Hounga allow her to profit from her wrongful conduct in entering into the contract? No, it was an award of compensation for injury to feelings consequent upon her dismissal, in particular the abusive nature of it.

b) Did the award permit evasion of a penalty prescribed by the criminal law? No, Miss Hounga has not been prosecuted for her entry into the contract and, even had a penalty been thus imposed upon her, it would not represent evasion of it.

c) Did the award compromise the integrity of the legal system by appearing to encourage those in the situation of Miss Hounga to enter into illegal contracts of employment? No, the idea is fanciful.

d) Conversely, would application of the defence of illegality so as to defeat the award compromise the integrity of the legal system by appearing to encourage those in the situation of Mrs Allen to enter into illegal contracts of employment? Yes, possibly: it might engender a belief that they could even discriminate against such employees with impunity' (paragraph 44).'

In answer to the second question, regarding whether there is another aspect of public policy to which application of the defence would run counter, Lord Wilson held that:

'[Even] if Miss Hounga's case was not one of trafficking on the part of Mrs Allen and her family, it was so close to it that the distinction will not matter for the purpose of what follows – In my view it would be a breach of the UK's international obligations under the Convention [i.e. The Council of Europe Convention on Action against Trafficking in Human Beings CETS No 197] for its law to cause Miss Hounga's complaint to be defeated by the defence of illegality' (paragraphs 49-50).

The facts of Hounga provided good reason to revisit what would otherwise have been a needlessly inflexible approach. As Lord Wilson set out at paragraph 23:

'[The complaint of discriminatory dismissal] may well be said not to capture the gravamen of Miss Hounga's case against Mrs Allen. Irrespective of whether all of it can form the subject of a civil claim, the case which, on the tribunal's exiguous findings, Miss Hounga makes against Mrs Allen relates centrally to her participation in the plan to secure her entry into the UK on a false basis; to Mrs Allen's failure to pay her the promised wages and, in particular, to secure for her the promised education (although the tribunal made no finding that Mrs Allen had never intended to secure it for her); and to her acts of serious violence towards Miss Hounga over 18 months, coupled with threats of imprisonment which were entirely convincing to Miss Hounga and which in effect disabled her from taking any steps to rescue herself from her situation in Mrs Allen's home. In the event it was Mrs Allen's eviction of her which precipitated her rescue. Cruel though the manner of its execution was, the dismissal was, in a real sense, a blessing for Miss Hounga.'

145

9.2.2 POLICE AND PRISON OFFICERS

Police officers are not employees within the meaning of the ERA 1996. Accordingly, they cannot claim, for example, unfair dismissal or unlawful deductions from wages under it.

Further, persons in 'police service' do not generally have the right to claim unfair dismissal, according to section 200 of the ERA 1996. Police service means 'service as a member of a constabulary maintained by virtue of an enactment', or any other service where the person has the power of a constable – but not including prison officers, according to section 126 of the *Criminal Justice and Public Order Act 1994*.

If internal police disciplinary rules are not followed, the police officers may have remedies under the law of judicial review (*R v Sec'y of State for Home Dep't, ex parte Benwell [1984] ICR 723*, and *Commissioner of the Metropolitan Police v Lowrey-Nesbit [1999] ICR 401*). Further, section 50 and section 85 of the *Police Act 1996* provide for disciplinary rules and appeals to a police appeals tribunal.

It is, however, important to note that police officers are expressly included in the definition of 'employee' for the purposes of protection against dismissal and detriment on the grounds of both protected disclosures and health and safety (section 43KA and section 134A of the ERA 1996).

9.2.3 STRIKING WORKERS

As a general rule, employees taking part in unofficial industrial action cannot claim unfair dismissal unless the reason for dismissal is pregnancy, maternity or another automatically unfair reason (section 237(1) of the TULR(C)A 1992).

An employee taking part in official industrial action can only complain of unfair dismissal if there has been selective dismissal of employees taking part in the action or there have been selective offers of re-engagement to employees taking part in the action. If the employer dismisses all employees taking part in the action, they cannot claim unfair dismissal (section 238 of the TULR(C)A 1992).

However, an employer cannot dismiss employees engaged in official industrial action during an initial protected period. The protected period is usually 12 weeks from the date when the industrial action started. This period is extended if the employer stonewalls or does not take reasonable steps to resolve the dispute. Dismissal of employees during the protected period is automatically unfair under section 238A of the TULR(C)A 1992.

9.2.4 WORKERS ORDINARILY OUTSIDE GREAT BRITAIN

Where employees are employed outside Great Britain, the important question is whether the employment tribunal has jurisdiction. This was considered by the House of Lords in *Lawson v Serco [2006] UKHL 3*.

Lord Hoffmann, who gave the leading judgment in *Lawson v Serco*, identified three categories of employees who would likely fall under the tribunal's jurisdiction:

1) The employee who was ordinarily working in Great Britain at the time of dismissal

2) The peripatetic employee who moved between jurisdictions but was based in Great Britain at the time of dismissal

3) The expatriate employee who was posted abroad by a British employer to further the business of that employer

He did not, however, suggest that these categories were exhaustive.

The Court of Session in Scotland held in *Ravat v Halliburton Manufacturing & Services Ltd [2010] IRLR 1053 ScotCS* that proper application of *Lawson v Serco* involves three principles:

- To invoke the jurisdiction successfully, it is not essential for a claimant whose employment contains a foreign element to demonstrate that they may properly be placed in one of the categories considered in detail by Lord Hoffmann in *Lawson v Serco*, since the categories are not exhaustive.

- An employee may have a place of work in a foreign country but carry it out in a manner and in circumstances in which they cannot properly be described as 'peripatetic' or 'expatriate'. Integral to the concept of 'expatriate' is the fact that the employee not only works abroad but also lives there in some form of stable place of residence: one who is 'being more faithful to the root, one who has forsaken his native land'.

- The jurisdictional criterion must be a 'strong connection' as opposed to a 'substantial connection'.

This decision was affirmed by the Supreme Court in *Ravat v Halliburton Manufacturing & Services Ltd [2012] UKSC 1*.

9.3 CAPABILITY OR QUALIFICATIONS

Under the ERA 1996, one of the potentially fair reasons for dismissal is that the reason 'relates to the capability or qualifications of the employee for performing work of the kind which he was employed by the employer to do' (section 98(2)(a) of the ERA 1996).

When relying on this reason, the employer needs to demonstrate that the employee's capability or qualifications were the reason, or principal reason, for the dismissal. The tribunal then has to be satisfied that the dismissal was fair in all the circumstances.

When dismissing for reasons relating to capability, an employer must bear in mind the effect of the disability discrimination provisions in the *Equality Act 2010* (EqA 2010). If the employee qualifies as disabled within the meaning of the EqA 2010 and it is possible to make reasonable adjustments to enable the employee to perform the job, then the employer will probably be in breach of those provisions if it fails to do so. In addition, the employer will probably be found to have acted unfairly in all the circumstances, thus also rendering the dismissal unfair under the ERA 1996. However, the tests for disability discrimination and unfair dismissal are separate, and a breach of one of the ERA 1999 or the EqA 2010 does not automatically entail a breach of the other (*Kent County Council v Mingo [2000] IRLR 90*).

9.3.1 QUALIFICATIONS

'Qualification' in relation to an employee is defined by section 98(3) of the ERA 1996 as 'any degree, diploma or other academic, technical or professional qualification relevant to the position which he held'.

There are very few cases dealing with a lack of qualifications as a reason for dismissal. Often, if an employee has misled an employer about qualifications on an application form, the matter will become clear – and the employee will be dismissed – before accruing the continuous employment needed to bring an unfair dismissal claim. Where the employee has accrued the necessary qualifying period, many employers will treat the case as one relating to conduct (in other words, lying on the application form) and deal with it under that route.

Qualification has been interpreted as relating to aptitude or ability. A mere licence, permit or other authorisation, does not fall within the definition of qualification unless it is substantially concerned with the aptitude or ability of the person to do the job. The dismissal of a seafarer who was not registered was thus not a reason relating to his qualifications (*Blue Star Ship Management Ltd v Williams [1979] IRLR 16*). However, the holding of a driving licence can be a qualification within the statutory definition (*Tayside Regional Council v McIntosh [1982] IRLR 272*), as can the holding of a pilot's licence (*Sayers v Loganair Ltd [2005] 5 WLUK 383*).

9.3.2 CAPABILITY: INCOMPETENCE

'Capability' in relation to an employee is defined in section 98(3) of the ERA 1996 as meaning 'capability assessed by reference to skill, aptitude, health or any other physical or mental quality'.

In practice, as well as in the statutory definition, a distinction is drawn between cases involving incapability due to the employee's incompetence and cases involving incapability due to their inability to work through ill health. This section deals with the former.

Issues of 'capability' and issues of 'conduct' should not be confused. Incompetence and laziness are not the same thing. Laziness will usually be conduct rather than capability. As Kilner Brown J said in *Sutton & Gates (Luton) v Boxall [1979] ICR 67*:

> 'Cases where a person has not come up to standard through his own carelessness, negligence or maybe idleness are much more appropriately dealt with as cases of conduct or misconduct rather than of capability.'

It is not for a tribunal to decide whether it thinks the employee is capable of doing the job. Provided the employer has formed a genuine and reasonably held belief that the employee is not meeting the required standards, the tribunal must not substitute its views for those of the employer. Accordingly, where an airline pilot was involved in a faulty landing, causing damage to the aircraft – and, as bad luck would have it, a senior executive from the airline was on the flight – the pilot's dismissal was held to be fair (*Taylor v Alidair Ltd [1978] IRLR 82*). As Lord Denning said:

> 'Whenever a man is dismissed for incapacity or incompetence it is sufficient that the employer honestly believes on reasonable grounds that the man is incapable and incompetent. It is not necessary for the employer to prove that he is in fact incapable or incompetent.'

In practice, to demonstrate that its belief was genuinely held on reasonable grounds, an employer will have to provide evidence of the employee's inability to perform adequately. Sometimes an assertion of the employee's incompetence by a sensible manager will suffice, and the courts have held that tribunals are entitled to accept such evidence at face value and not insist on corroboration. However, a tribunal would normally expect to see at least one warning letter to the employee setting out the ways in which the employer asserts that the employee is failing to meet standards (*Cook v Thomas Linnell & Sons Ltd [1977] IRLR 132*).

Evidence which may assist an employer in establishing its reasonable belief in the employee's incompetence includes staff appraisals (*Cook v Thomas Linnell & Sons Ltd*), complaints by customers (*Dunning & Sons (Shop Fitters) v Jacomb [1973] IRLR 206*) or staff members (*Hopper v Feedex Ltd [1974] IRLR 99*), or a general fall-off in trade (*Cook v Thomas Linnell & Sons Ltd* and *R & M Gaskarth v Mr S Campbell [2012] 5 WLUK 651*).

It is important that employees are judged only in respect of matters which are part and parcel of the job they were employed to do. Thus the dismissal of an assistant accountant for lacking management ability was held to be unfair because he had been employed to assist with accounts, not to be a manager (*Woods v Olympic Aluminium Co Ltd [1975] IRLR 356 IT*).

Warnings

The employer should warn an employee about the respects in which they are failing to do their job adequately and give them an opportunity to improve their performance. As Sir John Donaldson said in *James v Waltham Holy Cross UDC [1973] IRLR 202*:

> 'An employer should be very slow to dismiss upon the grounds that the employee is incapable of performing the work which he is employed to do without first telling the employee of the respects in which he is failing to do his job adequately, warning him of the possibility or likelihood of dismissal on this ground, and giving him an opportunity to improve his performance.'

It is uncommon for a dismissal to be found fair if the employer has not warned the employee that their performance is unsatisfactory. The authorities make it clear that a reasonable employer is expected to give the employee at least one opportunity to improve. An isolated careless act will rarely justify dismissal.

In rare circumstances, it can be reasonable for an employer to dismiss without giving a warning. Old authority exists suggesting that if the employee will not change their ways, and a warning would be futile, it is not necessary to warn them (*Retarded Children's Aid Society v Day [1978] IRLR 128* and *Grant v Ampex (Great Britain) Ltd [1980] IRLR 461*). It would, however, be dangerous to rely on these authorities nowadays, because – particularly in the light of cases such as *Polkey v AE Dayton Services Ltd [1988] AC 344* – a tribunal is likely to say that an employer cannot know that a warning would be futile until it has tried to warn. As Sir Hugh Griffiths said in a well-known passage in *Winterhalter Gastronom Ltd v Webb [1973] ICR 245*, 'many [employees] do not know that they are capable of jumping the five-barred gate until the bull is close behind them'.

Where an employer dismisses an employee for conduct or capability following past warnings, a tribunal is unlikely to look behind the earlier warnings unless there is evidence that they were issued in bad faith or were manifestly inappropriate (*Wincanton Group v Stone [2013] IRLR 178*).

Opportunity to improve

A warning is pointless without giving the employee an opportunity to improve. If no period is offered, then, subject to establishing one of the reasons for not giving any warning (see above), the dismissal will probably be unfair.

How long a period ought to be given? This is a question of fact, and a tribunal will decide whether it considers the period provided to be reasonably sufficient to allow the employee to achieve (or demonstrate) a satisfactory level of improvement. Factors taken into account include the nature of the job, the employee's length of satisfactory service, and the turnaround time for demonstrating improvement.

Alternative employment

An employer should be able to show that it has considered alternative employment, even if the end result is that it does not think that there is anything suitable for the incompetent employee. The extent of the obligation to seek alternative employment will depend on factors such as the size of the company and whether the employee had a history of being able to do another job competently. As Balcombe LJ said at paragraph 20 of *P v Nottinghamshire County Council [1992] IRLR 362*:

> 'In an appropriate case and where the size and administrative resources of the employer's undertaking permit, it may be unfair to dismiss an employee without the employer first considering whether the employee can be offered some other job, notwithstanding that it may be clear that he cannot be allowed to continue in his original job.'

9.3.3 CAPABILITY: ILL HEALTH

An employee will be incapable of performing their job properly if they are persistently absent through ill health, either through an ongoing series of short-term absences or because of a single lengthy episode of absence. Ill health dismissals are the most frequently encountered examples of capability dismissals.

Note that the disability discrimination provisions of the EqA 2010 must be considered when considering dismissal on grounds of long-term illness, in particular, the duty to make reasonable adjustments (see **Chapter 13.5**).

The key question in ill-health dismissals

The crucial point to bear in mind in ill-health dismissals is that tribunals are not particularly concerned with what has happened in the past. They are far more interested in whether the employer has taken reasonable steps to investigate what is likely to happen in the future. Even if an employee has been absent for many months, if their return is imminent, an employer will act unfairly in dismissing them.

The key question in ill-health dismissals is set out by Phillips J in *Spencer v Paragon Wallpapers Ltd [1977] ICR 301* (as applied and approved by the Court of Appeal in *O'Brien v Bolton St Catherine's Academy [2017] ICR 737*):

> 'Every case depends on its own circumstances. The basic question which has to be determined in every case is whether, in all the circumstances, the employer can be expected to wait any longer and, if so, how much longer? Every case will be different, depending upon the circumstances.'

The relevant circumstances

BS v Dundee City Council [2013] CSIH 91 provides a helpful summary of the existing case law. Here, the court set out three main themes or questions that an employment tribunal should consider before dismissing an employee on the grounds of ill health:

1) Whether the employer could have been expected to wait any longer and, if so, for how much longer. Relevant factors could include whether the employee had exhausted their sick pay, whether the employer was able to call on temporary staff during the employee's absence and the size of the employer.

2) Whether the employee had been properly consulted, and whether their views had been taken into account and appropriately balanced against the views of any medical professional. If the employee stated that they were anxious to return to work and hoped to do so in the near future, that would operate in their favour; whereas, if they stated that they were no better and did not know when they could return to work, that would be a significant factor operating against them.

3) Whether reasonable steps had been taken to discover the employee's medical condition and likely prognosis. It would not be necessary for the employer to pursue a detailed medical examination provided the correct question was asked and answered.

Particular difficulties can arise if the employee's illness was work-related (for example, inhalation of noxious fumes or – as now commonly seen – stress). The employer's treatment of the employee which caused the ill health, leading to incapability and subsequent dismissal, does not in itself make the dismissal unfair. The proper approach is to apply section 98 of the ERA 1996 in the normal way and decide whether dismissal was or was not within the range of reasonable responses for the employer in the circumstances. A factor that may properly be taken into account is whether the employer was responsible for the employee's incapacity, in which case it may be necessary for the employer to 'go the extra mile' to avoid the dismissal (*Royal Bank of Scotland v Aidie [2008] ICR 1087*).

A dismissal may be justified if the risk of future illness places the health and safety of other employees in jeopardy. Accordingly, a sole wireless operator at risk of a heart attack on a ship could be fairly dismissed due to the risk to his fellow sailors (*Converfoam (Darwen) Ltd v Bell [1981] IRLR 193*).

Timing

The relevant circumstances include 'the nature of the illness, the likely length of the continuing absence, the need of the employers to have done the work which the employee was engaged to do' (*Spencer v Paragon Wallpapers Ltd*

[1976] IRLR 373, quoted with approval by the Court of Appeal in *O'Donoghue v Elmbridge Housing Trust [2004] 6 WLUK 305*).

Making enquiries

The employer must make reasonable enquiries in order to form a view on the likelihood of the employee's return to work or the probability of continuing short-term absences. Failure to do so will almost always result in the dismissal being unfair. This involves two distinct stages.

First, the employer should consult fully with the employee to establish the reason for the absence(s) and the employee's view of when they are likely to return to work (*East Lindsey District Council v Daubney [1977] IRLR 181*). Note that the obligation to remain in contact is the employer's, and it cannot avoid this obligation by saying 'the employee never contacted me' (*Mitchell v Arkwood Plastics (Engineering) Ltd [1993] ICR 471*). The employer should make the employee aware that it is contemplating dismissal if there is no return to work. This is not so much a disciplinary warning as giving the employee full notice of the potential outcome if their health does not improve.

Second, the employer will normally be expected to undertake some level of consultation with a doctor. A good example is a case in which a bus driver suffered a suspected stroke. His PSV licence was rescinded, and his employers dismissed him without waiting for medical reports to confirm whether he was permanently incapacitated. The EAT agreed with an employment tribunal that this was unreasonable and that the dismissal was unfair (*First West Yorkshire t/a First Leeds v Haigh [2008] IRLR 182*). However, employees cannot be compelled to undergo a medical examination or submit to the disclosure of medical records – unless they have agreed to do so in the contract of employment. If they refuse to consent, the employer will not be criticised provided an attempt has been made to obtain medical advice.

However, employers will only be required to take such steps as are reasonable in the circumstances when deciding what medical evidence to obtain and when. As the Court of Session noted at paragraph 34 of *BS v Dundee City Council [2014] SC 254*:

> 'The obligation on a reasonable employer is only to carry out such medical investigations as are sensible in all the circumstances.'

Depending on the nature of the illness, the employer must decide whether to seek the opinion of a specialist or simply rely on a GP's report. There are risks for employers other than small companies in relying on a GP's report: a tribunal may consider that it was unreasonable to limit the investigation to a medical expert who does not specialise in the relevant medical field. Further, in practice, GPs' reports rarely contain clear prognoses, and an employer may be criticised for dismissing on the basis of an unclear prognosis (*Crampton v Dacorum Motors Ltd [1975] IRLR 168*).

153

If the medical opinion demonstrates that the employee is unlikely to return to work in the near future, and the employer is satisfied that its business interests require dismissal, it will normally be fair to dismiss. However, a tribunal is likely to take the view that it is incumbent on an employer to take reasonable steps, including getting proper medical reports, to satisfy itself that an employee is malingering if dismissal on those grounds is being considered. In this context, whether or not covert surveillance contravenes an employee's right to privacy under article 8 of the *European Convention on Human Rights* is a matter of proportionality (*McCann v Clydebank College (2010) UKEATS/0061/09*).

Alternative employment

An employer should always consider alternative employment in cases of ill-health dismissals (*McCann v Clydebank College*).

Is there a job the employee could undertake from home? Is there light work available the employee could do? A failure to consider alternatives will often render a dismissal unfair, although the compensatory award will be nil if there were, in fact, no suitable alternative positions available (*Merseyside & North Wales Electricity Board v Taylor [1975] IRLR 60*).

9.4 CONDUCT

9.4.1 GENERAL

Misconduct is a ground frequently relied on by employers to justify dismissal. If the principal reason for a dismissal is serious misconduct, which the employer reasonably believes has been committed by the employee, then the dismissal can be regarded as potentially fair (section 98(2)(b) of the ERA 1996).

Whether the dismissal is, in fact, fair or unfair will then turn on whether the employment tribunal considers that the employer acted reasonably in the circumstances – which include the size and administrative resources of the business – in treating it 'as a sufficient reason for dismissing the employee'. There is no onus of proof on the employer or employee here, and the matter has to be determined by the tribunal 'in accordance with equity and the substantial merits of the case'. Each case has to be looked at on its own particular facts, and although some general principles can be drawn from case law, these decisions should generally be treated only as examples and not as establishing that a particular type of misconduct does or does not justify dismissal (section 98(4) of the ERA 1996).

A well-established three-limb test known as the 'Burchell guidelines' shows that in coming to its decision, an employment tribunal must consider:

1) Whether the employer genuinely believed that the employee had been guilty of the misconduct when it dismissed him.

2) If so, whether there were reasonable grounds for the belief.

3) Whether the employer carried out as much investigation into the matter as was reasonable in all the circumstances before dismissing the employee (*British Home Stores v Burchell [1980] ICR 303*).

In *Hope v British Medical Association [2022] IRLR 206*, the EAT emphasised that in cases where the potentially fair reason relied on is 'conduct', the factual enquiry did not require a further finding of 'gross misconduct'. Mr Justice Choudhury, then President of the EAT, reiterated the importance of applying section 98 of the ERA 1996 and the familiar *Burchell* test. The question of whether or not dismissal by reason of conduct is fair or unfair within the meaning of section 98(4) of the ERA 1996 depends not on the label attached to or characterisation of the conduct as gross misconduct, but on whether, in the circumstances, including the size and administrative resources of the employer's undertaking, the employer acted reasonably or unreasonably in treating it as a sufficient reason for dismissing the employee. He held that it is equally well established that the determination of that question involves, in a case where the reason for dismissal is said to be the employee's misconduct, the following four-stage analysis:

1) Whether the employer had a genuine belief in the misconduct

2) Whether the employer had reached that belief on reasonable grounds

3) Whether the belief was reached following a reasonable investigation

4) Whether the dismissal of the claimant fell within the range of reasonable responses in the light of that misconduct

There is no requirement in the four-stage analysis to determine whether conduct amounts to 'gross misconduct', which involves a separate contractual concept. In addition, where the misconduct relied upon is said to have been in breach of the employer's policy, with such breach having been contractually stipulated to amount to gross misconduct, this is still not determinative, since the tribunal is still obliged to apply the statutory test.

Substitution and the band of reasonable responses

An employment tribunal must not substitute its own view for that of the employer (*London Ambulance Service NHS Trust v Small [2009] IRLR 563*). The correct test is not whether a reasonable employer would have dismissed the employee as opposed to imposing a lesser penalty, but whether dismissal fell within the range of reasonable responses of a reasonable employer in all the circumstances. It is arguably more accurate to refer to 'unfair' dismissal as 'unreasonable' dismissal.

The dismissal will be unfair only if the employer's decision was outside this band of reasonable responses (*Midland Bank plc v Madden [2000] 2 All ER 741* and *Post Office v Foley [2000] ICR 1283*). It is also established that the test of whether a decision to dismiss falls within the band of reasonable responses to the employee's conduct a reasonable employer could adopt is a test which applies to each of the three limbs of the Burchell guidelines.

However, there has arguably been some refinement of these principles. As Bean LJ held in *Thames Water Utilities Ltd v Newbound [2015] IRLR 734*, at paragraph 74:

'The "band of reasonable responses" has been a stock phrase in employment law for over 30 years, but the band is not infinitely wide. It is important not to overlook section 98(4)(b) of the 1996 Act, which directs employment tribunals to decide the question of whether the employer has acted reasonably or unreasonably in deciding to dismiss "in accordance with equity and the substantial merits of the case". This provision, originally contained in section 24(6) of the *Industrial Relations Act 1971*, indicates that in creating the statutory cause of action of unfair dismissal Parliament did not intend the tribunal's consideration of a case of this kind to be a matter of procedural box-ticking.'

A fair investigation

The band of reasonable responses test applies not only in determining whether it was procedurally or substantively fair or unfair to dismiss an employee but also in determining whether investigations carried out by the employer were reasonable in all the circumstances (*Sainsbury (J) Ltd v Hitt [2003] ICR 111*). The investigation should be considered as a whole. An employer is not required to consider each 'line of defence' that an employee may raise. As Richards LJ held in *Shrestha v Genesis Housing Association Limited [2015] IRLR 399*, at paragraph 23:

'The investigation should be looked at as a whole when assessing the question of reasonableness. As part of the process of investigation, the employer must of course consider any defences advanced by the employees, but whether and to what extent it is necessary to carry out specific inquiry into them in order to meet the Burchell test will depend on the circumstances as a whole.'

The real reason for dismissal

The basic rule is that it is for the employer to show the reason (or, if more than one, the principal reason) for a dismissal (section 98 of the ERA 1996). A particular danger for employers when dismissing an employee for misconduct is that the employee may claim misconduct was not the real reason. A good example is *East Lancashire Coachbuilders v Hilton [2006] 8 WLUK 229*, in which a director was dismissed ostensibly on the grounds of misconduct which had clearly taken place, but a tribunal found the real reason for his dismissal was quite different and had nothing to do with misconduct. Accordingly, the dismissal was unfair.

In *Queen Elizabeth Hospital NHS Trust v Ogunlana (2006) UKEAT/0372/06*, the EAT neatly summarised that '[t]he overall position is as follows:

i) It is for the employer to show a genuine belief in the misconduct alleged, and that that belief was the reason for dismissal;

ii) Having established that potentially fair reason for dismissal, it is for the tribunal to determine, the burden of proof being neutral, whether the employer carried out a reasonable investigation and had reasonable grounds for that belief. In answering those questions, the tribunal must apply the range of reasonable responses approach. It must not substitute its view as to whether a reasonable investigation was carried out or whether there were reasonable grounds for that belief, for that of the respondent employer;

iii) A similar approach must be taken to questions of procedural unfairness;

iv) Finally, the question is whether dismissal fell within the range of reasonable responses open to the employer.'

If an employee has admitted the misconduct in question, this may limit the extent to which the employer is required to investigate (*CRO Ports London v Wiltshire (2015) UKEAT/0344/14/DM*).

In *Uddin v London Borough of Ealing [2020] IRLR 332*, the EAT held that the knowledge (or conduct) of someone other than the person who took the decision to dismiss could be relevant to the fairness of a dismissal. In other words, if someone responsible for the investigation process did not share a relevant fact with the decision-maker, that could make the dismissal unfair.

Disparities in treatment

Tribunals may be slow to accept that unequal treatment of employees will be within the band of reasonable responses. As Brandon LJ said in *Post Office v Fennell [1981] IRLR 221*:

'I would stress in subsection (3) of section 57 the words in brackets, "having regard to equity and the substantial merits of the case". It seems to me that the expression "equity" as there used comprehends the concept that employees who misbehave in much the same way should have meted out to them much the same punishment, and it seems to me that an industrial tribunal is entitled to say that, where that is not done, and one man is penalised much more heavily than others who have committed similar offences in the past, the employer has not acted reasonably in treating whatever the offence is as a sufficient reason for dismissal.'

However, the fact that an individual can show that on a previous occasion, another employee had not been dismissed even though guilty of the same type of misconduct is simply one matter to take into account in deciding whether the dismissal was fair or unfair. In every case, what matters is the statutory test under section 98(4) of the ERA 1996 (*Hadjioannou v Coral Casinos Ltd [1981] IRLR 352*).

If one of a group of employees is guilty of misconduct but the employer – having made reasonable inquiries – genuinely cannot find out who, it can be fair to dismiss the whole group (*Monie v Coral Racing Ltd [1980] IRLR 464*), or the whole group other than any who the employer genuinely and justifiably believes were not responsible (*Frames Snooker Centre v Boyce [1992] IRLR 472*).

Similarly, if several employees are guilty of the same misconduct and some are dismissed but others are not, it does not follow that the dismissals are unfair. Disparity in treatment is just one of many factors to be taken into account. The employer can properly consider different circumstances, such as length of service and/or previous conduct, in deciding to dismiss some and not others. A good example is *UK Coal Mining Ltd v Raby (2003) EAT/1124/02*, in which two employees were caught fighting at work and one was dismissed while the other was not. The disparity in treatment was justifiable as the one not dismissed was acting in self-defence and had an unblemished record, which the other did not. Another example is *Enterprise Liverpool plc v Bauress UKEAT/0645/05* in which three joiners were caught 'doing a foreigner' – that is working for other employers and using their real employer's tools when doing so. Two were relatively new employees and were sacked, but the other was not. The EAT found that the dismissals were fair.

Misconduct and gross misconduct

The law differentiates between gross misconduct and misconduct generally. Gross misconduct is an old common law expression which refers to conduct so serious that it justifies instant dismissal without notice. Misconduct can justify dismissal even though it is not gross misconduct in that sense. However, a dismissal for misconduct not deemed to be gross misconduct will normally be unfair if the employer failed to discuss the matter properly with the employee, failed to apply any relevant disciplinary procedures or failed to give the employee a chance to correct matters.

If a tribunal decides in a particular case that the misconduct was not a sufficient reason for dismissing the employee, the dismissal will have been unfair. Nevertheless, if the misconduct contributed to the dismissal, it must be taken into account in assessing the compensatory award component and may be taken into account in assessing the basic award component (section 123(6) of the ERA 1996).

158

When determining the fairness or otherwise, a tribunal must consider the position as known to those responsible for the decision at the time of the dismissal. This, of course, does not include facts which only come to light afterwards, even if those facts were known to another member of staff at the time of the dismissal (*Orr v Milton Keynes Council [2011] ICR 704*).

9.4.2 EXAMPLES

1) An employee refused to work on a day which, under his contract, was a holiday. The work was commercially urgent: this could be conduct justifying dismissal (*Brandon and Goold v Murphy Bros [1983] IRLR 54*).

2) An employee refused to falsify invoices: this was not conduct justifying dismissal (*Morrish v Henlys (Folkestone) Ltd [1973] IRLR 61*).

3) A long-serving member of staff in a shop was caught shoplifting in another shop: this could be conduct justifying dismissal (*Moore v C&A Modes [1981] IRLR 71*).

4) Lateness for work without good reason can be conduct justifying dismissal if it continues over a period of time and is not corrected in spite of warnings (*Hallett & Want v MAT Transport Ltd [1976] IRLR 5*).

5) Being spotted at a function while allegedly absent on sick leave can be conduct justifying dismissal (*Hutchinson v Enfield Rolling Mills Ltd [1981] IRLR 318*).

6) Unauthorised use of the employer's computer equipment can be conduct justifying dismissal (*Denco Ltd v Joinson [1991] ICR 172*).

7) Unauthorised use of the employer's telephone system can be conduct justifying dismissal (*East Berkshire Health Authority v Matadeen [1992] ICR 724*).

8) A resident social worker slapped an inmate at a young person's residential home: this could be conduct justifying dismissal (*Boys & Girls Welfare v McDonald [1997] ICR 693*).

9) One-off use of obscene language is unlikely to amount to conduct justifying dismissal (*Wilson v Racher [1974] ICR 428*).

10) A foreman working for a cleaning company applied personally to one of the customers to carry out a cleaning contract for that customer: this was conduct justifying dismissal (*Adamson v B & L Cleaning Services Ltd [1995] IRLR 193*).

11) An employee normally worked overtime but was not obliged to do so by the terms of his contract. He decided that in future, he would work overtime only on days which suited him, which placed his

local authority employer in a difficult position. The EAT held that in the circumstances this amounted to conduct justifying his dismissal (*Horrigan v Lewisham Council [1978] ICR 15*).

12) A bank employee's contract provided that he could be required to work at any of the bank's branches in the UK. He refused to move at short notice from Leeds to Birmingham, resigned and claimed constructive unfair dismissal. The EAT held he had been constructively dismissed and his conduct did not justify that dismissal (*United Bank v Akhtar [1989] IRLR 507*).

13) A clause in a consultant's contract under which he could be dismissed if he was guilty of conduct tending to bring the 'employer' into disrepute entitled the 'employer' to dismiss him even though the misconduct had taken place before the date of the contract (*Bland v Sparkes (1999) The Times, 17 December*).

14) Fighting at work with a fellow employee is likely to be regarded as conduct justifying dismissal even if the employee concerned previously had a long unblemished record (*Beedell v West Ferry Printers [2000] IRLR 650*).

15) While unauthorised private use of a telephone at work might, in some circumstances, justify dismissal, this will depend on all the facts and would very seldom, if ever, justify dismissal without warning. The same thinking would no doubt apply to unauthorised use of the internet by an employee (*John Lewis plc v Coyne [2001] IRLR 139*).

16) An employee used a company vehicle for private purposes without permission. The EAT overruled the tribunal's finding of unfair dismissal largely because of the employee's previously unblemished long service but was itself overruled by the Court of Appeal (*Strouthos v London Underground Ltd [2004] IRLR 636*).

17) An employer did not have reasonable grounds for its belief that fraud had been committed and failed to carry out sufficient investigation (*Panama v London Borough of Hackney [2003] IRLR 278*).

18) An employer's use of covert surveillance to get evidence that an employee was falsifying timesheets was held to be proportionate and not an unlawful infringement of the employee's right to privacy under the *Human Rights Act 1998* (*McGowan v Scottish Water [2005] IRLR 167*).

19) Downloading pornography from the internet. An example is *London Borough of Hillingdon v Thomas (2002) EAT/1317/01*, in which the EAT held that an employer's decision to dismiss an HR manager with many years' unblemished service for downloading porn from the internet, in breach of the very rules he was meant to enforce, was within the

band of reasonable responses open to an employer and was therefore not unfair dismissal.

20) Pretending to be unfit to return to work when video footage showed that the employee was not so unfit is conduct justifying dismissal (*Corus UK Ltd v A M Mainwaring (2007) UKEAT/0053/07*), which also establishes that there is no absolute requirement for the employer to get a doctor's report in such circumstances).

21) A headteacher who had failed to disclose that she was in a relationship with an individual who had been convicted of making indecent images of children was fairly dismissed (*A v B Local Authority [2016] ELR 329*).

Breach of health and safety

One relatively common reason for conduct dismissals is a breach of health and safety procedures.

As Bean LJ held in *Newbound v Thames Water Utilities Limited [2015] IRLR 734*, 'there is no special rule about assessing the reasonableness of a dismissal on conduct grounds where the alleged misconduct involves a breach of health and safety requirements'. The gravity of the breach may make it more likely that a dismissal will be found to be reasonable, but proper investigations should be carried out and consideration given to the level of the employee's culpability and any mitigation they may have if the dismissal will be found to be fair.

Social media

Dismissals for inappropriate use of social media will follow ordinary principles (*The British Waterways Board v Smith (2015) UKEATS/0004/15* and *Game Retail Limited v Laws (2014) UKEAT/0188/14*).

Acas offers guidance on social networking, including suggestions as to what should be included in a social media policy (https://archive.acas.org.uk/index.aspx?articleid=3375).

9.5 RETIREMENT

The *Employment Equality (Repeal of Retirement Age Provisions) Regulations 2011* brought an end to the default retirement age and the possibility for employers to automatically retire employees at age 65.

9.6 REDUNDANCY

Redundancy is a potentially fair reason for dismissal. In order to qualify, the employer will need to have undergone a reasonable period of consultation and selection. This is addressed in detail in Chapter 10.

9.7 CONTRAVENTION OF A STATUTORY DUTY

Another potentially fair reason for dismissal, under section 98(2)(d) of the ERA 1996, is 'that the employee could not continue to work in the position which he held without contravention (either on his part or on that of his employer) of a duty or restriction imposed by or under an enactment'.

A variety of situations may lead to an employee being prohibited by statute from working in the position that they hold. For example, the expiry of a visa (*Kelly v University of Southampton [2008] ICR 357*), a regulator removing the employee's regulated status (*Sandhu v Department of Education and Science [1978] IRLR 208*) or a statutory ban from driving (*Nairne v Highland and Islands Fire Brigade [1989] IRLR 366*).

An employer will not be able to rely on section 98(2)(d) of the ERA 1996 if there is not, in fact, a statutory ban in place: the reasonableness of an employer's belief that a statutory ban was in place is irrelevant (*Bouchaala v Trusthouse Forte Hotels Ltd [1980] IRLR 382*). However, under section 98(1)(b) of the ERA 1996, such a genuine and reasonable belief can constitute 'some other substantial reason' and thus a dismissal based on an erroneous, but reasonable, belief that a statutory ban is in place may be fair.

The mere fact that it becomes a breach of statute to continue employing the worker in that position does not automatically mean any dismissal will be fair: it merely means it is potentially fair. A tribunal will still consider the overriding test of fairness in section 98(4) of the ERA 1996, with the principal factors being whether the employer considered the possibility of alternative employment and whether modifications to the job description would have removed the element of breach of duty (*Appleyard v Smith (Hull) Ltd [1972] IRLR 19, Fearn v Tayford Motor Co Ltd [1975] IRLR 336 IT, Sutcliffe & Eaton v Pinney [1977] IRLR 349* and *Sandhu v Department of Education and Science,* above).

9.8 DISMISSAL FOR SOME OTHER SUBSTANTIAL REASON

If an employer can show that the reason for dismissal of an employee was a 'substantial reason of a kind such as to justify the dismissal of an employee holding the position which the employee held' (section 98(1)(b) of the ERA 1996), then the dismissal is regarded as potentially fair. This is so even if it is not for one of the specific potentially fair reasons set out in section 98(2) of the ERA 1996 – that is, reasons related to capability, qualifications, conduct, retirement, redundancy or reasons which would lead to contravention of a statutory duty or restriction.

Whether the dismissal is, in fact, fair or unfair will then turn on whether the employment tribunal considers that the employer acted reasonably in the circumstances – which include the size and resources of their undertaking – in treating it 'as a sufficient reason for dismissing the employee' (section 98(4) of the ERA 1996). There is no onus of proof on the employer or employee here, and the matter has to be determined by the tribunal in accordance with equity and the substantial merits of the case.

'Some other substantial reason' is a wide mop-up provision designed to ensure that employers are not unduly restricted by having to consider detailed legalistic rules when deciding whether or not it is appropriate to dismiss. Some general principles can be drawn from case law, but past cases should generally be treated only as examples, and each new case must be considered on its own particular facts and merits.

Where the employee has caused a fundamental and irretrievable breakdown of trust and confidence between them and their colleagues but is dismissed because of the actual breakdown rather than the conduct causing it, then the dismissal is not for reasons of conduct. It is, instead, for 'some other substantial reason'. The conduct will, however, be a pertinent consideration when deciding the appropriate disciplinary procedures to be adopted (*Ezsias v North Glamorgan NHS Trust [2011] IRLR 550*).

9.8.1 EXAMPLES

1) Disclosure of information: an employee whose spouse worked for a competitor of the employer was fairly dismissed because of the risk of disclosure of confidential business information. However, the risk must be demonstrably real if dismissal is to be within the range of reasonable responses open to the employer (*Chandlers (Farm Equipment) Ltd v Rainthorpe (2005) UKEAT/0753/04*).

2) An employee changing their mind about a proposed resignation: an employee stated that he was intending to emigrate and would be resigning, so the employer recruited and trained a successor. The employee then decided not to emigrate but was dismissed. The industrial tribunal, the EAT and the Court of Appeal all found his claim that the dismissal was unfair failed on the basis that his expressed intention to resign was 'some other substantial reason' (*Ely v YKK Fasteners Ltd [1994] ICR 164*).

3) Business disruption: an employee was held to have been fairly dismissed when antagonism between him and another worker in a small business was causing disruption to the business (*Triangle Cars v Hook (1999) EAT/1340/98*).

4) A temporary worker covering for a woman on maternity leave, etc.: provided the temporary worker was informed in writing of the position before being taken on, dismissal when the permanent employee returns from maternity leave (or after a pregnancy or maternity-related absence) will be treated as a dismissal for 'some

other substantial reason' and thus be potentially fair. This also applies if a permanent employee has been suspended on medical grounds not connected with pregnancy or maternity (section 106 of the ERA 1996).

5) A customer objecting to an employee: provided the employer has been careful to take all the circumstances into account, including length of service, the likelihood of the employee being able to find alternative employment and the general quality of their work, the dismissal of an individual whose continued employment could result in loss of a valued customer can be 'some other substantial reason' (*Dobie v Burns International Security Services (UK) Ltd [1984] ICR 812*). The employer in such a situation is not required to justify the decision taken by the third party (*Scott Packing & Warehouse Co Ltd v Paterson [1978] IRLR 166* and *Grootcon (UK) Ltd v Keld [1984] IRLR 302*, quoted with approval by Burton P in *B v BAA plc [2005] IRLR 927*) but will have to do everything it can to mitigate any injustice caused by the third party's request (*Bancroft v Interserve (2012) UKEAT/0329/12*).

6) Pressure from a customer or an important third party on the employer: whether third-party pressure justifies dismissal in any particular case will, as always, depend on the particular circumstances. This will include whether the employee was warned on accepting the job that he might be dismissed if customers so requested. In *Dobie v Burns*, the Court of Appeal held that a security guard had been unfairly dismissed when the reason for his dismissal was the insistence of the local authority, which controlled Liverpool Airport, that his employer should not allow that particular individual to do the job. The EAT has said that in this type of situation failure by the employer to consider whether the dismissal would cause an injustice to the employee would be an indication of the fact that the employer had not acted reasonably in all the circumstances (*Greenwood v Whiteghyll Plastics Ltd (2007) UKEAT/0219/07*).

7) Company takeover: the Court of Appeal ruled that the dismissal of a chief executive by the new owners of the employing company was fair after a takeover battle in which the chief executive had strongly fought against the new owners and had even mounted a competing bid (*Cobley v Forward Technology Industries plc [2003] ICR 1050*).

8) Shift changes for business needs: the dismissal of an individual who refuses to work on a Sunday for religious reasons, when business needs necessitate that they occasionally do so, is fair provided the employer balances the prejudice to the business of not having the individual working on a Sunday against the prejudice to the individual of imposing the rule (*Copsey v WWB Devon Clays [2005] ICR 1789*).

9) New restrictive covenants: An employee's refusal to sign a new contract of employment containing restrictive covenants could be 'some other substantial reason' provided that the requirement for the covenants was genuine and not 'whimsical or capricious' or a put-up job designed to get rid of the employee (*Willow Oak Developments Ltd t/a Windsor Recruitment v Silverwood & ors [2006] ICR 1552*).

10) Unsuitability for work with children or vulnerable adults: an employee who was responsible for the care of children was dismissed after receipt by the employer of an enhanced disclosure letter containing adverse information about the employee. The EAT in Scotland said that an employment tribunal 'should have had no difficulty in holding that that was "some other substantial reason" for the purposes of section 98(1)(b) of the ERA 1996' (*B v A (2007) UKEAT/0029/06*). In a different case with a confusingly similar anonymised name, the EAT in England later held that an employee had been fairly dismissed by a public authority following a police 'disclosure' that he had been engaged in paedophile activity even though he had not been convicted of any offence (*A v B [2010] ICR 849*).

11) Dismissal because of a reasonable and genuine belief that an employee was not permitted to work in the UK: an employer who had attempted to establish an employee's immigration status and acted in a reasonable way was entitled to dismiss the employee (*Nayak v Royal Mail Group (2016) UKEATS/0011/15/SM*).

Note that the *Acas Code of Practice on Disciplinary and Grievance Procedures* (2015) (Acas Code) does not apply to dismissals on the basis of 'some other substantial reason' (*Phoenix House v Stockman [2016] ICR 84*), nor does it apply to capability dismissals unless there is culpable conduct (*Holmes v Qinitiq Ltd [2016] ICR 1016*).

9.9 REASONABLENESS OF THE DECISION TO DISMISS

As part of considering the overall fairness of a dismissal, the tribunal will consider whether it was an appropriate sanction. In cases not involving misconduct – for example, dismissal due to incapability or contravention of a statutory duty – an employer will not act reasonably without first considering whether there is any alternative employment available for the employee. This must cover alternative employment within both the employer's organisation and any associated employers.

However, in conduct dismissals, the tribunal will be concerned with reviewing the fairness of the level of sanction imposed. In other words, was dismissal excessive? Would a warning (or some other sanction) have sufficed?

In deciding this question, a tribunal should not substitute its own view for that of the employer. On any given set of facts, one employer might think dismissal is warranted whereas another might not. This does not mean that the stricter employer is acting unreasonably. An employer will only be found to have acted unreasonably if the tribunal thinks that *no* reasonable employer would have dismissed in those circumstances.

Thus the courts have developed the range of reasonable responses test. If the decision to dismiss falls within the band of reasonable responses to the employee's conduct which a reasonable employer could adopt, the dismissal would be fair (*Iceland Frozen Foods v Jones [1982] IRLR 439*).

A disciplinary sanction short of dismissal can entitle the employee to resign and claim unfair and/or wrongful constructive dismissal if the sanction is out of all proportion to the employee's offence (*Stanley Cole (Wainfleet) Ltd v Sheridan [2003] IRLR 52*).

Dismissal will usually be a fair sanction in cases of gross misconduct unless unusual circumstances exist – for example, particular mitigating circumstances or a history of the employer having a policy of overlooking such offences (*Post Office v Fennell [1981] IRLR 221*). Offences of violence or dishonesty will almost always amount to gross misconduct.

If an act of misconduct does not amount to gross misconduct, it will be rare for a tribunal to ratify as fair a decision to dismiss unless there are unambiguous disciplinary rules making it clear that breaches will result in dismissal, even for a first offence (*Meyer Dunmore International Ltd v Rogers [1978] IRLR 167, W Brooks & Son v Skinner [1984] IRLR 379* and *Asda Stores Ltd v Malyn (2001) EAT/0066/00 & EAT/1112/00*). The same holds true if there is a history of warnings for the employee in respect of either a similar or, indeed, wholly different, disciplinary matter (*Retarded Children's Aid Society v Day [1978] IRLR 128* and *Auguste Noel v Curtis [1990] IRLR 326*).

Importance of warnings

Warnings should lapse after a given period. The Acas Code says that a final written warning should normally be disregarded for disciplinary purposes after a specified period, for example, 12 months. Once a warning has expired, the employer should generally disregard it. However, the existence of an expired warning can, in some exceptional circumstances, be properly taken into account in deciding whether to dismiss an employee (*Airbus UK Ltd v Webb [2008] ICR 561*). However, as was noted in *Airbus v Webb*, this should not be taken as 'encouraging reliance on expired warnings as a matter of course'.

9.10 AUTOMATICALLY UNFAIR DISMISSALS

Employers are prohibited from dismissing employees for a number of proscribed reasons. Where an employee is dismissed for one of these reasons, the tribunal will find that the dismissal is 'automatically unfair' and will not consider the reasonableness of the employer's conduct.

A dismissal can be automatically unfair whether it is a dismissal in the ordinary sense or a dismissal in the form of a redundancy. In other words, if the employees concerned are selected for redundancy for an automatically unfair reason, the redundancy is automatically unfair (section 105 of the ERA 1996 and section 153 of the TULR(C)A 1992).

An important practical consequence of a dismissal being categorised as automatically unfair is that, in most cases, such claims can be brought by new employees who have not completed the minimum employment period required for normal unfair dismissal claims.

More specifically, the consequences of a dismissal being automatically unfair are:

- The normal criteria for determining whether a dismissal is fair do not apply.

- In almost all cases, the employee does not have to have completed any qualifying period of continuous employment.

- In certain cases (most commonly health & safety dismissals), the basic award has a minimum of £7,836 (as of 6 April 2023).

Many of the situations in which dismissal is automatically unfair provide for exceptions in particular circumstances. This does not mean that a dismissal in those circumstances is fair: it merely means that the dismissal is not *automatically* unfair and leaves the question of whether it is fair or unfair for a tribunal to decide, according to ordinary principles of unfair dismissal law.

9.10.1 REASONS

The main situations in which a dismissal is automatically unfair are set out below.

Family leave

If an employee is dismissed for exercising the right to take family leave of whatever type (adoption leave, maternity leave, paternity leave or shared parental leave), then the dismissal will be automatically unfair.

Assertion of statutory rights

If an employee is dismissed for making an allegation that the employer has infringed one or more of their relevant statutory rights, then the dismissal is automatically unfair (section 104 of the ERA 1996). This is the case whether or not the employee has taken proceedings to enforce the right. It is immaterial whether the employee has the right or whether it has been infringed provided the claim is made in good faith (section 104(3) of the ERA 1996 and *Mennell v Newell & Wright [1997] IRLR 519*).

The relevant statutory rights are set out in section 104(4) of the ERA 1996 by reference to other sections. Reference should be made to the ERA 1996 for the precise detail, but examples include:

- The right to a minimum notice period
- The statutory right to time off work
- The right to itemised pay statements or payslips
- The right to a written statement of particulars of employment
- The right not to have unlawful deductions from wages, etc.
- The rights under the WTR 1998 to annual paid holiday and not to be required to work excessive hours
- The right to time off work for trade union activities or duties or as a trade union learning representative
- The right not to have unauthorised deductions from wages in respect of union contributions or union political funds
- The right to be consulted under the terms of TUPE 2006

The EAT has set out three steps which must be considered to support an automatically unfair dismissal claim on the basis of the assertion of a statutory right:

1) Decide whether the employee has alleged that the employer infringed a right of theirs which is a relevant statutory right.

2) Decide whether or not the employee has that right and whether it has been infringed.

3) Decide whether the claim to the right and the claim to the fact that it has been infringed has been made in good faith (*Danlardy v Southwark Race Equalities Council (2006) UKEAT/0159/06*).

Even if the employee did not realise until after they had been dismissed that they had been asserting a statutory right, it is enough that they refused to accede to a requirement that would have breached regulations giving them statutory rights and that the dismissal is because of that refusal. In *McLean v Rainbow Homeloans Ltd [2007] IRLR 14 (Scot)*, an employment tribunal rejected an unfair dismissal claim on the basis that the employee had not completed the required qualifying period of continuous service. The EAT overruled the tribunal as the employee claimed he was dismissed for refusing to work more than the 48 hours per week referred to in the WTR 1998. This was an assertion of a statutory right covered by section 104(4) of the ERA 1996 and no qualification period was required (section 108(3(dd) of the ERA 1996).

Business transfers

Dismissal of an employee because of a sale or other transfer of a business is automatically unfair dismissal, unless the dismissal is for an economic, technical or organisational (ETO) reason involving changes in the workforce (regulation 7 of TUPE 2006).

It makes no difference whether the dismissal was an actual dismissal or a constructive dismissal (*Morris v John Grose Group Ltd [1998] IRLR 499* and *CAB Automotive Ltd v Blake, Singh & ors UKEAT/0298/07/1202*). If the dismissal was because of the transfer, it will be automatically unfair unless it can be justified on ETO grounds entailing changes in the workforce noted above.

It should be noted that the normal qualification period of continuous employment, which is currently two years, applies if an employee claims automatically unfair dismissal under TUPE 2006. This is provided for by regulation 7(6) of TUPE 2006, which makes it clear that the automatically unfair dismissal provisions in those regulations benefit only employees who are eligible to claim unfair dismissal in the 'ordinary way'. See **Chapter 11** for more about TUPE dismissals.

Companion at certain meetings with the employer

A worker (as defined by section 13 of the Employment Relations Act 1999 (ERA 1999)) has the right to be accompanied by a fellow worker or trade union representative of their choice at internal disciplinary procedure and grievance procedure hearings (section 10 of the ERA 1999). Dismissal for exercising this right or that of the companion for accompanying that employee is automatically unfair dismissal (section 12 of the ERA 1999).

Employee representatives

Elected employee representatives have certain rights to be consulted in the event of proposed multiple redundancies on the sale or transfer of the employing business. Dismissal of an elected employee for performing or proposing to perform any functions as an employee representative is automatically unfair. It is also automatically unfair to dismiss someone for being a candidate for election as an employee representative or for voting in an election of employee representatives (section 103 of the ERA 1996 and regulation 13 of the Transfer of Undertakings (Protection of Employment) Regulations 2006).

Fixed-term work regulations

Dismissal is automatically unfair if it is in connection with an attempt to exercise any right under the Fixed-term Employees (Prevention of Less Favourable Treatment) Regulations 2002.

Flexible working

If the reason or principal reason for dismissal is that the employee made (or proposed to make) an application for flexible working arrangements (under section 80F of the ERA 1996), or for related reasons, the dismissal will be automatically unfair (section 104C of the ERA 1996).

Health and safety

A dismissal is automatically unfair dismissal if it is for one of six specified health and safety-related reasons (section 100 of the ERA 1996):

1) The employee was carrying out or proposed to carry out activities in connection with the prevention of health and safety risks at work, having been designated to do so by the employer.

2) The employee, being one of the duly appointed safety representatives in the workforce, performed or proposed to perform their duties as such.

3) The employee was exercising rights under the *Health and Safety (Consultation with Employees) Regulations 1996.*

4) The employee brought directly to 'his employer's attention, by reasonable means, circumstances connected with his work which he reasonably believed were harmful or potentially harmful to health or safety' (section 100(1)(c) of the ERA 1996) if there was no safety representative or safety committee whose attention could be drawn to the matter. This refers to the raising of the health and safety issue rather than to the safety of the employee (*ABC News Intercontinental Inc v Gizbert (2006) UKEAT/0160/06*). In *ABC News v Gizbert*, a journalist had brought to ABC's attention the dangers of travelling to a war zone. But that was not the principal reason for his dismissal. The principal reason was his refusal to go to a war zone.

5) The employee left or proposed to leave their place of work because they reasonably believed there was serious and imminent danger which they could not reasonably be expected to avert. The fact that the employer did not agree with the employee that a danger exists was irrelevant (*Oudahar v Esporta Group Ltd (2011) UKEAT/0566/10*).

6) The employee took, or proposed to take, appropriate steps to protect themself or others from danger which they reasonably believed to be serious and imminent unless those steps were so negligent that dismissal would be justified because of them.

Industrial action

Dismissal of an employee for taking part in 'protected industrial action', which normally means an official strike, is automatically unfair dismissal (section 238A(2) and 283A(3) of the TULR(C)A 1992) if one of the following applies:

- It takes place within the period of 12 weeks beginning with the day on which the employee started to take protected industrial action.
- It takes place after the end of that period and the employee had stopped taking protected industrial action before the end of that period.
- It takes place after the end of that period and the employee had not stopped taking protected industrial action before the end of that period, and the employer had not taken such procedural steps as would have been reasonable for the purposes of resolving the dispute to which the protected industrial action relates.

Jury service

Dismissals as a result of carrying out jury service are automatically unfair, subject to exceptions and safeguards if the employer's business would be badly affected by allowing the employee to take time off (section 98B of the ERA 1996). No employment qualification period is required for claiming unfair dismissal (section 108(3)(aa) of the ERA 1996).

Maternity leave and pregnancy (and adoption, paternity or parental leave)

It is automatically unfair dismissal if a woman is dismissed for a reason connected with pregnancy, childbirth or maternity (or is selected for redundancy for that reason). Subject to the exemption noted below, this includes refusing to allow her to return to work at the end of maternity leave (section 99 of the ERA 1996 and regulation 20(3) of the Maternity and Parental Leave Regulations 1999 (MPLR 1999)). The nature of the right itself depends on whether the leave was compulsory, ordinary or additional maternity leave. It is similarly automatically unfair to dismiss an employee for taking paternity, adoption leave, or shared parental leave (regulation 29 of the Paternity and Adoption Leave Regulations 2002 (PAL 2002) and regulation 43 of the Shared Parental Leave Regulations 2014 (SPLR 2014)).

There is an exemption from the normal automatically unfair dismissal where it is 'not reasonably practicable' for the employee to return to a job with their original employer (for reasons other than redundancy). If this applies, the employee has then been offered a suitable and appropriate job with an 'associated' employer and has either accepted or unreasonably refused it, then dismissal will not be automatically unfair (regulation 20(7) of the MPLR 1999).

National minimum wage

Dismissal is automatically unfair if it is in connection with an attempt to exercise any right under the National Minimum Wage Act 1998 (NMWA 1998), to bring a defaulting employer to book or because the worker might qualify for the National Minimum Wage (section 104A of the ERA 1996 and section 25 of the NMWA 1998).

Part-time work regulations

Dismissal is automatically unfair if it is in connection with an attempt to exercise any right under the Part-time Workers (Prevention of Less Favourable Treatment) Regulations 2000.

Redundancy selection (improper)

If one employee rather than another is selected for redundancy for a reason treated in law as automatically unfair dismissal, then – subject to one condition – the resulting dismissal is automatically unfair. This is the case even though, technically, the reason was redundancy, which, under section 105 of the ERA 1996 is prima facie a fair reason for dismissing an employee. The condition is that 'the circumstances constituting the redundancy applied equally to one or more other employees in the same undertaking who held positions similar to that held by the employee and who have not been dismissed by the employer' (section 105(1)(b) of the ERA 1996).

Time off for dependants

Subject to the same exception as noted above in connection with additional maternity leave and parental leave, it is also automatically unfair dismissal if employees are dismissed for a reason connected with them exercising their rights to take time off work to look after dependants (section 57A and section 99(3)(d) of the ERA 1996).

Trade union activities

Under sections 152-154 of the TULR(C)A 1992, dismissal is automatically unfair if the principal reason for it (or for the selection for redundancy) was that the employee 'had taken part, or proposed to take part, in the activities of an independent trade union at an appropriate time'. The normal length of service requirement for exercising unfair dismissal rights does not apply.

Trade union membership

If employees are dismissed for the negative reason that they are not a member of either any trade union or a particular trade union, or because they refused, or proposed to refuse, to become or remain a member, this will automatically be unfair dismissal. It is also automatically unfair dismissal if they were dismissed for the positive reason that they were a member of (or proposed

172

to join) a union, or because they had taken part (or proposed to take part) in union activities 'at an appropriate time'. In these cases, the union must be an independent trade union for employees to have automatic unfair dismissal rights. The normal minimum service rule for unfair dismissal does not apply in such cases (sections 152-154 of the TULR(C)A 1992).

Refusal to employ a person because they are – or are not – a member of a trade union is obviously not dismissal at all. There is therefore separate provision to make this unlawful (section 137 of the TULR(C)A 1992).

Whistleblowing

It is automatically unfair dismissal if a worker is dismissed for making a qualifying disclosure to someone to whom they are entitled to make it (section 103A of the ERA 1996).

Working time regulations

Dismissal is automatically unfair if it is in connection with an attempt to exercise any right under the WTR 1998 (section 101A and section 104(4) of the ERA 1996, and regulation 32 of the WTR 1998).

9.11 PROTECTED SETTLEMENT CONVERSATIONS

Evidence of pre-termination negotiations is inadmissible in unfair dismissal claims (section 111A of the ERA 1996). Pre-termination negotiations are defined as 'any offer made or discussions held, before the termination of the employment in question, with a view to it being terminated on terms agreed between the employer and the employee'.

This does not appear to be limited to offers made, or discussions held, between the employer and employee. Offers or discussions with an employment agency, a trusted third party or a union representative may therefore fall within the definition of 'pre-termination negotiations'.

The Acas Code is taken into account by tribunals when interpreting the legislation   (www.acas.org.uk/code-of-practice-settlement-agreements). To support the Acas Code, Acas also provides non-statutory guidance on settlement agreements and how they can be drafted and negotiated (archive. acas.org.uk/media/3736/Settlement-Agreements-A-guide/pdf/Settlement_ agreements_Dec_18.pdf).

9.11.1 WHEN DOES SECTION 111A OF THE ERA 1996 APPLY?

Section 111A of the ERA 1996 only makes evidence of pre-termination negotiations inadmissible in unfair dismissal cases. It does not apply to other claims, including discrimination claims. Automatically unfair dismissals are excluded, so evidence of pre-termination negotiations is admissible for any dismissals for whistleblowing, maternity and trade union activities.

The provision provides that if 'anything said or done which in the tribunal's opinion was improper, or was connected with improper behaviour' then the evidence of pre-termination negotiations will only be inadmissible 'to the extent that the tribunal considers just' (section 111A(4) of the ERA 1996). Tribunals may therefore need to hear evidence about the pre-termination negotiations to determine whether something about them was 'improper' in order to make a decision on whether or not to admit the evidence.

Note that the fact that offers were made is inadmissible in addition to the contents of the offer and that intra-organisational discussion of offers or settlements is also caught by the provision in section 111A of the ERA 1996 (*Faithorn Farrell Timms LLP v Bailey [2016] ICR 1054*).

Improper behaviour

The meaning of 'improper behaviour' is addressed in the Acas Code. The following examples would normally result in the removal of legal protection. The list is not intended to be exhaustive:

- All forms of harassment, including intimidation through the use of offensive words or aggressive behaviour

- Physical assault and other criminal or wrongful behaviour

- All forms of victimisation

- Discrimination because of age, sex, race, disability, sexual orientation, religion or belief, gender reassignment, pregnancy and maternity, and marriage or civil partnership

- Putting 'undue pressure' on a party. The following behaviours are stated (non-exhaustively) to constitute undue pressure:

  o An employer not allowing an employee a reasonable period of time to consider an offer (a minimum of 10 calendar days)

  o An employer saying before any form of disciplinary process has begun that if the offer is rejected, then the employee will be dismissed

  o An employee threatening to undermine an organisation's public reputation if the organisation does not sign the agreement (unless the provisions of the *Public Interest Disclosure Act 1998* apply)

There is no legal right for an employee to be accompanied by a workplace colleague or trade union representative at a meeting to discuss termination offers. However, the Acas Code makes it clear that employees should be allowed to be accompanied at settlement meetings.

9.11.2 DIFFERENCES FROM 'WITHOUT PREJUDICE'

The protected conversations rule runs parallel to, but independently of, the existing 'without prejudice' rule. There is, however, significant overlap between the two, and coming within either rule will give rise to confidentiality for offers and settlement discussions.

The 'without prejudice' rule generally only protects negotiations when there is an existing dispute, whereas section 111A of the ERA 1996 has a wider application. This may be useful where, for example, one party is not aware at the outset of the negotiations that there is a problem. The wider coverage of the 'improper behaviour' exception under section 111A of the ERA 1996, however, might mean that its protection is more easily lost if, for example, the employer gives the employee less than seven days to consider an offer.

There is express provision in section 111A(5) of the ERA 1996 that offers will remain admissible in costs arguments, even if the offer is inadmissible for the purpose of the substantive unfair dismissal hearing.

9.12 WRONGFUL DISMISSAL

'Wrongful dismissal' means a dismissal which is in breach of contract. Note that breach of an employment contract does not necessarily result in dismissal (*Wetherill & ors v Birmingham City Council [2007] IRLR 781*). Constructive dismissal – that is, resignation by an employee in circumstances such that they are entitled to terminate their contract by reason of the employer's conduct – is, by definition, always wrongful dismissal. A wrongful dismissal may also be an unfair dismissal, but not necessarily. (An example of a dismissal which was held to be 'wrongful dismissal' but not 'unfair dismissal' is *Samuel v London Borough of Lewisham (2001) EAT/1015/00*).

Unfair dismissal does not exist in the common law. It is entirely a 'creature of statute' which can – and frequently does – occur even though there is no breach of contract. Many more unfair dismissal cases than wrongful dismissal cases are brought, but when relevant, wrongful dismissal is likely to be extremely important. Typically, wrongful dismissal is most relevant where employees are entitled to a long notice period – for example, footballers and company directors – or to a particularly valuable deferred remuneration package, and/or if they are subject to contractual obligations which may continue after their employment ends, such as restrictive covenants. It follows that wrongful dismissal is most likely to be particularly relevant if the employee concerned was, or is, in a senior position. However, as indicated below, it is also relatively common for employees in less senior positions to bring wrongful dismissal claims.

An employee who sues a former employer for wrongful dismissal is suing for that employer's wrongful repudiation of the employment contract. This is because as a matter of general law, a party to a contract who commits a serious breach of a fundamental term is said to 'repudiate' the contract. The result is that the other party is entitled to treat the contract as at an end.

9.12.1 WRONGFUL DISMISSAL AND CONSTRUCTIVE UNFAIR DISMISSAL

An employee who has not been dismissed can treat his contract as having been terminated if the employer acts – or omits to act – in a way which amounts to a serious breach of a fundamental term (whether express or implied). The employee will have been 'constructively dismissed' and will be entitled to resign and bring a wrongful dismissal claim.

The breach of contract must be serious and go to the root of the employment relationship for it to have this effect. For example, it was held that an employer's refusal to implement a pay increase 'promised' to an employee in casual conversation at a Christmas party was not intended to create a binding obligation and did not entitle the employee to resign and claim constructive wrongful dismissal (*Judge v Crown Leisure Ltd [2005] IRLR 823*).

9.12.2 WHERE TO BRING A WRONGFUL DISMISSAL CLAIM

The remedy for 'wrongful dismissal' was traditionally to sue the employer in the county court or High Court for damages for breach of contract. However, employment tribunals have jurisdiction to hear wrongful dismissals and can award compensation of up to £25,000 (*Industrial Tribunals Extension of Jurisdiction (England and Wales) Order 1994*). Higher value claims should always be brought in the civil courts for the reasons set out below.

This cap on the amount an employment tribunal can award in a wrongful dismissal case sits oddly with the much higher top limit of compensatory award they can make in unfair dismissal cases and the total absence of any cap on awards in discrimination cases (section 34(4) of the ERA 1999).

If an ex-employee includes a wrongful dismissal claim in their application to an employment tribunal worth more than £25,000, they may be able to apply to withdraw that claim so that they can pursue it in the High Court where the limit does not apply (*Sajid v Chowdhury [2002] IRLR 1334*). However, there may still be circumstances where it is an abuse of process to bring a claim for breach of contract in another forum (*London Borough of Enfield v Sivanandan [2005] EWCA Civ 10*).

If matters get to the stage where an employment tribunal has given judgment, the cause of action is then merged into that judgment. The claim ceases to exist independently of the judgment and the claimant no longer has a cause of action for any excess above £25,000. The case is then *res judicata*, the long-established rule preventing claimants having more than one bite at the cherry in respect of one claim (*Henderson v Henderson (1843) 3 Hare 100*, and *Sheriff v Klyne Tugs (Lowestoft) Ltd [1999] ICR 1170*). Even if the loss is considerably greater than the £25,000 maximum the tribunal awarded, the High Court will strike out any claim for the excess (*Fraser v HLMAD Ltd [2006] ICR 1395*). For this reason, Mummery LJ pointed out in that case:

> '… claimants and their legal advisers would be well advised to confine claims in employment tribunal proceedings to unfair dismissal, unless they are sure that the claimant is willing to limit the total damages claimed for wrongful dismissal to £25,000 or less. If the claimant wishes to recover over £25,000, the wrongful dismissal claim should only be made in High Court proceedings.'

9.12.3 TIME LIMITS

Different time limits apply for bringing wrongful dismissal cases in the courts and in the employment tribunal.

If a wrongful dismissal claim is brought in the courts, the normal *Limitation Act 1980* time limits apply. These provide that 'an action founded on simple contract shall not be brought after the expiration of six years from the date on which the cause of action accrued'. There can be extensions in special cases, for example, if fraud is involved (section 5 and section 32 of the *Limitation Act 1980*).

If a wrongful dismissal claim is brought in an employment tribunal, the relevant time limits are set out in article 7 of the *Industrial Tribunals Extension of Jurisdiction (England and Wales) Order 1994*. In essence, this allows the employee three months from dismissal to present their claim and gives the employer six weeks to make a counterclaim, beginning with the day on which it received a copy of the employee's originating application from the tribunal office.

Employment tribunals have the power to extend these three-month and six-week periods if satisfied that it was not reasonably practicable to have complied with them (articles 7 and 8 of the *Industrial Tribunals Extension of Jurisdiction (England and Wales) Order 1994*).

A difficult issue concerning the effective date of termination arose in the case of *Geys v Societe Generale [2013] ICR 117*. Mr Geys did not accept his summary dismissal as a repudiatory breach of contract. The Court of Appeal found that in light of his affirmation, Mr Geys' contract of employment continued until it ended in accordance with the correct contractual provisions. However, his employee status ended on the date of the repudiation, which for statutory purposes (that is, unfair dismissal) was the effective date of termination. This resulted in a peculiar situation where the employment contract continued without an employee – and presumably without any mutuality of obligation. The Supreme Court, however, disagreed with the Court of Appeal's analysis and held that a party's repudiation of an employment contract did not automatically terminate the contract, which instead only terminated if and when the other party elected to accept the repudiation.

CHAPTER 10

REDUNDANCY

10.0 OVERVIEW

The process involved in making redundancies – particularly where 20 or more are contemplated – can be complex. This chapter explores what is involved and how to minimise the risk of unfair dismissal claims, especially those triggered by failings at the consultation, selection pool, selection criteria, actual selection and alternative employment offer stages.

10.1 WHEN IS AN EMPLOYEE REDUNDANT?

The statutory definition of redundancy is defined in section 139(1) of the *Employment Rights Act 1996* (ERA 1996) as follows:

'...an employee who is dismissed shall be taken to be dismissed by reason of redundancy if the dismissal is wholly or mainly attributable to –

(a) the fact that his employer has ceased, or intends to cease –

    (i) to carry on the business for the purposes of which the employee was employed by him, or

    (ii) to carry on that business in the place where the employee was so employed, or

(b) the fact that the requirements of that business –

    (i) for employees to carry out work of a particular kind, or

    (ii) for employees to carry out work of a particular kind in the place where the employee was employed by the employer,

have ceased or diminished or are expected to cease or diminish'.

If a 'redundancy' does not fall within this definition, it will not count for ERA 1996 purposes (*Lesney Products & Co Ltd v Nolan [1977] IRLR 77*).

'Business' includes the business of an associated employer. 'Cease' and 'diminish' can each be either permanent or temporary within the definition in section 139(1) of the ERA 1996.

The Employment Appeal Tribunal (EAT) spelled out the practical position clearly in *Hachette Filipacchi UK Ltd v Johnson (2005) UKEAT/0452/05*, saying:

> 'It is now well-established that a three-stage process is involved in determining whether an employee is redundant under ERA 1996, section 139(1)(b). First, ask if the employee was dismissed. Second, ask if the requirements of the employer's business for employees to carry out work of a particular kind had ceased or diminished or were expected to cease or diminish. Third, ask whether the dismissal of the employee was caused wholly or mainly by that state of affairs.'

Note that a business reorganisation which does not entail a reduction in the number of employees, just a redistribution of responsibilities, may not fall within the definition in section 139 of the ERA 1996 if the same number of employees is still needed to carry out work of a particular kind. Subject to a fair procedure having been followed, a dismissal arising from a reorganisation will, however, probably count as 'some other substantial reason' within section 98(1) of the ERA 1996. In this situation, employees will not be entitled to any statutory redundancy payment. As an example, a general manager of a group of hotels was not dismissed by reason of redundancy when he was replaced following a business reorganisation by a combination of a senior area general manager and a junior resident manager. This was because, subject to slight changes, the hotel group's requirements for his work to be done had not ceased or diminished (*Corus & Regal Hotels plc v Wilkinson [2004] All ER (D) 370 (Mar)*).

However, the case of *Packman (t/a Packman Lucas Associates) v Fauchon [2012] ICR 1362* makes clear that a reduction in headcount is not a prerequisite to a redundancy situation. Dismissal for refusing to accept new terms is likely to amount to a redundancy where the change in terms is because of a reduction in the amount of work available for the same number of employees.

10.2 QUALIFYING FOR A STATUTORY REDUNDANCY PAYMENT

In order to qualify for a statutory redundancy payment, an individual must:

1) Be an employee, rather than self-employed (section 135 of the ERA 1996)

2) Have accrued two years' continuity of employment (section 155 of the ERA 1996)

Redundancy rights are available to fixed-term employees working under a contract if they meet these criteria.

10.3 CHALLENGING THE FAIRNESS OF REDUNDANCIES

The fact that an employee was dismissed by reason of redundancy does not, of course, mean that the dismissal was not unfair. Redundancy is no more than a *potentially* fair reason for dismissal (section 98(2)(c) of the ERA 1996).

It is important to bear in mind that an employee is normally only entitled to challenge the fairness of the decision to select them for redundancy and the failure to find alternative employment. The law generally regards the primary decision – that is, the decision to make redundancies in the first place – as a business decision on which tribunals should not sit in judgment. This is justified, rightly or wrongly, on the basis that it is not for employment tribunals to investigate the merits of industrial disputes (*Moon v Homeworthy Furniture (Northern) Ltd [1976] IRLR 298* and *James W Cook & Co (Wivenhoe) Ltd v Tipper [1990] IRLR 386*).

There are three basic methods of attacking the fairness of a redundancy dismissal:

1) Proving that the reason for selection was automatically unfair. This is usually a reason connected with pregnancy, trade union activities or the assertion of various statutory rights.

2) Where the reason for selection is not automatically unfair, proving that the dismissal was nevertheless unfair because of the method of selection. This is often the subject of arguments that the employer failed to utilise an objective method of selecting redundant candidates or that the employer had a hidden agenda and used the redundancy situation as a device to engineer the dismissal of particular employees.

3) Where the selection method is objective, proving that the redundancy process itself was unfair. This will most commonly be seen where inadequate consultation takes place or where alternative work exists but is not offered.

The EAT has recently emphasised the fact-sensitive nature of the redundancy procedure even where the employee has volunteered for redundancy. In *White v HC-One Oval Ltd [2022] IRLR 576*, Mrs Justice Eady DBE, President, held that although the claimant had requested redundancy and was then dismissed, the claimant's challenges to the redundancy procedure were not irrelevant. A claim of unfair dismissal in those circumstances could not be assumed to be 'fundamentally flawed', and therefore it was not a case capable of summary determination.

10.4 AUTOMATICALLY UNFAIR REASONS FOR REDUNDANCY

Where the reason – or principal reason – for selecting employees for redundancy falls within a prescribed category, the dismissals will be automatically unfair (section 105 of the ERA 1996). Questions of whether the

181

employer has acted reasonably in other ways – for example, by investigating alternative employment – simply do not arise.

10.5 UNREASONABLE METHOD OF SELECTION

Even if a redundancy situation exists, a dismissal will be unfair if it fails to meet the overriding test of fairness set out in section 98(4) of the ERA 1996:

'The determination of the question whether the dismissal is fair or unfair (having regard to the reason shown by the employer) –

a) depends on whether in the circumstances (including the size and

b) administrative resources of the employer's undertaking) the employer acted reasonably or unreasonably in treating it as a sufficient reason for dismissing the employee, and

c) shall be determined in accordance with equity and the substantial merits of the case.'

A tribunal may not substitute its own views of what constitutes reasonableness – either in respect of redundancy selection criteria or in respect of their implementation – for the views of the employer. Instead, it must ask itself the wider question of whether the selection was one a reasonable employer acting reasonably could have made (*Drake International t/a Drake Ports Distribution Services v O'Hare (2003) EAT 0384/03/TM, Look Ahead Housing & Care Ltd v Odili and Mendes UKEAT 0437/07* and *Amazon.co.uk Ltd v Hurdus UKEAT 0377/10*). For this reason, it is generally not appropriate for an employment tribunal to recalculate the scores of individuals in a redundancy selection process as this could lead to a substitution of the tribunal's view as to what was within the 'band of reasonable responses' open to a reasonable employer (*Semple Fraser LLP v Daly (2010) EATS/0045/09*).

By the same token, a properly conducted scoring exercise will afford an employee a fair and proper opportunity to understand it fully. An employment tribunal should not normally interfere with the outcome of such an exercise (*Pinewood Repro Ltd t/a County Print v Page [2011] ICR 508*). In a classic decision which has withstood the test of time, the EAT set out in *Williams v Compair Maxam Ltd [1982] IRLR 83* the core factors that will usually exist before an employer can be regarded as having acted fairly. These are:

1) The employer will seek to give as much warning as possible of impending redundancies to enable the union and affected employees to take early steps to inform themselves of the relevant facts, consider possible alternative solutions and, if necessary, find alternative employment in the undertaking or elsewhere.

2) The employer will consult the union as to the best means by which the desired result can be achieved fairly and with as little hardship to the employees as possible. In particular, the employer will seek to agree

with the union the criteria to be applied in selecting the employees to be made redundant. When a selection has been made, the employer will consider with the union whether the selection has been made in accordance with those criteria.

3) Whether or not criteria have been agreed with the union, the employer will seek to establish criteria for selection which, so far as is possible, do not depend solely upon the opinion of the person making the selection but can be objectively checked against such things as attendance record, efficiency at the job, experience and length of service.

4) The employer will seek to ensure that the selection is made fairly, in accordance with these criteria, and will consider any representations the union may make as to such selection.

5) The employer will seek to consider whether instead of dismissing an employee, it could offer alternative employment.

Three points must be noted:

1) If the case involved an employer where a union was recognised, the same basic principles apply where there is no recognition.

2) If the employer omits a stage, it will not automatically render the dismissal unfair.

3) The above test is not a substitute for the overriding test in the statute. Rather, it must be regarded as an indication of ordinary principles of fairness rather than a statement of legal hurdles which must be overcome (*Rolls-Royce Motors Ltd v Dewhurst [1985] IRLR 184*).

The requirements set out in *Williams* v *Compair Maxam* were restated, more succinctly, by the House of Lords in *Polkey v AE Dayton Services Ltd [1988] AC 344*, per Lord Bridge, in the following terms:

'In the case of redundancy, the employer will normally not act reasonably unless he warns and consults any employees affected or their representatives, adopts a fair decision on which to select for redundancy and takes such steps as may be reasonable to minimise a redundancy by redeployment within his own organisation.'

Finally, Acas offers extensive guidance to both employers and employees on managing redundancies (www.acas.org.uk/manage-staff-redundancies), including the selection process.

10.6 CONSULTATION

If an employer fails to consult with employees during the redundancy process, a tribunal is highly likely to find that it has failed to act reasonably. Any dismissals for redundancy will therefore be unfair.

There is a statutory obligation to consult with trade unions or elected employee representatives if an employer proposes to 'dismiss as redundant 20 or more employees at one establishment within a period of 90 days or less' (section 188 of the *Trade Union and Labour Relations (Consolidation) Act 1992* (TULR(C)A 1992)).

For consultation purposes, redundancy is given a much wider meaning in the TULR(C)A 1992 than in the ERA 1996 and is defined in section 195(1) of the TULR(C)A 1992 as a dismissal for 'a reason not related to the individual concerned or for a number of reasons all of which are not so related'.

What constitutes an 'establishment'?

In order to engage the consultation obligations under the strict wording of section 188(1) of the TULR(C)A 1992, there must be 20 or more redundancies 'at one establishment'. In *Seahorse Maritime Ltd (appellant) v Nautilus International [2019] IRLR 286*, the Court of Appeal clarified what constitutes an 'establishment' when considering whether 'support ships' could amount to 'establishments' or not. Lord Justice Underhill explained the meaning of the term at paragraphs 42-44:

> 'The identity of the employer is not in itself a relevant factor. More substantially, the reasoning in all three of the judgments from which I have quoted focuses on functional and organisational characteristics – essentially whether the putative establishment constitutes a unit – and also, which is related, whether it is a single 'place'. Employees of different subsidiaries may constitute an integrated workforce at a particular unit. There is no reason why idiosyncratic complications of that kind should govern whether a particular unit constitutes an establishment. It is enough in my view that the establishment should have a workforce assigned to it (together with the other elements in the definition [i.e. a unit to which the workers made redundant were assigned to carry out their duties]), irrespective of the identity of the employer or employers. [On the facts of the case] each ship was indeed an establishment. It is clearly a self-contained operating unit of the kind described in the case law. The only possible question is whether it can be said to have a workforce assigned to it.'

The TULR(C)A 1992 implements the *Collective Redundancies Directive 98/59/EC*, which does not refer to single establishments in the context of the duty to consult over collective redundancies. In *USDAW and anor v Ethel Austin Ltd [2015] ICR 67*, the European Court of Justice – on a reference from the Court of Appeal – held that the term 'establishment' in the Directive:

'... must be interpreted as not precluding national legislation that lays down an obligation to inform and consult workers in the event of the dismissal, within a period of 90 days, of at least 20 workers from a particular establishment of an undertaking, and not where the aggregate number of dismissals across all of the establishments or across some of the establishments of an undertaking over the same period reaches or exceeds the threshold of 20 workers'.

Whether an individual undertaking's location qualifies as an 'establishment' is a matter of fact for a national court. The key is to look at the permanence and stability of the unit that is claimed to qualify as an 'establishment' (*Athinaiki Charopoiia AE v Panagiotidis [2007] IRLR 284 ECJ*).

The obligation to consult

The statutory obligation to consult is absolute. In *Mugford v Midland Bank [1997] IRLR 208*, HHJ Peter Clark summarised the obligation as follows at paragraph 406F:

'(1) Where no consultation about redundancy has taken place with either the trade union or the employee, the dismissal will normally be unfair unless the industrial tribunal finds that a reasonable employer would have concluded that consultation would be an utterly futile exercise in the particular circumstances of the case.

(2) Consultation with the trade union over selection criteria does not of itself release the employer from considering with the employee individually his being identified for redundancy.

(3) It will be a question of fact and degree for the industrial tribunal to consider whether consultation with the individual and/or his union was so inadequate as to render the dismissal unfair. A lack of consultation in any particular respect will not automatically lead to that result. The overall picture must be viewed by the tribunal up to the date of termination to ascertain whether the employer has or has not acted reasonably in dismissing the employee on the grounds of redundancy.'

Employers should also take into account the *Information and Consultation of Employees Regulations 2004.* These require affected employers to have in place arrangements giving employees the opportunity to be informed and consulted on management decisions affecting their future, such as decisions relating to changes in work organisation or contractual relations, including redundancies. These regulations apply to any employer with 50 or more employees.

10.6.1 WITH WHOM SHOULD EMPLOYERS CONSULT?

An employer must consult with any trade union that it recognises. If there is no trade union, the employees must be given the opportunity to elect employee representatives. The procedure for this is set out in section 188A of the TULR(C)A 1992. If the employees fail to elect representatives, the employer must give all those affected the information it would have had to give to the representatives.

10.6.2 HOW LONG SHOULD CONSULTATION TAKE?

There is a statutory obligation to consult if an employer proposes to make 20 or more people redundant from one establishment within a period of 90 days (section 188 of the TULR(C)A 1992). Where the statutory rules apply – if 20 or more people are being dismissed at one establishment by reason of redundancy – section 188(1A) of the TULR(C)A 1992 requires that the employer must begin consultation 'in good time' and, in any event, 30 days before the first of the dismissals takes effect. This increases to 45 days if the number of redundancies is 100 or more.

Where collective consultation is required before redundancies are made, this must be completed before notice of dismissal is given to any of the employees concerned (*Junk v Wolfgang Kuhnel (Case C-188/03) [2005] ECR I-885 ECJ*). The effect of this is that an employer proposing to dismiss 20 or more employees by reason of redundancy must complete the required 30 or 45 days' consultation *before* notice of dismissal is given to any employee. This is reflected in the EAT's judgment in *Leicestershire County Council v Unison [2005] IRLR 920*. The test of 'in good time' is slightly less stringent than the old test of 'at the earliest opportunity' (*MSF v Refuge Assurance plc [2002] IRLR 324*, and *Amicus v Nissan Motor Manufacturing (UK) Ltd (2005) UKEAT/0184/05*). Failure to consult sufficiently early may lead to an enhanced compensatory award (*Elkouil v Coney Island Ltd [2002] IRLR 174*) in addition to a protective award under the statutory collective consultation requirements (section 188 of the TULR(C)A 1992).

In *Carillion Services Ltd v Benson [2022] IRLR 39*, the EAT found that the employment tribunal had not erred in concluding that there were no special circumstances capable of rendering it not reasonably practicable to comply with the duty of collective consultation. There are three distinct stages in the analysis: (1) were there special circumstances? If so, (2) did they render compliance with section 188 of the TULR(C)A 1992 not reasonably practicable? And, if so, (3) did the employers take all such steps towards compliance with section of the TULR(C)A 1992 as were reasonably practicable in the circumstances? Given the sequential analysis, the second question only falls to be considered if the burden of showing that there were special circumstances has been discharged.

There is no specific expiry time for consultation, although section 188 of the TULR(C)A 1992 is not indefinitely 'elastic'. In one case, an employer was held to have complied when consultation started in January 2003 but the redundancy dismissals did not take place until almost two years later. This was because, throughout the intervening period, there was an ongoing meaningful and effective consultation concerning the same employees and the same prospective redundancies (*Vauxhall Motors Ltd v Transport and General Workers Union [2006] IRLR 674*).

The adequacy of consultation required where the statutory provisions do not apply – for example, because fewer than 20 people are to be made redundant – is, of course, a matter of fact and degree for the tribunal to determine. The EAT has stated that 'in our judgment, it falls short of an adequate and reasonable standard of consultation for an employee to be told on Monday that he is selected for redundancy dismissal intended to take place on Friday' (*Chronos Richardson Ltd v Watson [2001] All ER (D) 319*).

An employer has a separate obligation, under section 193 of the TULR(C) A 1992 to give advance notice to the Department for Business, Energy and Industrial Strategy (BEIS) if the employer proposes to make 20 or more employees redundant. This notice should be given on Form HR1 (you can find Form HR1 easily with a web search). Failure to notify the BEIS is a criminal offence and is increasingly commonly prosecuted (section 194 of the TULR(C) A 1992). However, such a failure will not affect the fairness or unfairness of any dismissals.

10.6.3 WHAT SHOULD THE CONSULTATIONS COMPRISE?

The consultation must include specific items. These are ways of:

- Avoiding the dismissals
- Reducing the number of employees to be dismissed
- Mitigating the consequences of the dismissals

It is also common – albeit not obligatory – to consult with unions and representatives over the selection criteria. Many unions avoid discussion about selection criteria for internal political reasons – they do not want to be seen supporting criteria that might favour some members over others. Provided an employer has tried to consult over selection criteria, it will be likely to have acted reasonably (section 188(4) and 188(6) of the TULR(C)A 1992).

Consultation must be 'with a view to reaching agreement', so employers must give unions and/or employees adequate information and time to respond. Any response must be conscientiously considered by the employer. This does not mean that the employer is obliged to accede to the demands of the union and/or employees. Provided the employer acts in good faith, gives proper consideration to their arguments, and does not unreasonably reject suggestions, it will have complied with its duty to consult (section 18(6) of the TULR(C)A 1992, *R v British Coal Corp, ex parte Price (No.3) [1994] IRLR 72 Admin Ct* and *Rowell v Hubbard Group Services Ltd [1995] IRLR 195*).

In *Lambe v 186K Ltd [2005] ICR C307*, Wall LJ confirmed the criteria for fair consultation set out by the EAT in *King v Eaton [1996] IRLR 199 ScotCS*, saying that fair consultation means:

1) Consultation when the proposals are still at a formative stage;

2) Adequate information on which to respond;

3) Adequate time in which to respond; and

4) Conscientious consideration by the employer of the response to consultation.

The larger the employer (and the greater the number of proposed redundancies), the more formal the consultation process should be. Smallness does not justify a failure to consult, but it will justify less formality (*De Grasse v Stockwell Ltd [1992] IRLR 269*).

A dismissal by reason of redundancy will generally be unfair if the employer has failed to inform the employee how the selection criteria have been applied to them personally (*Bond v Urmet Gomus Communication & Security UK Ltd (2010) UKEAT/0103/10*).

Where a business is closing, consultation over redundancies must extend to the reasons for the closure causing them. On the basis of older authorities, notably *R v British Coal etc, ex parte Vardy & ors [1993] ICR 720 QBD*, it had seemed that the duty to consult is concerned only with how a redundancy programme would be carried out and never with whether there should be redundancies.

In *UK Coal Mining Ltd v National Union of Mineworkers [2008] ICR 163*, Elias J held that:

'[T]he obligation to consult over avoiding the proposed redundancies inevitably involves engaging with the reasons for the dismissals, and that in turn requires consultation over the reasons for the closure'.

Where redundancies follow from the closure of a business, it will therefore only be in the rare situation when they could be avoided that consultation over the closure decision itself will not be needed. The extent to which, if at all, this case has any application in a 'non-closure' context remains uncertain.

10.7 ESTABLISHING THE POOL OF REDUNDANCY CANDIDATES

Before the selection of employees can take place, the employer needs to establish the pool from which to select. Sometimes, this will be obvious. For example, if an entire workforce or building is closing down, the pool might be that workforce or those who work in the building. Alternatively, in a small company, if two secretaries are to be made redundant, the pool may comprise both secretaries. Failure to consider employees doing similar work from more than one division of an enterprise can be considered unreasonable (*Kvaerner Oil and Gas Ltd v Parker & ors (2003) EAT/0444/02*). Similarly, where a group of six workers skilled in operating a specific machine but also skilled in other activities were selected for redundancy when the machine was decommissioned, it was held that the selection pool should have included the department's other employees. The dismissals were therefore unfair (*Hendy Banks City Print Ltd v Fairbrother & ors (2004) UKEAT/0691/04*).

The pool from which the employee – or employees – is to be selected must include all relevant employees and not just those occupying the precise position being made redundant (*Fulcrum Pharma (Europe) Ltd v Bonassera & anor (2010) UKEAT/0198/10*).

Provided the employer can provide a sensible explanation for the pool, the employee cannot criticise this before the tribunal. Again, this is a fundamental business decision and not one with which tribunals will interfere unless the decision is perverse (for example, employees with red hair), discriminatory (for example, part-time workers) or taken in bad faith (*Earl of Bradford v Jowett (No.2) [1978] IRLR 16*).

In *Mogane v Bradford Teaching Hospitals NHS Foundation Trust and anor [2023] IRLR 44*, the EAT held that the implied term of mutual trust and confidence must mean that an employer will not act arbitrarily between employees. That requirement impacts the decision regarding the selection pool in order that any decision is fair between employees and not arbitrary. On the facts of the case, a decision to place the claimant in a pool of one purely on the basis that her contract was the one up for renewal the soonest was arbitrary.

In *Citibank NA and ors v Kirk [2022] IRLR 925*, the EAT held that although it is unusual for employees of different ranks to be included in a selection pool, it can occur and is not necessarily unfair when it does, if there is a realistic prospect of the lower-ranked person succeeding.

10.7.1 THE SELECTION PROCESS

The first stage in the selection process is to establish the selection criteria. If the employer is consulting with a union or employee representatives, this may form a significant part of the consultation process.

The crucial point about the criteria is that they should be capable of some element of objective assessment. 'Disciplinary record' is capable of objective assessment. 'Strategic implementation planning ability' would mean wholly different things to different people and any assessments could therefore be inconsistent and unfair.

An employment tribunal must not substitute its own views of what constitutes reasonableness in respect of either redundancy selection criteria or their implementation for the views of the employer. What matters is whether the selection was one that a reasonable employer acting reasonably could have made (*Look Ahead Housing & Care Ltd v (1) Odili (2) Mendes [2008] All ER (D) 229 (Feb)*).

10.7.2 LAST IN, FIRST OUT

'Last in, first out' (LIFO) was the standard redundancy criterion during the 1970s. It was a simple method of selection: employees would be selected for redundancy in the order in which they joined the company, the most recent joiners being dismissed first. Because of the difficulties this sometimes caused when employers found themselves employing a predominantly middle-aged/ elderly workforce, an occasional alternative was 'first in, first out' (FIFO).

Selection for redundancy on the basis of age has been unlawful since 1 October 2006 (*Employment Equality (Age) Regulations 2006* and now the *Equality Act 2010* (EqA 2010)). This will be especially likely if the 'last in' are generally the youngest. However, if the age discrimination can be justified as 'a proportionate means of achieving a legitimate aim', it will not be unlawful (section 13(2) of the EqA 2010).

There is also a risk that a LIFO approach might be regarded as indirect sex or race discrimination where the business has been traditionally dominated by one gender, or race, and a more diverse range of employees has only recently been employed. If a business had historically employed mainly white men, then LIFO may have a disproportionate impact on women, and/or non-white employees. To avoid a finding of discrimination, an employer would have to show that the choice of LIFO as the selection criterion was objectively justified.

Acas offers guidance on avoiding discrimination and other pitfalls while establishing selection criteria (www.acas.org.uk/manage-staff-redundancies/select-employees-for-redundancy).

10.7.3 THE MATRIX METHOD

A common method of redundancy selection is to draw up a list of criteria and assign scores to each employee under each one. The scores are added up, and the employees with the lowest cumulative score are selected for redundancy.

Common criteria include:

- Length of service
- Disciplinary record
- Qualifications
- Leadership skills

- Productivity
- Cost to the business

Some of these, notably leadership skills and productivity, run the risk that they may not be capable of objective assessment and – if used – the scores should be supported by independent evidence.

Attendance and time-keeping records should be used with caution as redundancy criteria. Any periods off work relating to maternity or parental leave should be ignored, as should any accrued when workers exercise their right to time off to care for dependants in an emergency.

Special consideration must be given to those who suffer from a disability within the meaning of the EqA 2010. Whether a disabled employee is at a substantial disadvantage in a redundancy selection process is a question of fact. That involves considering the extent to which the disabled employee's chances of scoring as well as an employee who is not disabled are adversely affected by the disability. It also requires making any reasonable adjustments needed to ensure that the disabled person is not at a disadvantage because of their disability. However, an employer is not obliged to make any adjustment to a role to remedy a 'substantial disadvantage' before a potential candidate had applied for a job (*NTL Group Ltd v Difolco [2006] EWCA Civ 1508*).

Selection of a part-time employee for redundancy in preference to a full-time employee would be a breach of the *Part-time Workers (Prevention of Less Favourable Treatment) Regulations 2000* unless it could be justified on objective grounds (*Hendrickson Europe Ltd v Pipe (2003) EAT/0272/02*).

10.7.4 CONSULTATION AND DISCLOSURE OF SELECTION CRITERIA TO EMPLOYEES

It is good practice to consult with individual employees on their scores so that they can comment on whether they feel they have been unfairly marked down in any categories. This raises a controversial question: is it necessary to show the employees the scores of others? To disclose other employees' scores breaches principles of confidentiality and can result in an enormous amount of management time justifying minor discrepancies in scores. Then again, to withhold details of other scorings renders the entire process of limited value, because it is difficult to comment on what are, effectively, comparative markings.

The authorities are not consistent, making it difficult to provide clear advice. One approach is seen in *Eaton v King [1995] IRLR 75*, upheld in *British Aerospace plc v Green [1995] IRLR 433*, in which it was held that there was no obligation to disclose scores to employees.

The opposite approach is seen in *John Brown Engineering Ltd v Brown [1997] IRLR 90*. In that case, employees were not even given their own assessments when invited to comment on their selection for redundancy. The tribunal described the process as a 'sham', and the EAT upheld that decision. The EAT commented that 'it may be invidious to publish the whole identified "league tables", but in choosing not to do so, the employer must run the risk that he is not acting fairly in respect of individual employees'. Similarly, in *Pinewood Repro Ltd (t/a County Print) v Page [2011] ICR 508*, the EAT held that while an employer was not obliged to justify the individual scores awarded, it was required to give employees adequate information to allow them to comment and respond.

A sensible compromise in a small company might be to make all scores available to employees while anonymising the identities. In a larger company, a representative sample of (anonymised) scores could be made available. The employees' own scores should always be given to them for comment.

10.7.5 ARE THERE EXCEPTIONS TO THE NEED TO CONSULT?

If an employer can persuade the tribunal that consultation would have been 'utterly useless or futile' (*Polkey*), then it might have acted reasonably in not consulting and the dismissals will be fair. A deliberate decision that consultation would be futile does not need to be taken at the time: the question is whether a reasonable employer would have dismissed without consultation in the circumstances.

One case in which a failure to consult was upheld as reasonable was where the employer's business was vulnerable to industrial espionage. As a result, it had been agreed with the unions that staff who were made redundant would leave the employer's premises immediately (*Duncan v Marconi Command & Control Systems Ltd (unreported, EAT, 1988)*). Similarly, an employer was able to justify departure from best practice where the business was small and failing and consultation was pointless (*Warner v Adnet Ltd [1998] ICR 1056*). These are exceptional cases, however, and in practice, it is very difficult to persuade a tribunal that consultation would have been 'utterly useless or futile' (*Polkey; Duffy v Yeomans & Partners Ltd [1994] IRLR 642*).

10.8 SUITABLE ALTERNATIVE EMPLOYMENT

Legal wisdom dictates that an employer will always strain to avoid dismissing employees. When the spectre of redundancy raises its head, any reasonable employer would always look for, and offer, suitable alternative employment to affected employees. Further, a reasonable employer would seek out suitable alternative employment within the companies of any associated employers. Any employer who fails to offer suitable alternative employment when it is available is therefore acting unreasonably and thus rendering the dismissal unfair.

Note that employees lose the right to claim a redundancy payment if they accept an offer of alternative employment (subject to a four-week trial period, see below) or unreasonably refuse an offer of suitable alternative employment from the employer or an associated employer (section 138 and section 141 of the ERA 1996).

In all but the smallest companies, the employer should be able to demonstrate that it has considered alternative employment (if appropriate, with associated employers) and discussed it with the employee. The employer should also raise alternative employment at the consultation stage: the employee may be aware of suitable work that the employer is not.

10.8.1 WHAT IS SUITABLE ALTERNATIVE EMPLOYMENT?

This is an objective test (*Jones v MEM Marketing Retail Services (2008) UKEAT0375/07*). It is for the employer to prove that the offered employment is suitable.

Suitability is a question of fact and degree for employment tribunals to consider. Employees disentitle themselves from receiving statutory redundancy pay if they unreasonably refuse an offer of suitable alternative employment. When deciding whether refusal is unreasonable, a tribunal may take into account matters specific to the employee, and a small reduction in pay or status may be more relevant here. Examples of relevant issues to both questions are:

- Loss of status (*Taylor v Kent County Council [1969] 2 QB 560* and *Cambridge & District Co-operative Society Ltd v Ruse [1993] IRLR 156*)

- Travel (*Bass Leisure Ltd v Thomas [1994] IRLR 104* and *Douce v F Bond & Sons Ltd [1966] 1 ITR 365*)

- Working arrangements (*Morrison & Poole v Cramic Engineering Co Ltd [1966] 1 ITR 404* and *O'Connor v Montrose Canned Foods Ltd [1966] 1 ITR 171*)

- Family circumstances (*Bainbridge v Westinghouse Brake & Signal Co Ltd [1966] 1 ITR 55*)

An employee who is made redundant following an unsuccessful application for an alternative role with his employer cannot be said to be unfairly dismissed where the appointment process for the alternative role was objective and fair (*Morgan v Welsh Rugby Union [2011] IRLR 376*).

To ensure an offer of suitable alternative employment is handled reasonably – failing which the redundancy dismissal will be unfair – an employer must give priority to potentially redundant employees and appoint them to vacancies for which they are suited even though there may be better external candidates (*Corus Hotels plc v Williams (2006) UKEAT/0014/06*). This obligation does not, of course, extend to meaning that an employer must appoint someone to a post for which they are not suitable.

Each case has to be considered on its own merits. Precedent is not of great help, but a redundancy dismissal will likely amount to unfair dismissal if the employer fails to provide the employee concerned with full information – including salary levels if known – about alternative jobs available within the same group. In such a case, the employee's failure to express interest or to request further information can be a factor to be considered to reduce any compensatory award on grounds of contributory fault (*Fisher v Hoopoe Finance Ltd (2005) UKEAT/0043/05*).

The offer of alternative employment need not be put in writing, although, for evidential purposes, it is prudent for an employer to do so. It should contain sufficient information for the employee to make a decision on whether or not to accept and should be made before the original employment ends. In order to qualify, and so disentitle the employee to a redundancy payment, the new job must start immediately or within four weeks of the old job finishing.

The EAT has held that the further up the seniority ladder an employee is, the more proactive an employer can expect the employee to be when it comes to suggesting alternative employment – particularly if the employee wishes to be considered for a less senior or well-paid post. In *Whittle v Parity Training (2003) EAT/0573/02*, the EAT approved the proposition that:

> 'The duty on an employer is only to take reasonable steps, not to take every conceivable step possible, to find the employee alternative employment' and that it follows that if an employee at senior management level who is being made redundant is prepared to accept a subordinate position, he ought, in fairness, to make this clear at an early stage so as to give his employer an opportunity to see if that is a feasible solution.'

In *Aramark Ltd v Fernandes [2020] IRLR 861*, the EAT recognised that section 98(4) of the ERA 1996 focuses on whether the employer has offered reasonable alternatives to dismissal such that dismissal would thereby be avoided. In *Aramark* the employer had a practice of maintaining a list of staff to whom it would offer ad hoc employment, providing, at best, a reasonable prospect of work. The employment tribunal had found it was unfair for the claimant to have been dismissed without being placed on the list. Lord Summer overturned the decision on the basis that being placed on the list merely opened the prospect of work; it did not secure work. Therefore, the employer's decision not to place him on the list was not a decision that fell within the scope of section 98(4) of the ERA 1996, which addressed the mischief of dismissal. It did not provide a statutory right to an alternative that might have had the potential to mitigate the adverse effects of dismissal.

10.8.2 EMPLOYEES ON MATERNITY, PARENTAL OR ADOPTION LEAVE

When selecting for redundancy, an employer must be careful not to use selection criteria which place those who have been off work on parental leave at a disadvantage. Additional special rules apply to parents on maternity or adoption leave (*Riezniece v Zemkopibas Ministrija (Case C-7/12) [2014] 1 CMLR 6*).

If a woman on maternity leave is to be made redundant, she 'is entitled to be offered' suitable alternative employment (regulation 10 of the *Maternity and Parental Leave Regulations 1999* (MPLR 1999)). It seems that this will be so even if she is not the best candidate (*Archibald v Fife Council [2004] ICR 954*). This is an important disability discrimination case, but the same general principle may well apply. In other words, a woman on maternity leave comes first in the queue and trumps all other employees when the employer decides to whom a limited number of suitable alternative posts should be offered. The same wording has been used in regulation 23(2) of the *Paternity and Adoption Leave Regulations 2002*, in the section which covers redundancy during adoption leave. Failure to offer suitable alternative employment will render the dismissal automatically unfair.

It is worth noting that the statutory protection which allows employers to afford special treatment to mothers is not an automatic blanket protection but must be interpreted in a way which is no more than 'reasonably necessary to compensate them for the disadvantages occasioned by their condition' (*Eversheds Legal Services Ltd v de Belin [2011] IRLR 448*). Further, in the process of establishing whether there is a 'suitable available vacancy', where an otherwise-redundant employee is returning to work after maternity leave, the employer can properly make its own fair, objective assessment of what is 'suitable' (regulation 10 of the MPLR 1999). In *Simpson v Endsleigh Insurance Services Ltd & ors [2011] ICR 75*, the dismissal was found not to be unfair.

It used to be that in the case of small employers – that is, employers with five or fewer employees, inclusive of employees of an associated employer – it was not automatically unfair dismissal if the employer could show it was not reasonably practicable to permit a woman on maternity leave to return. However, this is no longer the case as regulation 20(6) of the MPLR 1999 was revoked by the *Maternity and Parental Leave etc and the Paternity and Adoption Leave (Amendment) Regulations 2006*.

The Equality and Human Rights Commission, in association with Acas, has a Good Practice Guide on Managing Redundancy for Pregnant Employees or those on Maternity Leave (www.equalityhumanrights.com/sites/default/files/managing_redundancy_for_maternity_and_pregnancy_final.pdf).

10.8.3 TRIAL PERIOD

Anyone offered suitable alternative employment is entitled to a statutory trial period of four calendar (as opposed to working) weeks. This means time continues to run even when the workplace is closed for a seasonal holiday (section 138(2)(b) of the ERA 1996). If either party terminates the employment during the trial period, then the dismissal is deemed to be by reason of redundancy. However, if the employee unreasonably resigns, and if the alternative employment was suitable, they cease to be entitled to a redundancy payment (*Benton v Sanderson Kayser Ltd [1989] IRLR 19*).

It is unreasonable, and may render any constructive dismissal unfair, to insist that the employee accepts or rejects the new job offer without allowing a four-week trial period (*Elliott v Richard Stump Ltd [1987] IRLR 215*).

The statutory four-week trial period may be extended for longer than four weeks if, and only if:

- It is for the purpose of retraining the employee for the new job

- It is agreed in writing, setting out the date on which the period of retraining ends

- It was agreed before the employee started work in the new job

- The agreement specifies the terms and conditions of employment which will apply at the end of the trial period (section 138(6) of the ERA 1996)

Where there is an extended trial period beyond the four weeks, the specified conditions must be strictly observed for the employee to remain entitled to statutory redundancy pay if they decide not to continue (*O'Hara v Reality (White Arrow Express) Ltd (unreported, EAT, 18 November 2003)*).

There is no room for a 'common-law reasonable' period to run alongside the statutory four weeks (*Optical Express v Williams [2008] ICR 1*).

10.9 BUMPING

There is a question mark over whether 'transferred redundancies' – known as 'bumping' – fall within the statutory definition of redundancy. Bumping is where one employee is dismissed to make way for another whose position no longer exists.

There are two views regarding whether a 'bumped' employee has or has not been dismissed by reason of redundancy. Back in 1981, in *Elliott Turbomachinery Ltd v Bates [1981] ICR 218*, the EAT said:

'... experienced as we are in this general area of industrial relations law, our immediate reaction was that a dismissal on the grounds of redundancy must ... relate the cessation or diminution of work to the dismissal of the particular man. We were soon shown to be wrong when we were referred to *W Gimber & Sons Ltd v Spurrett (1967) 2 ITR 308* ... Lord Parker ... giving the leading judgment, quoted and approved the words used by the industrial tribunal:

> "If there is a reduction in the requirements for employees in one section of an employer's business and an employee who becomes surplus or redundant is transferred to another section of that business, an employee who is displaced by the transfer of the first employee and is dismissed by reason of that displacement is dismissed by reason of redundancy".

This seems to be the generally accepted position. However, in *Church v West Lancashire NHS Trust [1998] IRLR 4*, the EAT held that a bumped employee does not fall within the definition of redundancy because there was no diminution in the requirement for work of the particular kind they were employed to do. Although the EAT gave permission to appeal to the Court of Appeal, the case was not pursued further.

In a later House of Lords case, the generally accepted position seemed to be restored (*Murray & anor v Foyle Meats Ltd [1999] ICR 827*). *Murray* was not directly concerned with 'bumped redundancies', and as the House of Lords made no reference to *Church* in its judgment, there is perhaps still scope to argue that the EAT was right in ruling that a 'bumped redundancy' dismissal is not 'by reason of redundancy'.

10.10 TIME OFF WORK

An employee who is under notice of redundancy and who has accrued two years' continuity of employment is entitled to time off work to look for a new job or arrange training for future employment. There is no limit to how much time off work can be taken, save that it must be 'reasonable' (section 52 of the ERA 1996).

However, this time off is not well remunerated. Employees are entitled to be paid on a pro rata hourly basis for each hour taken off but only to an absolute maximum of 40% of one week's pay. (The statutory cap on a week's pay which applies for some purposes does not apply here.) This maximum applies to the entire notice period. So, an employee earning £52,000 per annum who is under one month's notice of redundancy, and who takes a total of two weeks off, will only be entitled to a maximum of £400 (that is, 40% of one week's pay). In such circumstances, it makes sense to investigate whether the contract provides greater rights to payment than does statute (section 53 of the ERA 1996).

10.11 APPEALS

There is no obligation, as a matter of general fairness, to provide an appeal against a redundancy decision. In *Gwynedd Council v Barratt [2021] IRLR 1028*, the Court of Appeal emphasised that if the original selection for redundancy was in accordance with a fair procedure, then the absence of an appeal is not fatal to the employer's defence. On the facts of *Gwynedd*, an employment tribunal was entitled to find that the failure to offer the right of appeal to staff was unfair, and to state that it would only be in 'truly exceptional circumstances' that an employer could dispense with an appeal without invalidating its conclusions on unfair dismissal. It remains the case that a failure to offer an appeal against selection for redundancy will not, on its own, render a dismissal unfair (*Robinson v Ulster Carpet Mills [1991] IRLR 348*). However, it remains good practice to offer an appeal, and it is something that Acas recommends (www.acas.org.uk/manage-staff-redundancies/select-employees-for-redundancy).

CHAPTER 11

TRANSFER OF UNDERTAKINGS

11.0 OVERVIEW

When a business, or part of a business, is taken over or a business's activities are moved from one employer to another, staff will inevitably be worried about their jobs and the conditions in which they work. Meanwhile, both the old and new employer need to understand their obligations and know whether and how working conditions can be changed.

The rules for this are found in the *Transfer of Undertakings (Protection of Employment) Regulations 2006* (TUPE Regulations 2006). They implement *EU Directive 2001/23/EC* (the Directive). The priority, as laid out in Recital 3 of the Directive, is to safeguard employees' rights when the identity of their employer changes.

The law which has grown up surrounding TUPE calls for a 'straightforward', 'common-sense' and 'pragmatic' approach to the statutory language. Unfortunately, the application of that language has turned out to be far from straightforward. It is important, therefore, to be precise when trying to determine where TUPE applies, to whom, what employers must do and what rights are protected.

11.1 WHEN DO THE REGULATIONS APPLY?

TUPE rights for employees arise in two situations:

1) The transfer of a business or undertaking from one employer to another

2) A service provision change, which covers contracting out and contracting in

11.1.1 THE TRANSFER OF A BUSINESS OR UNDERTAKING

Under Regulation 3(1)(a) of the TUPE Regulations 2006, TUPE applies where there has been:

'A transfer of an undertaking, business or part of an undertaking or business situated immediately before the transfer in the UK to another person where there is a transfer of an economic entity which retains its identity.'

Determining whether a change of employer from transferor to transferee (that is, the old and new employer respectively) falls under TUPE is a two-step question:

1) Is there an economic entity which counts as an undertaking, and retains its identity, or an 'identifiable economic entity'?

2) Is the transfer itself a 'relevant transfer' for the purpose of TUPE?

These questions should normally be considered separately, and in turn (*Whitewater Leisure Management Ltd v Barnes & ors [2000] IRLR 456 EAT*). A failure by a tribunal first to define the identifiable economic entity, if there is one, is likely to make it harder to work out whether a relevant transfer has taken place – and therefore to risk an error of law.

An identifiable economic entity?

As with most questions under TUPE, the courts treat this issue as highly fact-sensitive and have declined to identify any exhaustive list of factors. However, in *Cheesman v Brewer Contracts [2001] IRLR 144*, Lindsay J set out a number of points which later tribunals have taken as their starting point:

- There should be a stable economic entity: an organised grouping of persons and assets enabling, or facilitating, the exercise of an economic activity pursuing a single objective on more than a one-off or casual basis.

- It should be structured and autonomous (although it does not necessarily have to have significant assets). There should be a recognisable continuum in function and activity, although there is no need for the entity being transferred to be organisationally separate prior to the transfer, so long as it is once it is with the transferee (*Fairhurst Ward Abbotts Ltd v Botes Building Ltd & ors [2004] ICR 919 CA*).

- Depending on the sector in which it operates – for instance, in the service sector – the entity's identity may, in effect, be reduced to its staff and what they do rather than any non-human assets or property.

- An organised group of wage earners specifically and permanently assigned to a common task may be enough to amount to an entity. Indeed, a single wage earner may, in principle, suffice to comprise an entity – as the Employment Appeal Tribunal (EAT) found in *Dudley Bower Building Services Ltd v Lowe & ors [2003] ICR 843* – although that would require some underpinning of complexity in the activity being performed.

- But the activity in itself is not an entity. That must emerge from other factors, such as workforce, management, how its work is organised and carried out and the resources available to it.

The focus throughout is on the transferred entity, not on the transferor's or transferee's business as a whole: the activity the entity is undertaking can be 'ancillary' rather than central to the transferor's business, as regulation 3(2) of the TUPE Regulations 2006 states. The tribunal's job is to weigh up the *Cheesman* factors', as they are known, and whatever other factors appear to a tribunal to be relevant to decide whether a 'stable economic entity' exists. Since what is relevant will vary hugely depending on the facts of the matter, a tribunal's decision on this point is unlikely to be overturned on appeal unless it is so clearly wrong as to be perverse – for instance, by focusing on one factor to the exclusion of others which are clearly relevant.

A relevant transfer?

Cheesman v Brewer is also a key authority in working out whether a transfer has, for TUPE purposes, taken place, with Lindsay J providing a still longer list of matters to be taken into consideration – again, balancing all the relevant factors and not focusing on any one in isolation:

- A decisive factor is whether identity is preserved, indicated, among other things, by whether the entity has, in fact, continued or resumed its operations.

- A transfer is not precluded just because – in a labour-intensive sector the transferred entity not only continues its own activity but also absorbs employees already carrying out that activity in the transferee.

- The type of undertaking, whether or not tangible assets are transferred, the value of intangible assets, what proportion (a majority or not) of the entity's employees transfer, how similar the activities are before and after the transfer and for how long – if at all – they are suspended are all relevant factors if the facts require their consideration. The weight given to any one factor will vary depending on the nature of the entity and the activity it undertakes.

- A relevant transfer can still take place if assets required to run the undertaking are not passed from transferor to transferee. Conversely, if significant tangible or intangible assets are not required, logically the existence of a relevant transfer cannot depend on whether or not such assets changed hands.

- The mere fact that the service provided by the old and new undertaking is similar does not mean a relevant transfer has taken place.

- No direct contractual relationship between transferor and transferee is required. If there is no contractual link between transferor and transferee, that may be evidence that no relevant transfer has taken place, but it will not be conclusive.

- If no employees are transferred, the reasons why this is the case may be relevant to whether or not a relevant transfer took place.

- It is normal for work to be performed continuously without interruption or change across the time of transfer, but the existence of a gap is not necessarily important (*Inex Home Improvements Ltd v Hodgkins [2016] ICR 71 EAT*).

- A 'transfer of administrative functions between public administrative authorities' is not a relevant transfer – so a shake-up within the public sector of genuinely public functions is not a TUPE transfer. But as was analysed in detail by the EAT in *Nicholls v London Borough of Croydon [2019] ICR 542*, public authorities often carry out functions which amount to 'economic activities'; and unless the function is a 'core state activity' which is 'necessarily' carried out by public entities, to which commercial considerations would be alien, TUPE is likely to apply.

It may sound obvious, but a transfer must remove the transferor from the employment relationship altogether. If the transferor retains a role – for instance, if additional employers join the relationship without wholly supplanting the transferor – no relevant transfer has taken place (*Hyde Housing Association Ltd v Layton [2016] IRLR 107*).

Share sales

TUPE applies where the identity of one of the parties to an employment contract has changed. Because of this, under regulation 3(1)(a) of the TUPE Regulations 2006, a share sale – where ownership changes but the parties to the employment contract do not – will not normally be a TUPE transfer.

There are exceptions. Inevitably, when ownership changes, changes in strategy may follow, filtering down to changes in working practices, contracts and people. The more direct those changes are and the more the new owner assumes day-to-day control of the undertaking, the more likely the share sale is to be considered a TUPE transfer. In *Print Factory (London) 1991 Ltd v Millam [2007] ICR 1331*, the Court of Appeal found that the legal structure was not decisive where practical management of operations, not merely overall control, transfers to the new owner.

The *Millam* test was refined in *ICAP Management Services v Berry & anor [2017] IRLR 811*, in which Garnham J identified key questions as being the degree to which the new owner has become responsible for carrying on the business, has incurred the obligations of an employer and has taken over the day-to-day running of the business. But he also stressed that changes away from the front line, such as setting new targets or amalgamating duplicated services, were not in themselves indicators of a relevant transfer.

As with other TUPE issues, it is important not to fixate on any one factor or group of factors. The items on the *ICAP* list are not necessary factors, as the EAT found in *Guvera Ltd v Butler EAT/0265/16*, but simply some of those which should be considered. (The EAT also noted that it did not matter which entity paid staff wages.) The true test, the tribunal had found and the EAT agreed, was to look for control which:

> '... went beyond the mere exercise of ordinary supervision or information gathering between parent and subsidiary' and to look for 'the measure of practical influence or control which practically comes with being a parent company, and the greater degree of day-to-day control which must be assumed for a transfer to occur'.

11.1.2 SERVICE PROVISION CHANGES

In recent decades, an increasing number of organisations have sought to focus on 'core' activities, contracting out others to external service providers – in some cases, a succession of them. Sometimes, contracting out is reversed, and services are brought back in-house. So long as certain conditions are met, TUPE applies to all three such scenarios (regulation 3(1)(b) of the TUPE Regulations 2006):

1) First-generation outsourcing, where a 'client' transfers an activity to a 'contractor' which was previously done in-house

2) Second-generation outsourcing, where the service moves from one contractor to another (whether or not the client originally did it for itself)

3) Contracting in, or 'insourcing', where the client brings a contracted service in-house, whether for the first time or bringing it back

It should be noted that a TUPE transfer can take place where there are multiple clients, as well as where there is only one (*Ottimo Property Services Ltd v Duncan [2015] IRLR 806 EAT*). The key is to identify the 'real' client (or clients), not merely on the basis of strict legal relationships but also on the basis of the facts before the tribunal (*Horizon Security Services Ltd v Ndeze UKEAT/0071/14*). So, even if a subcontractor's only contractual relationship is with the contractor, the 'client' can still – depending on the facts – be the ultimate recipient of the services, even though no direct legal relationship exists between the two (*Jinks v Havering LBC UKEAT/0157/14/MC*).

However, the client must remain the same (*Hunter v McCarrick [2013] ICR 235 CA*) and the activity must also 'fundamentally or essentially' remain unchanged (*Metropolitan Resources Ltd v Churchill Dulwich Ltd [2009] ICR 1380 EAT*). So, essentially, must the work done: any significant 'change in scope', meaning a more than minor difference in what activities are carried out and how, is likely to put the transfer outside TUPE's reach (*Tuitt v London Borough of Richmond upon Thames [2022] EAT 124*). A further important consideration arising from *Metropolitan Resources* is that unlike the 'multi-factorial' approach required for business transfers, the right approach to the language of regulation 3(1)(b) of the TUPE Regulations 2006 was a 'common-sense and pragmatic one', taking the wording at face value rather than balancing a range of factors. Similarly, it is the reality of what happens in the business which defines the nature of the service provision, not just what the contracts say (*ALHCO Group Ltd v Griffin & another UKEAT/0007/14/BA*).

What conditions apply?

The conditions are found in regulation 3(3) of the TUPE Regulations 2006. All three must be met for a TUPE transfer to have taken place.

'An organised grouping of employees'

There must be, immediately before the change, an 'organised grouping of employees situated in Great Britain which has as its principal purpose the carrying out of the activities concerned on behalf of the client' (regulation 3(3)(a)(i) of the TUPE Regulations 2006). In other words, there must be some intentional rather than circumstantial grouping of staff whose main role is to perform the services in question (*Eddie Stobart Ltd v Moreman & ors [2012] ICR 919 EAT*) – although, as with the question of a relevant transfer, a gap in provision will not in itself stop TUPE applying to a service provision change (*Mustafa v Trek Highways Services Ltd [2016] IRLR 326 EAT*).

'Not a single specific event or short-term task'

The service to be supplied cannot be on a one-off basis: the client must intend for it to be carried out 'other than in connection with a single specific event or task of short-term duration' (regulation 3(3)(a)(ii) of the TUPE Regulations 2006).

What amounts to 'short-term' can be a matter of perception, as Langstaff J recognised in *SNR Denton UK LLP v Kirwan & anor [2013] ICR 101*. But the relevant point of view – as the regulation's wording demonstrates – is that of the client, not the transferee (or transferor, for a second-generation outsourcing or an insourcing). Expressions of intent made at the time may assist in determining just what the perception was (*ICTS UK Ltd v Mahdi [2016] ICR 274 EAT*).

'Not wholly or mainly the supply of goods for the client's use'

The activities must amount to the provision of a service. If, instead, they amount to supplying goods for the client to use, then TUPE will not apply (regulation 3(3)(a)(iii) of the TUPE Regulations 2006).

Sometimes, as part of a transfer, a number of different activities formerly undertaken as part of a 'package' may be split up between different service providers. Whether or not TUPE applies to such 'fragmentation', as it is known, will depend on just how extensive the division has been, on the basis of the facts of the matter at hand. A simple split between two contractors (*Kimberley Housing Group Ltd v Hambley [2008] ICR 1030*) or a division along functional lines (*Arch Initiatives v Greater Manchester West Mental Health NHS Foundation Trust [2016] IRLR 406*) may not amount to fragmentation. But if the way the activities are delivered has changed or the work is not apportioned according to a pattern familiar from the previous provision, the fragmentation may be too significant for TUPE to apply.

The traditional approach, based on *Kimberley*, has been to say that staff transfer to only one of the transferees if there is more than one. But following the decision of the Court of Justice of the European Union (CJEU) in *ISS Facilities Services NV v Govaerts [2020] ICR 1115*, it is now possible that in some circumstances, the rights and obligations will be split between transferees so long as it does not lead to worse working conditions or a threat to workers' rights. While this decision is not – thanks to Brexit – binding in the UK in relation to service provision changes (since those are a UK-only statutory innovation), a Scottish EAT found in 2021 that it would make little sense for this change only to apply to 'regular' TUPE transfers (*McTear & ors v Bennett & ors UKEATS/0023/19/SS*). Currently, therefore, it seems that staff may, in some (probably limited) circumstances, find themselves contracted to two or more new employers.

11.2 WHAT RIGHTS AND OBLIGATIONS ARE TRANSFERRED?

The essential rule, if TUPE applies to a transfer, is that the transferee 'steps into the shoes' of the transferor as far as its rights and obligations with respect to its employees are concerned. The text of regulation 4(2) of the TUPE Regulations 2006 is clear:

'(a) all the transferor's rights, powers, duties and liabilities under or in connection with any such contract [of employment] shall be transferred by virtue of this regulation to the transferee; and

(b) any act or omission before the transfer is completed, of or in relation to the transferor in respect of that contract or a person assigned to that organised grouping of resources or employees, shall be deemed to have been an act or omission of or in relation to the transferee. Employment contracts are thus treated as if they had been originally made with the new employer.'

205

So, for instance, any personal injury claim pending before the transfer becomes the responsibility of the transferee, as does a claim for discrimination (*DJM International Ltd v Nicholas [1996] ICR 214 EAT*). The benefit of any rights under the transferor's liability insurance also becomes the responsibility of the transferee (*Bernadone v Pall Mall Services Group Ltd [2001] ICR 197 CA*). Similarly, it now seems that rights to share incentive schemes can sometimes transfer as well (*Ponticelli UK Ltd v Gallagher [2021] IRLR 1031 EAT*), as an obligation which is 'in connection with' the contract of employment.

While in the vast majority of cases, the rights and obligations transferred will be clearly contractual, non-contractual benefits may – if an employer has, through custom and practice, led employees to believe they are a contractual right – also transfer (*CSC Computer Sciences Ltd v McAlinden [2013] EWCA Civ 1435*).

The transfer of rights and obligations is subject to several exceptions:

- Employees can object to their employment being automatically transferred – although such an objection will usually act to terminate their contracts (see **11.5**).

- Criminal liabilities are not transferred (regulation 4(6) of the TUPE Regulations 2006).

- Pension rights are not transferred in themselves (regulation 10 of the TUPE Regulations 2006) – although the transferee is not without obligations depending on what pension provision existed before the transfer (see **11.7**).

- Liability to pay sums due under statutory schemes relating to insolvency (regulation 8 of the TUPE Regulations 2006) does not transfer (see **11.8**).

- Restrictive covenants transfer – but their interpretation will depend on the circumstances. Since such covenants are presumptively unenforceable unless they protect a genuine interest of the employer at the time the contract is agreed, a transfer from a small local employer to a multinational might still prohibit dealings with the transferor's clients for a period – but would not extend to the far larger range of clients of the transferee (*Morris Angel & Son Ltd v Hollande [1993] IRLR 169 CA*).

11.2.1 EMPLOYEES OR WORKERS?

The traditional interpretation of TUPE is that it only applies to employees – those who, under section 230(1) of the *Employment Rights Act 1996* (ERA 1996), work under a 'contract of employment', defined as a contract of service or apprenticeship. With the growth in zero-hours contracts and casual employment, many people may find themselves instead classified as 'workers'

– those who, under section 230(3)(b) of the ERA 1996, work under 'any other contract, whether express or implied and (if express) whether oral or in writing, whereby the individual undertakes to do or perform personally any work or services for another party to the contract whose status is not by virtue of the contract that of a client or customer of any profession or business undertaking carried on by the individual'.

Hitherto, these so-called limb (b) workers have been outside the scope of TUPE, which, in regulation 2(1) of the TUPE Regulations 2006, defines 'employee' as 'any individual who works for another person whether under a contract of service or apprenticeship or otherwise but does not include anyone who provides services under a contract for services'. However, in *Dewhurst v Revisecatch Ltd t/a Ecourier & anor ET/2201909/2018*, the tribunal found that workers too could benefit from TUPE's protections, thanks to the words 'or otherwise' in regulation 2(1) of the TUPE Regulations 2006. The reasoning was that if it were otherwise, then the liability to workers under discrimination legislation – which extends to both employees and workers (see **chapters 12-15**) – would not be transferred.

11.3 CONSULTATION AND INFORMATION

11.3.1 FROM EMPLOYERS TO EMPLOYEES

TUPE requires both transferor and transferee not only to inform the representatives of affected employees – a term broadly defined in regulation 13 of the TUPE Regulations 2006 to include anyone affected in either transferor or transferee, whether or not their jobs will be transferred – that a transfer is impending, but also to consult them about it.

The information must include:

- The fact of the transfer and its date or proposed date.

- The 'legal, economic and social implications' of the transfer for affected employees.

- What measures the employer envisages taking and, for the transferor, what measures it envisages the transferee will take regarding affected employees – or it must state that none will be taken.

'Measures envisaged' is not defined, but it will be construed widely to include 'any action, step or arrangement' that is being considered which amounts to more than a mere hope or possibility (*IPCS v Secretary of State for Defence [1987] IRLR 373*).

Informing employees is not enough. If 'measures' are envisaged, employees must also be consulted, through their representatives, so as to 'seek … their agreement to the intended measures' (regulation 13(6) of the TUPE Regulations 2006). Any representations the representatives make must be accepted, or reasons must be given for their rejection.

If the workplace lacks recognised independent trade unions, the obligation to consult and inform is sufficiently strong that regulation 14 of the TUPE Regulations 2006 compels the employer to initiate an election of representatives and then inform and (if necessary) consult them. Where the workplace has fewer than 10 employees, instead, the employer may inform and consult affected employees individually (regulation 13A of the TUPE Regulations 2006).

There is no timeline for the process of information and consultation. However, regulation 13(2) of the TUPE Regulations 2006 requires information to be provided 'long enough before a relevant transfer to enable the employer of any affected employees to consult the appropriate representatives of any affected employees'. Since consultation is undertaken with a view to seeking agreement, it appears that an employer who leaves things until the last minute will breach TUPE.

Failures to inform or consult – at all or adequately – often form the basis of TUPE claims, because such failures, including a failure to arrange elections of representatives, can attract an award of 'such sum not exceeding 13 weeks' pay … as the tribunal considers just and equitable' (regulation 16(3) of the TUPE Regulations 2006). Given that the award is intended to punish the employer rather than to compensate the employee, the maximum award is the norm (*Sweetin v Coral Racing [2006] IRLR 252*). Unlike many awards under the ERA 1996, the employee's weekly pay used to calculate the award is not subject to a cap (*Zaman & ors v Kozee Sleep Products Ltd [2011] IRLR 196*).

Unusually, regulation 15(9) of the TUPE Regulations 2006 makes both transferor and transferee jointly and severally liable for a failure to inform or consult. Where a transferee becomes insolvent, therefore, this may be the only route to substantial compensation for affected employees.

It is conceivable that it may genuinely be impossible for an employer to carry out one or more of its duties to inform and (if necessary) consult as TUPE requires. If so, an employer will satisfy its obligations if it 'takes all such steps towards performing that duty as are reasonably practicable in the circumstances' (regulation 13(9) of the TUPE Regulations 2006).

One problem for a transferor may arise if the transferee has failed to provide it with the information that regulation 13(4) of the TUPE Regulations 2006 requires of it. In such circumstances, the correct approach – as set out in *Allen v Morrisons Facilities Services Ltd [2014] ICR 792* – for employees wanting to obtain compensation from the transferee is to bring proceedings against the transferor, which can then add the transferee as a respondent (regulation 15(5) of the TUPE Regulations 2006). The employees cannot sue the transferee directly.

11.3.2 BETWEEN TRANSFEROR AND TRANSFEREE

A transferee will naturally want to know about the employees it is absorbing: what they do, what the terms of their employment are and whether the transfer has, or is likely to have, any unexpected liability to them.

Regulation 11 of the TUPE Regulations 2006 therefore requires a transferor to provide a transferee with 'employee liability information' at least 28 days before the transfer (or as soon as reasonably practicable thereafter, if it is not practicable to do so by then). For each employee to be transferred, this comprises:

- Their identity and age.

- The particulars of their employment, including any pension rights.

- Information about any disciplinary procedures against them, or grievances they have raised, in the past two years to which the Acas Code of Practice on Disciplinary and Grievance Procedures applied.

- Any employment claims arising out of their employment by the transferor, whether in the courts or the employment tribunal, which have either been brought in the past two years or the transferor has reasonable grounds to believe may be brought.

- Information of any collective agreement which will have effect after the transfer and will apply to them.

The information must be correct as at a specified date, at least 14 days before the date of notification, and any changes thereafter must also be notified to the transferee.

A transferor which fails to comply can be punished heavily. The transferee can take the transferor to the tribunal, which can order compensation in any amount it considers just and equitable, having regard to 'any loss sustained by the transferee which is attributable to the matters complained of' and any relevant contractual terms (regulation 12(4-6) of the TUPE Regulations 2006). The regulation indicates that the minimum should normally be £500 for each employee, although the transferee should, as usual, have sought to mitigate its loss.

11.4 WHAT TERMS OF EMPLOYMENT CAN THE TRANSFEREE CHANGE, AND HOW?

A new employer will often want to change the terms under which its newly acquired employees work. Particularly with service provision changes, it may have gained the contract by promising savings and staffing may comprise the bulk of the cost base.

Since 2014, an employer cannot vary terms after a TUPE transfer if the 'sole or principal reason' for the variation is the transfer itself. Perhaps surprisingly, this can include both beneficial and adverse changes, particularly if (for instance) managers make them in their own interest (*Ferguson v Astrea Asset Management Ltd [2020] IRLR 577*). However, two exceptions apply, allowing terms to be changed:

1) If the sole or principal reason is 'an economic, technical or organisational (ETO) reason entailing changes in the workforce, provided that the employer and employee agree that variation' (regulation 4(5)(a) of the TUPE Regulations 2006).

2) If the terms of the employment contract allow the employer to make the variation, irrespective of the reason for the variation.

This is a significant change from the pre-2014 wording of TUPE, in which the second of these did not appear, and variations were void if they were made simply 'for a reason connected with the transfer that is not an ETO reason' – arguably a lower threshold.

The definition of 'ETO reason' is dealt with in section **11.6.2**, given its common application to unfair dismissals. However, it is worth noting that regulation 4(4) of the TUPE Regulations 2006 refers to variations of a contract that 'is, or will be, transferred'. In other words, changes made by the transferor to staff who will be moving in anticipation of the transfer are covered, as well as changes made afterwards by the transferee. Similarly, terms incorporated into individual contracts from a collective agreement are also included, at least initially. But regulation 4(5B) of the TUPE Regulations 2006 allows the employer to change such terms after a year, so long as the changes are no less favourable overall to the employee.

11.5 WHAT IF AN EMPLOYEE OBJECTS TO A TRANSFER?

Nothing in TUPE forces an employee to move to the new employer. However, if they object, their contract, and the rights they have under it, do not transfer and are terminated as a result (regulations 4(7) and 4(8) of the TUPE Regulations 2006). The termination is not a dismissal, so unless an objecting employee can show (under regulation 4(9) of the TUPE Regulations 2006) that the transfer 'involves or would involve a substantial change in working conditions' to their 'material detriment', they are unlikely to be able to claim constructive dismissal arising from the TUPE transfer.

As for what amounts to a 'substantial change' or 'material detriment', what matters is the impact of the change, or proposed change, from the employee's point of view, so long as that point of view is reasonable (*Tapere v South London & Maudsley NHS Trust [2009] ICR 1563*). The change does not have to be contractual: 'working conditions' is defined more broadly. The tribunal will be concerned on the impact of the change upon the employee in question. So (as was the case in *Tapere*, for instance), a change of location of only a few miles may amount to material detriment to an employee with childcare responsibilities but not to another. The concept of 'detriment' in the regulations is analogous to the word's meaning within the *Equality Act 2010* (see *Shamoon v Chief Constable of the Royal Ulster Constabulary [2003] ICR 337*, and the discussion at **13.4.1**).

11.6 CAN EMPLOYEES BE DISMISSED?

It is automatically unfair to dismiss an employee, whether before or after a relevant transfer, if the 'sole or principal reason for the dismissal is the transfer' (regulation 7(1) of the TUPE Regulations 2006). This is subject to two qualifications.

First, as with ordinary unfair dismissal under the ERA 1996, the employee needs two continuous years of service to make a claim under regulation 7(1) of the TUPE Regulations 2006, or, alternatively, needs to show (under section 104 of the ERA 1996) that they were dismissed because they complained that, or brought proceedings because, their employer had infringed their rights under TUPE.

Second, the employer may seek to deploy the 'ETO defence' under regulation 7(2)-7(3) of the TUPE Regulations 2006, by showing that the dismissal was for an 'economic, technical or organisational reason entailing changes in the workforce of either the transferor or the transferee before or after a relevant transfer'.

The ETO defence is not a complete one. It only means the dismissal was not automatically unfair. The dismissal is still subject to the usual 'reasonableness' test which arises under section 98(4) of the ERA 1996 for unfair dismissal claims, requiring the employer to show that it acted within the range of reasonable responses given all the circumstances, including obeying relevant procedures.

For the employer, the critical questions are therefore what the reason for dismissal really is, and whether it counts as an ETO reason entailing changes to the workforce.

11.6.1 THE REASON FOR DISMISSAL

If an employee claims they were unfairly dismissed by reason of a TUPE transfer, the court will need to determine the reason for the dismissal, and whether it was really 'solely or principally' the transfer itself.

The reason may not be the ostensible one. So long as the employee can show some evidence that they were dismissed because of the transfer, it is for the employer to prove that the reason operating on the employer's mind – that is, generally, the decision-maker's (although other managers can be considered if their ulterior motives are brought to bear on the decision-maker, following *Royal Mail Group Ltd v Jhuti [2020] IRLR 129 UKSC*) – when they dismissed the employee (as defined in *Manchester College v Hazel [2014] ICR 989 CA*) was, in fact, something else.

An example of how narrow this line may be can be seen in *Hare Wines v Kaur [2019] IRLR 555 CA*, in which an employee was dismissed at the time of a transfer ostensibly because of a personality conflict with their manager. The tribunal and EAT had found that, in fact, the employee had been fired because the transferee did not want them. The Court of Appeal agreed, pointing out that the poor relationship had persisted for some time without resulting in dismissal before the transfer and that the dismissal was on the day of the transfer – a point it said was evidential but often a powerful indicator of unfairness. Most of all, though, the Court of Appeal stressed that the existence of the personality conflict as an underlying reason did not take away from the core point: that the employee was dismissed so that the transferee would not need to have her on staff.

11.6.2 WHAT IS AN 'ETO REASON ENTAILING CHANGES IN THE WORKFORCE'?

The term 'ETO reason' is not defined in TUPE, but a substantial body of case law gives pointers as to how it should be interpreted, and the overarching point is that the interpretation should be narrow. Otherwise, as numerous courts have held, the term risks being so broad as effectively to encompass almost any transfer. More specifically:

- Changes in who fills roles do not amount to changes in the workforce if the number and function of employees working for the undertaking are unchanged (*Berriman v Delabole Slate [1985] ICR 546*).

- Changes to terms and conditions are, unsurprisingly, not 'changes in the workforce', unless employees' functions have substantively changed (*London Metropolitan University v Sackur and ors UKEAT/0286/06*).

- A wish to make a business more economically attractive to a purchaser is not an economic reason (*Spaceright Europe Ltd v Baillavoine and ors [2011] ICR 520*). What is required is a change in the workforce which enables the continued conduct of the business.

- If continuing to pay an unchanged workforce would mean a business could not continue to trade, dismissals may be for an ETO reason (*Kavanagh v Crystal Palace FC Ltd [2014] IRLR 139*).

- The phrase 'changes in the workforce' can generally be taken as a whole to mean a requirement for redundancies or redeployment (*Manchester College v Hazel [2014] ICR 989*).

- If a transferee operates machinery or systems that a transferring employee cannot or will not learn to use, that may amount to a technical reason – as long as it means changes to the workforce are necessary.

- If, as part of the transfer, the undertaking is reorganised and certain functions become unnecessary as a result – or (as in *Nationwide Building*

Society v Benn [2010] IRLR 922) roles are necessarily downgraded or diminished – that may amount to an organisational reason.

Whether a tribunal is likely to find that a dismissal was for an ETO reason is difficult to predict. In the words of Briggs LJ in *Kavanagh*, it requires a 'subjective fact-intensive analysis'.

11.6.3 TIMING OF THE DISMISSAL

Regulation 4(3) of the TUPE Regulations 2006 provides that employees benefit from TUPE if they were employed in the transferred undertaking 'immediately before the transfer'. Anyone dismissed at any time before the transfer will be treated as such, as long as the transfer was the reason for the dismissal. This rule was established in *Litster v Forth Dry Dock and Engineering Co Ltd [1989] ICR 341* and is now explicitly incorporated into the regulation – even if at the time of the dismissal the transferee had not specifically been identified (*Spaceright Europe Ltd v Baillavoine and ors [2011] ICR 520*).

However, if dismissals, in fact, took place because the business was insolvent and could only be made viable as a going concern by reducing the workforce, this is likely to be an ETO reason. The affected employees' only recourse would be to claim against the insolvent transferor, leaving them to fall back on the state 'insolvency guarantee' scheme noted at **8.8** (*Thompson v SCS Consulting Ltd & ors [2001] IRLR 801*).

11.7 DO PENSION RIGHTS TRANSFER?

Occupational pension rights have always been excepted from TUPE, albeit under several conditions.

First, this exception must be narrowly construed, as established by the CJEU case of *Beckmann v Dynamco Whicheloe MacFarlane Ltd [2003] ICR 50*. Any provisions of an occupational scheme which do not relate to old age, invalidity or survivors – for instance, as was the issue in *Beckmann*, benefits accruing on redundancy after a particular age but before the normal retirement age, such as an early retirement pension – do transfer.

Second, schemes other than occupational pension schemes – such as individual and group personal pension schemes – do transfer, so if the transferor pays a contribution into an employee's private pension, that obligation will move to the transferee.

Third, the *Pensions Act 2004* (sections 257-259) and the *Transfer of Employment (Pension Protection) Regulations 2005* together require a transferee to provide some form of pension arrangement to all eligible transferring employees if the transferor had previously done so. There is no requirement for the new arrangement to match the terms of the old one. Instead, as a general rule, at a minimum, the new employer must match employee contributions up to an upper limit of 6% of basic pay. Further, the transferee and its new employees may agree to opt out of this requirement, instead agreeing any pension terms they want at any time after the employee becomes employed by the transferee (section 258(6) of the *Pensions Act 2004*).

Finally, it is possible for pension rights to transfer by contract, rather than via TUPE. In the case of *Whitney v Monster Worldwide Ltd [2010] EWCA Civ 1312*, the employee had been promised by his old employer, some 20 years earlier, that he would suffer no detriment from the replacement of a final-salary scheme with a money purchase one. The Court of Appeal held this to be a contractually binding promise despite the complete lack of any formal documentation. It was therefore contractually binding on the transferee. *Whitney* was highly specific to the situation in question, but the case reinforces the critical importance of wide-ranging due diligence when taking over a business.

11.8 WHAT IF THE TRANSFEROR IS INSOLVENT?

When a business is failing, it is far harder to find new owners for its assets if they will be bound, through TUPE, to all the business's employment liabilities. There is provision for this in regulation 8(7) of the TUPE Regulations 2006, by which the transfer of liabilities under regulation 4 and the unfair dismissal rules in regulation 7:

> '... do not apply to any relevant transfer where the transferor is the subject of bankruptcy proceedings or any analogous insolvency proceedings which have been instituted with a view to the liquidation of the assets of the transferor and are under the supervision of an insolvency practitioner'.

The new employer is therefore not bound to keep any of the old employer's staff, and if it does decide to retain them, it can impose new terms without inheriting any of the old liabilities.

If, instead, an administration under Schedule B1 of the *Insolvency Act 1986* is underway, with a view to rescuing the business as a going concern, regulation 8(5) of the TUPE Regulations 2006 will apply, although some liabilities – including statutory redundancy payments, pay arrears and pay in lieu of notice – will remain with the now-insolvent transferor and will therefore be payable by the Government out of the National Insurance Fund.

In this case, it is possible for representatives of employees to agree 'permitted variations', which are, by regulation 9(7) of the TUPE Regulations 2006, those which are 'designed to safeguard employment opportunities by ensuring the survival of the undertaking, business or part of the undertaking or business that is the subject of the relevant transfer' – as long as the transfer has happened after the insolvency proceedings have started.

Where a 'pre-pack insolvency' takes place – the common procedure where an insolvency practitioner works with a business before it goes into administration to arrange a sale which is triggered as soon as the administration begins – TUPE will apply as under an administration. A CJEU case, *FNV v Smallsteps BV [2017] ICR 1316*, tested this point, with the argument being made that because the pre-pack was aimed at maximising the proceeds of the transfer, and thus protecting creditors, it was instituted with a view to the liquidation of assets. The CJEU disagreed. Even if that was an effect, the primary objective was to safeguard the insolvent business. A post-Brexit CJEU case, *Federatie Nederlandse Vakbeweging v Heiploeg Seafood International BV and anor C-237/20*, reached much the same conclusion, although, given its 2021 timing, it is not binding on UK courts and tribunals.

Where a pre-pack is being envisaged, therefore, it would be wise to assume that TUPE, subject to the provisions of regulation 8(5) of the TUPE Regulations 2006, will apply.

CHAPTER 12

PROTECTION FROM DISCRIMINATION: THE FRAMEWORK

12.0 OVERVIEW

Discrimination in the workplace is governed by the *Equality Act 2010* (EqA 2010) which brought together a complex web of previous legislation into a single piece of legislation. Although it codified and tidied existing law, it made few substantial changes – indeed, in at least one way, it in fact reverted the law to how it had been prior to a House of Lords case. As a result, Employment Appeal Tribunal (EAT) and court decisions on discrimination made before the EqA 2010 remain relevant.

This chapter discusses the main issues common to discrimination claims in general and explores who can claim, who can be liable and possible defences.

12.1 THE BASIC FRAMEWORK

Not all kinds of unequal treatment are covered by the EqA 2010. Instead, section 4 of the EqA 2010 defines nine 'protected characteristics' and makes it unlawful to treat individuals with any of those characteristics in a number of specific ways.

The protected characteristics, described in **Chapter 14**, are:

1) Age (section 5 of the EqA 2010)

2) Disability (section 6)

3) Gender reassignment (section 7)

4) Marriage and civil partnership (section 8)

5) Race (section 9)

6) Religion or belief (section 10)

217

7) Sex (section 11)

8) Sexual orientation (section 12)

9) Pregnancy and maternity (section 18)

The types of discriminatory treatment, detailed in **Chapter 13**, are:

- Direct discrimination (section 13 of the EqA 2010)
- Indirect discrimination (section 19)
- Harassment (section 26)
- Victimisation (section 27)
- Failure to make reasonable adjustments (section 21)
- Discrimination arising from disability (section 15)

With two exceptions, these types of discrimination apply in a similar fashion across all protected characteristics. The exceptions are:

1) Failure to make reasonable adjustments and discrimination arising from disability apply only to disability

2) Indirect discrimination does not apply to pregnancy and maternity

Issues of unequal terms between men and women, while included in the EqA 2010, are covered separately in **Chapter 15**.

The Equality and Human Rights Commission (EHRC), the public body set up under the EqA 2010 to oversee equality issues, issues three Codes of Practice which supplement the provisions of the EqA 2010, two of which are on employment and equal pay. These can be found on the EHRC's website at https://www.equalityhumanrights.com/en/advice-and-guidance/equality-act-codes-practice. They are not legally enforceable but are admissible in evidence. In practice, courts and tribunals frequently take the EHRC Codes of Practice into account.

12.2 THE SCOPE OF THE EQA 2010

The EqA 2010 sets out wide-ranging circumstances in which an employer can be liable if they discriminate:

- In how they decide who should be offered employment
- By not offering employment
- In the terms of employment
- In access to promotion, transfer or training opportunities or any other benefit
- By subjecting people to a detriment (see **13.4.1**) or dismissing them
- By harassing people

- By victimising people for having raised concerns about or taken action in relation to discrimination

A similar set of prohibited actions applies for contract workers.

Note that the protection offered by the EqA 2010 starts before the employment relationship, protecting job applicants, and continues after the employment relationship ends. So, if the employer later does something discriminatory – such as in relation to a job reference – it will be discrimination if the act arose out of, and is closely related to, the employment relationship (sections 108(1) and 108(2) of the EqA 2010 and *Onu v Akwiwu [2013] IRLR 523*). It will also be discrimination if the employer's action would have amounted to discrimination had it occurred during the employment (*Ford Motor Co Ltd v Elliott & ors UKEAT/0327/14*).

12.3 WHO CAN BRING A CLAIM?

12.3.1 EMPLOYEES, AGENCY WORKERS AND OTHERS

Only 'employees' can claim for discrimination under the EqA 2010 – but 'employee' is defined widely. It includes not only people working under contracts of employment or apprenticeship but also self-employed people who have a contract personally to do work, Crown employees, police officers, members of the armed forces and some Parliament staff.

This is still likely to exclude many self-employed workers, such as those who can send someone else to undertake their duties (see, for instance, *Jivraj v Hashwani [2011] ICR 1004 SC*). Where someone carries out a series of discrete tasks, the tribunal can look at any umbrella agreement to help determine whether there is an employment relationship but only to the extent that it helps identify whether the characteristics of employment are present (*Windle v Secretary of State for Justice [2016] ICR 721*). The self-employed distinction has been doubted at the European level (for instance, in *JK v TP Case C-356/21* at the Court of Justice of the European Union), but post-Brexit, such authority is persuasive at best. Meanwhile, domestic tribunals continue to resist extending the 'worker' definition to the self-employed, with one example (albeit from the point of view of whether an individual respondent is a 'worker') being *Alemi v Mitchell [2021] IRLR 262*.

There are explicit provisions for agency workers (section 41 of the EqA 2010); partners (sections 44 and 45 of the EqA 2010); barristers and (in Scotland) advocates, including trainees and pupils (sections 47 and 48 of the EqA 2010); and holders of public offices (sections 49-52 of the EqA 2010).

12.3.2 WHEN CAN SOMEONE MAKE A CLAIM?

There is no minimum length of service required to make a discrimination claim. Indeed, applicants for employment are also protected, although someone applying not so much to get a job as to make a claim if they do not get it will not be protected (*Kratzer v R+V Allgemeine Versicherung AG C-423/15; [2016] ICR 967*).

12.3.3 ILLEGALITY

The general rule is that an illegal contract of employment – one prohibited by statute (such as the employment of someone without the right to work in the UK) or for an illegal purpose, such as committing a crime – will not necessarily bar someone from making a discrimination claim (*Hall v Woolston Hall Leisure Ltd [2001] ICR 99*). However, if the claim is 'inextricably linked' to the illegal conduct, then without some strong public policy grounds (as in *Hounga v Allen [2014] IRLR 811*, where the claimant was seen as a victim of human trafficking) it should not be permitted to proceed to avoid appearing to condone the conduct.

12.4 ISSUES OF PROOF

12.4.1 THE BURDEN OF PROOF

In civil courts, claimants have to show their version of events is more likely to be true than the respondent's version. In discrimination claims under the EqA 2010, the claimant only has to provide enough evidence to show they were treated less favourably (or unfavourably).

The tribunal will then presume discrimination unless the respondent can provide, and prove, a non-discriminatory explanation for what happened.

This is often referred to, misleadingly, as the 'reverse burden of proof', whereas 'shifting burden' would be a better description. The claimant still carries an initial burden. As the Court of Appeal found in *Ayodele v CityLink & anor [2018] IRLR 114*, the tribunal cannot simply take the case presented by the two sides and then balance them up. Instead, there is a two-stage process, as explained in *Wong v Igen Ltd [2005] ICR 931* and approved by the Supreme Court in *Hewage v Grampian Health Board [2012] ICR 1054*.

The claimant must first show that facts exist which allow the tribunal to presume discrimination, including the acts or omissions complained of and the protected characteristic in question. If they cannot, the claim fails. The respondent can of course provide its own factual evidence to undermine the claimant's attempt to clear this first hurdle; as the Supreme Court held in *Efobi v Royal Mail Group [2021] IRLR 811*, a tribunal needs the claimant to prove enough facts to make this presumption and must also weigh anything put forward by the respondent (although without considering the respondent's explanations for the alleged conduct) before deciding whether stage one has been satisfied.

Only once that is done does the burden 'shift' to the employer, at which point the claim will succeed unless the employer can show that the treatment in question was not based on the protected characteristic to any substantial degree. Discrimination does not have to be the sole or main driver behind the treatment of which the claimant complains, as long as (in the words of *O'Neill v Governors of St Thomas More RC School [1997] ICR 33*) it is an 'effective cause'.

It is sometimes possible for a tribunal to go straight to stage two, the 'reason why', if the employer's reason is self-evidently sound and non-discriminatory. But this should be rare, as the EAT found in *Field v Steve Pye & Co (KL) Ltd [2022] IRLR 948*. If there is evidence that could indicate discrimination, that should usually be considered at the first stage; and if it is inadequate, then the second stage can be dealt with briefly.

The courts recognise that in discrimination cases, there may only be limited direct evidence. Few employers, after all, will explicitly discriminate. Instead, as explained in *Barton v Investec Henderson Crosthwaite Securities Ltd [2003] ICR 1205*, a tribunal may draw inferences from primary facts, including from evasiveness (or indeed wholly untruthful responses until late in the proceedings – *Base Childrenswear Ltd v Otshudi [2020] IRLR 118*) on the part of the employer, in deciding whether the claimant has proved the facts required to shift the burden. Because the mind of the decision-maker is often the focus, a respondent which chooses not to have the decision-maker give evidence, instead relying on documentary evidence, may struggle to make its case (*Bennett v MiTAC Europe Ltd [2022] IRLR 25*).

12.4.2 HOW CAN DISCRIMINATION BE PROVED?

As noted at **12.4.1**, claimants must frequently rely on inference, rather than direct evidence, to prove that unlawful discrimination has occurred. There is ample case law on what kinds of inferences are proper, such as (but not limited to) the following:

- If an employer fails to follow its own procedures or diverges without good reason from guidance found in the EHRC Codes of Practice, the tribunal is likely to infer discrimination (*Anya v University of Oxford [2001] ICR 847*).

- Statistical evidence can have a role to play in proving discrimination, particularly but by no means exclusively in cases of indirect discrimination (see **13.2**). But a tribunal must be wary of drawing conclusions from insufficiently strong statistical trends (*Appiah v Bishop Douglass Roman Catholic High School Governors [2007] IRLR 264*).

- Where the discrimination is alleged to arise from assumptions made by the employer about people with the relevant protected characteristics, it is not enough for claimants to allege that assumptions were made.

They must prove facts from which the tribunal can infer this was the case (*Stockton-on-Tees BC v Aylott [2010] ICR 1278*).

- The tribunal cannot infer discrimination where an employer treats all its staff, not just those with a particular protected characteristic, equally poorly (*Laing v Manchester City Council [2006] ICR 1519*).

- The tribunal must base its inferences on facts proved, not on assumptions arising from those facts (*BMA v Chaudhary (No 2) [2007] IRLR 800*).

- Although employers are no longer required to respond to statutory questionnaires from claimants, a failure reasonably to answer queries concerning allegations of discrimination may still lead to a negative inference (*Dattani v Chief Constable of West Mercia Police [2005] IRLR 327*).

- There is never a requirement for a claimant to present direct evidence of why the respondent acted as they are alleged to have done, as long as facts are proved from which the tribunal 'could conclude' (see the burden of proof discussion at **12.4.1**) that discrimination had happened (*Breslin v Loughrey [2021] IRLR 320*).

12.5 DEFENCES AND EXEMPTIONS

Some employers are exempted from some or all of the requirements of the EqA 2010 – the main ones are dealt with below. Some exemptions are specific to age discrimination (see **14.1.2**). First, however, it is worth dealing with a defence available to an employer across several forms of discrimination: justification.

12.5.1 JUSTIFICATION

In some circumstances, an employer which has discriminated can claim that it had a reasonable objective justification for having done so. This defence is available in all indirect discrimination claims except those concerning pregnancy and maternity, direct age discrimination and discrimination arising from disability.

For all but direct age discrimination, there is a common standard: the employer must show that the treatment alleged was 'a proportionate means of achieving a legitimate aim'. Proportionality, which means it is both appropriate to the aim and necessary to achieve it, will depend on the nature of the treatment alleged: the more discriminatory this was, the more important the aim will have to be, and the treatment may need to be particularly necessary and appropriate to achieving it. The aim itself needs to be 'legal and non-discriminatory', and must 'represent a real, objective consideration', as the EHRC's Employment Code puts it: one which is a real need on the part of the employer's business (*Bilka-Kaufhaus GmbH v Weber von Hartz [1987] ICR 110*).

It will help, although it does not suffice in itself, if the employer can show it considered proportionality at the time at which the treatment was imposed. Note that it is not enough that some underlying policy can be justified; the focus is on the treatment itself. Where the treatment comprises multiple acts, as was shown in *Buchanan v Commissioner of Police of the Metropolis UKEAT/0112/16*, each will have to be individually justified.

There is no authoritative list of aims which can be legitimate, although common ones cited include health and safety, client needs (as long as these are not in themselves discriminatory) and genuine operational necessity. Cost can be a factor, but no more than that – it can only form part of the justification, and only if there are other good reasons (that is, legitimate aims) for the practice in question (*Woodcock v Cumbria Primary Care Trust [2012] ICR 1126*).

In all cases, the tribunal will have to undertake a balancing exercise between 'the discriminatory effect of the condition and the reasonable needs of the party who applies the condition' (*Hampson v Department of Education and Science [1989] ICR 179*).

12.5.2 OCCUPATIONAL REQUIREMENTS

An employer can rely on an 'occupational requirement' (OR) if it can show a particular role genuinely requires (or bars) a particular protected characteristic – for instance, to cast a female actor for a female part. This defence only applies to direct discrimination (schedule 9, paragraph 6(2) of the EqA 2010), and even then only to recruitment, promotion, transfer, training and (other than in sex discrimination cases) dismissal. It cannot be used in relation to the terms on which employment is offered or conducted, in cases of victimisation or harassment or where the claimant is subject to any other detriment.

The application of the OR must be a 'proportionate means of achieving a legitimate aim' (see **12.5.1**), and the employer must also show that the person to whom it was applied did not meet it (or, other than in sex discrimination cases, there were reasonable grounds for not being satisfied that the person met it).

The OR provisions are clearly open to abuse by employers, so tribunals tend to apply them narrowly. An OR defence which, on closer inspection, is a sham or is not directly and closely linked to the role in question is likely to fail.

12.5.3 STATUTORY REQUIREMENTS AND NATIONAL SECURITY

A further exemption (section 191 and schedules 22 and 230 of the EqA 2010) applies for treatment which is necessary to comply with other legislation

– for instance, health and safety rules, religious education or roles where nationality may be relevant, such as those involving national security.

National security is the subject of a specific exemption in section 192 of the EqA 2010, which exempts discriminatory acts done 'for the purpose of safeguarding national security', although it requires the treatment to be proportionate to that purpose.

12.5.4 PARTICULAR TYPES OF EMPLOYMENT

The EqA 2010 exempts several specific kinds of employment from certain kinds of discrimination:

- Political parties are allowed to select election candidates on grounds of gender. The exemption was inserted into the *Sex Discrimination Act 1975* (at section 42A) in 2002, but section 105 of the EqA 2010 extended its application to 2030.

- Religions are allowed to insist on a minister being of a particular marital status, sexual orientation or gender (or not having undergone gender reassignment) to avoid offending religious doctrine (schedule 9, paragraph 2 of the EqA 2010).

- The armed forces are allowed to bar women and transsexuals (as discussed at **14.3**, this is the term used in the EqA 2010) from certain roles if this is a proportionate means of ensuring combat effectiveness (schedule 9, paragraph 4(1) of the EqA 2010).

- Sikh men may wear turbans unless an employer can show there is an objective requirement for them not to. This means an employer cannot otherwise rely on health and safety legislation to not employ Sikhs. However, a Sikh injured in circumstances where protective headgear would otherwise be required would only be entitled to limited compensation (section 11 of the *Employment Act 1989*).

- Single-sex sports events are lawful under section 195 of the EqA 2010 as long as they would otherwise put women at a disadvantage because of physical strength, stamina or physique. Similarly, it is lawful to select athletes to represent a country or place on the basis of their nationality, place of birth or residence.

12.5.5 POSITIVE ACTION

While discrimination in favour of people with one protected characteristic is unlawful, since, by definition, it discriminates against others, the EqA 2010 allows employers to undertake positive action (as did its precursors) to help under-represented groups in certain, limited circumstances.

They may do so (under section 158 of the EqA 2010) for persons who share a protected characteristic if they suffer a disadvantage connected to it or have needs different from those without it, or if their participation in an activity is disproportionately low. Further, they may do so if the action is a proportionate means of achieving the aim of (1) enabling or encouraging those who share the characteristic to overcome or minimise the disadvantage they face, (2) meeting their distinct needs, or (3) participating in the activity in which they are underrepresented.

An employer seeking to undertake positive action does not necessarily need an elaborate statistical basis for doing so, as long as they reasonably think the conditions are satisfied – for instance, by looking at the profile of their workforce or inquiring with comparable employers.

Prior to the EqA 2010, positive action applied only (in the employment context) to training opportunities. Section 159 of the EqA 2010 extended that to employment in general. It allows an employer to treat someone with a protected characteristic more favourably than someone without that characteristic when deciding who to recruit or promote, but only if:

- The candidates are as 'qualified' as each other.

- There is no blanket policy, such as a quota.

- The more favourable treatment is a proportionate means of achieving the aim in question.

The Government has a guide to positive action in recruitment and promotion (www.gov.uk/government/publications/employers-quick-start-guide-to-positive-action-in-recruitment-and-promotion).

12.6 VICARIOUS RESPONSIBILITY

People discriminate, so discrimination claims must be based on the actions of individuals – and an individual, say another employee or a manager, can themself be the subject of the claim (sections 110-112 of the EqA 2010). However, the employer is also liable for anything someone does 'in the course of their employment' (section 109 of the EqA 2010), whether or not it was done with the employer's knowledge or approval. In practice, it is rare for the employer not to be named as well as, or instead of, the individual(s) alleged to have perpetrated the discrimination in question: the employer's duties (and thus potential wrongs) are likely to be more wide-ranging, and its pockets – or those of its insurers – deeper.

The long-established two-stage test for vicarious liability in civil cases applies, with some modifications, to discrimination matters as well, as expressed by the Supreme Court in *Catholic Child Welfare Society v Various Claimants and Institute of the Brothers of the Christian Schools [2013] IRLR 219*, often referred to as the '*Christian Brothers*' case:

1) Was there a relationship akin to employment between the individual wrongdoer and the employer?

2) Was there a sufficiently close connection between the discriminatory act and that employment relationship?

12.6.1 'A RELATIONSHIP AKIN TO EMPLOYMENT'

For the first question, employees (on the broad EqA 2010 definition (see **12.3.1**)) will, of course, qualify. But self-employed individuals may too, as may agency workers. It all depends on how closely the shape of the relationship maps onto the employer-employee model. As was held by the Court of Appeal in *E v English Province of Our Lady of Charity [2012] IRLR 846*, the key is whether a wrongdoer 'is so much a part of the work, business or organisation' of the employer that it is just to make the latter answer for the wrongdoing.

The link only stretches so far. In *Barclays Bank v Various Claimants [2020] IRLR 481*, the Supreme Court made clear that the traditional barrier between people (whatever label is attached to them) who are working for someone else, and so-called 'independent contractors' conducting a 'recognisably independent business of their own', remains intact.

It is not just employees, defined broadly, who can trigger vicarious liability. The net stretches to include the liability of principals for their agents – for instance, an elected union official who is not an employee of the union (*Unite the Union v Naillard [2018] IRLR 730*) – so long as they acted with the principal's authority (although again not necessarily their knowledge or approval). Even a prisoner, if carrying out work assigned to them for the benefit of the assigner, can also be in a relationship 'akin to employment' (*Cox v Ministry of Justice [2016] ICR 470*).

However, employers are no longer liable for discrimination perpetrated by third parties. Sections 40(2) and 40(3) of the EqA 2010, which could (for instance) make a store owner liable if a racist customer harassed a member of staff, were repealed in 2013. It has been argued that this does not apply to harassment cases (see **13.3**) if the employer has failed to prevent the harassment or protect the employee from it (*Bessong v Pennine Care NHS Foundation Trust [2020] IRLR 4*) – but wholly unsuccessfully.

12.6.2 'IN THE COURSE OF EMPLOYMENT'

Once a 'relationship akin to employment' is identified, there still remains the question of whether the discrimination happened 'in the course' of that employment. The concept has a wide meaning, not limited to acts performed during working hours and as part of the tasks assigned to the perpetrator (as was found by the Court of Appeal in *Jones v Tower Boot Co Ltd [1997] IRLR 168*) but embracing acts done outside, so long as the connection to work is real. An example of this is harassment happening in the pub after work, or at a company Christmas party (*Chief Constable of Lincolnshire Police v Stubbs [1999] IRLR 81*). The tribunal must consider what 'the layman' would consider to be within the course of employment and not be overly concerned by excessively technical distinctions (*Sidhu v Aerospace Composite Technology Ltd [2001] ICR 167*).

The old distinction between acts which the employer had authorised – even if done in an unauthorised manner – and other acts (the former attracting liability, the latter not) is now disfavoured as a semantic rather than real distinction. This evolution came about from cases where children had suffered sexual abuse at the hands of school staff, the way being led by *Lister v Hesley Hall [2001] ICR 665* but now generally applied.

As the Supreme Court confirmed in *WM Morrison Supermarkets plc v Various Claimants [2020] IRLR 472* (*Morrisons*), which explored a number of recent authorities and is now the leading authority on the issue, the key is to identify whether there is a sufficiently 'close connection' between the act in question and the employment relationship. The employee does not need to be acting in a 'representative capacity' (as was held in *Mohamud v WM Morrison Supermarkets plc [2016] ICR 485*), but the act needs to grow out of more than simply a temporal or causal connection, or an opportunity presented by the employment. The motive may be relevant if it helps distinguish something connected with someone's job from something which is 'purely personal'. The latter was the case in *Morrisons*: an employee had leaked other employees' personal data entrusted to him to the papers as retaliation for having been disciplined at work.

12.6.3 THE 'ALL REASONABLE STEPS' DEFENCE

If an employer can show it took 'all reasonable steps' to prevent the discriminatory acts complained of, they may have a defence under section 109 of the EqA 2010, placing all liability personally on the employee who carried them out (*Yeboah v Crofton [2002] IRLR 634*).

This is a high bar to clear, and such a defence does not often succeed. While no exhaustive list of steps exists, the EHRC's Employment Code of Practice mentions implementing an equality policy, ensuring workers are aware of that policy, reviewing the policy when appropriate, providing equality training and dealing effectively with employee complaints. But even all of these steps may not suffice. The tribunal will ask itself what steps were taken before the alleged discrimination occurred (steps taken afterwards do not count), and then ask what other steps could reasonably have been taken. The defence will fail if any exist – even if, on analysis, they would not have changed the outcome (*Canniffe v East Riding of Yorkshire Council [2000] IRLR 555*). However, the defence does sometimes succeed – for instance, in *McCue v Civil Nuclear Police Authority ET/4111346/2021*, where in two out of three instances in which a Catholic police officer was subjected to instances of sectarian insult, his employer was found to have taken all reasonable steps by having previously delivered repeated training and consistent management messaging, taking the situation seriously and offering significant support to the claimant in the context of little history of such conduct in the claimant's unit. (The defence failed with respect to the third incident largely because the employer was, by then, on notice of the problem and failed to respond quickly enough after the second incident – for instance, by rapidly mounting a formal rather than informal investigation and instituting renewed training.)

12.7 CONFIDENTIALITY AGREEMENTS

An employer facing a discrimination claim under the EqA 2010 may well decide to try to settle it. Since allegations of discrimination can give rise to serious reputational damage, they may understandably want some clause requiring confidentiality to be included in any settlement agreement.

To the extent that any such clause 'purports to exclude or limit a provision of or made under' the EqA 2010, section 144 of the EqA 2010 renders it unenforceable. Unless it is therefore a 'qualifying settlement agreement', a confidentiality clause cannot be used to stop a worker from making a complaint or bringing a claim.

Under section 144(4) of the EqA 2010, a 'qualifying settlement agreement' (or one made with the assistance of Acas) is enforceable. Such an agreement is defined in section 147(2) of the EqA 2010 as one which:

- Is in writing.

- Relates to the particular complaint being settled.

- Is only entered into after the complainant has received advice from an independent adviser (such as a lawyer, a trade union official certified to give advice, or a worker at an advice centre who is so certified), who has appropriate insurance in place, about what the agreement's terms mean and what effect they have.

- Identifies the independent adviser in question within the agreement.

- States that the advice has been given and the insurance is in place.

Unsurprisingly, the adviser cannot work for, or be connected with, the employer (section 147(5) of the EqA 2010).

CHAPTER 13
TYPES OF DISCRIMINATION

13.0 OVERVIEW

The law covering discrimination is extensive and covers multiple types of potential claims. This chapter explores the detail of unlawful discrimination and the many forms it can potentially take.

13.1 DIRECT DISCRIMINATION

Direct discrimination under section 13(1) of the *Equality Act 2010* (EqA 2010) occurs when someone is treated less favourably than someone else and that treatment arises because of a protected characteristic, whether their own (actual or perceived by the wrongdoer) or someone else's. The treatment can take place before, during or after the employment relationship. The critical factor is that the thought process of the person making the allegedly discriminatory decision must be motivated by the presence of the characteristic in question (*CLFIS (UK) Ltd v Reynolds [2015] ICR 1010*).

13.1.1 THE COMPARATOR

Direct discrimination is about less favourable treatment – not unfavourable in the abstract, but worse than what someone else would receive. The 'someone else' is called the comparator.

(An employer does not discriminate unlawfully it if treats all its staff terribly, irrespective of protected characteristics – although its employees may have other claims.)

It is critical to identify the right comparator. They need to be in the same position as the claimant – going for the same job, doing the same work and with similar experience and qualifications – except that they lack the relevant protected characteristic. For example, they could be of another gender or nationality or hold a different set of beliefs. The comparator can be real (if a suitable person exists) or hypothetical, constructed to match the material circumstances. Care needs to be taken so that, for instance, a female clerical worker alleging sex discrimination is compared to a male clerical worker, not to the firm's male managing director. Even so, as was explained in *Chief Constable of West Yorkshire v Vento (No. 1) [2001] IRLR 124*: 'It is all too easy to become nit-picking and pedantic in the approach to comparators. It is not required that a minutely exact actual comparator has to be found. If that were to be the case, then isolated cases of discrimination would almost invariably go uncompensated.'

Tribunals which either misunderstand the need for a proper comparator, or fail clearly to identify one, tend to fall into error. An example is *Croydon Health Services NHS Trust v George UKEAT/0139/15*, in which a midwife alleged direct discrimination on the grounds of race when she was demoted and subjected to a disciplinary process. The employment tribunal had compared her situation to a former (white) midwife at the trust and found against her. But the EAT overturned the decision, finding significant material differences between the two, and noting that the woman had not been chosen as such by the claimant.

When the discrimination is against a woman on grounds of pregnancy or maternity, no comparator is required. The Court of Justice of the European Union (CJEU) has long held that since pregnancy and maternity are uniquely female conditions, no comparison with a man is appropriate (*Webb v Emo Air Cargo (UK) Ltd [1994] ICR 770*). Conversely, section 13(6)(b) of the EqA 2010 provides that a man cannot claim sex discrimination on the grounds that he has not received special treatment afforded to a pregnant woman or mother. Nor, under section 13(3) of the EqA 2010, can an employee claim discrimination because they have not benefited from adjustments made to assist a disabled colleague.

No comparator is required with racial segregation either. Section 13(5) of the EqA 2010 provides that this always amounts to less favourable treatment when imposed on a racial group – although, if a group chooses to segregate itself, this will not (without more) amount to discrimination (*FTATU v Modgill [1980] IRLR 142*).

13.1.2 'LESS FAVOURABLE TREATMENT'

Once the appropriate comparator (real or hypothetical) has been found, the next step is to identify the treatment that the claimant says was less favourable. In some cases, this will be clear: dismissal, for instance, or a lower pay rise than someone without the relevant characteristic. Denial of an opportunity (say, for training) would also qualify. Differences without material loss may also count: a mentor whose mentee is removed and not replaced could suffer a diminution in status.

The reason for the differential is irrelevant at this point. The employer may well have reasons, good or otherwise, for why two employees get different bonuses or pay rises: productivity, for example. However, that analysis comes at the next stage. At this point, a tribunal is simply trying to identify whether there is a material difference between the claimant's treatment and that of the comparator.

That difference must be to the claimant's disadvantage. Difference is not in itself discriminatory. The issue often arises in claims concerning uniform requirements, where a difference in required clothing – such as different uniforms for men and women – is not in itself enough to amount to discrimination. Similarly, a dress code would not on its own underpin a claim; what would matter was whether the overall requirements placed on men and women (as opposed to examining each item separately) amounted to different levels of stringency, judged by current societal attitudes (*Smith v Safeway plc [1996] ICR 868*).

13.1.3 'BECAUSE OF A PROTECTED CHARACTERISTIC'

For less favourable treatment to be discriminatory, it must have happened 'because of' the protected characteristic in question. As discussed at **13.1.5**, the characteristic does not have to be the claimant's own. But there must be a causal connection between the characteristic and the treatment, founded in the wrongdoer's conscious or subconscious reason for doing what they did (*Nagarajan v London Regional Transport [1999] IRLR 572*).

The need to look at why the respondent actually acted requires the tribunal to take a subjective approach, except in those cases (such as simply refusing to employ anyone with a particular characteristic) where the treatment is inherently discriminatory (*R (E) v JFS Governing Body & anor [2010] IRLR 136*). As such, the so-called 'reverse burden of proof' is likely to be important (see **12.4.1**). 'Reason' denotes whether the protected characteristic was a consideration (it does not have to be the only or even main consideration) for the decision-maker. Their motivation for including the characteristic in their thought process is irrelevant.

Normally, it is the decision-maker's state of mind which is determinative. There may be times, however, when a decision-maker is operating on information provided by another employee, which is 'tainted' by reason of that employee's conscious or unconscious prejudice. In such cases (of which *Reynolds*, mentioned at **13.1**, is a leading example; more on this kind of 'tainted information' can be found in relation to whistle-blowing in the Supreme Court's decision on *Jhuti v Royal Mail [2020] ICR 731*), the thought processes of the supplier of the information must be considered in relation to their own actions (rather than those of the 'primary' decision-maker).

Finally, someone whose less favourable treatment of another person arises from their own characteristic does not directly discriminate (the most prominent example outside the field of employment is *Lee v Ashers Baking Company Ltd [2018] IRLR 1116* – the so-called 'gay cake' case discussed at **14.7.3**). They may discriminate in other ways.

13.1.4 DEFENCES

An employer can seek to rely on an occupational requirement defence (see **12.6.2**), but except with age discrimination (see **14.1.1**), there is no justification defence to a direct discrimination claim.

13.1.5 ASSOCIATION AND PERCEPTION DISCRIMINATION

Most direct discrimination cases arise when someone is ill-treated because of a protected characteristic of their own, but this is not a requirement. The wording of section 13 of the EqA 2010 requires only that the treatment be 'because of a protected characteristic'. It does not specify whose.

As a result, someone discriminated against because they are mistakenly thought to be gay, or to be of a particular ethnicity or faith, has a claim just as if they, in fact, had that characteristic. The same applies to so-called associative discrimination; a person ill-treated because they are married to someone of a particular ethnicity could claim direct discrimination.

Note, however, that this does not apply where the discrimination arises from marriage or civil partnership status, in which case it is the claimant that must have the characteristic in question.

13.1.6 COMBINED DISCRIMINATION

In recent years, the concept of intersectionality has gained prominence in thinking about discrimination: the idea that characteristics or identities may combine to produce distinct patterns of discrimination. Section 14 of the EqA 2010 takes account of this kind of 'combined discrimination', but the section has never been brought into force. Until it is, while someone may make a claim based on several different characteristics, each is considered in isolation. Consequently, a claimant might allege both race and sex discrimination, but could not currently argue that the prejudice shown by their employer is against, say, Black women in particular.

13.1.7 PRE-EMPLOYMENT HEALTH INQUIRIES

For disabled people, a supplemental form of direct discrimination arises from section 60 of the EqA 2010, which stops employers from asking questions about someone's health before employing them. One cannot claim solely because such a question has been asked, but if a disabled person did not get the job, the question would be enough to shift the burden of proof (see **12.4.1**).

There are circumstances which can justify an employer asking such questions, listed in section 60(6) of the EqA 2010:

- Establishing whether a job applicant can comply with a requirement to undergo an assessment as part of the application process, or whether the employer will need to make reasonable adjustments to enable the applicant to do so.

- Establishing whether the applicant will be able to carry out a function intrinsic to the nature of the work concerned.

- Monitoring diversity.

- Taking action in relation to positive action (see **12.5.5**).

- If a particular disability is a requirement for the work, establishing whether the applicant has that disability.

13.2 INDIRECT DISCRIMINATION

Indirect discrimination arises when there is a requirement or condition imposed generally by an employer which may, on the surface, seem inoffensive – but, in fact, causes particular difficulties for a specific protected group. A classic example might be a minimum height requirement, which would disproportionately bar women and people from ethnicities who are generally less tall (such as in the CJEU case of *Ypourgos Esoterikon v Kalliri [2018] IRLR 77*, which concerned a bar on people shorter than 1.7 metres getting into Greek police training schools). Others (highlighted in the Equality and Human Rights Commission Employment Code (EHRC Employment Code)) might be a refusal to allow staff to cover their heads – which could discriminate against Muslim women and Sikh men – or a refusal to allow dreadlocks even when tied back, which could discriminate against Rastafarian men.

Less obvious requirements have also been found to be discriminatory. For example, a requirement for long or uncertain hours (*London Underground Ltd v Edwards (No.2) [1998] IRLR 364*) or a refusal to allow flexi-time or job sharing (*British Telecommunications plc v Roberts [1996] IRLR 601*) were found to discriminate against women, as – in 1977 – was a requirement for applicants for a job to have an engineering degree since at the time women were less likely than men to possess one.

Section 19 of the EqA 2010 says that indirect discrimination occurs when:

- An employer applies a 'provision, criterion or practice' (PCP) both to an employee with a protected characteristic and to others without it.

- The PCP's application puts (or would put) people with the employee's characteristic at a 'particular disadvantage' compared to those without it.

- The employee is also put (or would be put) at that disadvantage.

Unlike direct discrimination, employers can defend a potentially discriminatory PCP if they can objectively justify it (see **12.5.1**).

There is no room here for perception or associative discrimination. Only employees who themselves have the relevant characteristic can make a claim.

To activate the 'reverse burden of proof' (see **12.4.1**), an employee will need to provide proof of all three factors, at which point it is up to the employer to try to justify the PCP objectively.

13.2.1 PROVISION, CRITERION OR PRACTICE

'Provision, criterion or practice' (PCP) is undefined in the EqA 2010. The concept may sound more complicated than it is. Any policy or requirement which is applied broadly across a workforce or a subset of it – whether formal or informal, customary or written down, present or future – can be a PCP, as long as it is 'neutral on its face', as Baroness Hale put it in *Chief Constable of West Yorkshire Police v Homer [2012] IRLR 601*. So a requirement that all female employees undergo a health screening to keep their jobs would be direct, not indirect, discrimination. If the requirement applied to everyone (male and female) in one department but not to those in another, and the affected department had a far higher proportion of women in it, that might be indirectly discriminatory instead.

On the whole, a one-off incident will not constitute a PCP unless it is capable of being applied in future to employees in similar situations (*Ishola v TfL [2020] IRLR 368*). But a practice does not need to arise often to qualify, as *Pendleton v Derbyshire County Council [2016] IRLR 580* showed. A local authority had a policy that teachers whose spouses were convicted of particular sex offences had to leave their spouses or lose their jobs. A female teacher, a devout Christian, believed her marriage vows prevented her from leaving her husband, who was convicted of such an offence. Even though the policy would only extremely rarely be applied, it remained a generally applicable rule, and the particular nature of the claimant's beliefs persuaded the EAT to find indirect discrimination.

Whatever the PCP is, it needs to be defined precisely. Claimants should think carefully about the relationship between the PCP and the disadvantage claimed: it is not unknown for a tribunal to reject a claim, even if a different (but unpleaded) formulation might have succeeded.

13.2.2 PARTICULAR DISADVANTAGE

Without a comparison, there can be no indirect discrimination. Unlike direct discrimination, however, the primary comparison is group-based. There must be 'no material difference' (section 23(1) of the EqA 2010) between the two groups – the one with the protected characteristic and the one without – and both must have the same PCP applied to them at the same time. That does not mean they have to be identical – that would render section 19 of the EqA 2010 toothless.

So, for a case of race discrimination, two South Asian women of a similar age could be in the same group – even if one was a devout Muslim and the other a Jain, or one married and one divorced – unless religion or marital status was relevant to the application of the PCP.

In disability cases, care will need to be taken in identifying the groups, given the requirement in section 6(3) of the EqA 2010 for such a group to have 'the same disability'. Claimants will need to define the boundaries of the relevant disability or disabilities carefully, focusing primarily on their effects.

Once the groups are identified, the disadvantage must be specified. Although it must affect the group with the characteristic more than the 'control group', the control group need not be wholly unaffected. The rule about resigning or divorcing, mentioned in *Pendleton* (see **13.2.1**), clearly disadvantages all those to which it would apply, but it may be worse for those whose beliefs bar divorce.

As discussed elsewhere (see **13.4.1** and **13.6.1**), 'disadvantage' is not intended to be a complex concept. It denotes something that would make the employee, in their own view, worse off. This does not mean solely materially or financially: a loss of respect or authority would suffice. But the view must be a reasonable one.

The words 'would put' are important. They cover situations where a PCP may not yet have had a concrete effect but would do if activated. The EHRC Employment Code gives the example of a role with a mobility clause requiring short-notice international travel. A woman with young children might consider this to be discriminatory because women are more likely to be carers of children, but she would not need to wait until she is asked to travel at short notice before making a claim.

(Incidentally, this kind of so-called 'childcare disparity' – women generally bearing greater childcare obligations than men – remains something that tribunals are required to consider under the doctrine of 'judicial notice' if it is relevant: *Dobson v North Cumbria Integrated Care NHS Foundation Trust [2021] IRLR 729*.)

The group requirement does not need statistics to support its existence. A tribunal requiring a claimant to show numerically what proportion of a workforce is affected will err. Witness or expert evidence will usually suffice, although if statistics are available, it may well help the tribunal in its decision-making. The correct starting point is to examine the proportions of affected versus unaffected persons in each group, so evidence that 75% of, say, white people are unaffected by a PCP, but only 20% of BAME people, is likely to be persuasive. But where that comparison is not definitive, a tribunal may wish also to look at other forms of comparison (*Secretary of State for Trade and Industry v Rutherford (No 2) [2006] ICR 785*).

It is not enough for a claimant to show the group disadvantage exists. They must also show that it affects them specifically. Equally, a claimant who can identify their own particular disadvantage but cannot show that a group with the same characteristic also suffers that disadvantage is unlikely to succeed (*Gray v Mulberry Company (Design) Ltd [2019] ICR 715*). Group statistics may help a claimant here if they establish a group disadvantage but there is no other evidence to explain the alleged personal disadvantage (*Essop v Home Office [2017] ICR 640*).

Note, however, that where beliefs are concerned, and the claimant genuinely holds to a minority interpretation of that belief, then as long as there is a reasonably-interpreted detriment to them, and there is a group – even a small or hypothetical one – it will not matter if others holding to less demanding interpretations are not similarly affected (*Mba v Merton London Borough Council [2014] ICR 357*).

Finally, claimants only need to show that the particular disadvantage exists and that it arises from the PCP. There is no need for them to show any mechanism explaining how this comes to be the case (*Naeem v Secretary of State for Justice [2017] ICR 640*).

13.2.3 JUSTIFICATION

As highlighted at **12.5.1**, an employer accused of indirect discrimination can seek to justify it if it objectively amounts to a proportionate means of achieving a legitimate aim – whether social policy or 'a real need on the part of the employer's business' (*Chief Constable of West Yorkshire Police v Homer [2012] ICR 711*). The tribunal must ask itself what aim the PCP is intended to accomplish, then ask whether the PCP is, in fact, a proportionate (a term which includes the concept of necessity) way of achieving it. If there is a way of doing so which imposes less detriment, then the PCP is unlikely to be considered proportionate.

Finally, the tribunal must weigh each emanation of the PCP's unfavourable effect against the aim, considering how many people are affected and to what extent. The wider the effect, the higher the bar the employer will need to clear in justifying the PCP and its effects. There is no room for a 'band of reasonable responses' as in unfair dismissal cases (*Hardys & Hansons plc v Lax [2005] ICR 1565*). An employer does not have to demonstrate that the PCP was the only way of achieving the aim in question, but it cannot simply claim that the PCP falls within a range of possible reasonable options.

13.3 HARASSMENT

Harassment is defined in section 26 of the EqA 2010 as unwanted conduct which is related to a relevant protected characteristic and has one of the following purposes or effects:

- Violating the victim's dignity

- Creating an intimidating, hostile, degrading, humiliating or offensive environment for them

The word 'relevant' in the definition refers to the fact that harassment does not apply to all protected characteristics – pregnancy and maternity, and marriage and civil partnerships, are omitted.

13.3.1 UNWANTED CONDUCT

Conduct – which is defined broadly to include everything from written or spoken words to gestures, physical contact, images, practical jokes, or even music – does not have to be deliberate to be unwanted. Whether it is unwanted (which the EHRC Employment Code says means the same as 'unwelcome' or 'uninvited') is a question to be seen from the claimant's perspective; although the tribunal will consider whether it was reasonable to take offence, so hypersensitivity on the claimant's part would undermine the claim. There is no requirement for the claimant to voice their disquiet. The fact that the wrongdoer may not realise the conduct is unwanted is unlikely to make much of a difference (*Insitu Cleaning Co v Heads [1995] IRLR 4*). This is particularly so in cases where the undesirability of the conduct is self-evident (such as insinuating to a female employee that her chances of promotion are higher because she is physically attractive). Obviously, if the claimant genuinely does not object to the treatment, it is, by definition, not unwanted – as in *Mbuyi v Newpark Childcare (Shepherds Bush) Ltd ET/3300656/14*, when a claimant who was found to have been discriminated against when investigated for telling a lesbian colleague she believed homosexuality to be a sin was nonetheless found not to have been harassed, since she had said she welcomed the investigation as a chance to 'tell the gospel' and 'establish who I am'.

The tribunal must also consider other circumstances of the case, which may include the personal circumstances of the claimant (for example, their physical or mental health, mental capacity, cultural norms or previous experience of harassment) and also the environment in which the conduct takes place (see paragraph 7.18 of the EHRC Employment Code).

Respondents will sometimes claim that conduct amounts to nothing more than 'banter' between colleagues. This could constitute a defence if the respondent can show there was genuinely no intent to cause hurt and that the claimant understood and accepted this. But more frequently – especially with a power imbalance, such as between manager and staff (*Munchkins Restaurant Ltd v Karmazyn UKEAT/0359/09*) – the excuse is unlikely to work. Equally, there may be a 'tipping point' where, despite initial acquiescence in conduct by a claimant, the degree of insult crosses a line into unacceptable behaviour (*Thomas Sanderson Blinds Ltd v English UKEAT/0316/10*).

13.3.2 RELATED TO A PROTECTED CHARACTERISTIC

The unwanted conduct must be 'related to' the protected characteristic. This connection could arise from the form it takes (such as sexist banter), or because the conduct is targeted at someone with the characteristic in question. This includes situations where the victim is incorrectly perceived to have the characteristic, and so-called 'associative' harassment, where someone without the characteristic is nonetheless offended by a wrongdoer's discriminatory treatment of another.

A tribunal will consider whether it is reasonable for the conduct to be related to the characteristic. For example, in *Tees Esk & Wear Valleys NHS Foundation Trust v Aslam UKEAT/0039/19*, a claimant who complained of a comment made about Isis in her hearing was found by the EAT not to have been harassed, there having been no evidence to support her contention that there was a public perception tying Isis to people from South Asian backgrounds and that therefore the comment was related to race.

13.3.3 PURPOSE OR EFFECT

Unsurprisingly, it can be hard to show that a respondent deliberately violated an employee's dignity, or created an 'intimidating, hostile, degrading, humiliating or offensive environment for him or her' (section 26(1)(b) of the EqA 2010), although it is worth noting that where someone wants to do so but does not follow through, this would be enough to satisfy this element of the definition of harassment. It is far more common for successful claimants to persuade a tribunal that irrespective of intent, the conduct had the effect of doing so.

Either way, the tribunal will consider the question from the claimant's perspective. If effect is being considered, though, the employment tribunal is required by section 26(4) of the EqA 2010 to consider the surrounding circumstances (such as whether the injury to the claimant's feelings was inadvertent or whether there was any genuine attempt at amends) but also whether the claimant's perception was, in fact, reasonable (*Pemberton v Inwood [2018] ICR 1291*), taking into account – for instance – what the claimant appreciated or should have appreciated about the intent behind the conduct in question (*Ali v Heathrow Express Operating Company Ltd [2022] IRLR 558 EAT*).

This assessment will include examining the seriousness of the conduct. As the EAT found in *Betsi Cadwaladr University Health Board v Hughes UKEAT/0179/13*, words like 'intimidating' are strong ones, denoting 'effects which are serious and marked, and not those which are, though real, truly of lesser consequence'.

The tribunal should also consider the relevant conduct in its context. Particular conduct may create an offensive environment by being part of a series of acts, and a tribunal will err if it measures each incident in isolation rather than looking at the cumulative effect (*Reed and Bull Information Systems Ltd v* Stedman *[1999] IRLR 299*).

13.3.4 SEXUAL HARASSMENT

Section 26(2) of the EqA 2010 makes distinct provision for sexual harassment, providing that a person harasses another if they engage in unwanted conduct of a sexual nature and that conduct has the purpose or effect described above at **13.3.3**. No connection with a protected characteristic is necessary.

As with other forms of harassment, 'unwanted conduct' covers a wide spectrum of behaviour, including jokes (so-called), intrusive questions, gestures, physical contact, or the display of still or moving images (such as pornography), as long as it is connected to sexual activity in some way. Overtly sexual conduct will tend to be deliberate and will therefore amount to harassment without much further analysis. Where the conduct is less overt or not deliberately sexual, the tribunal will need to assess the reasonableness of the claimant's reaction.

Section 26(3) of the EqA 2010 protects people from being treated less favourably because they either rejected, or submitted to, unwanted sexual conduct, and from unwanted conduct related to gender reassignment or sex. The 'purpose or effect' condition applies, but the person applying the less favourable treatment does not have to be the same one perpetrating the unwanted conduct, or even an employee. An employee who refused advances from her manager's friend, and was denied a promotion by the manager as a result, would therefore have a claim.

13.4 VICTIMISATION

People who consider raising a concern at work about their own treatment, or someone else's, may well fear retaliation for having done so. Section 27 of the EqA 2010, the victimisation provision, is designed to mitigate this fear by prohibiting anyone from subjecting another person to detriment because they have done a 'protected act', most commonly making a complaint under the EqA 2010. The outcome of the protected act does not matter: as long as it is done in good faith, any detriment suffered on account of it is unlawful. The perpetrator of the detriment does not even need to be the subject of, say, the complaint. Therefore, an employer ill-treating an employee who had alleged an EqA 2010 breach elsewhere because they perceived the employee to be a potential troublemaker would be liable.

13.4.1 DETRIMENT

'Detriment' is a term used not only in the EqA 2010 with reference to victimisation but also as part of the definition of employment-related discrimination in general. The EqA 2010 does not define detriment, but the detriments commonly arising in victimisation and other discrimination claims include being turned down for jobs, losing promotion or training opportunities, being denied pay rises or bonuses, being threatened with disciplinary proceedings or being dismissed (including potentially constructive dismissal – *Driscoll v V&P Global Ltd [2021] IRLR 891*). Victimisation after employment has finished, for instance, by refusing a reference or providing an unfairly negative one, is also covered by section 27 of the EqA 2010. Even though this appears to be excluded by section 108(7) of the EqA 2010, the Court of Appeal found in *Rowstock Ltd v Jessemey [2014] ICR 550* that since European law required post-employment victimisation to be protected, and since precursor legislation had done so, section 108(7) of the EqA 2010 must have been a drafting error. Words should be implied into it to enable the protection to stand.

A claimant alleging victimisation need not identify a 'comparator'. The detriment itself, if proved, will suffice. Further, the motive of the employer is largely immaterial (*St Helens MBC v Derbyshire [2007] UKHL 16*), although, the motive of the complainant is: a protected act made falsely and 'in bad faith' (section 27(3) of the EqA 2010) is not protected.

Rather, what matters for the purposes of this element of victimisation is whether there is detriment. The term can generally, if not universally, be equated with concepts such as 'disadvantage' or 'unfavourable treatment', as was explored in *Williams v Trustees of Swansea University Pension and Assurance Scheme & anor [2019] ICR 230*. For more on this case, see **13.6.1**. This can be found if 'a reasonable worker would or might take the view that he had thereby been disadvantaged in the circumstances in which he had thereafter to work' (*Shamoon v Chief Constable of the Royal Ulster Constabulary [2003] ICR 337*).

13.4.2 'BECAUSE OF A PROTECTED ACT'

For the detriment to amount to victimisation, it must have been done 'because of a protected act', defined in section 27(2) of the EqA 2010 as one of the following:

- Bringing a claim under the EqA 2010, whether about the employer or not

- Giving evidence or information in connection with such a claim

- Doing any other thing for the purposes of, or in connection with, the EqA 2010 or its forerunners

- Alleging, expressly or otherwise, that someone (whether or not the employer) has breached the EqA 2010

'Doing any other thing' broadens the scope of victimisation considerably. Paragraph 9.8 of the EHRC Employment Code provides the example of a manager who upholds a harassment grievance and is denied an opportunity at work as a result.

It does not matter whether the protected act has, in fact, been done or whether the employer believes it has been done – or even may be done. However, there must be a chain of causation: the protected act needs to have been a trigger, more than trivial but not necessarily the only or even the main one, for the detriment (paragraph 9.10 of the EHRC Employment Code).

And a tribunal may have to take care that it identifies the real reason since sometimes there would be a reason separable from, say, an EqA 2010 complaint which, on proper analysis, was really why the detriment had occurred (*Martin v Devonshires Solicitors [2011] ICR 352 EAT*). For instance, in *Page v Lord Chancellor [2021] IRLR 377*, a magistrate was reprimanded and then removed from office after giving press interviews about opposition to same-sex adoption (although he sat on family panels deciding on such applications) in which he mentioned his reprimand. He was found not to have been victimised: it was his continued public statements about same-sex adoption, not his mention of the reprimand, which triggered his removal. (This case is discussed in the context of conflicts between characteristics at **14.7.3**.)

That said, the connection does not need to be a conscious one: an unconscious motivation for the detrimental treatment will suffice (*Nagarajan v London Regional Transport [1999] IRLR 572*).

Difficulties may arise as a result of pending litigation, where the scope for actions which – judged reasonably – cause detriment to an aggrieved employee is increased. Even so, an employer can take steps to protect its position, so long as on objective analysis the pending litigation, rather than the protected act itself, is the reason why. For example, in *Chief Constable of West Yorkshire Police v Khan [2001] ICR 1065*, the employer declined to provide the claimant with a reference, triggering a victimisation claim. The House of Lords found that the Chief Constable acted as he did because he 'honestly and reasonably' believed it was necessary to avoid prejudice to the proceedings.

13.5 FAILURE TO MAKE REASONABLE ADJUSTMENTS

The problems a disabled person may face in the workplace can be alleviated, or removed altogether, if their employer makes adjustments tailored to address a 'substantial disadvantage' that the person faces. Sections 20-22 of the EqA 2010 make this a duty on employers of all sizes, but the fact that an employer needs to do only what is reasonable, not everything possible, means the nature of the requirement will vary with the circumstances.

The duty to make reasonable adjustments applies to every stage of the employment relationship, including recruitment and dismissal. It can even continue after employment ends (section 108(4) of the EqA 2010) in certain circumstances – for instance, if a benefit granted to an employee continues after they leave or retire.

The onus to make reasonable adjustments, and to pay for them, is on the employer. The cost cannot be passed onto the employee (section 20(7) of the EqA 2010). A failure to obey the duty to make reasonable adjustments is discrimination.

However, the duty is not triggered until the employer knows – or ought to know, having done everything they could reasonably be expected to do – both that the employee is disabled, and that the disability is likely to place them at a substantial disadvantage (*Secretary of State for Work and Pensions v Alam UKEAT/0242/09*). The employer's process of finding out whether an employee has a disability does not have to be perfect (*Donelien v Liberata UK Ltd UKEAT/0297/14*), but a reliance, for instance, solely on an occupational health report which says there is no disability has been found not to be enough (*Gallop v Newport City Council [2014] IRLR 211*).

The duty does not apply associatively, so the parent of a child with a disability could not require their employer to make adjustments to help them accommodate their child's needs.

13.5.1 WHEN IS THE DUTY ENGAGED?

The duty is engaged in three situations, found in sections 20(3)-20(5) of the EqA 2010. Where a PCP (see **13.2.1**) or a physical feature puts a disabled person at a substantial disadvantage compared to non-disabled people, the duty requires the employer to 'take such steps as are reasonable' to avoid it. Alternatively, where the lack of an 'auxiliary aid or service' creates the disadvantage, the duty is to take reasonable steps to supply it. The comparison differs from indirect discrimination in that there is no need to identify a comparison group with 'no material difference' from the disabled person. This is not a group matter; rather, it is a matter of what is right for the individual employee.

A 'substantial disadvantage' is one that is more than minor or trivial (section 212(1) of the EqA 2010). Whether such a disadvantage exists in a particular case is a question of fact to be assessed on an objective basis.

The term 'physical feature' embraces both temporary and permanent features and covers the design or construction of a building; access to it (whether approach or exit); any fixtures or fittings, including furniture, equipment or materials; and 'any other physical element or quality'. Paragraph 6.12 of the EHRC Employment Code provides a lengthy list, including lifts, floor coverings, toilets and signs, and stresses that the list is not exhaustive. Avoiding such a feature means removing or altering it, or providing the disabled person with a means of avoiding having to use it (section 20(9) of the EqA 2010).

'Auxiliary services or aids' provide the person with support or assistance. Paragraph 6.13 of the EHRC Employment Code offers examples, ranging from adapted keyboards to sign language interpreters. Where information needs to be provided (under this or the PCP requirement), it must be provided in an accessible format – for example, in Braille for a partially-sighted person, if that is what they require.

The duty activates as soon as an employer is aware, actually or constructively, of the disability and its effects. However, if an employee is off work, it does not engage until the employee takes positive steps to suggest that they wish to return (*Doran v DWP UKEAT/0017/14*).

The EqA 2010 provides detailed descriptions in its schedules of what the duty entails across a number of scenarios (including premises, work and education). Consideration of these provisions is beyond the scope of this book.

13.5.2 WHAT IS 'REASONABLE'?

The duty to make adjustments is not absolute. Employers are not required to do anything which would (in the words of the relevant EU Directive) place a 'disproportionate burden' on them. An example often quoted is *Dyer v London Ambulance NHS Trust UKEAT/0500/13*, in which there were found to be no adjustments an employer could reasonably have made to accommodate an employee who could suffer life-threatening reactions to perfumes but worked in a busy call centre. (In the wake of Covid-19, with call centre workers routinely having worked from home for months on end, this case might now be decided differently.)

However, that still leaves a great deal of room for requirements to be considered reasonable. Often, the tribunal will have to undertake a 'balancing act' between policies, resources and the employee's needs. Cheap or non-invasive adjustments are highly likely to be considered reasonable, but the EHRC Employment Code points out that even more expensive or far-ranging ones need to be balanced against, for example, the cost of recruiting and training new staff.

The employer may also have to consider other people's interests, particularly if an adjustment might put others at risk even while it mitigates the claimant's disadvantage. For this reason, as well as on general risk management principles, an employer is well-advised to start the process of satisfying its duty with regard to reasonable adjustments by undertaking a risk assessment considering both the employee's situation and those of other stakeholders. In practice, it would be rare that a reasonable adjustment would put others at material risk. Thereafter, a sensible employer will document the steps that the employee suggests, as well as make its own suggestions, and assess their reasonableness. The EHRC Employment Code notes that factors which may be taken into account include not only the measures' cost and practicality (set against the size of the employer and the resources at its disposal) but also whether there is any financial or other assistance available to help implement them.

As to the kinds of adjustment which may be considered, paragraph 6.33 of the EHRC Employment Code provides a non-exhaustive list of possibilities, ranging from altered hours, different work locations or a change in role or adjustments to premises (such as a ramp or wider doors) to providing special equipment (such as furniture or computers) or adapting procedures.

Employers will sometimes seek to argue that a particular adjustment would not have helped mitigate the disadvantage in question. Certainly, a futile adjustment is an unreasonable one – but the requirement is only that the adjustment could possibly, at the time it was implemented, have been helpful. The tribunal will have to assess whether there was a 'prospect' – not necessarily a good one – that it would have succeeded in helping. If so, then it was reasonable, and therefore required (*Griffiths v DWP [2015] ICR 160*). Even a future benefit may, in some cases, be a reasonable adjustment – for instance, one promised if a specified set of circumstances which would exacerbate the employee's difficulties were to arise (*Hill v Lloyds Bank plc [2020] IRLR 652*).

Griffiths also showed that there may be times when an employer has to take positive steps beyond simply treating employees equally, such as providing more time off or continuing to pay a disabled employee the same salary even if they have moved, as a reasonable adjustment, to a less demanding, more junior role. However, there is no requirement to pay a disabled person more on long-term sick leave than a non-disabled person in similar circumstances (*O'Hanlon v HMRC [2007] ICR 1359*).

13.5.3 JUSTIFICATION

An employer cannot justify a failure to make reasonable adjustments.

13.6 DISCRIMINATION ARISING FROM DISABILITY

A claim for discrimination arising from disability (section 15 of the EqA 2010) often sits alongside a direct or indirect discrimination claim, and, in particular, together with one for a failure to make reasonable adjustments. It can also stand alone: in circumstances where a claimant cannot point to acts or omissions directly driven by their disability itself, or to a policy, criterion or practice with general application that disproportionately affects people with their disability, a claim under section 15 of the EqA 2010 may be the only option.

The EqA 2010 defines discrimination arising from disability as occurring when:

- An employer treats an employee unfavourably

- Because of 'something'

- That 'something' arises as a consequence of the employee's disability

- The employer cannot show that the treatment is justified (see **12.5.1**)

A tribunal should take each factor separately (*Pnaiser v NHS England [2016] IRLR 170*), although the order in which they are assessed – treatment, then 'something', or the other way around – does not necessarily matter (*Basildon and Thurrock NHS Foundation Trust v Weerasinghe [2016] ICR 305*).

For a claim to succeed, the employer must know the disability exists, or it must be reasonable for them to be aware of it.

Therefore, an employee whose disability means they need more time off than someone else, but who is disciplined for the excessive leave, has not suffered direct discrimination, since the disciplinary decision was not because of the disability itself, but because of its effect on the employee. The employee may, however, have a case under section 15 of the EqA 2010.

A claim under section 15 of the EqA 2010 can only be brought by a person with a disability. The statutory wording is clear: there is no room for perception or associative claims.

13.6.1 UNFAVOURABLE TREATMENT

Unfavourable treatment needs to be assessed on a free-standing basis. There is no need for a comparator.

Until recently, there was some disagreement about the relationship between this concept and other terms – such as 'detriment' or 'disadvantage' – used elsewhere in discrimination legislation. That confusion has been resolved by the Supreme Court in *Williams v Trustees of Swansea University Pension and Assurance Scheme & anor [2019] ICR 230*, previously mentioned at **13.4.1**. The Court found that for practical purposes, little was to be gained by parsing any 'narrow distinctions' between the terms and that the 'threshold of disadvantage' that the treatment would need to clear was 'relatively low'.

The Supreme Court also stressed that the treatment had to be evaluated in the round. In *Williams*, the core issue was that the claimant had been working part-time (a reasonable adjustment for his disabilities) when he had to retire, in his 30s, on ill-health grounds. His employer's pension scheme calculated his pension on the basis of his part-time earnings but credited him with almost three extra decades of work all the way to retirement age. Mr Williams claimed he had been unfavourably treated because his pension was based on his part-time salary. The Supreme Court disagreed: it said Mr Williams was cherry-picking a single effect while ignoring the fact that the scheme was actually advantageous, in that it credited him with 29 years of additional accruals.

A more recent example in the EAT was in *Cowie v Scottish Fire and Rescue Service [2022] IRLR 913*. The employer had a special leave policy allowing employees who had exhausted their time off in lieu (TOIL) from working overtime to take extra leave in, say, unexpected family emergencies. During 2020, it extended this policy to include those who were shielding or who had to stay home to look after children no longer able to attend school – as long as they exhausted their TOIL and normal leave first. The claimants (who had shielded) said this was unfair because they were forced to use up leave others would have kept. The EAT said this was well within the *Williams* situation: it was artificial to try to split off (and ignore) what was, in fact, a benefit – the extra leave – from the conditions for getting it.

13.6.2 BECAUSE OF 'SOMETHING'

A common, sometimes critical, error by claimants seeking redress for alleged discrimination arising from disability – and an opportunity consequently often taken by respondents – is to fail properly to identify the 'something arising from disability' on which their claim will rest. The requirement in section 15 of the EqA 2010 for a chain of causation – the 'because of' element – means that tribunals will routinely demand a clear description of the 'something' before a claim can proceed. If the 'something' that is identified does not naturally arise from the disability, or the connection between it and the treatment is not evident, the claim is likely to fail.

The 'something' does not need to be the only, or even the main, cause of the disadvantage suffered, nor does it need to be the only link in the causal chain. But it must have more than a trivial influence over the decision underpinning it (*Secretary of State for Justice v Dunn UKEAT/0234/16*). As the Court of Appeal found in *Robinson v DWP [2020] IRLR 884*, a tribunal will nearly always need to consider the conscious or unconscious thought processes of the decision-maker, to see just what influence the 'something' had – although their *motive* for thinking that way is irrelevant.

The range of possible 'somethings' is limitless, but a good example appears at paragraph 5.9 of the EHRC Employment Code. An employee is disciplined for losing her temper at work, but the loss of temper is out of character and results from the severe pain she is suffering caused by cancer. The punishment is caused by the 'something' that arose from her disability, not by the disability itself.

13.6.3 THE KNOWLEDGE REQUIREMENT

The wide variety of possible 'somethings', it could be argued, lowers the bar for employers' liability considerably. But a claim will nonetheless fail if the employee cannot show that the employer was aware of the disability in question, or that it is reasonable for the employer to have been aware of it, at the time of the unfavourable treatment complained of. Knowledge acquired after the unfavourable treatment complained of will not suffice, as the claimant found in *Stott v Ralli Ltd [2022] IRLR 148 EAT*. Ms Stott complained to the employment tribunal of discrimination under section 15 of the EqA 2010 after being dismissed, but her claim was rejected because, said the tribunal, the knowledge element was lacking. Ms Stott appealed, saying that she made the company aware of her disability during the subsequent grievance and appeal process, but the EAT pointed out that she had not complained about the grievance process – only about the dismissal.

The decision-maker does not necessarily have to be aware. If occupational health, HR or another person knows of the disability, then it is reasonable to expect the decision-maker to have been informed. Their ignorance may not be a defence.

Employers who ignore evidence of disability are also likely to be found to have constructive knowledge. However, that does not mean that a failure to ask about a possible disability is necessarily fatal to the employer's chances if inquiries would not reasonably have enlightened it – for instance, if an employee was embarrassed or ashamed about a condition and would not have revealed it if asked.

Note that it is the disability of which the employer must be aware. There is no requirement that they are aware of the specific consequence – the 'something' (*City of York Council v Grosset [2018] ICR 1492*).

13.6.4 JUSTIFICATION

The justification defence discussed at **12.6.1** is available in claims for discrimination arising from a disability. The requirement for proportionality and necessity can present serious difficulties for an employer relying on justification, especially in cases where there is also a claim for a failure to make reasonable adjustments. Where adjustments exist that could have been made, and they are less discriminatory than the treatment alleged, it is likely that the defence will fail (*Essop v Home Office [2017] ICR 640*). However, the justification can sometimes be after the fact: an employer can permissibly argue before a tribunal that its conduct was objectively justified even if it did not, in fact, have that justification in mind at the time of the alleged discrimination (*ICTS (UK) Ltd v Visram UKEAT/0344/15/LA*).

CHAPTER 14
PROTECTED CHARACTERISTICS

14.0 OVERVIEW

As established in Chapter 12, the *Equality Act 2010* (EqA 2010) covers nine protected characteristics. This chapter looks in detail at those characteristics and at how the UK and European courts have defined what does – and does not – amount to discrimination in relation to them.

14.1 AGE

The EqA 2010 defines the protected characteristic of age in terms of members of an 'age group'. This could be a specific age, but more usually refers to a range – whether narrow or wide and at any part of the spectrum from young to old. Logically, therefore, if a comparator (see **13.1.1**) is required to prove a claim, they must be someone facing the same circumstances but from a different age range. The difference in age does not have to be large, as long as less favourable treatment can be identified; although the significance (and thus the discriminatory effect) of a narrow difference may be more pronounced at some ages than others (*Citibank NA v Kirk [2022] EAT 103*). Age discrimination can also manifest as sex discrimination – for instance, if a job has different retirement ages for men and women without any objective justification for the gap (*Bullock v Alice Ottley School [1993] ICR 138*).

14.1.1 AGE DISCRIMINATION AND JUSTIFICATION

Uniquely, employers can claim a justification defence in the face of a direct age discrimination claim, but the standard they have to meet is demanding. The wording of the age justification test in section 13(2) of the EqA 2010 is similar to other such tests in the EqA 2010, requiring the employer to show the treatment in question was 'a proportionate means of achieving a legitimate aim'. However, the *EU Equality Framework Directive (2000/78/EC)*, on which the provision is based, calls for the difference in treatment to be 'objectively and reasonably justified by a legitimate aim' and 'appropriate and necessary'.

The Supreme Court has found (*Chief Constable of West Yorkshire Police v Homer [2012] ICR 711*) that this sets a higher bar: not only will the treatment need to be a proportionate means of achieving a legitimate aim, but it will also have to be reasonably necessary. The aim in question would also need to be justified by reference to the public interest, as opposed to simply with reference to the employer's business (*Seldon v Clarkson Wright & Jakes [2012] ICR 716*).

In practice, this means, as formulated by the employment tribunal in the case of *McCloud v Ministry of Justice ET/2201483/15* and later approved by both the Employment Appeal Tribunal (EAT) (*[2018] ICR 1039*) and the Court of Appeal (*[2019] ICR 1489*):

- The burden is on the employer to make out their justification defence to a high standard of proof.

- The employer must be able to articulate the aim which was being pursued, although absolute precision in stating the aim is not required.

- Social policy aims can be 'legitimately' pursued by a public employer, and the Government will be accorded a wide discretion in choosing between possible social aims and approaches, although that wide discretion does not extend into the private relationship between employer and employee.

- The measure must be an 'appropriate' way to achieve the legitimate aim.

- For the measure to be 'reasonably necessary', the employer must be able to explain how the measure will achieve the legitimate aim without going beyond what is required to meet it.

14.1.2 EXCEPTIONS TO AGE DISCRIMINATION

As well as the general exemptions outlined at **12.5**, a number of specific exceptions exist applying solely to age discrimination.

Retirement and 'employer justified retirement ages'

Since April 2011, forcing someone to retire at a default retirement age has amounted to unfair dismissal, unless an objective justification brings it within the bounds of 'some other substantial reason' for dismissal (section 98(1) of the *Employment Rights Act 1996* (ERA 1996). Such a justification creates an employer-justified retirement age (EJRA). The change in 2011 means cases from before then need to be treated with caution, particularly those which pre-date the Supreme Court's narrowing of the justification defence with specific reference to retirement ages in *Seldon*.

As with any objective justification, an employer wanting to put in place an EJRA will need to show it is a proportionate means of achieving a legitimate aim which is in the public interest, as well as that of the employer, and that the ERJA is reasonably necessary to achieve that aim.

This is a highly fact-contingent process, so much may depend on the evidence before the tribunal. This was shown by the EAT's decision in two cases involving the same EJRA policy of Oxford University but with different tribunal outcomes. In one (*Pitcher v Chancellor, Masters and Scholars of the University of Oxford [2021] IRLR 946*), the tribunal had found the EJRA-based refusal of a retirement extension to be justified. In the other (*Ewart v Chancellor, Masters and Scholars of the University of Oxford [2021] IRLR 946*), a different tribunal had found for the claimant. The EAT said both tribunals had been right: although the legitimate aims (see below) were the same, and were allowed, in both cases, there had been different evidence (leading to different outcomes) on the detriment caused to the claimant and the supposedly beneficial effects of the policy.

Legitimate aim

Establishing the 'legitimate aim' is probably the easier part of the defence. An employer might attempt to argue:

- The 'dead man's shoes' argument: promoting recruitment and retention by ensuring there is a clearly defined career path caused by the compulsory retirement of older workers.
- Collegiality: limiting the need to dismiss employees based on diminishing performance, and allowing people to retire with dignity.
- That it is facilitating long-term employment planning.

There may also be cost considerations, such as higher premiums for some forms of insurance for older employees (or, indeed, particularly young ones). Given the need to serve a social or employment policy aim, this is probably the most controversial, and the courts have not been entirely consistent in how they approach it. The dominant approach, more consistent with *Seldon*, is to allow cost to be a potential supporting reason but to reject the idea that cost savings are sufficiently a public interest issue to be an employer's primary motivation. This so-called 'costs-plus' standard, which the Court of Appeal approved in *Woodcock v Cumbria Primary Care Trust [2012] ICR 1126*, has come in for criticism as being too mechanistic: a better approach (said the Court of Appeal in *Heskett v Secretary of State for Justice [2021] IRLR 132*) is to reject a defence based on costs alone, but otherwise to see how the employer's reason should be fairly characterised (including cost, if that is genuinely part of the picture) and assess justification on the basis of that holistic picture.

Proportionality

Even if a legitimate aim with an adequate public interest element can be identified, the EJRA must still be a proportionate way of achieving it. This is usually harder, and UK courts have tended to take a strict approach – certainly more so than in Europe, where it has been held that a fire service could bar applicants over 30 due to the need for physical stamina (*Wolf v Stadt Frankfurt am Main [2010] IRLR 244*), or that dentists should retire at 68 to give way to younger generations (*Petersen v Berufungsausschuss für Zahnärtze für den Bezirk Westfalen-Lippe [2010] IRLR 254*).

For example, a retirement age of 48 for football referees was found by a tribunal to be unlawful (*Martin v Professional Game Match Officials (2009) ET/2082438/2009*), as was an age cap for trainee air traffic controllers at 35 (*Baker v National Air Traffic Services (2009) ET/2203501/2007*) and a compulsory retirement age of 65 for one group of judges (*Hampton v Lord Chancellor [2008] IRLR 258*).

As a general rule, therefore, employers would be wise to avoid compulsory retirement ages wherever possible. Instead, they might discuss options with employees reaching state pension age, such as retirement, a change to hours or role, job sharing or other amendments to working conditions. If done sensitively, without acting in such a way that the employee could reasonably perceive any pressure to step down, this is unlikely to amount to direct age discrimination. Acas's more cautious recommendation is to hold regular meetings to discuss career objectives with all workers, not just those, say, over 60, to avoid the risk of appearing to treat older employees differently.

An employer can still dismiss an older worker if they are unable to do their job, just as it would a younger one – provided, of course, that procedures are followed properly. Such a dismissal would not be discrimination on grounds of age, although the employer might need to justify the dismissal's fairness on capability grounds if the employee was to make a claim for unfair dismissal.

Length of service

It is not uncommon for the level of some benefits, such as redundancy, to change with an employee's length of service. Schedule 9, paragraph 10 of the EqA 2010 says that employees with five years' service or fewer cannot claim age discrimination if they are disadvantaged 'in relation to the provision of a benefit, facility or service' in comparison to someone with longer service. For other employees, an employer would need to justify the different levels of benefit on the basis of believing the distinction served a business need, such as encouraging loyalty or rewarding experience. Such a belief must be objectively reasonable.

This exemption does not extend to termination payments (Schedule 9, paragraph 10(7) of the EqA 2010). Redundancy payments linked to length of service are therefore generally subject to the usual objective justification requirement (see **14.1.1**). However, a more limited exception would apply to an employer offering different redundancy payments to different employees

252

if the amount paid is calculated on the same basis as the statutory redundancy scheme in section 162 of the ERA 1996.

The statutory scheme awards employees 1.5 weeks' pay for every year of employment in which the employee was at least 41 years old, one week for each year between 22 and 40, and half a week for each other year. The EqA 2010 exception differs from normal statutory redundancy pay calculations in three principal ways, allowing employers more flexibility:

1) There is no minimum term of service.

2) While the statutory scheme caps the weekly wage for the purposes of the calculation (£648 per week, as of 6 April 2023), employers can apply a higher cap or none.

3) As long as the age-related ratios remain unchanged, employers can apply a multiplier of more than one to the amount accrued for each year of service, or to the overall amount.

So, for instance, an employer could choose to base redundancy payments on workers' full weekly wages and double the multipliers (to pay three weeks a year for the older band, two for the middle and one for the younger band). It could not, however, set lower multipliers or a lower wage cap than the statutory scheme requires or change the ratios.

National Minimum Wage

The National Minimum Wage (NMW) is set at different levels for different age bands, and these are sometimes sharply different: as of April 2023, £10.42 an hour for those aged at least 25 but £5.28 for those under 18. On the face of it, this is discriminatory. The justification is that it makes it easier for the less experienced to find employment. In any case, the EqA 2s010 contains specific provisions at Schedule 9, paragraphs 11-12, exempting the NMW bands from the age discrimination rules.

Insurance benefits

As mentioned above, some kinds of insurance may be more expensive for older workers. In response to fears expressed by employers' organisations, in 2011, a new paragraph 14 was inserted by the government into Schedule 9 of the EqA 2010. This allows employers lawfully to stop providing insurance or 'a related financial service' to employees who reach the later of 65 or the state pensionable age (currently 66 for people born before 6 April 1960, but between 66 and 67 for people born between then and 5 April 1977).

The business justification is understandable, but the change has the effect of leaving employees without cover just when they might need it the most. In addition, the provision makes no distinction between insurance with a price that changes with age, and other kinds – legal expenses cover, for instance – where this is not the case.

Even if a discrimination claim is barred, an employee whose terms of employment include an entitlement to insurance cover may be able to claim breach of contract.

Pension schemes

As is the case with equal pay (see **15.1.5**), an analysis of pension schemes in the context of age discrimination is complex and beyond the scope of this book. It is worth mentioning that a large number of exceptions apply, principally arising from section 61 of the EqA 2010 (covered under equal pay) and the *Equality Act (Age Exceptions for Pension Schemes) Order 2010*. Readers needing to know more are advised to consult specialist texts on pensions law.

Childcare benefits

Conceivably, an age discrimination claim could arise if a parent sought redress because a childcare provider did not serve their child's age group. This would not succeed, at least not on age discrimination grounds: Schedule 9, paragraph 15 of the EqA 2010 provides that it is not a contravention of the Act to facilitate the provision of care for children of a particular age group.

14.2 DISABILITY

Section 6(1) of the EqA 2010 defines a disability as:

- A 'physical or mental impairment', which
- Adversely affects someone's ability to carry out normal day-to-day activities, where that adverse effect is
- Substantial, and
- Long-term

The points should be dealt with in turn, not all together (*Goodwin v Patent Office [1999] IRLR 4*).

This high-level definition is elaborated further at Schedule 1, part 1 of the EqA 2010, with statutory guidance providing further assistance. The guidance is not mandatory, but courts and tribunals are obliged to take it into account. It is available at https://www.gov.uk/government/publications/equality-act-guidance/disability-equality-act-2010-guidance-on-matters-to-be-taken-into-account-in-determining-questions-relating-to-the-definition-of-disability-html.

Employers defending a disability claim will frequently argue that the claimant does not satisfy the EqA 2010 definition. Tribunals will sometimes seek to settle the issue of whether a disability exists in a preliminary hearing.

This will not be necessary with some conditions, such as cancer, HIV and multiple sclerosis, which are deemed always to be disabilities (Schedule 1, paragraph 6(1) of the EqA 2010).

A key aspect of disability discrimination cases, and one which sets them apart from other discrimination claims, is that a successful claim will often provide a claimant with 'advantages' others do not have – at least insofar as a reasonable adjustment could be said to provide an 'advantage', given that its aim and effect is to counter disadvantages arising from the disability. In this, it differs from, say, sex or race discrimination cases, where the aim is to ensure equal treatment between the claimant and others. As Baroness Hale put it in *Archibald v Fife Council [2004] ICR 954*: 'The question ... is when that obligation arises, and how far it goes.'

'Physical or mental Impairment'

There is no statutory definition of 'physical or mental impairment'. Usually, a tribunal will focus less on the condition itself and more on the impact it has on the claimant.

This does not mean the identity of the condition is unimportant. Some conditions, such as additions to 'alcohol, nicotine or any other substance' are specifically excluded by the *Equality Act 2010 (Disability) Regulations 2010* (the 2010 Regulations), as are hay fever, body piercings and tattoos, as well as a number of personality disorders, including voyeurism and tendencies to criminal behaviour. However, if these are a symptom of an underlying disorder, or aggravate one (such as hay fever with asthma), a tribunal may take them into account in considering the effect of the alleged disability.

The key question for the tribunal will be what claimants cannot do as a function of their disability, not what they can do (*Aderemi v London & South East Railway Ltd [2013] ICR 591*). This is not an all-or-nothing question: someone who can carry out day-to-day activities may still only do so in an impaired fashion (*Ekpe v Commissioner of Police of the Metropolis [2001] ICR 1084*). Further, there is no question of comparison with an average able-bodied person (*Paterson v Metropolitan Police Commissioner [2007] ICR 1522*) or with a group of people or segment of the population (*Elliott v Dorset County Council [2021] IRLR 880*): the correct comparison is with what the claimant could do without their impairment.

The question may sometimes arise – for instance, with an insulin-dependent diabetic – of whether a claim can be made for a disability which would exist only if medical treatment ceased. Schedule 1, paragraph 5(1) of the EqA 2010 specifically permits this as long as the claimant can prove, not merely assert, what would happen without the treatment (*Woodrup v Southwark LBC [2003] IRLR 111*).

Is the effect 'substantial'?

An impairment's effect does not have to be overwhelming to be 'substantial'. Instead, it need only be 'more than minor or trivial' (section 212(1) of the EqA 2010). This is not a continuum: as the EAT found in *Aderemi*, an impairment will fall into one of two categories. If it cannot be classed as minor or trivial, it will be substantial for the purposes of the EqA 2010. That said, the effect does have to be caused by the impairment, even if the causal link is not necessarily direct.

A prospective effect – one which is likely to happen if treatment is absent – may qualify, with 'likely' given the meaning of 'could well happen' rather than 'more likely than not' (*Boyle v SCA Packaging Ltd [2009] ICR 1056*). Similarly, a progressive condition with likely future substantial effects – albeit ones which have not yet reached that degree – can also entitle a claimant to protection (Schedule 1, paragraph 8 of the EqA 2010).

Otherwise, the question of whether an effect is 'substantial' is one for the tribunal. Medical opinion may well provide valuable assistance, where it exists, but medical experts cannot make the decision for the tribunal (*Abadeh v BT plc [2001] ICR 156*), nor should they offer an opinion on whether the conditions and symptoms they have identified qualify as disabilities under the EqA 2010 (*Carden v Pickerings Europe Ltd [2005] IRLR 720*).

An exception to the need to determine whether an impairment is substantial is where the impairment is a severe disfigurement. In such a case, its substantial effect on day-to-day activities is assumed under Schedule 1, paragraph 3 of the EqA 2010, and a claimant need only prove the effect is long-term (see below).

Is it 'long-term'?

The key period for deciding whether an impairment is 'long-term' is 12 months. As Schedule 1, paragraph 2 of the EqA 2010 provides, the effect of the impairment needs to have lasted for 12 months already, to be likely to last for 12 more months or to last for the rest of the claimant's life (in case life expectancy is less than a year). Note that it is the longevity of the effect, not the condition which caused it, that the issue (*Swift v Chief Constable of Wiltshire Constabulary [2004] IRLR 540*). As with the House of Lords' decision in *Boyle*, an effect which is 'likely to recur' (meaning 'might well do so') will qualify (Schedule 1, paragraph 2(2) of the EqA 2010).

The key date here is the date on which the alleged discrimination occurred. As a result, a condition which was, at the time, expected only to have a short-term effect, but which later developed more chronic effects, will not qualify (*Elliott v Pertemps Recruitment Partnership Ltd EAT/0648/02*). The date on which the long-term effect is diagnosed or becomes apparent will therefore be critical (*Tesco Stores Ltd v Tennant EAT/0167/19*).

Similarly, in cases relying on recurring effects, recurrences after the date of the discriminatory event are not relevant. A tribunal must base its decision only on the likelihood of resurgence at that time, not on information which became available later (attractively referred to by the Court of Appeal in *Richmond Adult Community College v McDougall [2008] ICR 431* as requiring 'a prophecy to be made'). Where circumstances change soon after the event in question, this may mean that an employee's claim fails where it would have succeeded had the discriminatory event occurred just weeks later.

'Normal day-to-day activities'

When considering what activities are 'normal' and 'day-to-day', courts and tribunals will take a flexible approach. As the government's official Guidance (Guidance on Matters to be Taken into Account in Determining Questions Relating to the Definition of Disability) makes clear at paragraph D3, the activities in question are by no means limited to those which are work-related – far from it. The list offered there includes 'things people do on a regular basis', such as 'shopping, reading and writing, having a conversation, watching TV, and getting washed and dressed' and others, including work- and study-related activities such as keeping to a timetable or using a computer. As far as work-related activities are concerned, the fact that a particular condition may only occur at work is not a reason to exclude it from consideration when deciding whether it has an effect on day-to-day activities (*Cruickshank v VAW Motorcast Ltd [2002] ICR 729*).

Neither an over-inclusive nor too narrow approach is proper. So, while a tribunal should avoid taking account of activities which are normal only for one person or a small group, or highly specialised, such as playing a sport or musical instrument to a high level, equally they should not exclude activities which, say, are generally limited to one sex (*Ekpe v Commissioner of Police of the Metropolis [2001] ICR 1084*). As the EAT found in *Ekpe*, 'normal' really only excludes things which are unusual.

14.2.1 EXAMPLES OF IMPAIRMENT

It would be impossible to compile an exhaustive list of conditions which have been recognised as impairments. The following have been recognised, although it is important to take into account that in most cases, a tribunal's decision will rest on the particular facts and on how the condition affects a particular claimant.

- Achondroplasia, or dwarfism (*English v Kwik-Save ET/1501565/03*).

- Asthma (*Browne v Commissioner of Police of the Metropolis UKEAT/0278/17*).

- Autism in the shape of conditions such as autism spectrum disorder (ASD) or Asperger's Syndrome (*Hewett v Motorola Ltd [2004] IRLR 545*).

- Attention deficit hyperactivity disorder (ADHD) has been accepted as a disability by respondents in some cases, although in *JC v Gordonstoun Schools Ltd [2016] SC 758*, the Court of Session declined to accept that its effect was sufficiently substantial and long-term.

- Back injuries (*JP Morgan Europe Ltd v Chweidan [2012] ICR 268*).

- Blindness is automatically deemed to be a disability (by the 2010 Regulations) as long as the claimant has been certified blind or partially sighted or is registered as such on a local authority register. Sight problems which glasses or contact lenses can correct will not qualify.

- Depression (*J v DLA Piper UK LLP [2010] ICR 1052*).

- Diabetes (*Home Office v Collins [2005] EWCA Civ 598*).

- Dyslexia (*Holmes v Bolton Metropolitan Borough Council (unreported, IT, December 1988)*).

- Irritable bowel syndrome (*Hoyte v Jaguar Land Rover Ltd ET/1300211/2016*).

- Menopause (*Rooney v Leicester City Council [2022] IRLR 17*).

- Myalgic encephalomyelitis (ME), albeit together with chronic fatigue syndrome and schizophrenia (*O'Neill v Symm and Co Ltd [1998] ICR 481*).

- Obesity, by itself, is unlikely to render a person disabled. But it may exacerbate other conditions such that their effect amounts to an impairment (*Walker v Sita Information Networking Computing Ltd UKEAT/0097/12*).

- Panic disorders, albeit often as a symptom of depression or other mental disabilities.

- Post-traumatic stress disorder (*Blackledge v London General Transport Services Ltd UKEAT/1073/00*).

- Stress, without more, is unlikely to count as a disability (*J v DLA Piper [2010] ICR 1052*), although it may be a symptom of an underlying disorder, in which case it will be taken into account. Sometimes, though, it may be the result of work, not an underlying condition – in which case, it will probably not in itself qualify (*Herry v Dudley MBC [2017] ICR 610*).

- 'Long Covid' – the constellation of symptoms, often similar to those of chronic fatigue syndrome, suffered by some who have contracted Covid-19 – is only now appearing in tribunal judgments, and there have been no appeals about it. But at least one employment tribunal has ruled that effects attributed to Long Covid can be a disability (*Burke v Turning Point Scotland ET/4112457/2021*).

14.3 GENDER REASSIGNMENT

People who have undergone, are undergoing or are proposing to undergo a process (or part of one) of reassigning their sex are protected from discrimination by section 7 of the EqA 2010. The process in question is a personal one, not necessarily a medical or legal one. Paragraph 2.24 of The Equality and Human Rights Commission Employment Statutory Code of Practice (the EHRC Employment Code) says that it 'may include undergoing the medical gender reassignment treatments, but it does not require someone to undergo medical treatment in order to be protected'. Someone who starts such a process, whether medical or not, but stops before it is completed is also protected. Further, while the *Gender Recognition Act 2004* provides for someone to acquire a Gender Recognition Certificate (GRC) which changes their legal gender, no one needs a GRC to benefit from the protection of section 7 of the EqA 2010.

In addition, it is discriminatory to deny someone a period of absence to undergo gender reassignment treatment if they would have been permitted absence if ill or injured (section 16 of the EqA 2010).

It is important to note that the EqA 2010 as currently enacted protects gender reassignment, not gender identity, so as the law currently stands, a person who self-identifies as a gender other than their biological gender is unlikely to benefit from its protection unless a 'process' can be identified and proved. The EqA 2010 is also arguably – as highlighted in 2016 in a House of Commons Women and Equalities Committee report – outdated in its use of the word 'transsexual', not only in section 7 but also elsewhere. The report recommended updating it to 'transgender' or simply 'trans' to reflect the preferred usage of those with the characteristic. Thus far, there has been no statutory movement on this point.

The requirement for a 'process' has raised questions about when in a gender reassignment procedure a particular act may amount to discrimination. The leading case on the issue, *Croft v Royal Mail Group plc [2003] ICR 1425*, in fact, pre-dates the EqA 2010. In *Croft*, the Court of Appeal found that the employer had not unlawfully discriminated against a claimant who had been born male (and had worked for the employer for 10 years as such), but had started living as a woman, when they required her to use a unisex (disabled) toilet rather than the female toilets. The court stressed that the claimant was undergoing a process and that while the court had to have regard to her identification of where she was in that process, it was nonetheless for the court 'to make a judgment as to when the employee becomes a woman and entitled to the same facilities as other women'. Such an employee was not necessarily immediately entitled to the same facilities as women born female.

It is doubtful whether *Croft* would be decided the same way today. The Court of Appeal's decision was under precursor legislation which required the 'process' to be 'under medical supervision', and the fact that the claimant had only recently started to dress and live as a woman was, though not the deciding factor, certainly a significant one in the court's reasoning. However, while the question of access to facilities is likely to continue to require an assessment of progress in the 'process' – whatever form that takes for the individual in question – other forms of detriment (such as refusal of employment, insults, ostracism or dismissal) are less likely to need to rely on such an assessment.

The gender reassignment provisions of the EqA 2010 do not cover transvestites – that is, people who dress in clothing associated with their opposite sex for reasons other than gender reassignment, namely, pleasure (see paragraph 2.26 of the EHRC Employment Code). However, transvestites will be protected from discrimination if they are mistreated because they are mistakenly thought to be undergoing or proposing to undergo gender reassignment (see **13.1.5**).

14.4 MARRIAGE AND CIVIL PARTNERSHIP

Section 8 of the EqA 2010 prohibits discrimination on the grounds that someone is married or in a civil partnership. 'Marriage' covers any formal union legally recognised in the UK as a marriage, whether secular or sacred, and, since 2013 (2014 in Scotland), has included same-sex marriages. A civil partnership is a registered civil partnership under the *Civil Partnership Act 2004*, which also now allows for both same- and opposite-sex relationships.

The EqA 2010 is specific about the status of a marriage or civil partnership: it must be current for the Act's protection to engage. Divorced or cohabiting people, or people whose civil partnership is dissolved, are not covered. Nor are people intending to be married or have a partnership registered. Further, there is no provision in the EqA 2010 for harassment based on marriage or civil partnership to be unlawful discrimination. That said, in either case, a claim based on sex or sexual orientation discrimination (for instance, if someone was discriminated against for intending to marry someone of the same sex, or harassed for doing so) is conceivable.

14.4.1 EXAMPLES

Although discrimination on the grounds of marriage or civil partnership seems conceptually straightforward, it has not always proved so in practice. A few examples demonstrate the potential complexities:

- In *Graham v Chief Constable of the Bedfordshire Constabulary [2002] IRLR 239*, a female police inspector was denied a promotion opportunity because her husband would have become her commander. The reason was concern that, since spouses cannot be compelled to give evidence against one another, she could not be a witness should he find himself prosecuted. The EAT found this to be a 'marriage-specific' reason and thus discriminatory.

- In *Dunn v Institute of Cemetery and Crematorium Management [2012] ICR 941*, a female claimant was allegedly treated less favourably in the way a number of grievances were investigated because her employer was displeased with her husband. A tribunal rejected her claim of discrimination based on her marital status. On appeal, the EAT acknowledged that the claimant might have been treated in the same way if she had been in a non-marital but close relationship with her husband, but suggested that this did not defeat the marriage discrimination claim.

- However, in the later case of *Hawkins v Atex Group Ltd [2012] ICR 1315*, the EAT took issue with the approach taken in *Dunn* and ruled that less favourable treatment because a claimant is in a close relationship with another employee (which could include but is not limited to marriage) would not amount to marital discrimination.

- In *Gould v Trustees of St John's Downshire Hill UKEAT/0115/17*, a minister was dismissed from his church for suffering difficulties in his marriage. His claim was struck out on the grounds that it was the difficulties, rather than his being married, which was the issue, but the EAT overturned the decision on the basis that – as in *Graham* – the reason was 'marriage-specific'. In other words, problems in a non-marital relationship would, in these particular circumstances, not have put him in the same position.

The lesson to draw, it seems, would be that marriage and civil partnership discrimination claims are not impossible to bring, but require a particularly specific approach to pleading. Only if the detriment genuinely arises from the status of being married or in a civil partnership itself – rather than because of the identity of the partner or spouse, or something which could equally arise in a less formal relationship – is the claim likely to have a realistic chance of success.

14.4.2 OCCUPATIONAL REQUIREMENTS – THE RELIGION EXCEPTION

As noted at **12.5.4**, the EqA 2010 provides a specific occupational requirement to organised religions allowing discrimination involving marital status (as well as sex and sexual orientation), if the requirement is applied to comply with the religion's doctrines or to avoid conflict with strongly-held religious convictions of a significant number of its followers.

The most prominent example of this concerns marriage discrimination. Jeremy Pemberton, a Church of England priest, was denied a role as a hospital chaplain because he had married his same-sex partner and the church's doctrine held that marriage should only be between a man and a woman. He sued, but the Court of Appeal found that even though the proposed employer was not itself an organised religion, the role required a properly-licensed member of the clergy. The EqA 2010 exception therefore applied (*Pemberton v Inwood [2018] ICR 1291*).

14.5 PREGNANCY AND MATERNITY

Many employers continue to stigmatise pregnant women and mothers. Research by the Equality and Human Rights Commission (EHRC) in 2016 indicated that almost half of employers thought it was reasonable during a recruitment process to ask women (but not men) if they had young children. Roughly the same number felt women should not have children in their first year in a new organisation. More than one in 10 mothers surveyed said they had been dismissed, made compulsorily redundant unfairly or treated so poorly they had had to leave their job.

Specific provisions in the EqA 2010 provide protection against direct pregnancy and maternity discrimination. Section 18 of the EqA 2010 states that a woman is discriminated against if her employer treats her unfavourably because she is pregnant, because she suffers illness as a result of pregnancy, because she is on compulsory maternity leave or because she seeks to exercise a right to ordinary or additional maternity leave.

As discussed at **13.1.1**, women claiming under section 18 of the EqA 2010 do not need to identify a comparator. The EqA 2010 says they have to show 'unfavourable' treatment, not 'less favourable' treatment. In practice, it means much the same as 'detriment' or 'disadvantage' (terms explored at **13.4.1**) and is not considered to be an especially high bar to clear.

Among examples of unfavourable treatment (albeit mostly under precursor legislation) are:

- Dismissal (such as when a teacher at a Roman Catholic school was constructively dismissed for becoming pregnant by a Roman Catholic priest: *O'Neill v Governors of St Thomas More RC School [1997] ICR 33*).

- A failure to carry out a risk assessment for a pregnant employee in circumstances where a risk of harm existed or statute required it (*Hardman v Mallon (t/a Orchard Lodge Nursing Home) [2002] IRLR 516*; *O'Neill v Buckinghamshire County Council [2010] IRLR 384*).

- A reduction in a woman's bonus because she was absent during part of the year with pregnancy-related sickness and on maternity leave (*GUS Home Shopping Ltd v Green & McLaughlin [2001] IRLR 75*).

- Removing a woman from a list of 'bank staff' – those available for short-term work – because she had not worked for 12 months, even though the absence was maternity-related (*Johnson v Queen Elizabeth Hospital NHS Trust UKEAT/1331/01*).

Women do not have to disclose a pregnancy while applying for a job. While a pregnancy may be evident, an employer is likely to discriminate if it allows that information to influence decision-making. Pregnant women have the right to paid time off for antenatal appointments, and a refusal to allow this (or a detriment suffered because a woman insisted on it) would likely be discriminatory.

During maternity leave, a woman continues to be employed, and her terms of employment remain unchanged except for her wages (which are substituted by either Statutory Maternity Pay or the employer's own maternity pay scheme). Therefore, gym memberships, communications expenses, company cars (unless provided solely for business) and, perhaps most importantly, pension and other non-salary benefits must continue. Opportunities for promotion cannot be withheld, and applications cannot be discouraged or downgraded. Critically, the employer's obligation of trust and confidence also persists.

14.5.1 THE PROTECTED PERIOD

Uniquely among causes of action in the EqA 2010, a claim under section 18 is timebound and can only be made in relation to unfavourable treatment which happens during the 'protected period', as defined by section 18(6). The protected period starts when the pregnancy begins. For women entitled to maternity leave, the protected period ends either on the expiry of ordinary and additional maternity leave (at the time of writing, a total of 52 weeks) or when the woman returns to work, whichever is earlier. For women not entitled to maternity leave, such as job applicants or the self-employed, the protected period expires two weeks after the end of the woman's pregnancy.

14.5.2 RELATIONSHIP TO SEX DISCRIMINATION

One could argue that discrimination on the grounds of pregnancy or maternity is a subset of sex discrimination. Claimants will sometimes seek to argue both kinds of discrimination, and there is nothing to stop a claim under section 18 of the EqA 2010 co-existing with a claim for indirect sex discrimination (section 19 of the EqA 2010 makes no provision for indirect discrimination on the grounds of pregnancy or maternity). Such a claim under section 19 of the EqA 2010 succeeded in *Town v Devon & Cornwall Police [2021] IRLR*

235: a pregnant front-line officer compelled to transfer to a back office role because she had been placed on restricted duties for more than two weeks (the provision, criterion or practice (PCP) in question) was found to have been discriminated against because the PCP (since other pregnant officers might similarly be placed on restricted duties) would affect far more women than men.

However, so long as the detriment in question falls within the protected period, a claim for direct sex discrimination cannot be made. Section 17(6) of the EqA 2010 states that a claim for direct sex discrimination cannot be made in relation to a woman's pregnancy or maternity status if it could instead be made under section 18 of the EqA 2010. In any case, it is hard to see how a claim under section 13 of the EqA 2010 could be more beneficial, given that it would require a comparator.

If, on the other hand, the wrongdoing took place outside the protected period, a direct sex discrimination claim may still be made. There is nothing in section 13 of the EqA 2010 that explicitly prohibits such an approach; indeed, section 13(6)(a) of the EqA 2010 mentions that 'less favourable treatment' for the purposes of direct discrimination includes such treatment because a woman is breastfeeding. However, a suitable comparator will need to be identified, such as an ill male employee, as was the case in a claim dealing with post-natal depression (*Lyons v DWP Jobcentre Plus UKEAT/0348/13*).

14.6 RACE

For the purposes of discrimination law, 'race' is defined in section 9(1) of the EqA 2010 to include colour, nationality and ethnic or national origins. It acts to protect people who 'share the same racial group' from being treated poorly. Section 9(3) of the EqA 2010 recognises that the term 'racial group', when used for this purpose, is an iterative term. One racial group – for instance, Black British – can include two or more other racial groups. Note that any other racial group could be the comparator, and it is no defence for a discriminator to be from the same group as their victim.

An employee alleging race discrimination need not, unless relevant to the claim, define their racial group too narrowly so long as the group pleaded is one to which they genuinely belong, and whose treatment is recognisably distinct from another group. Indeed, it has been found – in *Orphanos v Queen Mary College [1985] IRLR 349*, confirmed later, albeit in the criminal sphere, in *R v Rogers [2007] 2 AC 62* – that 'non-British' or 'foreign' could, against the right factual background, count as a single racial group.

As the use of the word 'include' indicates, this list may not be a closed one, and employees who believe they have been discriminated against on other race-related grounds may still have a claim. One such, 'caste' (in the sense used in, among other places, South Asia), in fact, features explicitly at section 9(5) of the EqA 2010, which places a duty on the Government to legislate to include it in the list in section 9(1) of the EqA 2010. While the Government has declined to do so and has said it intends to repeal section 9(5) at some point, case law has taken up the slack in the meantime. The EAT confirmed in *Chandhok v Tirkey [2015] ICR 527* that discrimination on the grounds of caste falls within the ambit of section 9 of the EqA 2010.

As with other forms of discrimination, intent or motivation are irrelevant to the question of whether someone has been discriminated against on the grounds of race. It is therefore possible for a claim to rest on cultural assumptions made without proper evidence, however benign the discriminator's intentions may have been (*Bradford Hospitals NHS Trust v Al-Shabib [2003] IRLR 4*).

Colour

Discrimination on the grounds of colour appears self-evident. Whether it has occurred will be a question of fact in each case. Almost invariably, there will be an element of prejudice against a nationality or ethnic origin underpinning discrimination which is ostensibly because of someone's colour. In practice, the courts have deliberately avoided drawing fine distinctions, not least because they recognise (as in *Mandla v Dowell Lee [1983] ICR 385*) that assigning people to racial or colour categories is a 'rubbery and elusive' enterprise, not to mention a wholly unscientific and often abused one.

Nationality or citizenship

Nationality (or citizenship) is the specific legal relationship between a person and a state through birth or naturalisation. It is distinct from national origins (paragraph 2.38 of the EHRC Employment Code). So while the United Kingdom is a single state, and for the purposes of defining nationality within discrimination law is treated as such, a Scot could still be discriminated against on the basis of their national origins if they were treated less favourably than English people. The same is true the other way around: In *BBC Scotland v Souster [2001] IRLR 150*, an English BBC employee argued successfully before Scotland's Court of Session that losing his role as a rugby presenter to a Scottish woman was discrimination because he was of English origin.

Discrimination on the grounds of nationality or citizenship does not, however, stretch to include discrimination because of immigration status. As the Supreme Court found in the linked cases of *Taiwo v Olaigbe and Onu v Akwiwu [2016] ICR 756*, if the trigger for poor treatment is that someone is vulnerable because they are an immigrant, rather than because of what nationality they are, the treatment will not amount to race discrimination.

Ethnic or national origins

Where someone is mistreated because of the country they – or their family or ancestors – come from (often, but not necessarily, where they were born), things may be relatively straightforward. But not every ethnic origin, separate from a state or political jurisdiction, will attract protection from discrimination. For an 'ethnic group' to so qualify, it must amount to a separate and distinct community.

Needless to say, this is hard to quantify or identify, but in the case of *Mandla v Dowell Lee [1983] IRLR 209*, where a Sikh boy's claim of discrimination because his school would not let him wear his turban was upheld, the courts sought to lay down a yardstick. Confronting the argument that because there was nothing biological or political to distinguish Sikhs from anyone else in the Punjab, India, or indeed the UK, Lord Fraser identified two key characteristics an ethnic group needed to have:

1) A long-shared history, of which the group is conscious as distinguishing it from other groups, and the memory of which it keeps alive

2) A cultural tradition of its own, including family and social customs and manners, often but not necessarily associated with religious observance

Other characteristics relevant to determining whether a group was an ethnic group attracting protection from unlawful discrimination, but not essential, were:

- Either a common geographical origin or descent from a small number of common ancestors

- A common language, not necessarily peculiar to the group

- A common literature peculiar to the group

- A common religion different from that of neighbouring groups or from the general community surrounding it

- Being a minority or being an oppressed or a dominant group within a larger community

Aside from Sikhs, other groups which the courts have found to attract the law's protection include Jews (at least so far as the discrimination arises because of their cultural background, rather than their religious beliefs), Roma and Travellers (both Irish and Scottish). Not, however, Muslims. The position taken by the courts thus far (*Walker v Hussain [1996] IRLR 11*) arises from the distinction between a group which shares a faith but derives its identity from a common geographical origin and one where the faith may have a distinct geographical origin but its adherents do not. Put differently, the distinction is one between faiths spread as their adherents migrate and one spread by evangelism.

Rastafarians have failed to secure protection as an ethnic group (*Crown Suppliers (PSA) Ltd v Dawkins [1993] ICR 517*). Here, the court found that their shared history of less than a century was too short and that there was not

266

enough to distinguish them from the rest of the Afro-Caribbean community in the UK. Rastafarians have had more success in claiming discrimination on the grounds of belief (see **14.7**).

14.7 RELIGION AND BELIEF

Everyone believes in something. The contributors to this book may even believe that rock music died with David Bowie; that Glasgow Rangers is – or, as the case may be, is not – the greatest football team ever; or that Yoda's teachings furnish one with a philosophy worth living by.

Where that 'something' is a religion – whether a faith in general or a denomination or sect, such as Methodists within Christianity, or Sufis within Islam – and the faith has a clear system of beliefs and structure (as the EHRC Employment Code puts it), it may be relatively straightforward to ground a discrimination claim if adherence to that faith is a trigger for less favourable treatment. A lack of faith – for instance, atheism – is also expressly included (section 10(1) of the EqA 2010).

Things are less clear for non-religious beliefs. The above examples, for instance, would be unlikely to be enough (indeed, 'a belief in the supreme nature of the Jedi knights' was explicitly mentioned in Parliament when the EqA 2010 was being debated as something which would be excluded).

The question, therefore, is what qualifies as a belief for protection under section 10 of the EqA 2010. The courts now routinely rely on the 'Grainger criteria', five characteristics set out in *Grainger plc v Nicholson [2010] ICR 360*, which say that if a philosophical belief is to be protected it must:

1) Be genuinely held

2) Be a belief, not an opinion or viewpoint based on the present state of information available (in other words, it needs a quality of timelessness)

3) Be a belief as to a weighty and substantial aspect of human life and behaviour

4) Attain a certain level of cogency, seriousness, cohesion and importance

5) Be worthy of respect in a democratic society, not incompatible with human dignity and not conflict with the fundamental rights of others

The Grainger criteria have been the subject of many high-profile tribunal and appeal judgments in recent years. The trend is now to draw a bright line between *belief* on the one hand, which the Grainger criteria primarily govern, and *manifestation* of that belief on the other (see **14.7.1**); that is, between what one believes and how one shows it. In an important EAT judgment, since frequently followed, Mr Justice Choudhury (the president of the EAT) found in *Forstater v CGD Europe [2022] ICR 1* that the fifth criterion set a very low bar: that only the most extreme beliefs (Nazism, say) would fall short, and that tribunals should avoid straying into making judgments on the merits and validity of the belief itself. They should, he said, 'abide by the cardinal principle that everyone is entitled to believe whatever they wish, subject only to a few modest, minimum requirements' – but he stressed that because of this, no one should misinterpret a tribunal's acceptance that a belief satisfied the Grainger criteria as approval of that belief or as licence to manifest that belief however they desired.

That is not to say that the other four criteria are irrelevant; far from it. In *McClung v Doosan Babcock Ltd ET/4110538/2019*, an ardent supporter of Glasgow Rangers failed to convince a tribunal that this belief should be protected against discrimination, falling short on four criteria – although the tribunal, and the respondent, acknowledged that as an 'ardent fan', Mr McClung's belief was certainly genuinely held.

There is nothing to stop political beliefs from being protected, as in *Olivier v Department of Work and Pensions ET/1701407/2013*, in which a belief in 'democratic socialism' could found a civil servant's discrimination claim. Some may fall foul of the fifth Grainger criterion – as in *Redfearn v UK (47335/06) [2013] IRLR 51*, in which a train driver was summarily fired after becoming a local councillor for the British National Party, which is widely regarded as racist. UK courts upheld his dismissal. The European Court of Human Rights (ECtHR) held that his right to free assembly had been interfered with and that without due process (he did not have enough service to claim unfair dismissal) that right had not been protected. It made no finding or comment as to whether or not his beliefs were objectionable.

Rastafarianism has been found to be a philosophical belief (*Harris v NKL Automotive and Matrix Consultancy UK Ltd UKEAT/0134/07*). So has Freemasonry (*Conway v Secretary of State for the Home Office ET/2205162/13*), although not a religious belief, notwithstanding its requirement that its members believe in some 'higher power', although it does not specify which. Even a belief in the vital importance of public service broadcasting (*Maistry v BBC ET/1313142/10*) has qualified, although the right to hold the copyright in works one has made oneself did not (*Gray v Mulberry Company (Design) Ltd [2020] ICR 715*).

In *Maistry* – which ultimately the claimant lost because those alleged to be discriminating against him were found not to know about his belief, and thus could not have acted because of it – it was not enough simply that the claimant, a BBC employee, believed that public service broadcasting was important. The tribunal noted that the particular strength and coherence of the belief, founded in his past work as a journalist during apartheid-era South Africa, was a significant factor in its finding.

This point – the degree to which a person can show their belief infuses or affects their life and decision-making, and in other words demonstrates it is cogent and genuinely held – was critical in the case of *Casamitjana Costa v League Against Cruel Sports ET/3331129/2018*, which upheld the claimant's argument that his ethical veganism was a protected belief. Despite media coverage suggesting that anyone avoiding animal products could now claim the law's protection, the tribunal had, in fact, stressed just how deeply Mr Casamitjana had incorporated veganism into his life: he avoids all animal-related products, only stays in hotels where his views can be accommodated, wears no clothes and keeps no items in his home which incorporate animal products, and even avoids sitting on leather seats or using new banknotes made with animal products.

However, a fear of catching Covid-19 has thus far tended to fail to qualify. In *X v Y ET/2314947/2020*, concerning a worker who refused to return to work after lockdown in 2020 because of her health and safety fears, the fears were found not to be a belief but to be a reaction to a threat of physical harm. In other words, she failed to satisfy the second Grainger criterion.

14.7.1 MANIFESTATION OF RELIGION OR BELIEF

Inevitably, issues of discrimination on the ground of religion frequently intersect with the right to freedom of thought, conscience and religion under Article 9 of the *European Convention on Human Rights* (ECHR). This right is absolute, subject only to a limitation in Article 17 on the abuse of Convention rights (this being the ground on which Choudhury P defined the borderline of the fifth Grainger criterion in *Forstater* – see **14.7**).

However, the right to manifest one's religion – in other words, how one practises it – can be subject to limitations (among other things) to protect the rights and freedoms of others, so long as those limitations are necessary for the given purpose, prescribed by law, and are as minimal as possible.

Employers can therefore establish policies to limit manifestation of belief. But as a tribunal explored when the *Forstater* case was remitted to it in 2022 (*Forstater v CGD Europe ET/2200909/2019*), employers may get into trouble if these limitations are not clearly specified, so that they can be even-handedly applied. Manifestation is, after all, still protected; albeit that the *manner* of manifestation may be more apt to cause offence, and thus in cases of indirect discrimination, it may be subject to interference by a PCP (see **13.2.1**) if an objective justification can be established. This justification may be more straightforward for senior people whose views will inevitably be connected with their employer.

It should be noted that persistent and unwanted manifestation – such as what amounts to proselytisation in the workplace – is unlikely to be protected, as when an employee describing herself as a 'born-again Christian' was found to have several times imposed her beliefs on a more junior Muslim employee and was disciplined (*Wasteney v East London NHS Foundation Trust [2016] ICR 643*). The EAT found that while her conduct was clearly connected to her religion, the written warning she received was primarily because her conduct was objectively unprofessional; the employer would have done the same to someone who had similarly crossed professional boundaries for a non-belief reason.

Until 2013, the courts tended to view only practices which were mandatory as protected by the qualified right to manifest one's beliefs. Those which an individual chose, such as following a particular dress code or diet, or wearing jewellery (say, a crucifix) with specific religious meaning, were not.

That changed with the ECtHR's decision on four joined cases in January 2013 (*Eweida, Chaplin, Ladele and McFarlane v The United Kingdom [2013] IRLR 231*). In all four, the Court indicated that a manifestation or practice would attract the qualified protection of Article 9 whether it was mandatory or not, so long as it was motivated or inspired by, and sufficiently linked to, a religion or belief.

Eweida and *Chaplin* were about dress codes. Both claimants were prevented by their employers – British Airways and the NHS respectively – from wearing a crucifix overtly. The ECtHR upheld Ms Eweida's appeal, saying the domestic court had placed too much weight on its corporate image and not enough on her right while working as a check-in officer to show her faith. It dismissed Ms Chaplin's, finding that the health and safety implications of wearing her crucifix in a clinical setting (she was a nurse) outweighed her right to do so.

Following this decision, public sector workers – who are directly protected by the *Human Rights Act 1998* – have a direct right to manifest their religion or belief in the workplace, subject still to the potential limitations. In the private sector, a worker stopped from manifesting their religion may claim discrimination. This will usually be indirect discrimination, say, for a dress code (as in both *Eweida* and *Chaplin*), in which case they would need to show a 'particular disadvantage' (see **13.2.2**).

(*Ladele* and *McFarlane* both concerned the right to refuse to serve gay people as a result of religious belief and are dealt with at **14.7.3**.)

Similarly, and more recently, the Court of Justice of the European Union (CJEU) has upheld the right of Muslim women to wear the hijab if they so decide. In *Achbita v G4S Secure Solutions NV C-157/15* and *Bougnaoui v Micropole SA C-188/15*, the claimants were both dismissed, one for wearing a headscarf when a code of conduct prohibited the wearing of 'any religious, political or philosophical symbols' and the other for refusing to comply with a customer's request that she not wear a headscarf. Unsurprisingly, the CJEU found that the hijab was a manifestation of belief. While a general ban (as in *Achbita*) was not directly discriminatory, it could amount to indirect discrimination. A desire for a 'neutral' image could be a legitimate aim, but a national court would have to decide whether a less drastic solution than dismissal (such as a change of role) would have been reasonable, and any such 'neutral image' policy would have to be applied wholly even-handedly across faiths and beliefs (as found in the later cases of *IX v WABE eV* and *MH Müller Handels GmbH v MJ [2021] IRLR 832*). As for the customer's feelings in

Bougnaoui, this could not, the European Court of Justice said, be a genuine occupational requirement (see **12.5.2**); but legitimate customer wishes, as the CJEU held in *IX*, could nonetheless be taken into account by a court when considering whether objective justification was made out.

Guidance published by the EHRC following the 2013 cases suggests employers dealing with manifestations should take the following into account:

- The cost, disruption and wider impact on business or work if the request is accommodated

- The health and safety implications of the proposed change

- The disadvantage to the affected employee if the request is refused

- The impact of any change on other employees, including on those who have a different (or no) religion or belief

- The impact of any change on customers or service users

- Whether policies to ensure uniformity and consistency are justifiable

14.7.2 EXAMPLES

While it is impossible to state definitively what will or will not amount to discrimination, the following examples may provide an indication:

- A bus cleaner who took unpaid leave to perform Hajj, having asked for it but received no response, was found to have been discriminated against (*Khan v NIC Hygiene ET/1803250/04*).

- A Christian employee had told her employer at interview that she could not work on Sundays and resigned after she was required under a new rota system to do so and thus to miss church. The tribunal found she had been discriminated against and that her employer's conduct amounted to a breach of its duty of trust and confidence, making her constructive dismissal unfair (*Williams-Drabble v Pathway Care Solutions Ltd & anor ET/2601718/04*).

- A Christian nursery worker who was dismissed after telling a gay colleague that homosexuality was a sin was found to have been directly and indirectly discriminated against. The employer had, in effect, dismissed her after making assumptions about her belief, not merely because of her manifestation of it (*Mbuyi v Newpark Childcare (Shepherds Bush) Ltd ET/3300656/14*).

- A Sikh train driver lost both his tribunal case and his appeal to the EAT when he was dismissed after he refused to tidy his beard. The EAT said the dismissal was because of tidiness, not religion. The employer had shown it was happy to employ bearded Sikhs otherwise, so the driver had not raised a prima facie case sufficient to shift the burden of proof (*Mohmed v West Coast Trains Ltd UKEAT/0682/05*).

- A Muslim schoolteacher lost an appeal to the EAT after she had been required to remove her full-face veil while in class. This was found to be a proportionate means of achieving the legitimate aim of educating children (*Azmi v Kirklees MBC [2007] ICR 1154*).

- A Christian sacked for missing sales targets because he believed, thanks to his faith, that it was always wrong to lie was found to have been the subject of indirect discrimination, because his employer had said lying to potential customers was part of the job (*Hawkins v Universal Utilities Ltd t/a Unicom ET/2501234/12*).

- The EAT found that the question 'what's happened to the fucking Pope?', shouted in a pressured newsroom in the presence of a Catholic sub-editor, did not amount to harassment on grounds of religion. It had not been reasonable for the claimant to feel his dignity was violated or an adverse environment created (*Heafield v Times Newspaper Ltd UKEATPA/1305/12*).

- Being refused permission to wear a poppy at work during Remembrance Week was not a detriment, because the belief that one should lacked cogency and cohesion and could not be said to be a belief as to a 'weighty and substantial aspect of human life' (*Lisk v Shield Guardian Co Ltd ET/3300873/11*).

- In the *Forstater* case, the claimant was ultimately found to have been discriminated against because while her public statements of her belief in the immutability of sex (that is, that no one could *become* a woman if they had been born physically male) might and did cause offence to individuals, they were not objectively offensive or unreasonable.

- However, in *Mackereth v DWP [2022] EAT 99*, a claimant failed to convince a tribunal he had been discriminated against because of his views about trans people, although here the key was their religious foundation. He worked as an assessor of benefits claimants and refused to use people's preferred pronouns because he claimed his Christian faith prevented him from doing so. The EAT agreed with the tribunal: he had a right to his belief, but the DWP's conduct in accepting his resignation (in the DWP's view) or firing him (in the claimant's) was acceptable because, in the context of the service the claimant was hired to provide, his manifestation of his faith was unacceptable – and would have been unacceptable in someone who felt the same way without a religious underpinning.

14.7.3 CONFLICTS BETWEEN PROTECTED CHARACTERISTICS

There are times when different protected characteristics will clash. This has particularly been so in cases involving religious belief and sexual orientation, given a belief among some more traditionalist adherents of several faiths that homosexuality is a sin.

In *Ladele* and *McFarlane* – mentioned earlier at **14.7.1** – both claimants were dismissed by their employers for having refused to carry out certain work duties in respect of same-sex couples on the grounds of their religious beliefs. The court held that a balance had to be struck between their rights and those of the same-sex couples they refused to accommodate. In both cases, it was held that the UK courts had not exceeded their wide discretion to balance these competing rights, particularly where the action of the employer was intended to secure the implementation of a policy of providing a service without discrimination.

The Supreme Court has twice in the past decade considered this tension, albeit in spheres other than employment. Firstly, the court held in *Hall v Bull [2013] UKSC 73* that Christian hotel owners had discriminated against a gay couple in a civil partnership by refusing to let them share a double bed because they were not in a heterosexual marriage. At the time, only gay people could be in civil partnerships, and the court found that since civil partners had in law the same rights as married people, the hotel had discriminated against them.

In 2018, the court revisited the issue in what came to be known as the 'gay cake' case (*Lee v Ashers Baking Company Ltd [2018] UKSC 49*). A bakery in Northern Ireland refused to fulfil an order from a gay person for a cake because it was to bear the words 'Support Gay Marriage'. The Supreme Court ruled that the bakery had not discriminated on grounds of religion because it was their religion, not that of the claimant, that prompted their actions. As for sexual orientation discrimination, that too found no favour with the court: the bakery's objection was to the cake, not to the person ordering it. They would not have refused to sell him another cake, and they would have refused a similar order from a straight person. A later reference to the ECtHR by Mr Lee (*Lee v UK [2022] IRLR 371*) also failed: the Strasbourg court said Mr Lee had not complained to domestic courts about ECHR breaches, so his complaint to it was inadmissible.

Two connected cases in the Court of Appeal involving a view critical of adoption by same-sex couples voiced by an avowed Christian (*Page v Lord Chancellor [2021] IRLR 377* and *Page v NHS Trust Development Authority [2021] IRLR 391*) both rested on the impact of that view on others when repeatedly and publicly stated in media interviews: in one case, potential adoptive parents, and in the other, users of the NHS. The claimant was both a magistrate (making decisions about adoptions) and a non-executive director of an NHS Trust. After giving media interviews saying he disapproved of same-sex couples adopting (and refusing to not continue doing so), he was removed as a magistrate and later was not re-appointed as a director by the Trust. He complained of victimisation by the Lord Chancellor and discrimination by the Trust. Both claims failed: on appeal, the Court of Appeal agreed that it was the particularly inappropriate manner of manifestation which led to the Trust's decision (not the belief itself), and further, the Lord Chancellor's decision was not victimisation because Mr Page's removal was due to his continued public statements about adoption, not because he had complained after being disciplined for them.

14.8 SEX

Section 11(a) of the EqA 2010 defines the protected characteristic of sex as referring to 'a man or a woman'. It does not deal with, or protect against, discrimination arising from non-binary or any other gender status apart from being male or female. As such, it assumes only two, essentially biological, sexes. It is therefore important for both claimants and respondents to distinguish between instances when discrimination is on the grounds of sex and when it is (for instance) on grounds of gender reassignment or sexual orientation. The use of the adult terms is not restrictive: males and females of any age can be discriminated against and can claim.

Both women and men can be discriminated against under these grounds if they are treated less favourably than those of the opposite sex. (This does not apply where a man complains that a pregnant woman is getting advantages denied to him – see **13.1.1**.)

The range of detriments which can ground a claim for sex discrimination is immense, but it does not include equal pay. Under section 71 of the EqA 2010, claims that a woman is paid less than a man must generally be brought under separate equal pay provisions, for which see **Chapter 15**. There is, however, an exception for direct discrimination claims in which there is no actual male employee with whom the claimant can compare herself, only a hypothetical one (see **15.1.2**). It can, however, include breastfeeding, as easyJet discovered when it lost a claim related to rosters which compelled two breastfeeding employees to work shifts longer than eight hours (*McFarlane and anor v easyJet Airline Company ET/1401496/15 and ET3401933/15*). On at least one occasion, it has also involved discrimination arising from an employee's dismissal for poor performance despite medical evidence supplied to her employer that her work was being affected by the symptoms of menopause (*Merchant v BT plc ET/140135/11*).

One flashpoint in sex discrimination is the ability, under Schedule 3, paragraphs 26-28 of the EqA 2010, to offer single-sex services in some circumstances (that is, where the provision is a proportionate means of achieving a legitimate aim) without that amounting to sex discrimination. The key point of contention is whether transgender women should have access to women-only spaces. The nature and extent of the debate are beyond the scope of this book, and guiding judicial authority on the subject is as yet lacking. However, the EHRC has published guidance on separate or single-sex services in this context, which may be of assistance to employers.

14.9 SEXUAL ORIENTATION

Section 12 of the EqA 2010 acts to prohibit discrimination on the grounds that a person has a sexual orientation towards 'persons of the same sex, persons of the opposite sex or persons of either sex'. Any of these three groups can be the subject of discrimination under section 12 of the EqA 2010, so it is as unlawful to discriminate against a straight person for being heterosexual as to discriminate against a gay person for being homosexual.

It is unlawful for an employer to restrict benefits offered to staff solely to heterosexual partners. It is lawful (under section 18(2) of the EqA 2010) for an employer to offer benefits solely to married employees or those in civil partnerships, as long as these, again, are offered equally to those of any sexual orientation.

The definition in section 12 makes no stipulation as to sex, so gay men and lesbians belong, for the purposes of this provision, in the same category. This may, in some circumstances, be important, particularly with indirect discrimination, if a detriment affects only, for instance, gay women and not gay men. In such circumstances, a claim for sex discrimination might be possible instead. It also makes no mention of asexual people. Despite lobbying from some quarters, there has been no move to close this gap, and in a non-employment case (*Elan-Cane v Home Secretary [2021] UKSC 56*) the Supreme Court ruled against an asexual person who sought a passport with an 'X' for their gender instead of an 'M' or an 'F'.

It is also worth noting that it is the orientation that is protected, not – to the extent that the distinction may be relevant in any given case – how it is expressed. So, a preference for a sexual activity (or, for that matter, celibacy) is not protected unless, on analysis, the true root of any alleged discrimination is the orientation itself.

As with some other protected characteristics, discrimination on the grounds of sexual orientation can take place on the basis of a misperception – that someone is gay (or straight) when they are not. A claim may also rest on detriment connected with a perception that the perpetrators know is inaccurate. The classic example of this is *English v Thomas Sanderson [2009] ICR 543*, where colleagues levelled homophobic taunts at the claimant for characteristics they associated with gay men, even though they did not believe him to be gay. Although the tribunal and EAT went against him, the Court of Appeal found for the claimant, saying that it was the homophobic behaviour which rendered this discrimination on the grounds of sexual orientation, irrespective of whether the victim was thought to be gay or not.

The courts have seen significant cross-over between the protected characteristic of sexual orientation and that of religion or belief, given that some religions – or at least some strands of those religions – profess a belief that anything other than heterosexual behaviour may be sinful. This issue is discussed in more detail at **14.7.3**.

CHAPTER 15

OTHER FORMS OF DISCRIMINATION

15.0 OVERVIEW

The right to equal pay has been on the statute book for 50-plus years, but – now widened to cover terms as well as pay – generates a wide body of high-profile cases. This chapter explores this area of discrimination law before also looking at the types of claims open to fixed-term and part-time workers.

15.1 EQUALITY OF PAY AND TERMS OF EMPLOYMENT

The *Equal Pay Act* reached the statute books in 1970, aiming to redress the balance at a time when it was routine – indeed, unremarkable – for women to be paid far less than men. In 2010, the *Equal Pay Act 1970* was repealed, as its substantive provisions were replicated in sections 64-80 of the *Equality Act 2010* (EqA 2010). The heading is 'equality of terms', which, in practice, is a far more accurate description of the chapter's intent than simply 'equal pay'.

Half a century on, equality of terms remains a common problem put before employment tribunals. Research by DLA Piper in 2020 indicated that as of the end of 2019, 14% of claims included some equality of terms element. Further, this marked a rise in the long-run average of 12%. Gender pay gap statistics produced by the Office for National Statistics indicate some narrowing in recent years: the overall gap as at the most recent release in October 2022 stood at 14.9%, down 2.5 points since 2019. However, for full-time workers, the after-effects of the Covid-19 pandemic appear to have been harmful, with the full-time gender pay gap rising to 8.3% (from 7% in 2020).

The vast majority will be small claims, but in some, tens of thousands of claimants allege unequal treatment stretching back, in some cases, well before the EqA 2010 came into force. Probably the most prominent example of such a claim is *Asda Stores Ltd v Brierley & ors [2021] IRLR 456*, in which the Supreme Court found in favour of some 35,000 female retail supermarket employees. The decision is discussed in more detail at **15.1.2**.

While the UK was in the European Union (EU), equality of terms was also a right under Article 157 of the *Treaty on the Functioning of the European Union*. In 2019, an employment tribunal referred a case on whether this was a right which had 'direct effect' – that is, one which could be relied on by EU citizens without having to have recourse to specific domestic laws. In 2021, the Court of Justice of the European Union (CJEU) decided (in *K and ors v Tesco Stores Ltd [2021] ICR 1524 CJEU*) that it did; and because the reference took place before Brexit came into effect, this ruling is binding in the UK – at least absent any change in how retained EU law is applied and unless and until the Court of Appeal or Supreme Court decides otherwise.

15.1.1 EQUALITY OF TERMS: THE BASICS

Under the EqA 2010, men and women have the right to receive the same remuneration, and the same terms of employment, when they are doing the same work for the same employer. In construing the right, the courts consider not 'fairness', but simply whether a disparity in pay or terms arises from discrimination between the sexes.

Section 66 of the EqA 2010 seeks to protect this right by inserting a 'sex equality clause' into every contract of employment, as well as a 'sex equality rule' into every occupational pension scheme (see **15.1.5**), which does not explicitly or implicitly already have one. By section 66(2) of the EqA 2010, the clause modifies any term less favourable to one sex than the other to remove the disparity, or – if a term which benefits one sex is missing from the contract of someone from the other sex – adds such a term. (Note that this works in both directions, protecting a man whose terms are less favourable than a woman's. In practice, though, the vast majority of claims are brought by women.)

A tribunal will not take a 'package deal' approach to an equality of terms claim. Each term challenged needs to be looked at in isolation, comparing each provision in turn with one in the contract of a suitable comparator (see **15.1.2**) to see whether there is less favourable treatment. Employers cannot escape liability by pointing to other terms which they say are more favourable to a claimant in order to justify a less favourable term. That said, pay for normal working hours – even if, in effect, that aggregates terms covering both hourly rates and other items, such as guaranteed bonuses – is treated as a single term however the contract subdivides it (*Degnan v Redcar and Cleveland Borough Council [2005] IRLR 615*). This cuts both ways, however: the Court of Appeal has ruled that a claimant cannot seek to formulate an equality of terms claim by disaggregating a term into sub-terms which do not, in fact, exist (*McNeil & ors v Revenue and Customs Commissioners [2020] ICR 515*).

The modification takes whatever form is necessary to equalise terms with the relevant comparator, although it will not modify a term so that it becomes more favourable, for instance by adding benefits accruing to a level of seniority beyond that which the comparator already has (*Enderby v Frenchay Health Authority (No.2) [2000] ICR 612*).

However, it will only do so for a person whose work is 'equal' to that of someone of the opposite sex, working for the same or an associated employer (section 66(1) of the EqA 2010), with 'equal' being defined as one of the following:

- Like work – that is, the same job

- Work rated as equivalent

- Work of equal value

Where the hours worked differ between claimant and comparator – say, one is part-time and the other full-time – the court should aggregate wages, allowances and benefits before dividing that total by the number of hours worked to arrive at the appropriate hourly rate for comparison purposes (*Degnan v Redcar and Cleveland Borough Council [2005] IRLR 615*).

Who, and what, is covered?

As with other aspects of discrimination, 'employment' carries a wide meaning as far as equality of terms is concerned. A person is 'employed', and thus protected by the EqA 2010, not only if they are an 'employee' under a contract of service or apprenticeship but also if they are self-employed but providing services under 'a contract personally to do work' (section 83(2)(a) of the EqA 2010), a Crown employee or member of the armed forces.

As for what 'terms' can be equalised, anything that forms part of the contractual arrangement between employer and employee is covered, including:

- Ex gratia perks, even where they are post-retirement perks such as a travel concession (*Garland v British Rail Engineering [1982] ICR 420*)

- Severance payments, whether statutory or contractual (*R v Secretary of State for Employment, ex parte EOC and Day [1994] ICR 317*)

- Unfair dismissal compensation (*R v Secretary of State for Employment, ex parte Seymour-Smith [1999] ECR I623*)

However, discretionary benefits are not included: variable bonuses, for instance, would need to be dealt with as a normal sex discrimination claim.

The tribunal must ensure the equality of specific terms. It does not matter if doing so actually has the effect of giving the claimants a better remuneration package as a whole than their comparators: the focus of the law is not on the total pay or the contract in its entirety (*St Helens and Knowsley Hospitals NHS Trust v Brownbill [2012] ICR 68*).

What about transgender people? As things currently stand, trans people whose gender is legally recognised by means of the *Gender Recognition Act*

2004 (GRA 2004) should be able to make an equal pay claim in their acquired gender; but may not be able to if they do not have a gender recognition certificate under the GRA 2004. Although section 70 of the EqA 2010 prohibits claimants from bringing equality of terms claims under the 'normal' discrimination provisions covered in Chapters 12-14 of this book, that would not stop a claimant from claiming discrimination with gender reassignment as the protected characteristic.

What is 'equal work'?

The EqA 2010 protects people rewarded differently for doing 'equal' work. Where two individuals work side by side in the same role for the same company, the comparison is straightforward. In many claims, though, this is not the case. The following sections look at the three definitions of 'equal' work in section 65 of the EqA 2010: like work, work rated as equivalent and work of equal value. A claimant can – and often will – claim under more than one of these categories, although only one can succeed.

What is 'like work'?

'Like work' is work that is 'broadly similar' in nature, where 'such differences as there are between [the] work are not of practical importance in relation to the terms of [the] work' (section 65(2) of the EqA 2010). In practice, this category applies to jobs where the content of the work and the knowledge and experience needed to carry it out are closely matched.

Determining whether two roles are 'like work' is a two-stage process. Firstly, the employee will need to show that the work is 'broadly similar' in terms of knowledge and skill required. If they can, the onus shifts to the employer to show whether any differences of practical importance – with particular reference, as prescribed in section 65(3) of the EqA 2010, to the 'frequency with which differences ... occur in practice, and the nature and extent of the differences'.

Practical differences could include additional duties, level of responsibility, skills, qualifications, physical effort and the time at which the work is done (paragraph 36 of the *Equal Pay Code of Practice*). What matters is how the work is done in practice, not, say, how a contract or job description portrays it.

A difference in workload in itself will not preclude a finding of 'like work' unless the difference amounts to something more – a difference in responsibility, for example. The fact that a promoted woman undertakes more duties than her male predecessor in the same job cannot result in a conclusion that their work is not 'like work', and so justify her being paid less than him (*Sita UK Ltd v Hope UKEAT/0787/04*).

Paragraph 36 of the *Equal Pay Code of Practice* gives the following examples of successful 'like work' claims:

280

- Male and female drivers where the men are more likely to work at weekends (*Hatch v Wadham Stringer Commercials (Ashford) Ltd ET/40171/77*)

- A female cook preparing lunches for directors and a male chef cooking breakfast, lunch and tea for employees (*Capper Pass Ltd v Allan [1980] ICR 194*)

- Male and female supermarket employees performing similar tasks requiring similar skill levels, although the men may lift heavier objects from time to time

A more recent example, and one which attracted a good deal of publicity, came when BBC presenter Samira Ahmed complained to the tribunal that her work presenting Newswatch on the BBC's news channel was broadly similar to that of Jeremy Vine presenting Points of View. The BBC said Points of View (which paid some £3,000 an episode) was a qualitatively different task than Newswatch (for which Ahmed was paid £440 a show): among other things, the former was a high-profile entertainment show with a more experienced presenter on a terrestrial channel, while the latter played to a far smaller and more niche audience. The tribunal disagreed (in *Ahmed v BBC ET/2206858/2018*): both were 15-minute shows involving a presenter reading scripted content comprising viewers' critiques and questions and the BBC's responses. The task was broadly similar, and the BBC failed to demonstrate that any non-discriminatory differences had been actually taken into account when setting the different pay levels. It is worth noting that the BBC was not found to have discriminated, per se; what mattered was its inability to satisfy the burden of proof for the second stage.

What is 'work rated as equivalent'?

Many employers, particularly in the public sector, undertake a 'job evaluation study' (JES) to help them determine pay structures. Such a study is a technical process, involving a systematic analysis that ranks a group of roles into salary bands based on their value and the demands made on the employee. To be relied upon for a claim by either party, a JES must be objective and non-discriminatory (paragraphs 41 and 43 of the *Equal Pay Code of Practice*), and, as Phillips J put it in *Eaton Ltd v Nuttall [1977] ICR 272*, it must be 'thorough' in its analysis and 'capable of impartial application'. A JES which lacks rigour, or one which requires management to make subjective judgments in fitting jobs to bands, he said, is not a JES which a tribunal should accept. Further, both the claimant's role and that with which it is compared (see **15.1.2**) must be evaluated in the same study and using the same criteria (*Paterson & others v London Borough of Islington UKEAT/0347/03*).

Roles in the same band are 'rated as equivalent', and an employee whose terms are worse than those of opposite-sex workers in the same band, or a lower one (*Redcar and Cleveland Borough Council v Bainbridge & ors [2007] IRLR 984*), may have a claim in this category. However, a claim using a comparator in a lower band can only equalise terms to the level of that comparator, not raise them higher (*Evesham v North Herts Health Authority [2000] IRLR 257*).

Claims are usually based on the banding given in the JES. However, if a claimant can show that the banding is flawed – if its scoring incorporates 'sex-specific' factors, as section 65(4)(b) of the EqA 2010 puts it, meaning criteria which score men and women by different yardsticks, such as overweighting the importance of physical labour in a workplace where such roles are more likely to be occupied by men – they may still show the roles in question are equivalent even if the JES says otherwise.

Of course, the employer first needs to have carried out a JES. Employees can ask for one to be undertaken but have no right to require it.

What is 'work of equal value'?

Work may fall outside the categories of 'like work' and 'work rated as equivalent' but nevertheless be equal in terms of the demands it places on a worker. This category is the broadest of the three, and the most contentious and difficult to prove.

Equal value claims allow comparison of entirely different jobs (such as manual and administrative), which may ultimately be found to be equal in terms of the demands they place on workers. A claim may also be made if the claimant's work is of greater value than that of the comparator (*Murphy v Boyd Telecom [1988] ICR 445*), although, even in such a situation, the outcome will be parity with the comparator, not better terms. Assessing and weighing the demands of work requires rigorous (and usually expert) analysis – akin to a JES, but carried out only on the roles under examination rather than as part of a more general, even enterprise-wide, exercise.

If a JES has been carried out and has found the roles to be in different bands, that will normally provide a complete defence for an employer (section 131(6) of the EqA 2010), unless the employee can point to flaws in the JES, such as those highlighted above.

15.1.2 COMPARATORS

At the heart of any equal pay claim is the comparator: the worker(s) of the opposite sex whose better terms are the source of the injustice claimed. By section 79 of the EqA 2010, the claimant and the comparator must both:

- Be employed by the same, or an associated, employer
- Work at the same establishment, or at another establishment at which common terms apply

282

Generally, the comparator must be an actual (as opposed to hypothetical) person or persons, but the comparator does not need to have been working at the same time. A claim making a comparison with one's predecessor in a job can succeed (*McCarthys Ltd v Smith [1980] ECR 1275*), but not a comparison with one's successor, as this is seen as too speculative (*Walton Centre for Neurology and Neuro Surgery NHS Trust v Bewley [2008] ICR 1047*).

Where the only comparison is with a successor, a claimant may need to fall back on the exception provided by sections 70-71 of the EqA 2010, which provide – somewhat obscurely – that normal sex discrimination claims cannot be brought in relation to a term of an employment contract unless 'a sex equality clause or rule has no effect'. Instead, a claim for direct or indirect sex discrimination may be possible, although the normal three-month employment tribunal time limit for bringing a claim would apply as opposed to the six-month period permitted for equality of terms claims.

Where an equality of terms claim relates to pregnancy or maternity, any provision which requires a comparator is disapplied, since (as with pregnancy and maternity discrimination) the condition is uniquely female (*Alabaster v Woolwich plc & anor [2005] IRLR 576*).

'In the same employment'

For a comparison to be valid, the first condition is that both claimant and comparator must be 'in the same employment', a term which came from the *Equal Pay Act 1970* and – while it does not appear in the EqA 2010 – remains in common use. It means that both claimant and comparator work either for the same employer or with 'associated employers'.

The 'same employer' seems a straightforward definition, but complexities have arisen because the English test appears to differ from the one used by the CJEU. Thanks to the case of *Lawrence v Regent Office Care Ltd [2002] ICR 1092*, European jurisprudence allows a comparison as long as any difference in terms is attributable to a 'single source', which can be held responsible for the disparity and can rectify it. For some time, there was friction between English and EU law in this area, but the situation was alleviated somewhat by the Employment Appeal Tribunal (EAT) in *Fox Cross Claimants v Glasgow City Council [2013] ICR 954*, in which the tribunal set out helpful obiter advice on how to interpret the 'single source' requirement. The proper approach, it said, was to take the test in two steps. First, ask whether there was a body responsible for the ongoing disparity in treatment, and second, ask whether that body could restore equal treatment. The EAT added that the focus should be on the responsibilities and powers of the body alleged to be the 'single source' rather than on the immediate employer (if different).

Alternatively, a claimant may rely on the comparator being employed by their employer's 'associate'. Section 79(9) of the EqA 2010 provides that for employers to be associated, either both are companies controlled by the same third party or one is a company controlled by the other. In either case, the control can be direct or indirect. 'Company' is not defined, but *Fox Cross* held the term to include limited liability partnerships (a finding later upheld by the Scottish Court of Session), and *Yildiz v Barking & Dagenham ET 3202029/19* found that this could extend to a public body such as a local authority (although, on the facts, the tribunal in that case found the necessary element of control did not exist).

'Establishments' and common terms

Being in the 'same employment' will not suffice on its own. The claimant and comparator must either work at the 'same establishment' – meaning simply the same workplace – or at different establishments but on common terms. Where the establishment is the same, there is no need for common terms (*Lawson v Britfish Ltd [1988] IRLR 53*).

The requirement for common terms across different establishments is rather inelegantly drafted in section 79(4) of the EqA 2010. But – as the Supreme Court found in the case of *Asda Stores Ltd v Brierley & ors* mentioned at **15.1** – that does not provide a loophole for employers. Confirming the Court of Appeal's view of the matter, the Supreme Court found that there was no need for different establishments to have the same employment regimes. That, Lady Arden said, would have turned the provision into a high bar to clear rather than a relatively liberal threshold test. Instead of undertaking a provision-by-provision comparison to see if the claimants' terms at one site were the same as the comparators' at another, as the first-instance tribunal had done, a tribunal should look at whether the comparators would have been on broadly similar terms to their own had they been employed, in their own roles, at the same location as the claimants – whether or not, in fact, they could, in reality, have been transferred there. In other words, the EqA 2010 had not changed the fundamentals of this test: it remained as it had been under the *Equal Pay Act 1970*.

Moreover, Lady Arden made it clear that the 'common terms' test was not intended as a major hurdle for claimants. Rather, tribunals should look at it simply as a way to identify and 'weed out' those claims where the comparator was clearly inappropriate – say, because the differences were genuinely geographical – and avoid allowing 'markedly over-complicated' factual explorations.

Terms do not have to be identical, or even nearly so. Instead, the test is that they should be substantially comparable, or broadly similar (*British Coal Corporation v Smith [1996] ICR 515*).

15.1.3 DEFENCES AND EXCEPTIONS

The most obvious defence an employer has to an equal pay claim is whether it can show that the claimant and comparator are not doing equal work. Failing that, section 69 of the EqA 2010 provides a defence if the employer can show the inequality in terms is genuinely due to a 'material factor' which is not related to the sex of the jobholders.

The 'material factor' defence

An employer seeking to rely on the 'material factor' defence must show that the reason they put forward for the disparity is:

- Genuine and not a 'sham or pretence', meaning a deliberate fabrication (*Bury MBC v Hamilton [2011] ICR 655*) rather than simply something that had not worked as intended.

- A significant and relevant factor causing the less favourable treatment.

- Not 'the difference of sex' – in other words, not directly or indirectly discriminatory.

- A material difference between the situations of the claimant and comparator (*Glasgow City Council & ors v Marshall & ors [2000] IRLR 737*).

The defence disappears altogether if the 'difference of sex' is directly discriminatory. If it is indirectly discriminatory, the employer may still be able to use the defence – but only if it can show that the material factor is a proportionate means of achieving a legitimate aim (section 69(1)(b) and section 69(2) of the EqA 2010 and see **13.2.3**). However, in this situation, it is for the employee – as usual with indirect discrimination – to raise enough evidence to show that the factor is 'tainted by sex' by showing a provision, criterion or practice (PCP (see **13.2.1**)) or producing statistical evidence (*Enderby v Frenchay Health Authority [1994] ICR 112*), before the employer has to prove justification. (Note here that, as with indirect discrimination, what needs to be shown is the *fact* of the discriminatory effect; a claimant does not have to explain why the effect has been produced by the PCP, or why the statistical anomaly has arisen, although, in the latter case, the statistical methods used may well come in for stringent analysis, as was the case in the Court of Appeal in *McNeil*.) Section 69(3) of the EqA 2010 provides that a long-term objective of reducing inequality between the employment terms of men and women will always be a legitimate aim. In the example given at paragraph 89 of the *Equal Pay Code of Practice*, an employer who has a process of phasing out disparities but protects men's pay and conditions for a period to cushion the effect of the new arrangements may be able to rely on the defence – but only if it can show its implementation of the process is proportionate, meaning the smoothing period would have to be short.

Employers will often want to argue that they simply could not, or still cannot, afford equality of terms. A 'costs' argument alone will not suffice to justify an indirectly discriminatory disparity. However, a 'costs plus' justification – that is, an affordability issue alongside other permissible material factors – can, in some circumstances, succeed: as Underhill LJ put it in *Heskett v Secretary of State for Justice [2021] IRLR 132*, quoting the case of *O'Brien* (see below with reference to part-time working at **15.3.1**), 'the distinction involved [between a pure wish to save money and economic necessity influenced by other factors] may sometimes be subtle … but it is real.'

Sometimes, a material factor will explain some, but not all, of the disparity in pay and terms. In such claims, as was the case in *Enderby*, the tribunal will calculate how much of the difference is accounted for by the material factor and award the claimant the remainder.

It would be impractical, and perhaps impossible, to offer any exhaustive list of potential material factors – there are simply too many candidates. Among those which have succeeded in some circumstances – although, of course, their success in other cases will depend wholly on the facts of the matter at hand – are:

- Location (where a disparity was the product of long-established different practices, rather than because the workers were of different sexes)

- TUPE (where terms have been protected following a transfer of undertakings)

- Unsocial hours

- Pay increases to retain staff

- A genuine mistake where a woman has been put into the wrong grade by accident

Several factors, in contrast, have tended to fail to qualify:

- Market forces will often not provide a good reason: for instance, an employer claiming it is simply doing the same as a competitor in paying women less will not succeed (*Ratcliffe v North Yorks CC [1995] IRLR 439*). If the market rate is affected by the fact that most people doing a job are women, any decision on pay taking that market rate into account will be 'tainted by sex' and directly discriminatory (*Newcastle Upon Tyne NHS Hospitals Trust v Armstrong [2010] ICR 674*). However, if the differential is in response to a genuine need, is not in itself tainted by sex, and can be transparently evidenced, the defence may succeed (*Bradley v Royal Holloway and Bedford New College EAT 0459/13*).

- Historical reasons alone are unlikely to suffice without some other good reason (*South Tyneside MBC v Anderson [2007] ICR 1581*).

- A material factor which was once valid but has now ceased to apply (paragraph 90 of the *Equal Pay Code of Practice*) is unlikely to suffice – although the Court of Appeal has recently pointed out that where there are other material factors, the 'evaporation' of one will not necessarily render the others inapplicable (*Co-operative Group Ltd v Walker [2020] ICR 1450*).

Proof and transparency can sometimes make the difference between an employer successfully relying on the material factor defence and failing to do so. *Ahmed v BBC* was one of the latter (see above at **15.1.1**): the BBC relied on multiple factors but was unable to prove that they had, in fact, played any part in the decision to pay almost 10 times as much for Points of View as for Newswatch.

Many factors can go either way. The CJEU has held that pay systems offering better remuneration to those with long service may be unlawful if the claimant can produce evidence to cast 'serious doubts' on whether the criterion is really appropriate – with 'serious doubts' seen as a relatively low bar to clear (*HSE v Cadman [2006] ICR 1623*). The 'serious doubts' threshold was considered to be a low one by the Court of Appeal in *Wilson v HSE [2010] ICR 302*. However, the European Court of Justice has also held that paying employees on different pay scales can be lawful even if most of the higher-paid are men and most of the lower-paid are women, and even if they are doing the same work, as long as the reason is a difference in qualifications rather than sex (*Angestelltenbetriebsrat der Wiener Gebietskrankenkasse v Wiener Gebietskrankenkasse [1999] IRLR 804*).

15.1.4 PREGNANCY AND MATERNITY

The EqA 2010 does not provide women on maternity leave with a free-standing right to full pay. However, following the CJEU decision in *Gillespie v Northern Health and Social Services Board (Case C-342/93) [1996] IRLR 214* that there was a need to ensure that those women were afforded special protection, section 73 of the EqA does provide some specific protection by implying a 'maternity equality clause'.

Its effect is set out in section 74 of the EqA 2010, which provides that a woman's contractual maternity pay is calculated with reference to any pay rises she would otherwise receive, and further provides that if a woman would have received the following contractual benefits but for her maternity leave, she will receive them during it:

- Pay (including pay by way of bonus) in respect of times before the woman is on maternity leave

- Pay by way of bonus in respect of times when she is on compulsory maternity leave

- Pay by way of bonus in respect of times after the end of the protected period (as outlined in section 18 of the EqA 2010)

Section 74(8) of the EqA 2010 provides that when a woman returns to work following maternity leave, her pay will be subject to any increases she would have received had she not taken that leave.

15.1.5 OCCUPATIONAL PENSION SCHEMES

Pensions law is an immensely complex and detailed topic which is beyond the scope of this book.

Insofar as equality law covers pensions schemes, however, the starting point is the implication, under section 67 of the EqA 2010, of a 'sex equality rule' into every occupational pension scheme. The effect is to modify any term which is less favourable to one employee than to another of the opposite sex doing similar work by removing that discrepancy. This applies to new and existing members. It also protects the dependants of scheme members. Where the effect of the term in question differs according to a person's family, marital or civil partnership status, the comparison must be with someone of the opposite sex with the same status (section 67(7) of the EqA 2010).

A 'maternity equality rule' is similarly implied into every scheme by section 75 of the EqA 2010 to protect women on maternity leave from any treatment different from how they would be treated if not on maternity leave.

Where a scheme's rules do not allow trustees or managers to make 'sex equality alterations' to those rules, or the process of doing so is likely to be unduly 'complex or protracted' or requires consent from members who cannot reasonably be traced, section 68 of the EqA 2010 gives them the power to do so with retroactive effect.

As far as the age of entitlement to pension benefits is concerned, all new schemes must adopt equal pension ages for males and females. All existing schemes must ensure that benefits accruing after 17 May 1990 are equally available to men and women. The age at which someone can claim state retirement pensions fully equalised in 2018 at 65. For people born on or after 6 October 1954, it is currently 66, but those born on or after 6 April 1960 qualify at gradually increasing ages, topping out, currently, at 68 for those born from 6 April 1978 onwards.

The 'material factor defence' applies to pension schemes broadly as it does to employment terms (see **15.1.3**). The wording is slightly different, but the effect – as the Court of Appeal found in *Lord Chancellor v McCloud [2019] IRLR 477* – is essentially the same.

The sex equality rule does not apply to pensionable service before 8 April 1976 (section 67(9) of the EqA 2010). Nor does it apply (by Schedule 7, Part 2 of the EqA 2010) to situations:

- Where men and women are entitled to different pension payments because of the provisions of the *Social Security Contributions and Benefits Act 1992*

- Where a difference in entitlement is based on actuarial calculations

15.1.6 GENDER PAY REPORTING

Under rules which came into force in 2017, any employer with at least 250 employees subject to English, Welsh or Scottish employment law must publish annual statistics about the 'gender pay gap' in their organisation. The requirement carries with it no obligation to achieve pay parity between male and female employees in the aggregate, although this does not, of course, change the obligations discussed above in relation to individual workers and roles. Note that 'employee' here is the broader definition used in the EqA 2010 that includes workers and agency workers as well as some self-employed people.

The gender pay reporting (GPR) regulations require the publication of six 'calculations' both on the employer's own website and on a Government website (https://www.gov.uk/report-gender-pay-gap-data). The calculation must be performed annually, covering the year to a 'snapshot date' of 5 April (for businesses and charities) and 31 March (for public sector organisations). The publication must take place within a year of the snapshot date, so by 4 April or 30 March respectively.

- The calculations required are:
- The mean average gender pay gap
- The median average gender pay gap
- The mean average bonus gender pay gap
- The median average bonus gender pay gap
- The proportion of males and females receiving a bonus payment
- The proportion of males and females in each pay quartile (when employees are ordered from lowest to highest pay)

Employers may, if they wish, accompany the calculations with a written narrative explaining the calculations and setting out plans for improvement, but this is not a requirement.

15.1.7 SECRECY CLAUSES

Secrecy or 'gagging' clauses have become a prominent employment law concern. While the EqA 2010 does not address the generality of gagging clause issues, it does act to protect employees who try to identify any discriminatory features in their terms of employment. It does so by rendering unenforceable any term which prevents or restricts a person from making a 'relevant pay disclosure' (section 77(1) of the EqA 2010) or seeking one from a current or former colleague (section 77(2) of the EqA 2010).

A 'relevant pay disclosure' is defined in section 77(3) of the EqA 2010 as one made for the purpose of enabling the person making it, or the person to whom it is made, to find out whether or to what extent there is, in relation to the work in question, a connection between pay and having (or not having) a particular protected characteristic. So (as the Equal Pay Guide explains), a discussion between a woman and a man for the purpose of establishing whether the man is being paid more than the woman could involve a relevant pay disclosure. However, a similar discussion between two men comparing their salaries would not unless they were doing so in relation to another protected characteristic.

Employees making or asking for a relevant pay disclosure are also protected from victimisation (section 77(4) of the EqA 2010).

15.1.8 WRONGFUL DEDUCTION FROM WAGES CLAIMS

The complexity of equal pay claims means that sometimes, a claim for unlawful deduction of wages, contrary to section 13 of the *Equal Rights Act 1996* (ERA 1996), may be more suitable.

When deciding which route to take, though, it is worth bearing in mind that an EqA 2010 equal pay claim can have distinct procedural advantages, as well as providing additional protection against victimisation. A useful summary of the differences between the two routes is provided at paragraph 30 of *Alabaster v Woolwich Plc & anor [2005] IRLR 576*. Although the case predates the EqA 2010, its equal pay provisions replicate those of the precursor legislation sufficiently closely that the advice remains relevant. Among the most important points are:

- The ERA 1996 time limit is three months, subject to a power to extend if it was not reasonably practicable to present a claim within time, whereas, under the EqA 2010, it is six months, except in cases of 'concealment or disability' (although it extends to six years for a claim brought in the civil courts).

- Advice may be available from the EHRC for an EqA 2010 claim, while none is available under the ERA 1996.

- An EqA 2010 claim allows interest on an award to be claimed immediately from the decision (if it is not paid within 14 days), and for the period up to the date of judgment from halfway between the date of the contravention and the date of judgment. An ERA 1996 claim has no pre-judgment interest, and interest only runs from 42 days after judgment.

- The burden of proof in an ERA 1996 claim remains on the claimant, whereas in an EqA 2010 claim, it passes to the employer once the claimant has established a prima facie case.

- Dismissal of an employee making an ERA 1996 claim for alleging their statutory rights have been infringed is unfair dismissal. The protection is wider in an EqA 2010 claim: both employees and workers are protected in such a circumstance, which would constitute victimisation. Further, post-employment victimisation in an EqA 2010 claim may constitute discrimination, while ERA 1996 claimants are only protected from victimisation while they are still employed.

15.2 FIXED-TERM EMPLOYEES

Employees whose contracts are for a fixed term may find themselves treated less favourably than those doing comparable ('the same or broadly similar') work but under a permanent contract. The *Fixed-Term Employees (Prevention of Less Favourable Treatment) Regulations 2002* (FTER) prohibit such discrimination if the employer cannot show an objective justification for the distinction.

15.2.1 WHO IS COVERED?

For the purposes of the FTER, 'employee' has the same (narrow) meaning as in an unfair dismissal claim, rather than the more expansive EqA 2010 definition. Further, those on government training schemes, attending work experience lasting less than a year as part of a higher education course, apprentices and agency workers are excluded from protection under the FTER.

'Fixed-term contract' refers both to a contract for a specific period, and one which terminates on the completion of a specific task or the occurrence (or non-occurrence) of a specific event other than the employee reaching retirement age (regulation 1(2) of the FTER).

One unfortunate side-effect of the FTER is that an employer could conceivably re-employ fixed-term employees onto permanent contracts but on different (presumably less favourable) terms than their existing permanently employed counterparts, as long as other discrimination rules were not contravened. However, disaffected employees might be able to claim parity by relying on the implied contractual term of trust and confidence rather than on the regulations, so this must be seen as dangerous territory.

15.2.2 THE BASIC RIGHT

Under the FTER, fixed-term employees have the right not to be treated less favourably than comparable permanent employees, whether in terms of their contract or by being dismissed or subjected to any other detriment by an act or deliberate failure to act on the part of their employer. As with discrimination, 'detriment' is construed broadly but can include – for instance – being denied extra benefits keyed to length of service, access to training or the ability to secure a permanent position.

Dismissal, in this situation, refers to dismissal before the date stipulated as the end of the fixed term. Such a dismissal because the employee was on a fixed-term contract is unlawful. A failure to renew the contract once its term has ended is not, without more, either dismissal or a detriment (*DWP v Webley [2005] IRLR 288*).

The right also includes pension eligibility. An occupational pension scheme cannot exclude fixed-term employees if comparable permanent employees are eligible for membership.

An important caveat is that difference in treatment will not in itself be enough to found a claim. The difference must be 'on the ground' of being on a fixed-term contract (Regulation 3(3)(a) of the FTER).

15.2.3 THE DEFENCE OF OBJECTIVE JUSTIFICATION

There are two ways in which an employer can claim that different treatment of a fixed-term employee is objectively justified, and thus defend a claim.

First, if the terms of the fixed-term employee's contract, taken as a whole, are at least as favourable as those of a comparable permanent employee (the 'total package' defence), any individual less favourable term is considered objectively justified, providing the employer with a defence to a claim under regulation 4(1) of the FTER. This will only work if the difference in treatment relates to a contractual term.

Alongside this definition, European case law suggests that the 'standard' definition of objectively justified treatment used in discrimination cases can also apply (*Del Cerro Alonso v Osakidetza (Servicio Vasco de Salud) [2008] ICR 145*). If, therefore, an employer can show that the different treatment responds to a genuine need, is appropriate for achieving it and is necessary for doing so, then the defence may be made out. Employers should be aware that any reliance on this limb of the defence is likely to require very specific reasoning and cannot rest on the mere fact that the work in question is temporary in nature.

Finally, the simple fact that short-term and permanent workers may have different expectations about their work can be an objective justification (*Montero Mateos v Agencia Madrilena de Atencion Social de la Consejeria de Politicas Sociales y Familia de la Comunidad Autonoma de Madrid [2019] ICR 63*) – but, clearly, this is an area where an employer would need to tread extremely carefully.

15.2.4 OTHER RIGHTS

As well as the basic right prohibiting less favourable treatment, fixed-term employees have the following rights:

- To have their contract converted to a permanent one after four years (regulation 8 of the FTER), although periods such as apprenticeship, which are excluded from the protection of the FTER, do not count towards the four years (*Hudson v DWP [2013] ICR 329*).

- To require a written statement from their employer setting out the reasons for their treatment if they consider they are being treated unfairly (regulation 5 of the FTER).

- To be considered to have been dismissed at the expiry of the contract for the purposes of considering whether an unfair dismissal has taken place (regulation 1(2) and Schedule 2, paragraph 3 of the FTER).

15.3 PART-TIME WORKERS

Part-time workers are also protected from less favourable treatment, in this case by the *Part-Time Workers (Prevention of Less Favourable Treatment) Regulations 2000* (PTWR).

15.3.1 WHO IS COVERED?

The PTWR cover 'workers' as well as employees and allow either to make a claim (under regulation 5 of the PTWR) if:

- They are part-time.

- They are treated less favourably than a comparable full-timer.

- The treatment is on the grounds that they are part-time.

- The employer cannot objectively justify the treatment.

Unhelpfully, the PTWR do not define a 'part-time worker' particularly clearly, instead describing them as someone 'paid wholly or in part by reference to the time he works' and who 'having regard to the custom and practice of the employer … is not identifiable as a full-time worker' (regulation 2 of the PTWR). The key, therefore, is to identify a full-time comparator, who must be a real person rather than a hypothetical one (*Carl v University of Sheffield [2009] ICR 1286*), and who must, under regulation 2(4) of the PTWR:

- Be employed by the same employer under the same type of contract.

- Be engaged in the same or broadly similar work, having regard where relevant to qualifications, skills and experience.

- Be based at the same establishment – unless there is no full-time worker at that establishment, and there is one at another establishment who otherwise satisfies these requirements.

Regulation 2(3) of the PTWR provides a list of types of contracts which will not be regarded as the 'same' as one another for the purposes of the first test above:

- Employees employed under a contract that is not a contract of apprenticeship.

- Employees employed under a contract of apprenticeship.

- Workers who are not employees.

- Any other description of worker that it is 'reasonable for the employer to treat differently from other workers on the ground that workers of that description have a different type of contract'.

The test for whether work is 'the same or broadly similar' was clarified by the House of Lords in *Matthews v Kent and Medway Towns Fire Authority [2006] ICR 365*. This said that once it had been determined that the full-time and part-time workers were in the same broad category in regulation 2(3) of the PTWR, the comparison as to the kind of work had to look at the whole of the work done and not focus (for instance) solely or predominantly on differences which arose simply because of the extra hours worked by full-timers. As long as those differences did not materially detract from the similarities, the work done should be regarded as the 'same or broadly similar'. This finding was relied upon by the EAT in relation to zero-hours contracts in *Roddis v Sheffield Hallam University [2018] IRLR 706*: the mere fact that someone is not guaranteed a specific amount of work (or indeed any work at all) does not stop them from being found to do 'broadly similar' work to that of a colleague doing a comparable job pursuant to regulation 2(4) of the PTWR.

One particular variety of part-time work has been the subject of extensive litigation, up to both the Supreme Court and the CJEU. Regulation 17 of the PTWR provides that it does not apply to 'any individual in his capacity as the holder of a judicial office if he is remunerated on a daily fee-paid basis'. In 2010, the Supreme Court found itself considering whether, despite that regulation, part-time recorders could satisfy the definition of 'worker' in the PTWR so as to be entitled, upon retirement, to a pension on terms equivalent to those applicable to full-time judges. After referring the matter to the CJEU, the court determined that they could (*O'Brien v Ministry of Justice [2013] ICR 499*).

While *O'Brien* has generally been found binding as to the position of part-time judges with reference to the PTWR, it should be noted that their inclusion in the 'worker' category by the Supreme Court was because the definition in this case derived from European legislation. Where the law is wholly domestic, as, for instance, with the protection under the ERA 1996 of whistleblowers, judicial office-holders are not workers (*Gilham v Ministry of Justice [2017] IRLR 23*).

15.3.2 THE BASIC RIGHT

Under the PTWR, part-time workers have the right not to be treated any less favourably than comparable full-time workers, as regards the terms of their employment or by being subjected to any detriment, on the grounds of their part-time status. They are thus entitled, for example, to:

- The same hourly rate of pay

- The same access to company pension schemes

- The same entitlements to annual leave and maternity/parental leave on a pro rata basis

- The same entitlement to contractual sick pay

- No less favourable treatment in access to training

The entitlements under the PTWR are intended to prevent part-time workers from getting a raw deal compared to their colleagues. Nothing in the PTWR prevents the opposite – as in *Brazel v Harpur Trust [2018] ICR D10*, where a part-time teacher employed only during term time was found by the EAT to be entitled to the same holiday pay (pro rata) as full-timers or part-timers employed all year round, even though that meant more of her overall pay was made up of holiday pay than theirs was.

Provided that a part-time worker can show that their part-time status was the effective and predominant cause of the less favourable treatment – not necessarily the only cause, as the case of *Carl* shows – they will succeed (subject to the objective justification defence).

The employer is liable under the PTWR for anything done by one of its workers or agents, irrespective of whether it was done with the employer's knowledge or approval unless the employer can prove it took such steps as were reasonably practicable to prevent it from happening.

15.3.3 THE DEFENCE OF OBJECTIVE JUSTIFICATION

Employers can claim the defence of objective justification (regulation 5(2)(b) of the PTWR), as they can under the FTER, although there is no equivalent of the 'total package' defence in the PTWR. Objective justification in this context is not defined, and while the explanatory notes to the PTWR originally provided a definition analogous to that used in indirect discrimination, they have no legal force. However, in 2013, the Supreme Court in *O'Brien* noted that the CJEU had used the indirect discrimination test – that treatment had to be in service of a legitimate aim, be suitable for achieving it and be reasonably necessary to do so. It seems likely, therefore, that tribunals will apply this standard to an employer seeking to rely on the defence.

15.3.4 OTHER RIGHTS

Part-time *employees* – that is, the narrow ERA 1996 definition, not the broader EqA 2010 definition to which the rest of the PTWR apply – also have a right not to be dismissed or subjected to a detriment because they have either tried to enforce their rights under the PTWR, alleged that their employer has breached a right or refused to forgo a right. Any dismissal for these reasons will be automatically unfair unless the employee's allegation was false and made in bad faith (regulation 7 of the PTWR).

Finally, if part-time workers consider that an employer has infringed their rights under PTWR, they are entitled to receive a written statement of reasons for the less favourable treatment (regulation 5 of the PTWR).

CHAPTER 16

REMEDIES AND COMPENSATION

To learn more about employment tribunal compensation, visit
go.danielbarnett.com/compensation

16.0 OVERVIEW

This chapter concentrates on remedies for four common types of claims
brought in employment tribunals: unfair dismissal, discrimination,
whistleblowing detriment and redundancy. Damages for wrongful dismissal
are dealt with in **Chapter 8**.

16.1 UNFAIR DISMISSAL

Tribunals have three remedies available for unfair dismissal: reinstatement,
re-engagement and compensation. When ordering reinstatement or re-
engagement, the tribunal will also order the employer to pay the employee
a sum reflecting the income lost during the period of unemployment.
Exceptionally, there is a fourth remedy – interim relief – which can be ordered
in a few specified cases (see **16.1.6**).

On the ET1 Form to bring a claim, there is a box where the claimant can
indicate whether they are interested in re-engagement or reinstatement as
a remedy. Even if the claimant does not express such an interest, tribunals
are under a statutory duty to explain the options of reinstatement and re-
engagement and to ask whether the claimant wants the tribunal to make an
appropriate order (section 112(2) of the *Employment Rights Act 1996* (ERA
1996)). However, if the tribunal fails to comply with this obligation, it does
not automatically mean the decision will be set aside (*Cowley v Manson
Timber Ltd [1995] IRLR 153 CA*).

The fact that an unfair dismissal was genuinely on the grounds of
redundancy does not remove the tribunal's duty to explain these two remedies
and to ask whether the claimant wishes to see the appropriate order. For
example, the situation with regard to possible vacancies may have changed
between dismissal and the hearing date (*King v Royal Bank of Canada Europe
Ltd [2012] IRLR 280 EAT*).

The tribunal cannot order reinstatement or re-engagement if the employee does not wish it and, in any event, is not obliged to do so (section 112(3) of the ERA 1996). In this situation, it must instead make an order for compensation (section 112(4) of the ERA 1996).

16.1.1 REINSTATEMENT AND RE-ENGAGEMENT

An order for reinstatement, as the name suggests, orders that the employee be reinstated in the same job as the one they occupied before dismissal. On re-engagement, the employee may be employed in similar work subject to different terms. Importantly, an order for re-engagement must specify the identity of the employer (section 115(2)(a) of the ERA 1996).

The tribunal is obliged to consider making an order for reinstatement or (if reinstatement is not appropriate) re-engagement before considering simply awarding compensation (section 116 of the ERA 1996). In practice, these orders are not often made. Few employees request them (other than as a negotiating tactic) and even fewer tribunals accede to the request. A tribunal's decision on the practicability of reinstatement or re-engagement will almost never be overturned on appeal (*Clancy v Cannock Chase Technical College [2001] IRLR 331 EAT*).

When will reinstatement and re-engagement be ordered?

The tribunal must take into account the employee's preferred remedy, whether it is practicable for the employer to comply with an order for reinstatement or re-engagement and whether it is just to make such an order if the employee contributed to their dismissal (section 116 of the ERA 1996).

Re-engagement must be reasonably practicable and the nature of the role in which the employee is being re-engaged must be sufficiently detailed and precise for the tribunal to make an order (*Lincolnshire County Council v Lupton [2016] IRLR 576*).

Factors which will influence a tribunal in deciding whether to grant reinstatement or re-engagement include:

- The likelihood of industrial strife if the order is made and complied with (*Bateman v British Leyland (UK) Ltd [1974] ICR 403 NIRC*)

- The disruption to personal relationships in a small company (*Enessy Co SA v Minoprio [1978] IRLR 489 EAT*)

- Distrust between the parties (*Nothman v London Borough of Barnet (No.2) [1980] IRLR 65 CA*)

- An inability to trust the employee when coming into contact with the public (*Inner London Education Authority v Gravett [1988] IRLR 497 EAT*)

- A genuine absence of vacancies (*Cold Drawn Tubes Ltd v Middleton [1992] ICR 318 EAT*)

In deciding whether to order reinstatement or re-engagement, the tribunal must disregard the fact that the employer has replaced the employee, save in two cases (sections 116(5) and 116(6) of the ERA 1996). These are:

1) Where the employer can demonstrate that the only way of arranging for the dismissed employee's work to be done was by taking on a permanent (as opposed to a temporary) replacement.

2) Where the employer has engaged the replacement after the lapse of a reasonable time without hearing that the dismissed employee sought reinstatement or re-engagement, and it was reasonable at that stage to engage a permanent replacement.

If a replacement employee has to be dismissed to make way for a reinstated or re-employed worker, that dismissal will usually be fair as being 'for some other substantial reason' under section 98(1)(b) of the ERA 1996, subject to the employer considering suitable alternative employment for the bumped replacement worker.

Terms of order

When ordering reinstatement or re-engagement, the tribunal must also order the employer to pay compensation reflecting the employee's lost earnings. This includes the value of all benefits. The tribunal must give credit for any sums received, such as payments in lieu of notice or salary received from another employment (sections 114(2)(a) and 115(2)(d) of the ERA 1996).

Reinstatement may mean being re-employed on the de-facto terms (rather than on the written terms) of employment prior to an unlawful dismissal, in which case the employer will be required to re-employ the claimant on the same restricted duties which they had been carrying out before the dismissal (*McBride v Scottish Police Authority [2016] UKSC 27*).

The tribunal must also state the date by which the order must be complied with and any rights and privileges (including seniority and pension rights) which must be restored to the employee (sections 114(2) and 115(2) of the ERA 1996).

When ordering re-engagement, the tribunal must also specify the terms of re-engagement, including the identity of the employer and the employee's remuneration (section 115(2) of the ERA 1996).

What if the employer does not comply?

Where the employee is re-engaged or reinstated but the employer does not comply with all the terms of the order, the employer will be ordered to pay the employee such compensation as the tribunal thinks fit (section 117(2) of the ERA 1996). Where the employee is not re-engaged or reinstated at all, they will be regarded as having been unfairly dismissed (section 117(3) of the ERA 1996). The tribunal must then make a compensatory award plus an additional award of between 26 and 52 weeks' pay.

A week's pay is capped for these purposes (sections 117(3)(b) and 227(1)(b) of the ERA 1996). Where the effective date of termination is on or after 6 April 2023, but before 6 April 2024, the cap is £643 per week. This figure changes every year on 6 April (section 227 ERA 1996). The most important factor in determining where in the 26-52 week range an order should be made is the employer's motive for not complying. A deliberate flouting of the order will warrant a higher additional award than a genuine belief that it was not practicable to comply (*Mabirizi v National Hospital for Nervous Diseases [1990] IRLR 133 EAT*). However, if there has already been an award of four weeks' wages when the order for reinstatement or re-engagement was made, this must be deducted from any 'additional award' (see section 117(3)(b) of the ERA 1996, and for non-compliance, see section 117(2A) of the ERA 1996).

The normal duty of an employee to mitigate their loss applies. Therefore, if the employer fails to provide reinstatement as ordered but offers appropriate alternative employment instead, which the employee unreasonably rejects, the employee will not be able to insist on reinstatement. Whether the alternative employment offered is appropriate and whether the employee acted unreasonably in not accepting it are matters of fact for the tribunal. It follows that, as a general rule, no appeal can be entertained against the employment tribunal's decision (*Sarieddine v Abou Zaki Holding Company [2008] EWCA Civ 453*).

Under section 124 of the ERA 1996, the compensatory award is subject to a statutory maximum as 'the lower of –

a) £105,707; and

b) 52 multiplied by a week's [gross] pay of the person concerned'

This figure is for claims where the effective date of termination is on or after 6 April 2023. This figure changes each year on 6 April.

This figure also applies to the part of the compensatory award that reflects arrears of pay and other benefits made under sections 114 and 115 of the ERA 1996 provided they total less than the statutory cap. This expressly includes pension contributions (*University of Sunderland v Drossou (2017) UKEAT/0341/16*). If an award under sections 114 or 115 of the ERA 1996 alone would exceed the statutory cap, then that sum is recoverable so as to allow 'full reflection' of the employee's losses in terms of section 124(4) of the ERA 1996. However, no further compensatory award can then be made since the statutory cap has been exceeded (*Parry v National Westminster Bank plc [2005] ICR 396*). It is debatable whether this approach is consistent with the purpose of section 114(2) of the ERA 1996, which 'was inserted to prevent employers from benefiting from the statutory limit simply by not reinstating an employee when ordered by a tribunal' (*Awotona v South Tyneside Healthcare NHS Trust [2005] ICR 958*).

However, there is a defence to the additional award if the employer can establish that it was not practicable to comply with the order. An employer will normally have difficulty in showing this because to order the reinstatement or re-engagement, the tribunal must have decided that it *was* practicable to comply (section 117(4) of the ERA 1996). In effect, the 'practicability' defence allows employers a second bite at the cherry, perhaps to introduce new evidence or to argue that their circumstances have changed since the order was made (*Mabirizi v National Hospital for Nervous Diseases [1990] IRLR 133 EAT*).

Where an order for interim reinstatement under section 164 of the *Trade Union and Labour Relations (Consolidation) Act 1992* (TULR(C)A 1992) is made against an undertaking which is then TUPE transferred, the order does not transmit to the transferee (*Dowling v ME Ilic Haulage [2004] ICR 1176 EAT*). However, it is likely that if an order for reinstatement were made under sections 113-116 of the ERA 1996, this is a liability which would transfer, as would liabilities arising out of any failure to comply.

Effect on continuity of employment

If a tribunal orders reinstatement or re-engagement – or if the parties agree reinstatement or re-engagement through Acas or as a term of a settlement agreement – then continuity of employment is deemed to be preserved (*Employment Protection (Continuity of Employment) Regulations 1996*). However, if the parties simply agree to reinstate or re-engage without commencing proceedings, going through Acas or entering into a formal settlement agreement, then normal rules on continuity of employment apply.

16.1.2 COMPENSATION: BASIC AWARD

Compensation for unfair dismissal is split into two parts, both of which the unfairly dismissed employee is entitled to. The (usually) smaller part – the basic award – is very similar to statutory redundancy pay and is calculated according to a strict mathematical formula. The (usually) larger part – the compensatory award – is harder to predict as it is intended to compensate the employee for their financial losses and often involves speculation as to future losses.

Normal calculation

The basic award is calculated by multiplying the number of years' continuous employment by a week's pay, adjusted according to the employee's age (section 220-229 of the ERA 1996). A week's pay is calculated according to a strict formula set out in the legislation. In summary, this is the gross standard weekly wage, or average wage if it fluctuates from week to week, ignoring overtime (section 119 of the ERA 1996).

The week's pay is capped, for these purposes, at £643 per week where the effective date of termination is on or after 6 April 2023 but before 6 April 2024 (section 227 of the ERA 1996). Thus, if an employee earns £655 per week, £12 of that is disregarded when calculating the basic award using the April 2023 cap. The maximum is index linked and is adjusted each year on 6 April.

The calculation varies according to the age of the employee:

- For each complete year of continuous employment, working backwards from dismissal, that the employee was aged over 41, they receive 1.5 weeks' pay.

- For each complete year of continuous employment that they were aged between 22 and 41, the employee receives one week's pay.

- For each complete year of continuous employment that they were aged below 21, the employee receives half a week's pay.

A maximum of the most recent 20 years' work can be taken into account for the basic award calculation (section 119 of the ERA 1996). The maximum possible basic award is therefore £19,290 (i.e. 20 × 1.5 × £643). The rate must not be calculated on a figure lower than the National Minimum Wage (*Paggetti v Cobb [2002] IRLR 861 EAT*).

Contributory conduct

The basic award can be reduced in certain circumstances. First, 'where the tribunal finds that the complainant has unreasonably refused an offer by the employer which (if accepted) would have the effect of reinstating the complainant in his employment in all respects as if he had not been dismissed the tribunal shall reduce or further reduce the amount of the basic award to such extent as it considers just and equitable having regard to that finding' (section 122(1) of the ERA 1996).

Second, 'where the tribunal considers that any conduct of the complainant before the dismissal (or, where the dismissal was with notice before the notice was given) was such that it would be just and equitable to reduce or further reduce the amount of the basic award to any extent, the tribunal shall reduce or further reduce that amount accordingly' (section 122(2) of the ERA 1996). This statutory reduction does not require the tribunal to identify any causal connection between the claimant's conduct and the reduction to the basic award.

However, in order to make a reduction under section 122(2) of the ERA 1996, the tribunal must first identify conduct which is 'culpable or blameworthy' in the sense defined in *Nelson v British Broadcasting Corpn (No 2) [1980] ICR 110*. Here. Brandon LJ clarified that 'culpable or blameworthy' included conduct which is perverse, foolish or bloody-minded. In *Gibson v British Transport Docks Board [1982] IRLR 228*, Browne-Wilkinson J, as President of the Employment Appeal Tribunal (EAT), thought that the conduct had to be 'improper'. In *Frith Accountants Ltd v Law [2014] ICR 805*, Langstaff J, President of the EAT (as he then was), held at paragraph 4 that:

> 'It is not sufficient merely that the conduct be unreasonable, though it may be so unreasonable as to be culpable or blameworthy or fit within that class of conduct. But it is plain that what is required is more than just conduct of which the tribunal disapproves or conduct which might, on reflection, have been better. And it is important not to water down the test, bearing in mind that contributory fault reduces the amount of compensation to be awarded for the primary fault, which remains the primary fault of the party responsible.'

Section 122(2) of the ERA 1996 does not apply in a redundancy case unless 'the reason for selecting the employee for dismissal was one of those specified in section 100(1)(a) and (b), [F1101A(d),] 102(1) or 103; and in such a case subsection (2) applies only to so much of the basic award as is payable because of section 120'.

In *Phoenix House Ltd v Stockman [2019] IRLR 960* the EAT held that just as there is a subjective and an objective element to a *Polkey* assessment (see step 3 below), so too must there be a subjective and an objective element to the tribunal's approach to sections 122(2) and 123(1) of the ERA 1996 where the issue is whether and to what extent it is just and equitable to make an award in light of conduct of which the employer subsequently learns. The question is whether and to what extent it is just and equitable to reduce an award given the actual employer and employee, not a hypothetical employee. However, the tribunal must then make its own assessment of what justice and equity require.

Special cases

If the employee received a redundancy payment at the time of dismissal, this must be set against the basic award. In most cases, the two payments will be precisely the same (section 122(4) of the ERA 1996).

Where the employee was dismissed for redundancy, and unreasonably refused an offer of suitable alternative employment, the basic award is limited to two weeks' pay (section 121 of the ERA 1996).

16.1.3 ACAS CODE UPLIFTS

A failure to follow the proper disciplinary and grievance procedures set out in the Acas Code of Practice on Disciplinary and Grievance Procedures (Acas Code) can lead to an adjustment of up to 25% in 'any award' the tribunal makes to an employee (section 207A of the TULR(C)A 1992). An Acas Code uplift is only possible for employees (*Local Government Yorkshire and Humber v Shah (2012) UKEAT/0587/11*).

Where the claimant is an employee, they can claim an uplift for whistleblowing detriment. In *Timis v Osipov (2017) UKEAT/0058/17* (before the EAT, and not challenged in the Court of Appeal) it was held that compensation for whistleblowing detriment could be awarded together with a 12.5% uplift on damages against the two individual respondents under section 207A of the TULR(C)A for failing to use the procedures laid down in the Acas Code.

Section 207A of the TULR(C)A 1992 provides that in 'proceedings before an employment tribunal relating to a claim by an employee under any of the jurisdictions listed in Schedule A2 [which includes unfair dismissal] ...

(2) [where] it appears to the employment tribunal that –

(a) the claim to which the proceedings relate concerns a matter to which a relevant Code of Practice applies;

(b) the employer has failed to comply with that Code in relation to that matter, and

(c) that failure was unreasonable, the employment tribunal may, if it considers it just and equitable in all the circumstances to do so, increase any award it makes to the employee by no more than 25%.

(4) In sub-ss (2) and (3), 'relevant Code of Practice' means a Code of Practice issued under this Chapter which relates exclusively or primarily to procedure for the resolution of disputes. The Code does not apply to dismissals due to redundancy or to the non-renewal of fixed-term contracts on expiry (for full details of when the Code applies, see Schedule A2 TULR(C)A 1992 itself (set out in Employment Act 2008, section 3(3)).'

In certain circumstances, the law provides for a minimum basic award, set at £7,836 from 6 April 2023 (section 120 of the ERA 1996). This occurs if the employee is dismissed for any of the following reasons:

- Being a safety representative
- Being a trustee of an occupational pension fund
- Being an employee representative (for consultation purposes)
- Because of trade union activities or membership
- Or because they insist on taking advantage of their rights under the *Working Time Regulations 1998* (WTR 1998) (section 101A of the ERA 1996)

The £7,836 minimum can be reduced if the employee unreasonably refused reinstatement or contributed to the dismissal, or to take account of redundancy pay already received (section 120 of the ERA 1996).

16.1.4 COMPENSATION: COMPENSATORY AWARD

The compensatory award is usually the larger part of unfair dismissal compensation. It is 'such amount as the tribunal considers just and equitable in all the circumstances having regard to the loss sustained by the complainant in consequence of the dismissal in so far as that loss is attributable to action taken by the employer' (section 123(1) of the ERA 1996).

There is normally a maximum award that a tribunal can order to be paid by way of the compensatory award (often referred to as 'the statutory cap on compensation'). The compensatory award is subject to a statutory maximum of £105,707 (as of 6 April 2022) or 52 weeks' gross pay where lower (section 124 of the ERA 1996).

However, the statutory cap does not apply in cases where the reason for the dismissal was related to whistleblowing, pregnancy or health and safety.

Unlike the basic award, under section 123(6) of the ERA 1996, and to reflect 'any extent [to which the claimant has] caused or contributed to [the dismissal], it [the tribunal] shall reduce the amount of the compensatory award by such proportion as it considers just and equitable having regard to that finding'. The tribunal must first identify conduct of the claimant which is 'culpable or blameworthy' in the sense defined in *Nelson v British Broadcasting Corpn (No 2) [1980] ICR 110*. It must then determine the extent to which *that* conduct has caused or contributed to the dismissal, and reflect that with an appropriate percentage reduction.

There is a vast body of jurisprudence on calculation of the compensatory award but – in the overwhelming majority of cases – it consists of a relatively straightforward mathematical calculation (albeit involving speculation as to the employee's future income).

Normally, the greatest difficulties arise when determining the order of deductions. To take a simple example, say an employee suffered a £105,000 loss but the award was subject to a 50% reduction for contributory fault (section 123(6) of the ERA 1996). If the reduction is applied before the statutory maximum, the employee will receive £52,500. However, if the statutory maximum is applied before the reduction, the employee will receive only £46,939 (i.e. 50% of £93,878), a difference of £5,561. The correct order in which deductions should be made is set out in *Digital Equipment Co Ltd v Clements (No.2) [1998] ICR 258 CA*. These steps are described in detail at **16.1.5**. The steps include an additional Step 7, which deals with compensatory awards in excess of (the normally tax-free) £30,000. This was not considered in *Digital Equipment Co Ltd v Clements* because, at that time, the limit on compensatory awards was £11,000, so the issue did not arise. Step 4 has been extended to take into account any adjustment for failure to comply with the Acas Code.

Acas Code

If an employer fails to comply with the Acas Code, the tribunal can increase the award it makes by up to 25% (section 207A of the TULR(C)A 1992). Conversely, if an employee fails to comply, the compensation is subject to the same percentage reduction. In exercising its discretion, the tribunal should have regard to 'all the circumstances' of the case, including the 'size and resources of an employer' (paragraph 3 of the Acas Code).

The Acas Code applies in most types of tribunal claims, but redundancy dismissals, breach of contract and expiry of fixed-term contract claims are excluded. (For full details of when the Acas Code applies, see Schedule A2 of the TULR(C)A 1992, set out in section 3(3) of the *Employment Act 2008*.) For the Acas Code to apply, there must have been 'culpable conduct' by the employee. This means that it is unlikely to apply where a dismissal arises out of illness (*Holmes v Qinetiq Ltd [2016] ICR 1016 EAT*) or where dismissal is for some other substantial reason if the reason is an irretrievable breakdown in the employer/employee relationship (*Phoenix House Ltd v Stockman [2016] IRLR 848 EAT*).

No award for injury to feelings on unfair dismissal

Compensation for unfair dismissal covers only pecuniary losses. There can be no award for injury to feelings arising out of the dismissal (*Dunnachie v Kingston upon Hull Council [2004] UKHL 36*). Matters can therefore be complicated where there is a dual claim based in part on dismissal and in part on breach of a statutory right which does allow an award for injury to feelings. For example, where a worker has been subjected to a detriment for making a protected disclosure, an award for injury to feelings is permitted (section 49(2) of the ERA 1996). But what is the position if an employee has been subject to a detriment but then dismissed? Where the detriment in question amounts to dismissal, the employee can claim that the taking of the decision is a detriment under section 47B of the ERA 1996, against (a) the individual who took the decision and (b) the employer, only in so far as it is vicariously liable for the actions of the dismissing individual (*Timis v Osipov [2019] IRLR 52*). Where the principal reason for the dismissal is the disclosure, the employee can also bring a claim directly against the employer on the basis they have been unfairly dismissed (section 103A of the ERA 1996).

In *Melia v Magna Kansei Ltd [2006] ICR 410*, the employee had been subjected to a detriment for making a protected disclosure. By June 2001, the employer's conduct amounted to a repudiatory breach of contract. The claimant resigned in November 2001 and claimed constructive dismissal. He argued that an award for injury to feelings should be made up to November

2001, when he terminated his contract. The EAT disagreed, finding that if an employee is dismissed for making a protected disclosure, the right not to be subjected to a detriment is lost (section 47B (2) of the ERA 1996). This meant that the cut-off date for any award for injury to feelings was the moment at which the employer's conduct became repudiatory, not the date when the repudiation was accepted. The Court of Appeal, however, held that the EAT had erred in construing the words 'amounts to dismissal' in section 47B (2) of the ERA 1996 as excluding a detriment suffered before the actual dismissal. In a constructive dismissal case, it was not the employer's breach of contract that amounts to a dismissal, but the employee's resignation in response to that breach. Accordingly, the claimant was entitled to an award for injury to feelings in respect of the detriment he suffered before 9 November 2001, and to compensation for the loss he sustained in consequence of the dismissal under the unfair dismissal provisions from that date.

No damages for loss of chance to claim unfair dismissal

Two years' continuity of employment is required to claim unfair dismissal. Where an employee is wrongfully dismissed before the necessary two years have been acquired, no damages can be awarded at common law in respect of the loss of the chance to claim unfair dismissal (*Wise Group v Mitchell [2005] ICR 896 EAT*).

16.1.5 CALCULATING THE COMPENSATORY AWARD

Step 1: Calculate what the employee would have earned if they had remained employed

The first step is to establish precisely what the employee would have earned had they not been unfairly dismissed. This entails establishing the employee's net (not gross) salary and factoring in the value of any benefits or pay rises they would have received. It is expressly provided that the compensatory award payable to an unfairly dismissed employee shall include compensation for 'loss of any benefit which he might reasonably be expected to have had but for the dismissal' (section 123(2)(b) of the ERA 1996). This refers to loss of benefits to which the employee was not contractually entitled, as well as those to which they were entitled under their contract (*Gould v Governors of Haileybury and Imperial Service College (2002) EAT/635/00 EAT/1191/00*). This is calculated to the date of the tribunal hearing. Matters are complicated if the employer is entitled to an insurance payment to which the employee did not contribute (see step 2, below).

In a case where a dismissal has been found to be unfair on the basis of features of the procedure (most frequently seen in redundancy or conduct cases), the tribunal will award compensation to put the claimant in the financial position they would have been in had those procedural defects been remedied. This aspect of section 123 of the ERA 1996 is commonly referred to as a *Polkey* reduction (see step 3 below). It can be used to reduce damages by reflecting the time it would have taken to complete a procedural element (such as additional interviews of witnesses) which was omitted and had led to a finding of unfair dismissal. For example, if going through a fair procedure would have taken four weeks, thus deferring the date of dismissal by four weeks, the tribunal will only award loss of earnings sustained in that four-week period (*Polkey v AE Dayton Services [1987] IRLR 504 HL* and *Steel Stockholders (Birmingham) Ltd v Kirkwood [1993] IRLR 515 EAT*). If an employee would, in any event, have been dismissed in the future because of closure of the business, the compensatory award will be limited by the date of the closure (*James W Cook & Co (Wivenhoe) Ltd v Tipper [1990] IRLR 386 CA*). In asking the hypothetical question 'what would have happened anyway?', the tribunal must also consider whether any subsequent decision to dismiss would have been fair or unfair (*Panama v London Borough of Hackney [2003] IRLR 278*).

The tribunal should then consider whether there are any ongoing losses – for example, if the employee remains unemployed or is now earning a lower salary. Where the statutory cap on compensation applies, the extent of the claimant's ongoing losses is less significant because the compensatory award will be limited to the lower of a maximum index-linked figure or 12 months' salary (see Step 8). However, section 124 of the ERA 1996 removes the statutory cap in certain circumstances and, in those cases in particular, the period of the claimant's ongoing loss is likely to be of fundamental importance.

In *Shittu v South London & Maudsley NHS Foundation Trust [2022] IRLR 382*, the EAT held that since the introduction of the statutory right not to be unfairly dismissed, tribunals have discharged the task of assessing the counterfactual situation of what might have happened had an employee not been unfairly dismissed by applying a percentage loss approach. Therefore, if the tribunal is satisfied that there was a 100% chance that the employee would have been dismissed anyway on the same date, or if the tribunal is able to reach any other conclusions with equal certainty (for example that the employee had a 100% chance of not being dismissed for a particular period of time, such as the length of time it would take for a fair procedure to be followed by the employer), compensation will be reduced accordingly. Similarly, the tribunal may conclude that there is no chance that the employment would have ended absent the unfair dismissal and make no percentage deduction.

There can therefore be an 'all or nothing' result, but it will be because the tribunal is 100% satisfied that a future chance would or would not have happened. In practice there are a number of possibilities: (1) there was a less than 100% chance of indefinite continued employment in which case the tribunal must assess the percentage chance and apply that percentage reduction; (2) the tribunal is satisfied, on the evidence, that there was a 100%

chance that the employment would have ended anyway by a certain time or at the same time as the dismissal, in which case compensation is limited to that period and the claimant is awarded 100% of whatever that period is (or receives nothing for loss of earnings if it was the same date as the dismissal occurred); (3) employment would have continued indefinitely, in which case there is no percentage reduction applied; (4) there was a 100% chance that the employment would have continued for a certain period followed by a lesser percentage chance thereafter. There may be other possible categories, but in each category, the exercise is the same – the assessment from 0 to 100 of the percentage chance of what might have been or what will be.

Generally, tribunals do not look further than 12 months beyond the hearing date unless the employee was within, say, two or three years of retirement age, in which case compensation will be awarded up until the anticipated retirement date. On occasion, a younger or middle-aged employee has been able to demonstrate a long-term future loss of earnings – perhaps because they were being paid significantly above the going market rate before being unfairly dismissed or because their dismissal caused an illness which prevented them from seeking work. In such circumstances, awards for long-term loss of earnings have been made, but they should be subject to an appropriate discount for accelerated receipt of monies. This has been presumed to be 2.5%, though this could be argued with today (*Bentwood Bros (Manchester) Ltd v Shepherd [2003] ICR 1000*). *Melia v Magna Kansei Ltd [2006] IRLR 117* is the authority for the proposition that if a reduction has been made to reflect accelerated receipt, then the claimant could obtain an enhancement of sums awarded in respect of past lost earnings.

When calculating the current value of future losses, tribunals have traditionally cautioned against using – or relying on – the Government's 'Actuarial Tables for use in Personal Injury and Fatal Accident cases' (the Ogden Tables), and their use in employment cases remains rare.

The EAT has pointed out that these tables are designed for use in personal injury cases and has warned against the danger of using them in other employment-related cases, save for calculating pension loss, unless it has been established that the claimant is unlikely to get another job before retirement age or that any job they get is likely to be at a lower rate of remuneration (*Dunnachie v Kingston upon Hull City Council (No.3) [2003] IRLR 843 EAT*) and *Birmingham City Council v Jaddoo (2004) UKEAT/0448/04*).

The claimant's ongoing losses are added to the past loss of earnings figure. The tribunal will also add any ancillary losses, for example, costs in seeking new employment and loss of pension rights. In *Bentwood Bros (Manchester) Ltd v Shepherd [2003] ICR 1000*, the Court of Appeal held that it was neither perverse nor an error of law for a tribunal to find an employee was entitled to 10 years' loss of pension.

Finally, the tribunal will award a sum for loss of statutory rights to reflect the fact that the employee's continuity of employment will have reset to zero with a new job and there will be a period during which they are without some protection. This loss is customarily assessed in the region of £500.

Step 2: Deduct monies received (with exceptions)

Next, the tribunal will deduct any (net) monies actually earned by the employee. The employee is under an express duty to mitigate their loss (section 123(4) of the ERA 1996). If the tribunal considers that the employee has taken inadequate steps to find new employment between the dismissal and the hearing, it will only award compensation to the point at which it thinks the employee ought to have found a new job had they been searching properly (*Gardiner-Hill v Roland Berger Technics Ltd [1982] IRLR 498 EAT*). Alternatively, the tribunal might award ongoing losses on the basis that the employee ought to have been in receipt of some salary, even if not at the level of their previous job, if they had been acting reasonably in searching for work (*Addison v Babcock FATA Ltd [1987] ICR 805 CA*). Sometimes, an employee will be entitled to take a long-term view and will not breach the duty to mitigate if they engage in retraining or enrol in higher education – provided always that they would take any suitable job that would provide the same standard of living as their old one, should one arise (*Orthet Ltd v Vince-Cain [2005] ICR 374 EAT*). It may be reasonable for an employee to mitigate their loss by starting up their own business. If so, the appropriate course for the tribunal is to:

1) Calculate what sum represents loss of remuneration.

2) Add any costs incurred by the claimant in starting up the business.

3) Subtract from the aggregate of (1) and (2) any earnings from the new business (*AON Training Ltd v Dore [2005] IRLR 891*).

If remuneration from a new job is greater than that from the old job, the excess is not to be taken into account to reduce the compensatory award for unfair dismissal from the old job (*Whelan (Cheers Off Licence) v Richardson [1998] ICR 318 EAT*).

If the employee gets a new job shortly after dismissal but is dismissed after a few months from that new job and does not get another for some time, compensation for loss of earnings may include compensation for a reasonable period after the second job ended (*Cowen v Rentokil Initial Facility Services (UK) Ltd t/a Initial Transport Services (2008) UKEAT/0473/07* and *Dench v Flynn & Partners [1998] IRLR 653 CA*).

Deductions may be made to reflect any extent to which a claimant has failed to mitigate their loss – for example, if there is a period of ongoing loss during which the claimant has failed to look for work. In *Kyndal Spirits v Burns (unreported, EAT 27 June 2002)*, the EAT pointed out that the onus is on the party alleging that another has failed to mitigate their loss to prove it.

310

The tribunal will also deduct any ex gratia sums received from the ex-employer as compensation for dismissal. It is worth noting that an ex gratia payment, if expressed as such in relevant documentation, cannot be set off against payment in lieu of notice (PILON) (*Publicis Consultants Ltd v O'Farrell (2011) UKEAT/0430/10*).

Any contractual redundancy payments which exceed the basic award will not be deducted at this stage – see Step 6 below and *Digital Equipment Co Ltd v Clements (No.2) [1998] ICR 258 CA*.

No deduction is made in respect of insurance payouts or early pension benefits received as a result of the dismissal (*Hopkins v Norcros plc [1994] ICR 11 CA*).

Further, no deduction is made in respect of universal credit or other income-related benefits, or housing benefit received while the employee was unemployed. This is because it will be recouped by the Department for Work and Pensions (DWP) from the compensatory award after the tribunal hearing (*Employment Protection (Recoupment of Benefits) Regulations 1996*). It seems that incapacity benefit should be deducted from the compensatory award on the basis that the compensatory award should fully compensate the claimant but should not provide a bonus (*Morgans v Alpha Plus Security Ltd [2005] ICR 525 EAT*).

Where an employee has been dismissed, they do not have to account for sums earned during their notice period (*Norton Tool Co Ltd v Tewson [1972] ICR 501*). Deductions should also not be made from any PILON where an employee finds new employment during what would have been a notice period (*Voith Turbo Ltd v Stowe [2005] ICR 543 EAT*). However, the decision in *Voith Turbo* does not fit easily with that in *Morgans v Alpha Plus Security Ltd [2005] ICR 525 EAT*.

The uncertainty has been recognised as unsatisfactory. Dealing with this and related points in *Langley & anor v Burlo [2007] ICR 390*, the Court of Appeal (Mummery LJ) said at paragraphs 87-89:

> 'I do not think that *Dunnachie* [*Dunnachie v Kingston upon Hull City Council [2004] ICR 1052 HL*] is express or implied authority for the proposition that the ET, in calculating compensation under [section 123 of the ERA 1996] for unfair dismissal, must ... require the employee to give credit for wages that were, or could have been, earned by the employee during the notice period ...

> I appreciate that uncertainty about an everyday legal point like this is not satisfactory for tribunals, practitioners, employers or employees. The sooner that the House of Lords can settle the law one way or the other the better, dealing also, if possible, with a related controversy on the duty to mitigate under [section 123(4) of the ERA 1996], another point which has not arisen for decision in this case (see, for example, the decisions of

the EAT in *Hardy v Polk (Leeds) Ltd [2005] ICR 557* and *Morgans v Alpha Plus Security Ltd [2005] ICR 525*; cf *Voith Turbo Ltd v Stowe EAT [2005] ICR 453*).'

There is conflicting authority on whether deductions should be made from any PILON if the employee finds new employment within the period for which they were entitled to PILON. In *Voith Turbo Ltd v Stowe [2005] ICR 453*, the EAT suggested that there should be no deduction for monies earned during the notice period, but in so doing, the tribunal refused to follow a decision – *Hardy v Polk (Leeds) Ltd [2004] IRLR 420 EAT* – that any monies earned are deductible.

Step 3: Adjust for the risk of dismissal in any event

A tribunal can consider whether, even had a fair procedure been followed, the employee may still have been dismissed. It is then entitled to apply a percentage reduction to the award to reflect the chance that dismissal would have occurred in any event. This is the aspect of section 123 ERA 1996 also often referred to as a '*Polkey* reduction' (*Polkey v AE Dayton Services [1988] ICR 142*).

A tribunal can, and will, adjust by a percentage (sometimes even 100%) to reflect the chance that dismissal would have been the outcome in any event. So if the loss of earnings is, say, £20,000, and the tribunal thinks there was a 50% chance the claimant would have been dismissed in any event, it will award £10,000.

Step 4: Adjust for non-compliance with the Acas Code

A failure to comply with the Acas Code may result in the tribunal adjusting the award by up to 25%. Likewise, if the employee has failed to comply with the Acas Code, the award will be reduced by up to 25% (section 207A of the TULR(C)A 1992). Any adjustment under this provision must be made before reductions for contributory fault or redundancy are made (section 124A of the ERA 1996).

Step 5: Reduce for contributory fault

If the dismissal was 'caused or contributed to by any action of the complainant', then the tribunal must 'reduce the amount of the compensatory award by such proportion as it considers just and equitable having regard to that finding' (section 123(6) of the ERA 1996). When assessing the compensatory award, the tribunal, having found that there was conduct considered blameworthy on the part of the unfairly dismissed employee, is bound by the wording of section 123 of the ERA 1996 to consider contributory fault even if the employer has not raised the point (*Swallow Security v Millicent (2009) UKEAT/0297/08*).

312

The tribunal can reduce the award by such percentage as it considers appropriate to reflect the employee's fault, even, on occasion, by 100% (*Perkin v St Georges Healthcare NHS [2006] ICR 617*). However, a 100% reduction does not sit well with the concept of *contributory* fault and will only be made in exceptional cases. It is rare for the EAT to change the percentage reduction applied by a tribunal for contributory fault.

Misconduct by an employee which is not serious enough to justify dismissal may still amount to 'contributory fault' warranting a reduction in unfair dismissal compensation (*Trafford Housing v (1) Hughes (2) Burke (2007) UKEAT/0310/07*). However, there must be an element of moral culpability or 'blameworthiness' (*Gibson v British Transport Docks Board [1982] IRLR 228 EAT* and *Langstone v Dept of BERR (2010) UKEAT/0534/09*). For example, it would not be correct to reduce the compensatory award when an employee was unfairly dismissed for refusing to obey the employer's instructions to falsify records (*Morrish v Henlys (Folkestone) Ltd [1973] IRLR 61 NIRC*), but drunkenness at work, even if the employee is an alcoholic, can amount to relevant contributory conduct (*Sinclair v Wandsworth Council (2007) UKEAT/0145/07*).

The tribunal may take into account the conduct of an employee during a disciplinary process to support a finding of contributory fault, but a mere issue with an employee's disposition or unhelpfulness in dealing with the process is not in itself sufficient to amount to contributory fault (*Bell v The Governing Body of Grampian Primary School (2007) UKEAT/0142/07*).

Although engaging in lawful industrial action cannot be treated as contributory fault (section 123(5) of the ERA 1996), if the employee's conduct has gone beyond ordinary industrial action, this may bring the contributory fault reduction into play (*Tracey v Crosville Wales Ltd [1997] ICR 862 HL*).

In deciding whether a dismissal is unfair, a tribunal cannot have regard to matters of which the employer was unaware at the time of the dismissal. However, the position is different when it comes to assessing compensation. Here, a tribunal can take into account evidence of misconduct which occurred before the dismissal, but which only came to light afterwards, and reduce the compensation which would otherwise have been awarded, even to zero (*W Devis & Sons v Atkins [1977] IRLR 314 HL*). Pre-dismissal conduct which is discovered after the dismissal must be distinguished from post-dismissal conduct: post-dismissal conduct is not relevant when considering any reduction in the compensation awarded (*Soros & Soros v Davison & Davison [1994] ICR 590 EAT* and *Nixon v Ross Coates Solicitors (2010) UKEAT/0108/10*).

Step 6: Deduct contractual redundancy pay

Under Step 2 (deductions), contractual redundancy payments are specifically excepted from the rule that monies received from the employer should be deducted, to the extent that they exceed the statutory basic award. The excess is deducted after any reductions for *Polkey* reasons and contributory fault. Thus, if an employee is entitled to a basic award of £1,000, but received a contractual redundancy payment of £2,500, the first £1,000 is offset against the basic award (so that the employee receives no basic award). The excess of £1,500 is deducted from the compensatory award after the *Polkey* reduction and contributory fault reduction are applied. The reason for this is that under statute, the employer is entitled to have any compensation payment reduced by the full amount by which a redundancy payment exceeds the basic award (section 123(7) of the ERA 1996). If an award of four weeks' wages was made at the time an order for reinstatement was made – and the employee was treated as being unfairly dismissed as a result of the employer's subsequent failure to comply with the order – this should also be deducted at this stage (section 123(8) of the ERA 1996).

Step 7: Gross up the award if it exceeds £30,000

Although an employee's losses are calculated on a net basis, the employee is liable to pay tax on any tribunal award over £30,000 (except in respect of some awards for injury to feelings). Accordingly, it is necessary to gross up any award in excess of this sum (section 403 of the *Income Tax (Earnings and Pensions) Act 2003*). Thus, if an employee who falls into the higher rate tax bracket has net losses of £36,000, the tribunal should gross this up to £40,000 (because 40% tax is payable on the excess over £30,000 – that is, on £10,000 of the award, thus resulting in an HMRC charge of £4,000 once the money is in the employee's hands (*Richardson (HM Inspector of Taxes) v Delaney [2001] IRLR 663 HC* and *Shove v Downs Surgical plc [1984] ICR 532 HC*).

Where a claim for unfair dismissal is settled, any payment made in consideration for the settlement agreement is not generally taxable as an emolument. Providing that it is less than £30,000, it will not be subject to tax under the sweeping-up provision of section 401 of the *Income Tax (Earnings and Pensions) Act 2003* (*Wilson (Inspector of Taxes) v Clayton [2005] IRLR 108*).

(This step was not considered in *Digital Equipment Co Ltd v Clements (No.2) [1998] ICR 258 CA* – which sets out the order of deductions – because, at the time of that case, the maximum compensatory award was set at a level significantly below £30,000 and the issue did not arise.)

Step 8: Apply the statutory 'cap'

The last stage is to apply the statutory maximum for the compensatory award. This is capped at either an index-linked figure (£105,707 in respect of dismissals on or after 6 April 2023 – this figure changes each year on 6 April) or '52 multiplied by a week's [gross] pay of the person concerned', whichever is the lower (section 124(1ZA) of the ERA 1996). A week's pay for this purpose is calculated in accordance with sections 221-229 of the ERA

1996 (without applying the limit set out in section 227 of the ERA 1996). In other words, it is a week's gross pay.

Note, however, that if the dismissal was for health and safety reasons or because the employee was a whistleblower making a protected disclosure, then no statutory maximum is applied (section 124(1A) of the ERA 1996).

16.1.6 INTERIM RELIEF

Interim relief is an exceptional remedy in employment law cases. If an employee considers that they have been unfairly dismissed on certain specified grounds, they can make an application to a tribunal (section 128 of the ERA 1996). In *Steer v Stormsure Ltd [2021] IRLR 762*, the Court of Appeal confirmed that interim relief is not available in discrimination/victimisation cases, and there is no obligation to read in such a right to the relevant provisions. Lord Justice Bean explained that the availability of this particular remedy in whistleblowing, which (as far as was known to the court) was brought by women and men in roughly equal numbers, did not mean that the unavailability of the same remedy in a sex discrimination claim constituted a difference of treatment on the grounds of sex or some form of indirect discrimination against women.

An interim relief order has the effect of ensuring that the dismissed employee continues to be paid their wages or salary pending a full tribunal hearing. The original underlying purpose was to enable an employment tribunal to give a preliminary ruling at an emergency hearing to head off industrial trouble before it began or became too serious. This means that, first, the relief is generally available only in cases where collective industrial action is likely and, second, the employee must move quickly: there is a seven-day window from the date of dismissal for making an interim relief application (section 128(2) of the ERA 1996).

The specified grounds on which an application for interim relief can be made are set out in section 128(1)(b) of the ERA 1996, section 12 of the *Employment Relations Act 1999* and section 152 of the TULR(C)A 1992. They are:

- Whistleblowing – dismissal for whistleblowing

- Disciplinary and grievance hearings – dismissal for seeking to exercise the right to be accompanied at (or to accompany someone else to) a disciplinary or grievance hearing

- Workers' representatives:

  o Dismissal of a member of a safety committee for a reason connected with that role

  o Dismissal of a workers' representative in connection with the WTR 1998

- o Dismissal of an employee-trustee of an occupational pension scheme for a reason connected with that role
- o Dismissal of an employee representative for a reason connected with that role

- Trade union-related reasons – dismissal for reasons related to trade union membership or non-membership or trade union activity
- Dismissal resulting from obstruction or promotion of official recognition of a trade union

It follows that, generally, interim relief cannot be granted following a redundancy dismissal. If, however, an employer asserts that the principal reason for the dismissal was redundancy, the employee can succeed in a claim for interim relief by establishing that the principal reason was instead one of the grounds set out in section 128 of the ERA 1996 – their trade union activity, for example (*Bombardier Aerospace-Shorts Brothers plc v McConnell [2008] IRLR 51 NICA* and *McConnell v Bombardier Aerospace Short Bros plc [2009] IRLR 201 NICA*). This must be distinguished from the situation where an employee is selected for redundancy because of their trade union activity (when the principal reason would be redundancy).

An application for interim relief is summary in character, so it can properly proceed without full evidence from both sides. A prerequisite for ordering interim relief is that the tribunal must think it 'likely' that at a full hearing, it will find that the reason for dismissal is one of the specified grounds listed above (*Dandpat v University of Bath (2009) UKEAT/0408/09*).

16.1.7 COMPENSATION: OTHER AWARDS

An employment tribunal can make a number of other awards in an unfair dismissal claim. The names are confusing and are often mixed up. Here, they are summarised only – refer to the statutory provisions for more detail.

Additional award

This is an award of between 26 and 52 weeks' pay made to the employee when the employer fails to comply with an order for reinstatement or re-engagement (section 117(3)(b) of the ERA 1996). This is addressed in more detail at **16.1.1**.

Protective award

This is an award of up to 90 days' pay to individuals whom an employer has failed to consult properly during redundancy consultations (section 189 of the TULR(C)A 1992). There is a statutory cap on the amount payable if the employer is insolvent and the liability to pay the protective award moves to the Secretary of State (section 186 of the ERA 1996).

This award is designed to provide a sanction for a breach of the provisions, not damages. In other words, the award is punitive, not compensatory. Because the protective award is punitive, a deduction must not be made by reason of the fact that the employees concerned continued to work and to receive salary during the protected period (*Cranswick Country Foods plc v Beall & ors [2007] ICR 691 EAT*, in which the EAT ruled that section 190(4) of the TULR(C)A 1992 should not be construed to mean the contrary).

The Court of Appeal has suggested that where there has been a complete failure to consult, the tribunal should start with the maximum period and reduce it only if there are mitigating factors. That the consultation would have made no difference anyway will not in itself lead to any reduction in the award (*Susie Radin Ltd v GMB [2004] ICR 893*).

An application for the protective award must be made by appropriate representatives. These will be representatives of the union if a trade union is recognised (sections 189(1) and 189(1B)(a) of the TULR(C)A 1992). Only employees in respect of whom the union concerned was recognised can then benefit. Other employees have to make a separate claim (*TGWU v Brauer Coley Ltd (in administration) [2007] ICR 226 EAT*).

Award for failure to consult during a TUPE transfer

Under regulations 13-16 of the *Transfer of Undertakings (Protection of Employment) Regulations 2006* (TUPE 2006), employers with ten or more employees are obliged to inform and consult about the implications of a TUPE transfer with any recognised trade union or, if no union is recognised, with specially appointed employee representatives. Where no employee representatives have been appointed, the onus is on the employer to initiate the elections of representatives. Where none have been appointed, the obligation is to consult with the employees (*Howard v Millrise Ltd [2005] ICR 435 EAT*).

Employers with fewer than 10 employees are permitted to inform and consult directly with employees where there are no pre-existing employee representatives, and the employees have not been invited to elect such representatives (regulation 13A of TUPE 2006).

Failure to comply will result in an award of up to 13 weeks' pay for each affected employee (regulation 16(3) of TUPE 2006). A week's pay for this purpose is not subject to the statutory cap set out in section 227 of the ERA 1996 (*Zaman v Kozee Sleep Products [2011] IRLR 196 EAT*). Because compensation for failure to consult is punitive and meant to be a deterrent rather than compensation for loss, the award should be the maximum 13 weeks' pay unless there are mitigating factors (*Sweetin v Coral Racing [2006] IRLR 252 EAT*).

16.2 DISCRIMINATION AND WHISTLEBLOWING DETRIMENT

In discrimination and whistleblowing detriment claims, there are four broad categories of compensation:

1) Compensation for financial losses

2) 'Injury to feelings' awards

3) Personal injury awards

4) Interest

With the exception of a tribunal's ability to make a 25% reduction to reflect that disclosures have not been made in 'good faith', the approach to these claims is identical in whistleblowing detriment claims – see section 49(6A) of the ERA 1996.

Awards for financial losses in discrimination/whistleblowing detriment claims are unlimited – there is no statutory cap. The concepts of 'basic' and 'compensatory' award do not exist in discrimination cases, and a tribunal will adopt principles of compensation from the law of tort.

In addition to ordering compensation, in discrimination claims tribunals have jurisdiction to make a declaration as to the parties' rights and to make recommendations as to actions to be taken within a specific period (sections 124(2)(a) and 124(2)(c) of the *Equality Act 2010* (EqA 2010)).

16.2.1 COMPENSATION

The tribunal has the power to order the payment of compensation, with the damages being assessed as if the act of discrimination were a tort (section 119 and section 124(2)(b) of the EqA 2010). For whistleblowing claims, the equivalent provision is found under section 49 of the ERA 1996.

Both kinds of awards can be made jointly and severally against both the employer and any person who has actually committed the acts of discrimination/detriment. The tribunal should not, however, apportion blame between the respondents, as when a claimant has suffered discrimination from multiple respondents, the damage is likely to be indivisible (*Sivanandan v Hackney LBC [2013] ICR 672*).

The award normally comprises two elements: injury to feelings and loss of earnings. In addition, tribunals have jurisdiction to award damages for personal injury. Further, interest falls to be awarded on compensation awards for discrimination.

Injury to feelings

The statutory provisions governing compensation expressly state that 'an award of damages may include compensation for injured feelings (whether or not it includes compensation on any other basis)' (section 119(4) of the EqA 2010).

It is difficult to estimate the value of awards for injury to feelings. However, the Court of Appeal set out clear guidelines in *Vento v Chief Constable of West Yorkshire (No.2) [2003] ICR 318*, which provides three rough award 'bands'. The *Vento* bands can be increased by the tribunal to account for inflation (*AA Solicitors Ltd (t/a Aa Solicitors) v Majid (2016) UKEAT/0217/15*). In *De Souza v Vinci Construction UK Ltd [2015] ICR 1034*, it was determined that the 10% *Simmons v Castle [2013] 1 WLR 1239* uplift should be applied to the amounts of the *Vento* bands after they have been adjusted for Retail Price Index inflation; specifically, the adjustment for inflation is applied to reflect inflation to the date on which the ET1 Form was issued. Applying the *Simmons v Castle* uplift of 10% to the *Vento* scale adjusted for inflation, the bands as of 6 April 2023 were as follows:

- a lower band of £1,100 to £11,200 (less serious cases);

- a middle band of £11,200 to £33,700 (cases that do not merit an award in the upper band); and,

- an upper band of £33,700 to £56,200 (the most serious cases), with the most exceptional cases capable of exceeding £56,200.

As the guidelines suggest, one-off incidents of verbal abuse are likely to fall within the lower Vento band (*Kemeh v Ministry of Defence [2014] ICR 625*) and an award for injury to feelings will only exceed the upper limit in the most exceptional cases.

It is legitimate to treat some degree of stress and depression as part of the injury to be compensated under the 'injury to feelings' head of loss, though each case turns on its own facts. If an employer's actions have caused a claimant to develop stress and depression to a very severe extent for the first time, then a separate award for personal injury is possible. If a separate award is made for psychiatric injury (see below), then tribunals must ensure that they do not award compensation for the same loss twice (*HM Prison Service v Salmon [2001] IRLR 425 EAT*). Injury to feelings is different in kind from anxiety. Anxiety may be an element within injury to feelings but is not compensable on its own (*Johnston v NEI International Combustion Ltd* and *Rothwell v Chemical & Insulating Co Ltd [2007] UKHL 39*).

Loss of earnings

The bulk of a tribunal's award is usually for loss of earnings. This is assessed in the ordinary way (see **16.1**) and claimants have a duty to mitigate their losses. In discrimination cases, tribunals tend to be more sympathetic to employees' claims that they will have difficulty obtaining further employment – particularly if they have developed psychological problems as a result of bullying, harassment or employment-related stress. In some cases, tribunals will award a loss of earnings for many years into the future.

An employer cannot rely on a subsequent dismissal that was unfair as a break in the chain of causation between the discrimination and a future loss of earnings (*HM Prison Service v Beart (No.2) [2005] ICR 1206*). Where there is an award for loss of earnings, the same deductions as would be made for an award of personal injuries must be made. Whether insurance payments to which the employer is entitled should be deducted can be problematic and is beyond the scope of this book. However, some of the difficulties surrounding deductions can be avoided if the tribunal instead recommends that the employee is retained under their contract of employment until retirement age and paid their contractual salary. Such an order can, for example, require the employee to attend medical examinations required by an insurance company. The tribunal can only make this recommendation if the employee requests it (see, generally, *Atos Origin IT Services UK Ltd v Haddock [2005] ICR 277 EAT*).

Personal injury

Since compensation is assessed on a tortious basis, tribunals have jurisdiction to award damages for personal injuries as well as injury to feelings. Most claims for damages for personal injury on dismissal are for psychiatric injuries, such as depression or stress. An employee should support any claim for personal injuries with medical evidence. Note that if an employee brings a claim for discrimination in the employment tribunal, the right to bring a claim for personal injuries in the civil courts (in so far as they arise from the same facts) will be lost because of the doctrines of *estoppel*, *res judicata* and abuse of process (*Sheriff v Klyne Tugs (Lowestoft) Ltd [1999] IRLR 481 CA*).

An employer is liable to pay compensation for psychiatric injury if the unlawful discrimination has caused the injury suffered by an employee. It is not necessary for the psychiatric injury to have been reasonably foreseeable (*Essa v Laing Ltd [2003] IRLR 346 EAT*). However, there are some limits to this rule and broadly, injury must have been reasonably foreseeable, even if the particular type of harm was not. In *Simmons v British Steel plc [2004] UKHL 20*, Lord Rodger of Earlsferry set out a test for determining questions of remoteness which limits when a psychiatric injury can be said to have been 'caused' by the unlawful act:

1) The respondent is not liable for a consequence of a kind which is not reasonably foreseeable.

2) While a respondent is not liable for damage that was not reasonably foreseeable, it does not follow that the respondent is liable for all damage that was reasonably foreseeable: depending on the circumstances, the respondent may not be liable for damage caused by a *novus actus interveniens* or unreasonable conduct on the part of the claimant, even if it was reasonably foreseeable.

3) Subject to the qualification in (2), if the claimant's injury is of a kind that was foreseeable, the respondent is liable, even if the damage is greater in extent than was foreseeable or it was caused in a way that could not have been foreseen.

4) The respondent must take the victim as they find them.

5) Subject again to the qualification in (2), where personal injury to the claimant was reasonably foreseeable, the respondent is liable for any personal injury, whether physical or psychiatric, which the claimant suffers as a result of the respondent's wrongdoing.

Tribunals can also award aggravated damages as an ancillary award to the injury to feelings. This is a smaller sum, rarely exceeding £5,000, to be awarded if the employer's conduct has been exceptionally high-handed, malicious or oppressive, such that an ordinary injury to feelings award will not suffice. While the authorities suggest that it should not be regarded as a punitive award so as to express the tribunal's disapproval of the employer's conduct, in practice, this is precisely what it tends to be used for (*Alexander v Home Office [1988] IRLR 396 CA*, *HM Prison Service v Salmon [2001] IRLR 425 EAT*, *Zaiwalla & Co v Walia [2002] IRLR 697 EAT* and *Leeds Rhinos Rugby Club v Sterling (2002) EAT/267/01*).

Ancillary losses

Ancillary losses, such as loss of pension rights or expenses in seeking new employment, can also be recovered.

Interest

Tribunals have the power to order interest at 8% on compensation awards for discrimination/whistleblowing detriment – unlike for unfair dismissal. This accrues daily on a simple basis, from the date of first discrimination/whistleblowing detriment (for the award for injury to feelings) or from the mid-point between the act of discrimination and the hearing (for all other heads of loss). In discrimination claims, 8% is essentially a starting point to be disapplied only if 'serious injustice' would occur, then the tribunal may calculate interest differently (*Employment Tribunals (Interest on Awards in Discrimination Cases) Regulations 1996*), applying the 8% rate from section 17 of the *Judgments Act 1838* in England and Wales. By contrast, 8% interest in whistleblowing claims is possible, but not a starting point since the quoted regulations do not apply to whistleblowing claims.

16.2.2 DECLARATIONS AND RECOMMENDATIONS

In addition to ordering compensation, tribunals have the power to:

321

- Make an order declaring the rights of the complainant and respondent in relation to the act to which the complaint relates.

- Make a recommendation that the respondent takes, within a specified period, specified steps for the purpose of obviating or reducing the adverse effect on the complainant of any act of discrimination to which the complaint relates (sections 124(2)(c) and 124(3) of the EqA 2010).

These remedies are not frequently pursued, often because the employee has left the respondent's employ by the time the claim is heard. If the tribunal makes a recommendation that the employer take action, and it fails to comply, the tribunal has the power to increase the level of compensation (or to order it if not previously ordered) (section 124(7) of the EqA 2010).

CHAPTER 17

TIME LIMITS, PROCEDURE AND SETTLEMENT

17.0 OVERVIEW

This chapter deals with procedures in employment tribunals but not the Employment Appeal Tribunal (EAT) or subsequent appeals. (Note that it is possible to 'leapfrog appeal' directly from the EAT to the Supreme Court in certain limited circumstances (section 65 of the *Criminal Justice and Courts Act 2015*)). The employment tribunal is governed by the *Employment Tribunals (Constitution and Rules of Procedure) Regulations 2013*. These rules were intended to streamline and simplify the previous rules, but they have not come close to creating a non-legalistic and informal process.

Previous editions of this Handbook dealt with tribunal fees for issuing claims and holding hearings. The fees regime introduced by the *Employment Tribunals and the Employment Appeal Tribunal Fees Order 2013* was ruled unlawful by the Supreme Court in *R (Unison) v Lord Chancellor [2017] ICR 1037*. As a result, no fees are payable for issuing or pursuing claims, and claimants who paid fees (and respondents who had been ordered to reimburse claimants' fees) have been refunded. However, it should be noted that the Supreme Court only found that the particular fee structure was unlawfully high; it did not hold that fees per se were necessarily unlawful.

17.1 TIME LIMITS

The majority of employment claims must be presented at the tribunal within three months of dismissal, or of the act (say, of discrimination) about which the employee is complaining (section 123 of the *Equality Act 2010* (EqA 2010)). Some claims have a slightly longer limitation period – for example, six months in which to bring a claim for a statutory redundancy payment (section 164 of the *Employment Rights Act 1996* (ERA 1996)) or an equal pay claim under section 129 of the EqA 2010. There is discretion to extend time for some claims. Claims in the civil courts (for tort and breach of contract) attract the normal six-year limitation period set out in the *Limitation Act 1980.*

Nearly all tribunal claims must be accompanied by a certificate from Acas, confirming that early conciliation has been undertaken. For such claims, the period of early conciliation – provided that it begins before the end of the primary limitation period – has the effect of 'stopping the clock'. This allows the time limit to be extended by the equivalent period, and the claimant always has a minimum of one month from the end of conciliation (see **17.2.1**).

Time limits go to the tribunal's jurisdiction to hear a claim and they cannot be waived just because a respondent fails to notice or decides not to rely on the fact that they are out of time. The tribunal should refuse to hear a claim at any stage of proceedings if it becomes aware of a time limit point unless it can exercise discretion to extend the time limit (*Radakovits v Abbey National plc [2010] IRLR 307 CA*).

Discretion for the tribunal to extend a time limit takes two forms, which apply to different types of claims:

- It was not reasonably practicable for the claim to be presented in time, and the claim was presented within a further reasonable period

- It is just and equitable to extend the time limit

Generally speaking, the 'not reasonably practicable' test is stricter and harder for a claimant to meet. The 'just and equitable' test considers all the circumstances, and it might allow a claim to proceed even if the claimant should have brought it sooner, provided that the 'balance of prejudice' favours the claimant. This can have the result that, where a claim is brought out of time for a dismissal which is alleged to be both unfair and discriminatory, the unfair dismissal claim may be struck out while the discrimination claim is allowed to proceed (as happened in *Trusthouse Forte (UK) Ltd v Halstead (1986) EAT/213/86*).

17.1.1 'NOT REASONABLY PRACTICABLE' EXTENSIONS OF TIME

This discretion applies most significantly to unfair dismissal claims from which nearly all the relevant case law arises. However, the same test and related case law applies more broadly to claims under the ERA 1996, including unlawful detriments (for example, for whistleblowing), deductions from wages and rights to time off work. It also governs claims for breaches of the *Working Time Regulations 1998* and contractual claims brought in the tribunal under the *Employment Tribunals Extension of Jurisdiction (England and Wales) Order 1994.*

Calculating time limits for unfair dismissal claims

An unfair dismissal claim must normally be presented to an employment tribunal before the end of three months, beginning with the effective date of termination (EDT). The EDT is included in calculating the three months (*Joshi v Manchester City Council (2008) UKEAT/0235/07*). Accordingly, if the EDT is 12 February, the claim must be presented by 11 May (section 111 of the ERA 1996).

The claim can be presented once notice of dismissal has been given, even before the EDT has occurred. This encourages claims to be brought as early as possible (section 111(3) of the ERA 1996).

Where it is unclear whether the employee has the legal right to bring a claim, it is prudent to lodge the claim form and apply for a stay. If the employee waits more than three months, they are unlikely to obtain an extension of time (*Biggs v Somerset County Council [1996] ICR 364 CA*).

Calculating time limits for other claims

The time limit for detriment claims under the ERA 1996 runs from the last of any series of similar acts or failures to act (section 48(3) of the ERA 1996). This can cover detriments perpetrated by different people, but there must be a connection and reasonable degree of similarity between the acts complained of (*Arthur v London Eastern Railway Ltd [2007] ICR 193 CA*).

For deduction from wages claims, the test is 'a series of deductions' (section 23(3) of the ERA 1996), but this is subject to a two-year backstop under the *Deduction from Wages (Limitation) Regulations 2014* (see further at **4.5.5**).

General points under the 'not reasonably practicable' extension

A late claimant has to persuade the tribunal that (a) it was not reasonably practicable for them to have presented their claim in time, and (b) it was eventually presented within a period which was reasonable. The burden of proof is on the claimant.

'Reasonably practicable' means somewhere between 'possible' and 'reasonable' (*Palmer v Southend-on-Sea Borough Council [1984] ICR 372 CA*). 'Practicable' means 'feasible'. It is primarily a question of fact, which means that there is normally no way to appeal the employment tribunal's decision regarding an extension of time unless the tribunal's decision is so unreasonable that it is 'perverse'. For example, in *Agrico UK Ltd v Amanda Ireland (2005) UKEAT/0024/05*, the EAT held that it had been perverse for a tribunal to allow a claim to be filed out of time where a solicitor had not filed before going on holiday. He instructed his secretary to file the claim instead, but she went off sick and failed to do so.

Ignorance of rights/time limit

A claimant who pleads that they were initially unaware of their right to make a tribunal claim will be expected to explain the opportunities they had to find out, whether they took those opportunities and how they eventually found out. The tribunal will assess whether the ignorance was reasonable (*Porter v Banbridge [1978] ICR 943 CA*). Judges will now often ask why a dismissed employee did not simply search 'what are my rights?' on Google.

Ignorance of the three-month limit is rarely an excuse because once a potential claimant is aware of their right to make a claim, they are expected to find out what the time limits are for doing so (*Trevelyans (Birmingham) Ltd v Norton [1991] ICR 488 EAT*). However, a combination of the claimant's special circumstances and lack of clarity from the employer about the precise date of termination may be a sufficient excuse (*John Lewis Partnership v Charman (2011) UKEAT/0079/11* and *Lowri Beck Services v Brophy [2019] EWCA Civ 2490 CA*). Misleading information from the employer might also excuse a late claim (*Andrews v Kings College Hospital NHS Foundation Trust (2012) UKEAT/0614/11*).

Ignorance of a fact that is 'fundamental' to the claim – meaning the claimant genuinely and reasonably changed their belief about whether they had a viable claim once they became aware of it – will usually excuse late presentation, provided that the initial ignorance was itself reasonable (*Cambridge and Peterborough NHS Foundation Trust v Crouchman [2009] ICR 1306 EAT*).

Reliance on incorrect advice

An 'innocent' employee will not be allowed an extension of time because they relied on advisers who advised incorrectly about time limits (*London International College Ltd v Sen [1993] IRLR 333 CA*). The 'Dedman principle' – from *Dedman v British Building and Engineering Appliances Ltd [1974] ICR 53 CA* – states that a claimant cannot rely on the fault of professional advisers in not giving the claimant such information as they should reasonably, as professionals, have given. The usual answer to such a claimant is that they should sue their advisers for negligence.

In general, it will make no difference whether the advice came from a solicitor or someone else – an employment law consultant, for example, or Citizens Advice advisor or trade union representative – who would reasonably be expected to know the applicable time limit (*Ashcroft v Haberdashers Aske's Boys School [2008] IRLR 375 EAT* and *London Borough of Islington v Brown (2008) UKEAT/0155/08*). In *Alliance & Leicester plc v Kidd (2007) UKEAT/0078/0*, a trade union representative wrongly advised Ms Kidd that time for lodging an unfair dismissal claim ran from when her internal appeal to her employer had been rejected, whereas the correct position is that time runs from the EDT. The EAT overturned the tribunal's decision to allow the claim to proceed.

However, erroneous advice from tribunal staff or Job Centre staff might be an acceptable excuse entitling a claimant to an extension of time (*Marks & Spencer v Williams-Ryan [2005] ICR 1293 CA*).

Claimant's personal circumstances

A claimant's illness or disability (physical or mental) can render it not reasonably practicable to make a claim in time. However, the tribunal will usually expect to see supporting medical evidence and an explanation of the particular difficulties that prevented the claimant from acting sooner. Simply being 'stressed', rather than having clinical anxiety or depression, is unlikely to suffice (*Asda Stores Ltd v Kauser (2007) UKEAT/0165/07*). However, even in the circumstances where an individual has a disability which may affect their ability to file a claim, the tribunal may consider what else the claimant did in the relevant period, including formal steps, such as participating in internal appeals and early conciliation, and other matters in their personal life (*Cygnet Behaviour Health Ltd v Britton [2022] EAT 108*).

Internal appeals

The effective date of termination runs from the date of dismissal and not from the outcome of any appeal process unless the contract specifically provides for the employee to remain employed pending the appeal. This can catch out a claimant who is waiting for a protracted appeal process to conclude before making a claim. As above, claimants are usually expected to know, or find out about, the time limit for making a claim, including that it runs from the date of dismissal.

Problems with presenting the claim

Solicitors have a duty to check that the claim form has arrived if they have not received an acknowledgement from the tribunal (*Capital Foods Retail v Corrigan [1993] IRLR 430 EAT*). If a letter is sent by first-class post, it is safe to assume it will arrive on the second day after it was posted, excluding Sundays and bank holidays. If it arrives later due to postal delays, an extension of time will normally be granted (*Consignia plc v Sealy [2002] ICR 1193 CA*, in which, ironically, the claimant was a postman and the employer opposing his application for extension of time was the organisation responsible for the postal delay).

The same guidelines apply, in principle, to the electronic submission of claims. In *Initial Electronic Security Systems Ltd v Avdic [2005] ICR 1598*, the EAT held that a claimant who had emailed her claim form to the tribunal eight hours before the expiry of the time limit was entitled to assume that it would arrive within an hour, in the absence of any indication that it had not been sent or delivered. However, claimants and their representatives are still well advised to seek confirmation that a last-minute claim has been received or consider delivering it by hand to the tribunal office.

'Such further period as is reasonable'

If an extension of time is granted, it will only be for such further period as the tribunal considers reasonable beyond the initial three-month period (section 111 of the ERA 1996). The mere fact that it was not reasonably practicable to present the claim within three months does not give applicants the right to an indefinite period in which to do so. There is no absolute limit to the length of time which will be considered reasonable, although tribunals will expect employees to act swiftly once it becomes practicable to lodge a claim (*Marley (UK) Ltd v Anderson [1996] ICR 728 CA*).

Additionally, there is an automatic extension to six months if the employee is taking part in official industrial action – or was locked out by the employer – and other employees dismissed at the same time have been offered re-engagement but the employee in question has not (section 239(2) of the TULR(C)A 1992).

17.1.2 'JUST AND EQUITABLE' EXTENSIONS OF TIME

This discretion applies to claims under the EqA 2010 (for example, discrimination, victimisation and harassment); the various regulations protecting fixed-term employees, part-time workers and agency workers; and redundancy pay claims under section 164 of the ERA 1996.

Calculating time limits for claims under the EqA 2010

The basic rule is that time starts to run when the act complained of was done. However, there are three additional points to bear in mind:

1) Where an unlawful act is attributable to a term in a contract, it is to be treated as extending throughout the duration of the contract.

2) Any conduct extending over a period shall be treated as done at the end of that period.

3) A deliberate omission is treated as done when the person in question decided upon it (section 123 of the EqA 2010, *Barclays Bank v Kapur [1991] ICR 208 HL* and *Cast v Croydon College [1998] ICR 500 CA*).

In *Hendricks v Metropolitan Police Commissioner [2003] ICR 530*, the Court of Appeal considered the meaning of the phrase 'any act extending over a period' (the wording of the *Sex Discrimination Act 1975*). It held that ongoing acts of harassment which evidenced a general culture of discrimination will amount to an 'ongoing state of affairs'. Accordingly, on the basis that the last act of harassment fell within the three-month period, the claimant could claim in respect of acts of harassment extending back over many years. It has sometimes been argued that there must have been a 'policy, practice or regime' of unlawful behaviour to be able to take advantage of the principle established in *Hendricks* (see, for example, *Robertson v Bexley Community*

Centre [2003] IRLR 434 EAT). However, the EAT has said this is wrong and that provided the employee could show – as the employee did in *Hendricks* – that they have a good arguable *prima facie* case, then a tribunal should accept that it has jurisdiction to consider the matter (*Pugh v National Assembly for Wales (2006) UKEAT/0251/06*).

The EAT applied this principle in *Hale v Brighton and Sussex University Hospitals NHS Trust (2017) UKEAT/0342/16*, holding that an entire disciplinary procedure amounted to conduct extending over a period, rather than a one-off decision (to instigate disciplinary proceedings) with ongoing consequences.

Extension of time

The tribunal's discretion is very wide and there is no definition of the factors that should be considered. This means that there is limited scope to challenge a tribunal's finding on the just and equitable extension on appeal (*Abertawe Bro Morgannwg University Local Health Board v Morgan [2018] ICR 1194 CA*). The 'checklist' in section 33 of the Limitation Act 1980 (which governs extensions of time for personal injury claims) is often referred to, but it is only a guide (*Southwark LBC v Afolabi [2003] ICR 800 CA*). However, tribunals will nearly always need to consider at least:

1) The length of and reasons for the delay

2) Whether the delay has prejudiced the respondent's ability to investigate the claim and/or respond to it effectively

When considering the length of and reasons for the delay, the same points as discussed above for 'not reasonably practicable' extensions of time may be relevant. However, given the wider nature of the discretion, the tribunal is more likely to be sympathetic to a claimant who reasonably relied on incorrect advice from a solicitor or other professional adviser (*Chohan v Derby Law Centre [2004] IRLR 685 EAT* and *Wright v Wolverhampton City Council (2008) UKEAT/0117/08*).

A solicitor's failure to file in time might be relevant in deciding whether an extension of time should be allowed in discrimination cases. In the combined race and disability discrimination case of *Virdi v Commissioner of Police of the Metropolis [2007] IRLR 24*, the EAT overruled an employment tribunal's refusal to allow an extension of time for submission of a claim when the failure to submit on time was the fault of the solicitors concerned. The EAT said that 'if the failings are those of the solicitor and not the claimant that is highly material. But the errors of his solicitors should not be visited on [the claimant's] head'. The EAT ruled that the race discrimination claim which had been submitted just one day out of time should be allowed to proceed and that, in relation to the disability discrimination claim which was three months out of time, the question of whether an extension should be allowed should be remitted back to the tribunal for reconsideration.

The second point is part of the 'balance of prejudice' test: does the prejudice to the claimant (from not being allowed to pursue their claim) outweigh the prejudice to the respondent (caused by the delay)? For this reason, a respondent opposing a late claim is well advised to present evidence showing that the delay has led – for example – to relevant documents being lost, or key witnesses becoming untraceable or unable to recall events. In the absence of any such prejudice, an extension of time may be granted even if there is no good reason for the lateness (*Abertawe Bro Morgannwg University Local Health Board v Morgan [2018] ICR 1194 CA* at paragraphs 17-26).

A tribunal can weigh into the balance the strength of the claimant's claims when considering whether to extend time. In *Kumari v Greater Manchester Mental Health NHS Foundation Trust [2022] EAT 132*, the EAT dismissed the claimant's appeal that the tribunal was wrong to take into account that the claimant's claims appeared to be weak, but cautioned that the tribunal must identify a reasoned basis for doing so, bearing in mind that it does have before it the full evidence that the tribunal would have at a full hearing, and that the tribunal needs to avoid becoming drawn into conducting a mini-trial.

Members of the armed forces have longer (six months) to bring a claim (section 123(3) of the EqA 2010).

17.1.3 EQUAL PAY CLAIMS

Equal pay claims in the employment tribunal must generally be brought within six months of the end of employment (section 129 of the EqA 2010). It is possible for an equal pay claim to be brought in a civil court if it is out of time in the employment tribunal, meaning that a limitation period of six years will apply (*Abdulla & ors v Birmingham City Council [2012] UKSC 47*).

Where employment has been under a series of short fixed-term contracts – typically a teacher employed on a series of contracts reflecting the terms of the school year – the six-month period runs from the end of the last contract forming part of that 'stable employment relationship', not from the end of the individual contracts (*Jeffery & ors v Secretary of State for Education & anor [2006] ICR 1062 EAT* and *Slack & ors v Cumbria County Council & anor [2009] ICR 1217*).

In establishing whether the 'stable employment relationship' has ended, the essential requirement is whether the nature of the work has changed and/ or whether there has been a break in the employment relationship. Changes to contract terms, even fundamental ones, do not in themselves cause the relationship to end (*North Cumbria University Hospitals NHS Trust v Fox & ors [2010] IRLR 804*). Further, a move onto a permanent contract following a succession of fixed-term contracts can ensure that a 'stable employment relationship' continues (see *Martyn v Essex County Council & ors (2009) UKEAT/0138/09*).

Where an employee has an equal pay claim against a transferor under the *Transfer of Undertakings (Protection of Employment) Regulations 2006* (TUPE 2006), the six-month time limit runs from the date of the transfer notwithstanding that enforcement will be against the transferee (*Gutridge & ors v (1) Sodexo, (2) North Tees & Hartlepool NHS Trust [2009] ICR 1486 CA*).

17.1.4 STATUTORY REDUNDANCY CLAIMS

Claims for a statutory redundancy payment must generally be made within six months of the termination of employment, although there is a discretion to extend time for a further six months if it is just and equitable to do so (section 164 of the ERA 1996).

If an employee has made a claim for payment by notice in writing to their employer within the six-month period, the employee retains their right to a redundancy payment even if a claim has not been issued in the employment tribunal (section 164(1)(b) of the ERA 1996). Although Crown and civil servants are not eligible for statutory redundancy pay (section 159 of the ERA 1996), their terms and conditions of service usually give them equivalent or better rights, albeit they are contractual, not statutory.

17.1.5 CONTRACTUAL CLAIMS

A contractual claim (including a claim for contractual redundancy payments) must be brought in the employment tribunal within three months of the effective date of termination of employment.

There is discretion to extend time if it was not reasonably practicable to present the claim within three months (see **17.1.1** (article 7 of the *Employment Tribunals Extension of Jurisdiction (England and Wales) Order 1994*).

However, an employee remains entitled to bring a contract claim in the county court or High Court, where the normal limitation period of six years will apply.

17.1.6 PROCEDURE FOR DEALING WITH TIME LIMIT ISSUES

In unfair dismissal claims, or claims arising from a single act of discrimination or detriment, it will usually be clear that the claim is out of time. The tribunal will normally fix a preliminary hearing to consider whether an extension should be granted under the applicable test.

However, in many cases, there are multiple allegations of discrimination or detriments, some of which are 'in time' and others 'out of time', or the claimant may allege that there was an ongoing state of affairs that amounted to discrimination. The tribunal may be unable to assess whether there was conduct extending over a period or a series of similar acts (such as to bring the earlier allegations in time) without first hearing extensive evidence on the allegations. In such cases, it is common to leave time limit issues to be considered at the final hearing. Doing so may cause the respondent difficulties in adducing evidence to meet old allegations. However, the tribunal is unlikely to 'sever' – effectively, to strike out – the older allegations unless the respondent can show at a preliminary stage that the claimant has no reasonable prospects of establishing that they were part of conduct extending over a period or a series of similar acts (*Arthur v London Eastern Railway Ltd [2007] ICR 193 CA*).

The case management judge has a very broad discretion regarding whether to deal with time limits as a preliminary issue, balancing the likely implications of each course of action for the parties' time and costs and the tribunal's resources (*Santander UK plc v Valverde (2015) UKEAT/0181/15*).

17.1.7 REFORM TO THE LAW ON TIME LIMITS

In its report on Employment Law Hearing Structures (April 2020), the Law Commission recommended reforms to loosen the strict time limits in favour of workers. Its key recommendations were to increase the time limit for all claims to six months and to use the 'just and equitable' test for extending time in all cases.

The Government responded to the report in June 2021. At the time, the Government's primary focus was on addressing the legislative and practical challenges of COVID-19 (discussed below). With regards to increasing the time limit for all claims to six months, the Government stated that it is unclear what impact an extended period would have on litigation behaviours and relied on the tribunal's discretion to allow claims to be submitted out of time on a case-by-case basis. As to the 'just and equitable' extension, the Government's response was that there were some reservations as to whether this affords judges greater discretion and whether there was a lack of justification for greater discretion outside of the discrimination field. The Government noted this recommendation and stated that it will consider this as part of any future work on extending time limits.

17.1.8 TIME FOR APPEALS TO THE EAT

The time within which an appeal must be instituted depends on whether it is against a judgment or against an order or decision of the employment tribunal (see paragraph 4 of the *Practice Direction (Employment Appeal Tribunal - Procedure) 2018*).

An appeal against an order or decision must be instituted within 42 days of the date it was made. The EAT will treat a tribunal's refusal to make an order or decision as itself constituting an order or decision. The date of an order or decision is the date when the order or decision was sent to the parties.

If the appeal is against a judgment, the appeal must be instituted within 42 days from the date on which the written record of the judgment was sent to the parties. However, in three situations, the time for appealing against a judgment will be 42 days from the date when written reasons (as opposed to the written record of judgment) were sent to the parties. This will be the case only if:

1) Written reasons were requested orally at the hearing before the tribunal.

2) Written reasons were requested in writing within 14 days of the date on which the written record of the judgment was sent to the parties.

3) The tribunal itself reserved its reasons and gave them subsequently in writing.

4) A request for written reasons was made out of time and granted.

Time runs from the date the written reasons or written record of the judgment were sent, not from the date they were received (see *Sian v Abbey National plc [2004] ICR 55 EAT*). Papers must be received by the EAT by 4pm on the relevant day for a notice of appeal to be in time. Any document received after 4pm will be deemed to be lodged on the next working day (see paragraph 1.8.2 of the 2018 EAT Practice Direction).

The 42-day time limit is strictly applied. The EAT has discretion to extend time but will exercise this only in rare and exceptional cases (*United Arab Emirates v Abdelghafar [1995] ICR 65 EAT*). This means it will only be appropriate to extend time in rare and exceptional cases, *not* that the case itself must be a rare and exceptional one (*Jurkowska v Hlmad Ltd [2008] ICR 841*).

The written reasons, the claim form and the response form must be sent with the notice of appeal for the appeal to be valid. Thus, if they are not all attached to the notice of appeal as required by the rules, the appeal will not have been properly lodged and no extension of time will ordinarily be granted (*Kanapathiar v London Borough of Harrow [2003] IRLR 571 EAT*). However, in *Jurkowska v Hlmad Ltd [2008] ICR 841*, the employer filed the main papers for appeal in time but omitted to include an essential attachment. The attachment was filed 33 minutes late. The EAT exercised its discretion to allow the employer's appeal to go ahead. It was pointed out that the *Practice Direction (Employment Appeal Tribunal - Procedure) 2018* specifically provide that dealing with a case 'justly' is the 'overriding objective', and the decision was confirmed by the Court of Appeal.

17.2 TRIBUNAL PROCEDURES

Tribunal procedure is governed by procedural rules set out in Schedule 1 of the *Employment Tribunals (Constitution and Rules of Procedure) Regulations*

2013. This section deals with the significant stages of a typical case, but it is not an exhaustive guide to every aspect of the rules.

Rule 7 gives the president of the employment tribunals (in England and Wales and, separately, Scotland) the power to issue non-binding guidance for judges as to how to exercise discretionary powers. The aim of this provision is to help ensure consistency of practice across the tribunal system. Significant guidance has been issued on general case management, postponements of hearings, alternative dispute resolution and remote hearings in light of the COVID-19 Pandemic.

17.2.1 EARLY CONCILIATION

In the vast majority of cases, claimants are not permitted to present their claim until they have alerted Acas to their potential dispute and a conciliation officer has certified that either the early conciliation period has expired without a settlement being reached or settlement is not possible. Generally, Acas has up to one month to attempt to resolve the dispute, and it may extend the period by a further two weeks if there is a reasonable prospect of settlement and the parties agree.

The requirement for early conciliation is set out in Sections 18-19A of the *Employment Tribunals Act 1996* (ETA 1996) and is governed by the *Employment Tribunals (Early Conciliation: Exemptions and Rules of Procedure) Regulations 2014* (EC Regulations) which set out the Early Conciliation Rules of Procedure (EC Rules). A claimant who fails to comply with the early conciliation procedure when they are required to do so may not present a claim (section 18A(8) of the ETA 1996).

When is early conciliation required?

Early conciliation is required before commencing almost all claims in the employment tribunal. However, there are some limited exceptions, including employer contract claims and applications for interim relief in unfair dismissal claims. The list of 'relevant proceedings' in which early conciliation is required is set out in section 18 of the ETA 1996.

Additionally, under regulation 3 of the EC Regulations, a tribunal claim does not have to be preceded by the early conciliation procedure if any of the following apply:

1) The requirement has been complied with by another person instituting relevant proceedings 'relating to the same matter'.

2) Proceedings that are not relevant proceedings are instituted by means of the same form as proceedings that are.

3) Acas has already been contacted by the potential respondent to the proceedings.

What must the potential claimant do?

A prospective claimant must present the 'prescribed information' to Acas in order to initiate early conciliation. The prescribed information is set out in rule 3(1) of the EC Rules:

- The name and address of the prospective claimant
- The name and address of their employer (the prospective respondent)

The Acas EC form also asks a prospective claimant to provide:

- The dates the employment started and (where applicable) ended
- The date of the matter complained of
- Whether the claimant is aware of other claimants making similar claims against the same employer
- Details of how Acas should seek to contact them

Separate EC notifications to Acas in respect of technically different claims are not required, even if some of the claims arise from events that occurred after the conciliation period. The legislation requires a prospective claimant, before starting proceedings 'relating to any matter', to provide information to Acas 'about that matter' (section 18A(1) of the ETA 1996). This requirement is given a flexible interpretation. In *Compass Group UK & Ireland Ltd v Morgan [2017] ICR 73*, for example, an early conciliation certificate was issued in respect of an employee who was still employed. Between the issuing of the conciliation certificate and the presentation of the claim form, the employee resigned, claiming that the resignation arose out of the conduct set out in the conciliation form. The claim form included a claim for constructive dismissal. The EAT held that the original early conciliation certificate covered the constructive dismissal claim.

Rule 4 of the EC Rules requires the prospective claimant to submit separate EC forms in respect of each prospective respondent (where there are several). However, it is permissible for Acas to then issue a single EC certificate with all of the prospective respondents' names and for the claimant to rely on this when submitting their claim to the tribunal (*De Mota v ADR Network [2018] ICR D6 EAT*).

Limitation periods

Entering into early conciliation by submitting the prescribed information to Acas effectively 'stops the clock' for limitation. Section 207B of the ERA 1996 provides two fairly simple but unwieldy rules which achieve this:

- The day the conciliation form is presented to Acas is day A.
- The day the conciliation officer's certificate is received (or, if earlier, deemed received) by the potential claimant is day B.

335

- Rule 1: The period from day A to day B does not count in calculating the relevant limitation period (section 207B(3) of the ERA 1996).

- Rule 2: If the limitation period would have expired during the period beginning with day A and ending one month after day B, then it is extended to expire one month after day B instead (section 207B(4) of the ERA 1996).

However, these provisions do not help a claimant who contacts Acas after the expiry of the primary limitation period (*Pearce v Bank of America (2019) UKEAT/0067/19*). Such a claimant is advised to ask Acas to issue the EC certificate immediately, then present the claim to the tribunal without further delay and seek an extension of time.

Once an EC certificate is issued, there is nothing to stop a prospective claimant from contacting Acas for a second time to assist with conciliation, but a second period of early conciliation will not 'stop the clock' again (*Romero v Nottingham City Council (2018) UKEAT/0303/17*).

Where the conciliation form is submitted after notice of dismissal is given but before the termination date, time spent in conciliation before the termination date does not 'stop the clock' because the clock has not yet started to run. In other words, it will not prospectively extend the three-month time limit that runs after the termination date (*Revenue and Customs Commissioners v Serra Garau [2017] ICR 1121 EAT*).

17.2.2 STARTING A CLAIM

The claim form

A claim is commenced by a claimant presenting a claim form (known as an ET1). See **17.1** for the time limits for presenting an ET1. A claim form may not be presented unless and until the early conciliation requirements have been complied with (see **17.2.1**).

Claim forms must be on the prescribed form and contain the following information (rule 10):

- Each claimant's name

- Each claimant's address

- Each respondent's name

- Each respondent's address

- The early conciliation certificate number provided by Acas as part of the early conciliation process (or an indication that early conciliation is not required because the case falls within one of the exceptions).

The ET1 contains space for the claimant to set out details of their claim, but it is usually sensible to submit a separate attachment containing the 'particulars of claim' or 'grounds of complaint'.

Errors on the claim form

A claim form that is missing any of the prescribed information above will be rejected and returned to the claimant by the tribunal office. Further, under rule 12, it will be referred to a judge and rejected if:

- The claim is one which the tribunal has no jurisdiction to consider;
- It is in a form which cannot sensibly be responded to or is otherwise an abuse of process; or
- It states erroneously that early conciliation is not required.

Under rule 12 a judge will also reject a claim form if the name or address of the prospective claimant/respondent on the early conciliation certificate and the claimant/respondent on the claim form is not the same – unless the judge considers that the claimant made a minor error in relation to a name or address and it would not be in the interests of justice to reject the claim.

If the claim is rejected for any of the above reasons, the tribunal will return it to the claimant with a notice giving the reason and information on how to apply for reconsideration. Rule 13 gives the claimant 14 days to apply for reconsideration on the basis that the decision to reject the claim was wrong or the defect can be rectified. However, if a judge accepts that the defect can be rectified, the claim is treated as having been presented on the date of rectification (which may mean it is out of time and the claimant has to seek an extension of time).

The requirement to have a valid early conciliation certificate and reference number is applied strictly. An inaccurate or incomplete reference number means the claim must be rejected, and the claimant cannot invoke rules 6 or 29 to amend the claim or waive this requirement (*E.ON Control Solutions Ltd v Caspall [2020] ICR 552 EAT*). The same goes for a mistaken indication that the claim is exempt from early conciliation (*Cranwell v Cullen (2015) UKEATPAS/0046/14*).

There is conflicting case law on situations where a judge can excuse a 'minor error' in relation to a name or address on the EC certificate and claim form: compare *Giny v SNA Transport Ltd (2017) UKEAT/0317/16* and *Chard v Trowbridge Office Cleaning Services Ltd [2017] ICR D21 EAT*.

How to submit the claim form

The ET1 can be submitted in hard copy or online. A hard copy can be downloaded, completed and then submitted by post (www.gov.uk/government/publications/make-a-claim-to-an-employment-tribunal-form-et1). Where a claim is submitted by post, it should be sent to the appropriate central office (which differs between England and Wales, and Scotland). In addition, claims can be taken by hand to certain individual employment tribunal offices. Putting the form through the tribunal letterbox will qualify (*Swainston v Hetton Victory Club Ltd [1983] ICR 341 CA* and *Consignia plc v Sealy [2002] ICR 1193*) at any time up to midnight on the last day for presentation (*Post Office v Moore [1981] ICR 621 EAT* and *Initial Electronic Security Systems Ltd v Avdic [2005] IRLR 671 EAT*). Proof of postage is insufficient *(Secretary of State v Banks [1983] ICR 48 EAT*) but it is not necessary that the tribunal opens or processes the originating application within that time period.

Submitting a claim online is generally the quickest and easiest way of presenting it to the tribunal – the official step-by-step guide to submitting a claim can be found online at www.gov.uk/employment-tribunals. Electronic submission of an ET1 does not constitute presentation for the purposes of the employment tribunal rules until it is received by the tribunal. However, as soon as an application has been accepted by the tribunal website, it will be treated as having been validly presented, even if there is a subsequent delay in forwarding it on within the tribunal service (*Tyne and Wear Autistic Society v Smith [2005] ICR 663*). Additionally, a claimant is entitled to assume that claim forms submitted electronically will arrive within an hour or so and will be able to rely on the 'not reasonably practicable' argument to extend time if the claim form is delayed or lost in the ether (*Initial Electronic Security Systems v Avdic [2005] IRLR 671 EAT*).

The time limit is strictly imposed. In one case, a claim 'submitted' on the ET website at 23:59:59 on the last day of the three-month time limit was received at 00:00:08 – nine seconds late. The employment tribunal rejected it as out of time and the EAT upheld that decision (*Miller v Community Links Trust (2007) UKEAT/0486/07*). Similarly, both the Court of Appeal and the EAT upheld a tribunal's decision not to accept an unfair dismissal claim that was presented one minute and 22 seconds late in *Beasley v National Grid [2008] EWCA Civ 742*.

17.2.3 THE RESPONSE FORM

Unless the claim is rejected, it will be sent to each named respondent with a prescribed response form (known as the ET3) and a notice which will include the time limit for submitting the response (rule 15), which by default is 28 days from the date the tribunal sent the copy of the claim form (rule 16).

The response must contain the following minimum information (rule 17):

- The respondent's full name
- The respondent's address
- Whether the respondent wishes to resist any part of the claim

In practice, respondents or their representatives will usually attach a separate document to the ET3, titled 'grounds of resistance' or similar, which sets out the full details of their answer to the claim.

If, and only if, the claimant has included a claim for breach of contract, then the respondent may include a counterclaim (known as an employer's contract claim – see rules 23 to 25).

If the respondent wants extra time to present its response, it must apply to the tribunal in writing for an extension of time (rule 20). If the time limit has already expired, the respondent must also submit a draft of the response that it wishes to present or an explanation of why that is not possible.

A response will be rejected if it does not contain the required minimum information or is presented out of time and without an application for an extension (rules 17 and 18). A similar process of reconsideration is available for a rejected claim form (rule 19).

17.2.4 EFFECT OF NO RESPONSE

Where the date for submitting the response has passed and no response has been presented, or any response received has been rejected and no application for a reconsideration is outstanding, an employment judge will proceed under rule 21 to do one of the following:

1) Issue judgment on the claim, if the available material allows a proper determination to be made

2) Require further information from the parties before making a determination

3) Fix a hearing before an employment judge alone, at which the respondent will only be entitled to participate to the extent permitted by the judge

If judgment is issued against the respondent, it can apply for reconsideration in accordance with rules 70-72. The judgment can then be confirmed, varied or revoked where it is in the 'interests of justice' (rule 70). It is also open to the tribunal to reconsider a judgment of its own volition (rule 73).

17.2.5 INITIAL SIFT

If the respondent has presented a valid response in time, a judge will conduct an initial 'sift' of the case under rules 26-28. If the judge considers any part of the claim/response has no reasonable prospect of success or is one that the tribunal has no jurisdiction to consider, the parties will be sent a notice to that effect. The claimant/respondent will be given a deadline by which to make written representations explaining why the claim/response (or part of it) should not be dismissed. If representations are received in time, a judge will either permit the matter to proceed or fix a hearing to decide the issue.

Otherwise, the judge conducting the initial sift will make an order to either list a preliminary hearing to consider case management or list a final hearing with full case management directions. Although it is not set out in the rules, the tribunals' practice is to allocate cases to one of three 'tracks':

1) Short-track cases are immediately set down for a one- or two-hour final hearing, with little or no case management orders. These include simple money claims (for example, unpaid wages or notice pay).

2) Standard track cases, for unfair dismissal claims, are given a one- or two-day final hearing, with standard case management orders. These typically include service of a schedule of loss, disclosure of documents, preparation of a final hearing bundle and exchange of witness statements.

3) Open track cases cover any other type of claim – for example, discrimination or whistleblowing. A preliminary hearing is listed to consider case management in detail. Some tribunals have a practice of immediately fixing dates for a final hearing based on the sift judge's estimate of how many days the case will need, but the listing may require revision at the preliminary hearing.

If the tribunal has not listed a preliminary hearing, and the time allocated for the final hearing appears insufficient, the parties should immediately contact the tribunal with a revised time estimate and their dates to avoid.

17.2.6 CASE MANAGEMENT

Tribunals have wide powers to manage their own procedure. In doing so, they are governed by the overriding objective to deal with cases justly. This includes – so far as is practicable – ensuring the parties are on an equal footing; dealing with cases in ways which are proportionate to the complexity and importance of the issues; avoiding unnecessary formality; seeking flexibility in the proceedings; avoiding delay, so far as is compatible with proper consideration of the issues; and saving expense (rule 2).

Tribunals can make directions or vary, suspend or set aside earlier directions, either following the application of a party or of their own initiative (rule 29). Rule 30 provides that a party applying for a case management order must notify the other parties that any objections to the application should be sent to the tribunal 'as soon as possible'. Under rule 92, each party must provide all the other parties in the claim with a copy of all its communications to the tribunal (except witness summons applications under rule 32).

Under rule 62 the tribunal must give reasons for any decision on any disputed issue, whether substantive or procedural. However, the reasons should be proportionate to the issue in question and so may be very short.

The reasons can be given in writing or orally unless a party requests that the reasons are given in writing.

17.2.7 PRELIMINARY HEARING

A preliminary hearing may be directed by the tribunal on its own initiative or on application from any party to the proceedings. At a preliminary hearing, the tribunal may do one or more of the following (rule 53):

- Conduct a preliminary consideration of the claim with the parties and make a case management order (including an order relating to the conduct of the final hearing)

- Determine a preliminary issue

- Consider whether a claim or response, or any part, should be struck out

- Make a deposit order

- Explore the possibility of settlement or alternative dispute resolution (including judicial mediation)

Preliminary hearings are generally referred to as 'closed' or 'case management' hearings if they are listed to deal only with case management orders or deposit orders. If a hearing is listed to determine a preliminary issue or consider striking out the claim or response, it is referred to as an 'open' hearing (because rule 56 requires it to be held in public). Preliminary issues can include, for example:

- Whether an out-of-time claim should be allowed to proceed.

- The disputed employment status of a claimant.

- Whether a claimant in a disability discrimination claim was, in fact, disabled. The claimant will usually be required to serve relevant medical records and an 'impact statement' explaining the effects of their condition.

17.2.8 FURTHER INFORMATION AND AMENDMENTS TO THE CLAIM/RESPONSE

It is common for tribunals to order further and better particulars or answers to questions put by the other party if they will help clarify the issues in the proceedings. However, an order will not normally be made unless the asking party has first given the other side an opportunity to provide the information voluntarily and the other side has failed to do so. Anyone who persistently fails to provide satisfactory information runs the risk of having their claim or response struck out.

Tribunals have a broad discretion to allow parties to amend their claim or response at any stage of the proceedings. An application for permission to amend can be made orally at a hearing or in writing, and it can be dealt with by a judge on the papers or at a hearing. The *Selkent* criteria (from *Selkent Bus Co Ltd v Moore [1996] ICR 836 EAT*) provide that the tribunal should assess the relative hardship to the parties that would be caused by refusing or allowing the amendment, and consider in particular:

- The nature of the amendment (correction of a clerical error, addition of factual details to existing allegations, re-labelling the legal claim for facts already alleged, making entirely new factual allegations that change the basis of the existing claim).

- If a new claim is to be added, whether it is out of time and whether the time limit should be extended under the applicable principles.

- The timing and manner of the application and the reasons for any delay. The closer a substantial amendment is made to trial, the more likely it is to prejudice the other party.

17.2.9 STRIKE OUT AND DEPOSIT ORDERS

At any stage of the proceedings, either on its own initiative or on the application of a party, the tribunal may strike out all or part of a claim or response under rule 37 on any of the following grounds:

- That it is scandalous or vexatious or has no reasonable prospect of success

- That the manner in which the proceedings have been conducted has been scandalous, unreasonable or vexatious

- For non-compliance with any of the procedural rules or with an order of the tribunal

- That it has not been actively pursued

- That the tribunal considers it is no longer possible to have a fair hearing in respect of the claim or response (or the part to be struck out).

A claim or response may not be struck out unless the party in question has been given a reasonable opportunity to make representations either in writing or, if requested by the party, at a hearing. A respondent seeking to strike out a claim at a preliminary stage should make its application well in advance of the case management hearing and ask the tribunal to convert the hearing to an open hearing (or to list a further hearing for this purpose).

Although rule 12(1)(b) provides that the tribunal must reject a claim form without a hearing where the claim form is in terms which cannot sensibly be responded to, the EAT has held that the tribunal must still provide the party in question with a hearing if requested to do so (*Trustees of the William Jones Schools Foundation v Parry [2016] ICR 1140*). Where a response is struck out, the effect shall be as if no response had been presented.

Striking out orders for breaches of rules or directions will only be made in exceptional circumstances. In *Marcan Shipping v Kefalas [2007] EWCA Civ 463*, the Court of Appeal specifically said that a judge should:

'... consider carefully whether the sanction being imposed is appropriate to all the circumstances of the case. Of course ... the party in default can always apply for relief, but a conditional order striking out a statement of claim or dismissing the claim or counterclaim is one of the most powerful weapons in the court's case management armoury and should not be deployed unless its consequences can be justified'.

A less draconian step is to issue an 'unless order' under rule 38. This alternative will often be favoured in cases of non-compliance with any of the procedural rules or with an order of the tribunal.

Generally speaking, a claim will not be struck out for having no reasonable prospects of success if there is a disputed point of fact that requires oral evidence from witnesses before it can be resolved. Tribunals are particularly reluctant to strike out discrimination and whistleblowing claims, where the motive of the alleged discriminator has to be established (*Ezsias v North Glamorgan NHS Trust [2007] ICR 1126 CA*).

Deposit orders under rule 39 are an alternative to strike out where a claim or response, or a specific part of it, has little (rather than no) reasonable prospects of success. The deposit can be fixed at up to £1,000, depending on the party's ability to pay. Failure to pay the deposit will mean the relevant allegation is struck out. If the party proceeds to a final hearing and loses on the relevant point, they will forfeit the deposit and be at risk of a costs order against them.

17.2.10 PREPARATION FOR FINAL HEARING

When listing the final hearing, the judge will decide whether it should cover all matters including remedy, or liability only, and make case management orders on this basis. A split final hearing is more likely to be appropriate where there are complex remedy issues, such as long-term loss of earnings or pension loss.

Disclosure

There is no general duty of disclosure in the employment tribunal, but tribunals nearly always make an order for 'standard disclosure' – that is, to disclose any relevant documents, whether they support or undermine the party's own case. In simple cases, the parties may be ordered to provide each other with copies and lists of documents at the same time. Otherwise, a two-stage process (disclosure by list, followed by requests for inspection of copies) will be ordered. Once an order for disclosure has been made, the parties remain under a continuing duty of disclosure in respect of any documents that later come to light.

A party that has unsuccessfully sought disclosure of a particular document may apply to the tribunal for a specific disclosure order under rule 31. The tribunal will assess whether the document is relevant and necessary for fairly disposing of the proceedings, but it will not permit 'fishing expeditions' intended simply to find out whether there is any foundation for a claim (*Canadian Imperial Bank of Commerce v Beck [2009] IRLR 740 CA*). Particular considerations apply to disclosure in discrimination claims (*West Midlands Passenger Transport Executive v Singh [1988] ICR 614 CA*).

Parties can claim to withhold inspection of documents under the same principles that apply in civil courts – for example, confidentiality, public interest immunity and legal professional privilege.

Rule 31 enables the tribunal to order any person in Great Britain to provide disclosure or inspection of a document. This allows for third-party disclosure orders, and, despite the wording, it has been interpreted to cover persons who are physically outside of Great Britain (*Sarnoff v YZ (2020) UKEAT/0252/19*).

Bundles

The parties will nearly always be ordered to agree a joint bundle for the final hearing. Preparation of the bundle will usually be the responsibility of the represented party if the other party is acting in person, or of the respondent if both sides are represented. In all cases, the parties are expected to cooperate and agree the contents. A document should only be included if a party intends to refer to it (in submissions or evidence) at the final hearing. A tribunal can also limit the length of a bundle (*Miron v Adecco UKEATPA/0471/20/AT*). In light of the increased utilisation of remote hearings, bundles are often submitted electronically to the tribunal. The tribunal issues guidance as to the format of electronic bundles and instructions for sending them to the tribunal. It is advised that careful attention is paid to this guidance, particularly as to formatting and page numbering within bundles.

Witness statements

In England and Wales, the standard practice is to simultaneously exchange witness statements after the bundle has been finalised, and for the statements to be taken as read at the final hearing. Tribunals usually issue detailed requirements for the form and content of statements (including references to page numbers in the bundle). The tribunal may permit limited or no supplementary questions at the final hearing, so the statement should cover all relevant matters in appropriate detail. In particular, comment as to remedy and mitigation is frequently omitted from claimants' witness statements and should be addressed.

344

If the other party's witness statements contain new allegations that were not raised in their statement of case, it is usually sensible to serve a supplementary witness statement in response.

In Scotland, full examination-in-chief in place of witness statements continues to be the standard procedure. Parties will often take proofs of evidence from their witnesses to assist with examination-in-chief.

Rule 32 enables the tribunal to order any person in Great Britain to attend a hearing to give evidence or produce documents or information. This allows for witness orders to compel a reluctant witness, or a willing witness whose employer will not release them from work, to attend. Applications for witness orders do not have to be copied to the other party (rule 92). The tribunal will apply a test of relevance and necessity in deciding whether to make an order (*Dada v Metal Box Co Ltd [1974] ICR 559*). Where a witness order is made, the parties should be notified in writing of the same and provided with the name of the person required to attend.

Schedules of loss

Tribunals usually order the claimant to serve a schedule of loss at an early stage if none was served with the claim form. There may be provision for the respondent to serve a counter-schedule and/or for an updated schedule of loss closer to the final hearing. The Presidential Guidance on General Case Management sets out the typical heads of loss that should be included.

Other preparation

In cases of any complexity, the tribunal will require a list of the issues to be addressed at the final hearing. Professionally represented parties are usually expected to draw up a draft list ahead of a preliminary hearing, with the intention of having it approved by the judge, and/or agree a final list of issues afterwards. The document should cover the legal tests and the key factual issues in dispute. Once agreed, the issues at the final hearing will generally be limited to those on the list, but it should not be followed slavishly or treated as a replacement for the formal pleadings (*Parekh v London Borough of Brent [2012] EWCA Civ 1630*).

The tribunal will often require the parties to agree a neutral chronology of relevant events and/or a cast list of key players, particularly in factually complex cases. In longer cases with professionally represented parties, a core reading list and/or a suggested timetable for the hearing should be agreed between the parties.

In discrimination claims with multiple allegations, it is common for tribunals to order the claimant to produce a 'Scott schedule'. This is a table setting out, for each allegation, the date, details, type of discrimination and relevant paragraph number of the particulars of claim.

17.2.11 FINAL HEARING

Composition of the tribunal

The final hearing will be conducted by a panel of three or a judge sitting alone. A judge can sit alone in the types of claims listed in section 4(3)(c) of the ETA 1996, which include ordinary unfair dismissal claims and unpaid wages claims (*Employment Tribunals Act 1996 (Tribunal Composition) Order 2012*).

In other claims (including discrimination claims) the case will be heard by a panel of three, which will include a legally qualified employment judge and two lay 'wing' members, one with experience from an employer's perspective and the other with experience from an employee's perspective, often a trade union official.

Procedure for final hearing

Despite the original aim of relative informality within tribunal proceedings, they have become increasingly formal and have a remarkably similar procedure to cases in the civil courts. Opening statements are seen only in the most complex of cases and the parties usually proceed straight to evidence. However, the pattern of examination-in-chief, cross-examination, re-examination and closing speeches mirrors that of civil courts. Under rule 45, a tribunal can impose and enforce limits on the presentation of evidence and submissions. Tribunal judges often take a strict approach to timetabling, limiting parties' questioning and submissions to pre-agreed time limits.

The order of presenting the cases is determined by the burden of proof, with the side with the primary burden of proof presenting evidence first and making the last closing submission. Usually, the claimant has the burden of proof in discrimination cases, even though the burden later shifts to the respondent if the claimant can show a prima facie case of discrimination. In unfair dismissal cases, the claimant goes first if the dismissal is not admitted (usually in constructive dismissal cases) and the respondent goes first if dismissal is admitted because they have the burden of proving a potentially fair reason. In cases where there are different allegations with different burdens of proof, representatives often agree in advance whose evidence will go first.

Technically, the tribunal is not 'bound by any rule of law relating to the admissibility of evidence in proceedings before the courts' (rule 41). In practice, the only real difference between the employment tribunal and other courts is that tribunals accept hearsay evidence. They will not permit leading questions, cross-examination of one's own witnesses or irrelevant or scandalous questions.

Witness statements are normally pre-read by the tribunal. Accordingly, rule 44 requires that any witness statement which is to stand as evidence-in-chief be made available to members of the public for inspection during the course of the hearing – unless the tribunal decides otherwise. It is normally incumbent on the parties to bring additional copies of the statements to the hearing for this purpose.

Witness evidence from abroad

Presidential guidance entitled 'Taking Oral Evidence by Video or Telephone from Persons Located Abroad', dated 25 July 2022, was issued in response to the decision of the Upper Tribunal (Immigration and Asylum Chamber) in *Agbabiaka (Evidence from Abroad, Nare Guidance) UK UT 286*, which stated, in essence, that enquiries must be made of the foreign state where the person is located to ascertain whether it objects to evidence being given orally to a tribunal in the United Kingdom from within its territory. The guidance stated that in any case where a party wishes to rely on oral evidence by video or telephone from a person located abroad, that party or their representative must notify the employment tribunal office which is dealing with the case of the following:

a) The case number

b) Confirmation that the party wishes to rely on evidence from a person located abroad

c) The dates of any listed hearing(s) in respect of which the request for the person to give evidence from abroad is being made

d) The state from whose territory that person would, if permitted, be giving oral evidence

The party or their representative does not need to provide the name of the person located abroad or any summary of what their oral evidence will be about. Other parties do not need to be copied into this communication. On receipt of this information, HMCTS will contact the Taking of Evidence Unit on behalf of the party. It should be noted that the process of seeking approval can take months (in the circumstances where an enquiry has to be made via the British Embassy or British High Commission). Therefore, it is crucial that a tribunal is informed as soon as possible.

The decision

Decisions are usually unanimous in the case of a panel, although they can be by a majority with the employment judge possessing the casting vote when just two members sit.

The tribunal will usually give oral reasons for its judgment at the end of the hearing, except in complex cases or where the remaining time is insufficient to consider and deliver the judgment. Either party has the right to request full written reasons for the judgment, either orally at the hearing or in writing, within 14 days of the date on which the judgment was sent to the parties (rule 62(3)).

Privacy and reporting restrictions

Final hearings and open preliminary hearings are, by default, held in public. Under rule 50, such hearings should only be held in private, and reporting should only be restricted, where it is in the 'interests of justice' to do so. This gives judges significant discretion and flexibility when deciding whether an order for privacy is required, balancing the rights to a fair and public hearing, respect for private and family life and freedom of expression (articles 6, 8 and 10 of the *European Convention on Human Rights*, respectively). In response to concerns from media groups, the rule explicitly refers to the need to give full weight to the principle of open justice when determining an application for a privacy or restricted reporting order.

17.2.12 COSTS

There is a fundamental difference between the civil courts and tribunals in relation to costs. In the courts, the general rule is that costs follow the event – in other words, reasonable costs are awarded against the losing party. In tribunals, the general rule is that no costs are awarded.

However, it will be different if a party in an employment tribunal case can show that the other side has, in bringing or conducting proceedings, acted vexatiously, abusively, disruptively or otherwise unreasonably, or if any part of the claim or response was without reasonable prospects of success. In any such case, a tribunal can – and with increasing frequency does – award costs (rule 76(1)).

Costs may be awarded even where the party concerned has won the claim. Thus, in *Wolff v Kingston upon Hull City Council & anor (2007) UKEAT/0631/06*, an employee won a constructive unfair dismissal case but had costs awarded against him because he unreasonably demanded, and persisted in demanding, that a re-engagement order should be made in his favour when this was quite inappropriate.

If an adjournment is caused by the default of one party, or because of an application made less than seven days before the hearing, the other party will often have a good argument for a contribution to costs (rules 76(1)(c) and 76(2)). Indeed, if the adjournment is caused because the employer has not come prepared with evidence to resist a reinstatement/re-engagement application in an unfair dismissal claim, of which it had at least seven days' notice, costs must be awarded against the employer unless special circumstances apply (rule 76(3)).

Even if one of the grounds in rule 76 is made out, the tribunal retains a discretion whether to make a costs order and if so, for how much. Relevant factors may include:

- The principle that cost orders are compensatory rather than punitive and should be the exception rather than the rule.

- The paying party's ability to pay. However, the fact that a party is currently unable to pay an order for costs will not necessarily preclude an order being made (*Habinteg Housing Association Ltd v Holleron (2015) UKEAT/0274/14*). The fact that an otherwise impecunious claimant has recovered a sum of money in the proceedings or is backed by an organisation such as a union or insurance company can be taken into account when deciding whether (and how much) to award against that claimant (*Walker v Heathrow Refuelling Services (2004) UKEAT/0366/04*).

- Whether the paying party is legally represented or has taken legal advice. However, litigants in person are not immune from costs orders. The EAT awarded costs against a litigant in person who had failed to properly particularise the claim, despite being given multiple opportunities at preliminary hearings to provide the relevant information (*Liddington v 2gether NHS Foundation Trust (2016) UKEAT/0002/16*).

- Whether the receiving party or the tribunal has previously made a 'costs warning' in respect of the paying party's conduct or the low merits of their case, although this is not a prerequisite.

- Any settlement offers that the parties have made or rejected. Rejection of a reasonable offer is not by itself grounds for making a costs order, but it may be indicative of unreasonable conduct.

The rules distinguish between 'preparation time orders', 'costs orders' and 'wasted costs orders':

- *Preparation time orders* can only be made if the receiving party has not been legally represented. They do not extend to covering the time involved in the final hearing itself. Preparation time costs are subject to a fixed hourly rate (£43 as at 6 April 2023, and increasing by £1 on 6 April each year) (rules 75 and 79).

- *Costs orders* can only be awarded where the receiving party is legally represented at the hearing (or, if earlier, when the proceedings are determined). The amount of the costs can be agreed or, in the absence of agreement, costs of up to £20,000 can be summarily assessed. Costs exceeding £20,000 can be ordered after detailed assessment by an employment judge (rule 78).

- *Wasted costs orders* can be made against a party's representative (unless a 'not for profit' organisation, such as a union or Citizens Advice) who has caused unnecessary costs. The party may even be ordered to pay their own client if they have acted improperly, unreasonably or negligently and the tribunal considers it reasonable to make such an order (rule 80).

If the issue of costs is disputed, the tribunal must provide written reasons for a costs order within 14 days of making it (rule 62(1)). A tribunal's failure (under the old 2001 rules) to provide clear reasons for a costs order resulted in the order being overruled by the Court of Appeal in *Lodwick v London Borough of Southwark [2004] ICR 884 CA*.

17.3 SETTLEMENT OF CLAIMS

To prevent employees being pressured into signing away their rights, perhaps as a condition of being given employment or receiving a final salary payment, the employment legislation provides that clauses in agreements which have the effect of contracting out of, disapplying or compromising an employee's rights are void (section 18 of the ETA 1996, section 203 of the ERA 1996 and section 144 of the EqA 2010).

There are three main exceptions to this:

1) Where the parties enter into a formal settlement agreement to settle a dispute

2) Where the settlement has been concluded through Acas

3) Settlement via the tribunal

17.3.1 SETTLEMENT AGREEMENTS

To settle an employee's claims, the parties can enter into a formal settlement agreement (previously known as a compromise agreement). The requirements for the settlement agreement to be effective are as follows (section 203 of the ERA 1996 and section 147 of the EqA 2010):

1) It must be in writing.

2) It must relate to the particular proceedings.

3) The employee must have received advice from a relevant independent adviser as to the terms and effect of the proposed agreement and, in particular, its effect on the employee's ability to pursue a claim before an employment tribunal. A relevant independent adviser must be a qualified lawyer, an advice centre adviser or a trade union official who is certified as competent to give advice.

4) The adviser must be covered by professional indemnity insurance.

5) The adviser must be identified in the agreement.

6) The agreement must state that the above requirements are satisfied.

Note that a settlement agreement is, by default, only binding in respect of the particular proceedings being settled. If the parties wish to enter into a blanket full and final settlement agreement, they must state this clearly. Some commentators suggest it is safer to enter into such a blanket settlement via Acas; others doubt whether parties have the ability to enter into very wide-ranging settlements. Ultimately, there is no real difference caused by the method of settlement: what is important is the precise words used in the agreement (*Lunt v Merseyside TEC Ltd [1999] ICR 17 EAT* and *Royal National Orthopaedic Hospital Trust v Howard [2002] IRLR 849 EAT*). The parties must expressly identify the particular type of claim to which the settlement agreement relates, either by generic description (for example, 'unfair dismissal') or by reference to the section of the relevant statute. It is not enough to use a rolled-up expression such as 'all statutory rights', nor to simply refer to the title of the statute, nor that the 'particular proceedings' were identified in correspondence before the settlement agreement was concluded (*Hinton v University of East London [2005] ICR 1260*).

To be valid, a settlement agreement must state that the conditions regulating settlement agreements set out in the relevant statute are satisfied. The absence of a clause confirming that the conditions are satisfied is fatal. The EAT has held that a settlement agreement that confirmed the conditions in section 203 of the ERA 1996 had been satisfied but did not specifically confirm that the conditions in relevant discrimination statutes – section 77 of the *Sex Discrimination Act 1975* and section 72 of the *Race Relations Act 1976* – had also been satisfied was therefore not valid to cover claims of race and sex discrimination. This was so even though the conditions had, in fact, been satisfied and even though, for practical purposes, the conditions are the same in all of them (*Palihakkara v British Telecommunications plc (2006) UKEAT/0185/06*). The consolidation of discrimination legislation in section 147(3) of the EqA 2010 makes this requirement simpler, but it must still be met.

If a representative has neither actual nor ostensible authority to negotiate a settlement, it will not be binding (*Gloystarne & Co Ltd v Martin [2001] IRLR 15 EAT*).

In *Sheriff v Klyne Tugs (Lowestoft) Ltd [1999] IRLR 481 CA*, the courts held that the settlement of a race discrimination claim prevented the employee from bringing a personal injury claim arising out of the same facts in the county court since damages for personal injury are available for race discrimination claims and the settlement must be taken to have settled that as well. It is highly likely that the same principle will hold true for other discrimination settlements. An employee who may wish to bring a separate personal injury claim should ensure that this right is expressly reserved.

A point of considerable practical importance for employers is to ensure that any settlement agreement is made subject to the employee giving warranties to the effect that they are not in breach of any significant term of their employment contract (except as might be specified). This must include, in particular, any breach which would have entitled the employer to terminate the contract without notice or payment in lieu of notice. A clause along these lines can give valuable protection to an employer (*Collidge v Freeport plc [2008] IRLR 697*). Other useful warranties might include one confirming that the employee has returned any property (computers, for example) belonging to the employer and/or that they have not found other employment. Of course, even without specific warranties, an employer will have rights if it turns out that representations by the employee on which they relied in agreeing to enter a settlement agreement were fraudulently untrue (*Crystal Palace FC (2000) Ltd v Dowie [2007] EWHC 1392 QB*).

A current area of concern is the use of 'gagging clauses' or 'non-disclosure agreements' in settlement agreements, particularly to prevent victims of alleged workplace harassment from making disclosures. The Government has indicated that it will bring forward legislation to ensure that such clauses cannot prevent someone from making a disclosure to the police or a healthcare or legal professional and that the limitations of any confidentiality clause are clearly spelt out in the agreement. The Solicitors Regulation Authority has also issued a warning notice reminding practitioners not to use non-disclosure agreements to prevent disclosures that are protected by whistleblowing legislation or reportable to regulators.

17.3.2 SETTLEMENT THROUGH ACAS

Acas is a non-departmental body governed by an independent council and publicly funded. It is best known for its involvement in attempts to settle collective disputes, but it also has a statutory duty, under section 18 of the ETA 1996, to endeavour to promote a settlement of most disputes of a kind falling within the jurisdiction of employment tribunals 'without their being determined by an employment tribunal'. This statutory duty exists regardless of whether tribunal proceedings have been started.

In individual disputes, Acas fulfils two key functions. First, Acas is responsible for facilitating early conciliations (see **17.2.2**). Second, Acas conciliation officers can be a useful go-between among the parties, particularly when one or more parties are unrepresented.

If the parties reach a settlement through Acas 'where a conciliation officer has taken action under section 18 of the Employment Tribunals Act 1996' (section 203(2)(e) of the ERA 1996), then it will be recorded in a document known as a COT3. Such a settlement is binding. It does not need to comply with the formalities of a statutory settlement agreement (see **17.3.1**). Acas will notify the tribunal that the parties have settled. However, conciliation officers will not simply rubber-stamp an agreement reached between the parties: Acas must have played some part in bringing that agreement about.

17.3.3 SETTLEMENT VIA THE TRIBUNAL

Cases frequently settle at the door of the tribunal. When that occurs, there are two common methods of effecting the settlement. The first, and least desirable, is asking the tribunal to make an order by consent. This is disadvantageous to the employer because the tribunal will record a finding against the employer (which the employer is usually keen to avoid). It is also disadvantageous to many employees because when the tribunal makes a formal order, the recoupment regulations apply (*Employment Protection (Recoupment of Benefits) Regulations 1996*). Under these regulations, benefits paid – for example, while a dismissed employee was out of work – will be clawed back by the Department for Work and Pensions out of the settlement monies.

The preferred method is for the parties to draft a 'Tomlin order' (named after Mr Justice Tomlin, dating from *Dashwood v Dashwood [1927] WN 276*). This is a short consent order providing for an application to be stayed upon terms attached in a schedule to the order with the parties having permission to apply to reinstate the application. The schedule contains the terms of agreement between the parties, which will usually include a provision that their liabilities to each other shall be discharged on payment of the sums agreed and/or if no application to reinstate is made within a defined period, say 28 days. If the employer fails to pay any monies under the order, the employee can apply to reinstate the claim. This has the advantage that, technically, the tribunal has not ordered payment of any monies and the recoupment regulations do not apply.

17.3.4 JUDICIAL MEDIATION

Rule 3 places a duty on employment tribunals to encourage and facilitate alternative dispute resolution and to propose mediation (where appropriate) at the case management stage. This makes it clear that it is proper and appropriate for an employment judge to raise matters relating to mediation and conciliation with the parties and reduces the risk of allegations of bias where a judge does so.

Judicial mediation involves the parties attending the tribunal for a mediation session at which a judge will attempt to facilitate the parties in reaching a settlement. This usually lasts between half a day and a day, although two-day mediation can also be offered.

As part of the case management process, the parties are asked whether they consider the case suitable for judicial mediation and, if so, whether they are willing to consider it. If one party is not willing to consider judicial mediation, the case progresses towards a final hearing.

If both parties are willing to consider judicial mediation, the case file is passed to the Regional Employment Judge, who decides whether or not the case should be submitted for judicial mediation. A working rule is that cases listed for more than three days, particularly discrimination claims or cases where the claimant is still employed by the respondent, are suitable. Usually, if the Regional Employment Judge considers that judicial mediation is appropriate, a telephone preliminary hearing will be held. At this, the parties will be offered judicial mediation and case management orders will be made to arrange the mediation and to alter the timetable towards a final hearing.

The mediation is conducted by an experienced judge who has been trained in mediation. It is done in private, and the procedure is flexible. The parties are each given their own room, and the judge moves between the parties. It is now frequently done online, which allows judges to switch between different remote 'rooms'. Often, the session will start with a joint meeting at which the issues will be outlined and each side may be given a brief opportunity to explain their position and what they are hoping to achieve. The judge does not pass judgment or rule on any aspects of the case. Rather, the judge acts as a mediator, conveying offers and counter-offers and attempting to assist the parties in finding common ground to reach an agreement with which both are happy.

If a settlement is reached, it is then finalised by Acas (see **17.3.2**).

17.3.5 JUDICIAL ASSESSMENT

This is not a method of alternative dispute resolution itself, but it is an option available to parties at case management hearings to help guide their settlement negotiations. A protocol and guidance for parties on judicial assessment are set out in Appendices 1 and 2 of the Presidential Guidance on Rule 3 – Alternative Dispute Resolution (22 January 2018).

Judicial assessment will only take place if the parties have indicated that they agree to take part in it, either in their case management agendas completed ahead of the hearing or when asked by the judge on the day. The case management part of the hearing will be conducted as normal, following which the judge will express a provisional view on the strengths and weaknesses of the case and any possible ranges of compensation if liability is established. The judge must make clear that their assessment is non-binding and based on a reading of the allegations rather than an evaluation of the evidence. Parties may then be given time to discuss settlement privately if there is a reasonable prospect of settling at the tribunal.

If no settlement is reached, the judge will have no further involvement in the proceedings (save for conducting any judicial mediation). The judge's comments cannot be disclosed to any other judge.

In practice, it appears that judicial assessment is rarely used. Parties are often unaware of it or unwilling to 'show their hand' at an early stage. Simpler cases, which may be more amenable to early assessment, are less likely to have a preliminary hearing, meaning that the opportunity never arises.

17.4 COVID-19 AND ITS EFFECT ON EMPLOYMENT TRIBUNAL PROCEEDINGS

The COVID-19 pandemic significantly disrupted and altered the running of employment tribunal claims. Whilst there was extensive guidance issued throughout the pandemic, the most important guidance, which will likely have a continuing lasting effect, is the guidance surrounding remote hearings.

In March 2020, the 'Presidential Guidance in Connection with the Conduct of Employment Tribunal Proceedings During the COVID-19 Pandemic' was issued. This reminded tribunals to put rule 46 at the forefront of their minds, which permits hearings of any kind to be conducted, in whole or in part, by use of electronic communication provided that the tribunal considers it just and equitable to do so and, where a hearing is to be in public, members of the public can hear what the tribunal can hear and see any witnesses as seen by the tribunal. The guidance stated that the starting point for case management preliminary hearings should take place by telephone or electronic means unless this is contrary to the overriding objective. Substantive preliminary hearings and final hearings should also be held via video hearings so long as they are in accordance with the overriding objective.

In September 2020, the 'Presidential Guidance on remote and in-person hearings' and the 'Presidential Practice Direction on remote hearings and open justice' were published. This guidance was issued to address the backlog of cases awaiting a decision, COVID-19 safety measures and the concern that the winding down of the Coronavirus Job Retention Scheme would lead to an increase in the number of cases presented. The guidance states that 'as a matter of principle', where there is disputed evidence that requires witness examination, 'a hearing held in person is usually the best way to experience the delivery of justice'. However, the guidance does state a temporary need for remote hearings in greater numbers to minimise the delay in cases being heard.

The guidance and accompanying practice direction highlight three options for the format of hearings: a wholly remote hearing, a partly remote hearing or an in-person hearing.

When considering whether a hearing should be in-person or conducted remotely, the guidance highlights the following considerations for the tribunal:

- The availability of enough space in safe, clean and risk-assessed venues, having regard to distancing measures required to ensure public safety

- Whether safe travel to the employment tribunal venue is possible, especially for those using public transport

- The availability of suitable hardware and software for use by the tribunal in the conduct of remote hearings

- The availability of HMCTS staff to support remote hearings

- The length of the delay that will likely result if the hearing of the case is to be held in person rather than remotely

- The personal circumstances, disability or vulnerability of any participant, including whether a litigation friend or interpreter is required. In some cases, the participant's circumstances will mean that an in-person hearing (or a partly remote hearing with the participant in attendance at the venue) may be fairer because it allows for more effective participation. In other cases, for example, because of clinical vulnerability or shielding or because of the risk associated with using public transport to travel to the venue, remote participation may be fairer.

- Whether the parties are legally represented, which may favour holding the hearing remotely.

- The ability of any participant to engage meaningfully with a remote hearing, which includes access to and familiarity with the necessary technology.

- Whether the nature of the disputed evidence is such that fairness and justice require it to be evaluated by the tribunal in a face-to-face environment.

The *Employment Tribunals (Constitution and Rules of Procedure) (Early Conciliation: Exemptions and Rules of Procedure) (Amendment) Regulations 2020* introduced further flexibility in tribunal proceedings in an effort to reduce the backlog further. This introduced measures such as widening the scope for multiple claims and respondents to use the same ET1 and ET3 forms, allowing claim forms to be accepted despite an error in the early conciliation number and allowing tribunals to list cases for hearing before the deadline for responding to the claim has passed.

In March 2022, further guidance was issued entitled 'A road map for 2021-2022'. The guidance highlights that, unlike other jurisdictions, the number of employment tribunal claims increased during the pandemic. Therefore, video hearings will continue to be used for at least two years to help to reduce the backlog.

TABLE OF CASES

Table of Cases

Table of Cases

Table of Cases

Table of Cases

INDEX

Index   393

Dear HR Professional,

I take my hat off to you.

Having supported the HR community for so many years, I know It's a challenging job you do, sometimes under really difficult circumstances.

The tricky HR issues you have to handle must take up a tremendous amount of your time, your energy and your brain power. I bet it can be exhausting for you to work under that level of pressure.

Being An HR Professional In Today's Business Environment Is TOUGH!

Maintaining your high standards of professionalism must be a real struggle, especially when your efforts and expertise often go unappreciated.

I'll wager you have to make decisions on challenging HR situations you've sometimes never encountered before. Even if you're part of a team, it must sometimes feel like you're working in isolation.

With so much complexity and ambiguity, do you ever find you're not clear whether you're doing the right thing when there's so much to think about?

I expect it can be draining too. You've got to make tough decisions which may be unpopular.

The pressure's on you to ensure people are treated fairly while the business complies with its legal obligations.

It's a thankless task, especially if you've got grief coming at you from all sides.

Doubt can creep in too. Even though you're an extremely competent professional, you might even begin to question yourself...What if you've got it wrong?

You've got to cope with all that, whilst constantly having to convince any doubting stakeholders you're adding value to the business.

That pressure must take its toll on you.

You wouldn't be human if it didn't cause you tension, stress or even worse!

Being the caring professional you are, I bet you often take work home with you.

If You're Not Careful The Stress WILL Creep Up On You

And I don't just mean opening your laptop on your couch when everyone else is watching Eastenders.

We all know of families and relationships that come a poor second to the pressures and challenges faced at work.

Yours too..?

But does it have to be that way?

Should you feel the responsibility of the HR world is entirely on your shoulders and that you've got to bear that burden alone?

The answer is a firm no.

It doesn't have to be like that.

There Is An Answer To Help Make Your Work & Your Life Much Easier For You

There's a place you can get all the help, support, advice and encouragement you need to ease the constant pressure you have to bear.

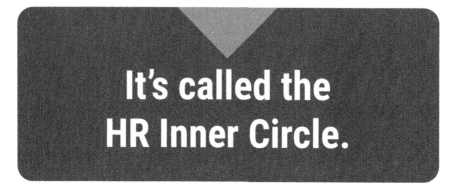

It will lift the burden you're carrying by giving you swift access to comprehensive resources and live practical guidance you can implement right away.

It's information I know will save you time, energy and effort.

It's a vibrant, active community of caring, like minded HR professionals willing to help you.

There are resources packed full of practical, actionable advice for you that's difficult to find anywhere else.

And it doesn't matter what you're working on.

Whether it be workforce engagement, attracting and keeping talent, diversity and inclusion or employee health and well being, you'll find support for all of that.

You're covered even if you're working on one of those tricky, sensitive, people problems you never see coming until they land squarely on your plate.

Timely Support To Make Your Job Easier, Can Be Rapidly Found In The HR Inner Circle

As a member of the HR Inner Circle, to get the support you want…

…just ask.

Your first port of call is the vibrant Facebook group, bursting at the seams with incredible HR professionals like you.

Just post your question and let it bubble and simmer in the collective genius of the group.

By the end of the day, you'll have at least 3-5 comments on your post, often more.

You'll get relevant, insightful and practical guidance that comes from the hard earned experience of your fellow members.

Often you'll get a response within a couple of hours. Sometimes you'll get an answer within minutes - even if it's late in the evening!

This highly active community never fails to astound me with just how willing they are to help fellow HR professionals like you.

They readily and generously share their hard earned knowledge and experience.

You Can Get Answers From <u>Real People</u> Quickly AND From Our Extensive Resource Library Too

...really important for someone working on their own who needs to check things out, or just bounce a few ideas around.

- Quentin Colborn
Director, QC People Management Ltd

While you wait for a response from the Facebook group, you'll likely find answers in the resource-rich members' vault on our secure online portal as well.

It takes just 2 clicks and a quick keyword search using our Rapid Results Search Tool.

You'll instantly find precisely where your topic is covered in our extensive back catalogue of monthly magazines and audio seminars.

In under 30 seconds you can find exactly what you're after.

It's that quick and easy.

…And if you need a specific legal insight?

Then pose your question live to an expert employment lawyer in our monthly Q&A session.

It'll either be me or one of my prominent contemporaries. You'll get your answer immediately without having to pay any legal costs.

If you can't wait, you'll find where it's been answered before with a quick search of previous Q&A sessions.

Our clever index system means you can find a question, and in a single click get straight to the recorded answer.

But perhaps you need to dive deep and explore the different options open to you to solve a particularly tricky problem?

Then join one of our monthly HR Huddles. There you can run your specific situation past other HR professionals.

They'll offer their insights, share their experience and work WITH you to find a solution that works FOR you.

You'll find all of this in one convenient place - the HR Inner Circle.

It's Been A
Labour Of Love
Putting The HR Inner Circle Together So It Works For Professionals Like You

I've spent years practising law and have become recognised as one of the UK's leading employment law barristers. I've even got my own radio show!

But more importantly for you, I've also developed another skill.

It's bringing useful employment expertise AND practical experience together in a way that supports busy, overworked (and sometimes stressed) HR professionals like you.

Everything you're likely to need is **literally at your fingertips**.

This will save you **time**, **energy** and **effort**.

Being a member also means your business and clients will see you as even MORE INFORMED about the intricacies of employment law.

They'll marvel at how well you keep up to date when you're busy working so hard for them.

You'll be seen making quicker decisions and implementing effective solutions to accelerate the growth of the organisation.

You'll make impressive time and cost savings for the business.

And those tricky, off-piste situations you've never come across before..?

Well, nothing will faze you, because you're backed up by an HR support system second to none.

But more importantly, you'll feel that pressure gently ease off.

With the relief you'll feel knowing that such great help and guidance is just a few minutes, you'll wonder how you survived without it!

That's Why I'm Inviting You To Join And Reap The Many Rewards Of Membership

▶ WWW.HRINNERCIRCLE.CO.UK ◀

Here's what you get when you join the HR Inner Circle:

Benefit #1- you'll get unlimited access to the hugely popular HR Inner Circle Facebook Private Group

- Tap into the vast wealth of knowledge, experience, insight and wisdom of the top 0.5% of your profession at any time, day or night.

- In less than 5 minutes you can post ANY HR question and get insightful answers and suggestions in a couple of hours or less, from some of the best in your profession.

- Fast track your impact by discovering effective shortcuts and workarounds from HR people who've been "there" and done "it".

- Expand and deepen your network of like minded individuals, secure in the knowledge they're as dedicated and as ambitious as you.

- Increase your prestige with your colleagues and stakeholders by being part of such an exclusive and prominent HR community.

- Gain confidence in your judgment and decisions by using the highly responsive community as a sounding board for your ideas.

Benefit #2 - you'll receive 11 copies of the HR Inner Circular Magazine every year

- Enjoy that satisfying "THUD" on your door mat every month when the postman delivers your very own copy of the HR Inner Circular magazine.

- Quickly discover exactly what the law says about key issues affecting HR professionals around the UK like you.

- Get concise and practical guidance on how employment law applies to the challenging situations and circumstances you deal with every day.

- Avoid the mistakes of others by applying the lessons from the in depth analysis of real life case studies.

- Benefit from a legal deep dive by the UK's leading employment law barrister into a topical employment question posed by a fellow member (perhaps you!).

- Review a summary of recent important Facebook Group discussions worthy of sharing, that you may have missed.

- Explore a range of related and relevant topics useful for your practice and your broader professional development.

> The magazine is really informative, the Facebook group such a community, and I think exceptional value for money.
>
> - Lis Moore
> Head of Advisory & Support Services,
> Society of Local Council Clerks

Benefit #3 - Monthly Audio Seminars

- A 60 minute legal deep dive by me into an important subject relevant to you and your practice.

- Professionally recorded content recorded exclusively for the HR Inner Circle - you'll not find this information anywhere else.

- Carefully structured content that's easy to consume, understand and apply in your work as an HR professional.

- Episodes delivered every month so you can stay current on the latest issues affecting HR professionals.

- The convenience of listening to the recording online or downloading the mp3 for later enjoyment at a time suitable to your busy schedule (perfect for any commute).

Benefit #4 - you get an exclusive invite to a live online Q&A Session every fortnight, led by an expert employment lawyer

- Gain 60 minutes of live and direct access to the sharpest legal minds from my secret little black book of contacts.

- Get answers to your knottiest employment law questions, and solutions to your trickiest HR problems, from some of the brightest employment lawyers in the UK.

- Avoid having to pay the £300-£400 it would cost you to ask a lawyer your question outside of the HR Inner Circle.

- Benefit from valuable insights from the answers given to other members.

- If you can't attend live, watch the recording when it's convenient for you.

- Quickly access the recorded answer to any question asked in the session by simply clicking the question index for that session.

- Save time by downloading the session transcription to scan-read at a time suitable for you.

Benefit #5 - join a live Monthly Huddle with other HR Professionals to solve your most challenging HR problems

- Attend your very own mini-mastermind group of highly qualified, highly regarded and experienced fellow HR professionals to "group think" through an issue you're facing right now.

- Develop bespoke solutions to the unique problems and challenges you have to deal with in a safe, supportive and confidential environment.

- Feel safe knowing these online zoom calls are NOT recorded to respect the sensitivity of issues addressed and the privacy of those involved. [NOTE - a professional transcriber attends and takes written notes. An anonymised summary is then made available to the membership]

- Recent Huddle topics included changing employee benefits, mandatory vaccination, career breaks, sickness during disciplinaries, effective worker forums and hybrid working arrangements.

Benefit #6 - access our Templates & Resources Centre

- Gain immediate access to our library of the most popular and frequently used forms, assessments, agreements, checklists, letter templates, questionnaires and reports to help the busiest HR professionals save time and get things done quicker and easier.

- Download them as Word documents, so you can edit and personalise them to fit your business needs

- New templates added every single month

Benefit #7 - build your own Employment Law Library

- We send you several brand-new books on employment law several times each year

- Acquire your own physical library of concise, easy-to-read and fully updated textbooks

- Recent titles include Hiring Staff, Managing Sickness Absence, Spotting Malingering and Resolving Grievances

Benefit #8 - free Ticket to our Annual Conference

- The perfect opportunity to extend your personal network of fellow HR professionals.

- Meet up face to face with the people who've been supporting you in the Facebook Group and HR Huddles so you can deepen those connections even further.

- Gather key insights and takeaways to help you personally and professionally from some of the best speakers on the circuit. Previous speakers have covered motivation, dealing with difficult people, goal setting and productivity, decision making and social media marketing.

- Get instant access to recordings of all previous conferences so even if you can't attend in person, you can benefit from the event in your own time.

- Includes probably the best conference lunch you'll ever have - a bold claim I know, but we use outstanding caterers.

> It never ceases to amaze me the amount of time and effort people put into the Facebook group, sharing their experiences, advice, and sage words of wisdom.
>
> - Emma Lister
> HR Consultant, SME HR Services

Benefit #9 - your Personal Concierge will help you get the best out of your membership

- You get personal access to Nina who'll point you in the direction of exactly where to find what you need. She's supported hundreds of members over the 5 years she's been part of the team.

- Nina also works closely with the 11 back office staff that support the operation. In the extremely unlikely event she doesn't know where something is, she knows who will.

HOW MUCH DOES JOINING THE HR INNER CIRCLE COST?

There's no doubt in my mind the annual value of membership benefits is in the many thousands of pounds range.

But you're not going to pay anywhere near that.

Let me remind you of what that small monthly fee gives you every year

Access to the private Facebook Group	INCLUDED
HR Inner Circular Magazine subscription	INCLUDED
Monthly Audio Seminars	INCLUDED
Live Q&A sessions	INCLUDED
Monthly HR Huddles	INCLUDED
Templates & Resources Centre	INCLUDED
Employment Law Library	INCLUDED
Free ticket to the HR Inner Circle Annual Conference	INCLUDED
Your Personal Membership Concierge	INCLUDED

TOTAL
PRICELESS

Another way of looking at your investment is this:

Because access to what you need is so quick…

Join today and that price is fixed for as long as you remain a member. You'll always pay the same, even if we increase the price to new members (which we regularly do).

…it's like having your very own part time, legally trained, assistant HR Business Partner, just waiting to provide you with all the answers you need…

►WWW.HRINNERCIRCLE.CO.UK◄

Plus, With Membership Of The HR Inner Circle, You'll Also Get These 4 Additional Resources For FREE!

Additional Resource #1 - Handling Awkward Conversations

A video case study masterclass you can share with managers to train them to handle awkward staff disciplinary, performance and attitude problems. A huge time saver for you.

Additional Resource #2 - 6 x HR Employment Online Courses

Immediate, on demand access to six thorough, online HR courses (with more constantly added), including Employment Tribunal Compensation, Chat GPT for HR Professionals, Deconstructing TUPE, Changing Terms & Conditions, Unconscious Bias At Work and Handling Grievances.

Additional Resource #3 - Free listing on the Register of Investigators

Advertise your professional investigations service in our member's portal.

Additional Resource #4 - Significant discounts on sets of policies, contracts, and other courses.

Get member discounts on my Getting Redundancy Right and HR Policies products as well as other price reductions as new products are released.

► WWW.HRINNERCIRCLE.CO.UK ◄

I'm So Confident Joining The HR Inner Circle Is The Right Decision For You, Here's My

NO LIMITS GUARANTEE

Take action and join the HR Inner Circle **now**.

If you're not 100% satisfied with your investment, you can cancel at ANY time.

Just tell us, and your membership will end immediately. No long-term contracts. No notice periods. No fuss.

I'm comfortable doing this because I know once you join, you'll find the support, the information and the strategies so useful, you'll never want to leave.

Before you decide though, let me be very clear about membership of the HR Inner Circle.

It's only for ambitious and dedicated HR professionals who want to accelerate and increase their impact by plugging into an HR ecosystem with its finger firmly on the pulse of what's working right now in HR.

If you're just plodding along and are content with just getting by, then this is probably not for you.

But if you're drawn to benefiting from standing shoulder to shoulder with some of the giants in the HR community who will help you solve your toughest problems, then joining the HR Inner Circle is the RIGHT decision for you.

Join here now:

WWW.HRINNERCIRCLE.CO.UK

Daniel Barnett

P.S. Remember when you join you get unrestricted access to the private Facebook group, the monthly magazine delivered direct to your door, the monthly audio seminar, regular free books, templates, checklists and resources, on-demand video courses, over 100 audio seminars and back copies of magazines, live interactive Q&A sessions with a lawyer, focused monthly huddles with other HR professionals, a free ticket to the annual conference, your personal concierge plus a bunch of additional resources…